ADVANCES
IN CHILD DEVELOPMENT
AND BEHAVIOR

Volume 18

Contributors to This Volume

Peter Barker
Harry Beilin
Sharon R. Garber
Barry Gholson
Howard V. Meredith
James L. Mosley
Willis F. Overton
David S. Palermo
Scott G. Paris
Herbert L. Pick, Jr.
Hayne W. Reese
Constance R. Schmidt
Gerald M. Siegel
Eileen A. Stan

ADVANCES IN CHILD DEVELOPMENT AND BEHAVIOR

edited by

Hayne W. Reese
Department of Psychology
West Virginia University
Morgantown, West Virginia

Volume 18

1984

ACADEMIC PRESS, INC.
(Harcourt Brace Jovanovich, Publishers)
Orlando • San Diego • San Francisco
New York • London • Toronto • Montreal • Sydney • Tokyo • São Paulo

ACADEMIC PRESS, INC.
Orlando, Florida 32887

United Kingdom Edition published by
ACADEMIC PRESS, INC. (LONDON) LTD.
24/28 Oval Road, London NW1 7DX

LIBRARY OF CONGRESS CATALOG CARD NUMBER: 63-23237
ISBN 0-12-009718-4

PRINTED IN THE UNITED STATES OF AMERICA

84 85 86 87   9 8 7 6 5 4 3 2 1

Contents

Contributors

Numbers in parentheses indicate the pages on which the authors' contributions begin.

PETER BARKER
Department of Philosophy, Memphis State University, Memphis, Tennessee 38152 (227, 277)

HARRY BEILIN
Developmental Psychology Program, City University of New York Graduate School and University Center, New York, New York 10036-8099 (245, 285)

SHARON R. GARBER
Center for Research in Human Learning, University of Minnesota, Minneapolis, Minnesota 55455 (49)

BARRY GHOLSON
Department of Psychology, Memphis State University, Memphis, Tennessee 38152 (227, 277)

HOWARD V. MEREDITH
Department of Physical Education, University of South Carolina, Columbia, South Carolina 29208 (81)

JAMES L. MOSLEY
Department of Psychology, The University of Calgary, Calgary, Alberta T2N 1N4, Canada (147)

WILLIS F. OVERTON
Department of Psychology, Temple University, Philadelphia, Pennsylvania 19122 (191, 273)

DAVID S. PALERMO
Department of Psychology, The Pennsylvania State University, University Park, Pennsylvania 16802 (259)

SCOTT G. PARIS
Department of Psychology, The University of Michigan, Ann Arbor, Michigan 48109 (1)

HERBERT L. PICK, JR.
Center for Research in Human Learning, University of Minnesota, Minneapolis, Minnesota 55455 (49)

HAYNE W. REESE
Department of Psychology, West Virginia University, Morgantown, West Virginia 26506-6040 (189)

CONSTANCE R. SCHMIDT
Department of Psychology, Virginia Polytechnic Institute and State University, Blacksburg, Virginia 24061 (1)

GERALD M. SIEGEL
Center for Research in Human Learning, University of Minnesota, Minneapolis, Minnesota 55455 (49)
EILEEN A. STAN
Department of Psychology, The University of Calgary, Calgary, Alberta T2N 1N4, Canada (147)

Preface

The amount of research and theoretical discussion in the field of child development and behavior is so vast that researchers, instructors, and students are confronted with a formidable task in both keeping abreast of new developments within their areas of specialization through the use of primary sources, and being knowledgeable in areas peripheral to their primary focus of interest. Moreover, journal space is often too limited to permit publication of more speculative kinds of analyses that might spark extended interest in a problem area or stimulate new modes of attack on a problem.

The serial publication *Advances in Child Development and Behavior* is intended to ease the burden by providing scholarly technical articles serving as reference material and by providing a place for the publication of scholarly speculation. In these documented critical reviews, recent advances in the field are summarized and integrated, complexities are exposed, and fresh viewpoints are offered. They should be useful not only to the expert in the area but also to the general reader.

No attempt is made to organize each volume around a particular theme or topic, nor is the series intended to reflect the development of new fads. Manuscripts are solicited from investigators conducting programmatic work on problems of current and significant interest. The editor often encourages the preparation of critical syntheses dealing intensively with topics of relatively narrow scope but of considerable potential interest to the scientific community. Contributors are encouraged to criticize, integrate, and stimulate, but always within a framework of high scholarship. Although appearance in the volumes is ordinarily by invitation, unsolicited manuscripts will be accepted for review if submitted first in outline form to the editor. All papers—whether invited or submitted—receive careful editorial scrutiny. Invited papers are automatically accepted for publication in principle, but may require revision before final acceptance. Submitted papers receive the same treatment except that they are not automatically accepted for publication even in principle, and may be rejected. The *Advances* series is usually not a suitable place of publication for reports of a single study, or a short series of studies, even if the report is necessarily long because of the nature of the research.

The use of sexist language, such as "he" or "she" as the general singular pronoun, in contributions to the *Advances* series is strongly discouraged. The use of "he or she" (or the like) is acceptable; it is widespread and no longer seems cumbersome or self-conscious.

I wish to acknowledge with gratitude the aid of my home institution, West Virginia University, which generously provided time and facilities for the preparation of this volume. I also wish to thank Drs. Kathleen Bloom, Robert Kail, Walter Manning, Willis Overton, and Carolyn Rovee-Collier for their editorial assistance.

Hayne W. Reese

ADVANCES IN CHILD DEVELOPMENT AND BEHAVIOR

Volume 18

THE DEVELOPMENT OF VERBAL COMMUNICATIVE SKILLS IN CHILDREN

Constance R. Schmidt

DEPARTMENT OF PSYCHOLOGY
VIRGINIA POLYTECHNIC INSTITUTE AND STATE UNIVERSITY
BLACKSBURG, VIRGINIA

Scott G. Paris

DEPARTMENT OF PSYCHOLOGY
THE UNIVERSITY OF MICHIGAN
ANN ARBOR, MICHIGAN

ADVANCES IN CHILD DEVELOPMENT
AND BEHAVIOR, VOL. 18

ISBN 0-12-009718-4

I. Introduction

As children acquire the words and grammars of their native languages, they learn how to communicate information, needs, and feelings more effectively. Linguistic, social, and cognitive aspects of development converge in the acquisition of oral communicative skills. Since the pioneering investigations of Piaget (1926) and Vygotsky (1962), the communication of young children has often been characterized as "egocentric" or "private," that is, neither socialized nor adapted to the audience. Recent research, however, has shown that 3–5 year olds often engage in reciprocal conversations and can take the listener's perspective into account (Bloom, Rocissano, & Hood, 1976; Garvey & Hogan, 1973; Maratsos, 1973). The controversy over the extent to which young children's communication is egocentric, and the related issue regarding the developmental fate of egocentric speech, have stimulated a great deal of research during the last 10 years. Much of this research contradicts the early hypotheses of Piaget (1926) and Vygotsky (1962).

We believe that a dichotomization of speech into egocentric and socialized categories is nonproductive because it leads researchers to ignore the developmental continuity and diversity of communicative skills. Communication is a multidimensional phenomenon reflecting many developmental accomplishments. Even simple conversations might involve social perspective taking, knowledge of linguistic forms and conventions, perceptual and cognitive analysis of the topic, memory for prior utterances, attention to the physical and social context, and the ability to process these features simultaneously in order to fulfill social goals. Clearly, unitary constructs such as egocentric or socialized speech cannot provide a detailed description or adequate developmental interpretation of these abilities. Furthermore, Ford (1979) has shown that egocentrism is not a "valid" construct in the sense that the intercorrelations among measures of egocentrism—even within a single domain such as communication research—tend to be insignificant.

In the present article, we review the early contributions of Piaget and Vygotsky, identifying shortcomings of the two approaches where appropriate. Both theorists failed to deal explicitly with the diverse motivations behind the communication of children, focusing instead on a single form of early speech and its function in social interaction. Their concern for the influence of social context on the communication of children was also limited. Finally, neither theorist considered in detail how children control their communicative efforts, select skills appropriate in given communicative settings, and evaluate the success of those skills for accomplishing social goals.

The first step in going beyond these early approaches is to identify a data base that encompasses the wide diversity of communicative skills that develops during early childhood. To accomplish this task, we outline four classes of communicative skills and trace their development during the preschool and early elementary school years. Following a selective review of relevant literature, we discuss some theoretical alternatives to the approaches of Piaget and Vygotsky. Finally, we propose a new framework for interpreting communicative development that integrates and extends aspects of several recent approaches. In this framework, developmental changes are proposed in the goals children bring to communicative tasks, in the plans they adopt for achieving these goals, and in the means available for implementing these plans. We hope to demonstrate that our analysis of the four classes of skills involved in communication coupled with the goals/plans/means framework provides a powerful tool for interpreting communicative development. Let us begin, however, with a review of Piaget and Vygotsky's original investigations of communicative development.

II. Two Early Approaches to Communicative Development: Piaget and Vygotsky

A. PIAGET'S ANALYSIS

Piaget described the development of communication as a gradual progression from egocentric to socialized speech, usually accomplished by 7 years of age. A child's speech is egocentric when the child "fails to place himself at the point of view of his hearer" (Piaget, 1926, p. 32). Socialized speech, in contrast, is adapted to the needs and perspectives of the listener. Piaget identified three categories of egocentric speech: repetition, monologue, and collective monologue. The categories of socialized speech included adapted information, argument, collaboration and criticism, commands, requests, threats, and questions.

Piaget posited three stages in the development of socialized speech. During the first stage (ages 3 to 5), children are totally egocentric in their speech and are capable only of monologues and collective monologues. Conversations are not yet possible because successive utterances are not adapted or even related to one another. Social attitudes are present "in form" but not "in substance" (Piaget, 1926, p. 76). In other words, despite some desire to communicate, the function of speech in Stage I is nonsocial.

During the second stage of communicative development (ages 5 to 7), some progress toward the socialization of speech is evident. Although children still talk about themselves and from their own points of view, they are heard and understood by their compatriots. The second stage is also characterized by collaboration in action or in nonabstract thought. In social situations, the subject of successive remarks "instead of being the activities of the respective speakers, is an activity in which they all share" (Piaget, 1926, p. 79). Thus, each child's utterance is in some way related to previous utterances by fellow interlocutors. In addition to the onset of collaboration, primitive forms of argument also appear during Stage II. Primitive arguments are clashes of opinion in which no justifications are given in support of conflicting views.

The final stage of communicative development is marked by the onset of truly socialized speech. After age 7, the child is capable of collaboration in abstract thought and can engage in "genuine arguments," arguments that include logical justifications for contrasting opinions. In his observations of spontaneous interactions among nursery school children, Piaget (1926) found that prior to age 7 approximately half of the children's utterances were egocentric.

According to Piaget, the transition from egocentric to socialized speech is influenced by two general factors, decentration and peer interaction. Cognitive decentration involves the "construction of transitive, associative, and reversible operations" that permit a conversion of egocentricity "into a system of relations and classes that are decentralized with respect to the self" (Piaget, 1950, pp. 122–123). Peer interaction is the major impetus for developing cognitive decentration. Children are forced to abandon egocentric orientations when they attempt to coordinate their behavioral goals with equally powerful peer goals. Piaget argued that interactions with adults will not lead to reductions in egocentric speech because children view adults as omniscient and as sharing identical goals with them. In support of this hypothesis, Piaget reported that children are more egocentric in their speech to adults than to peers.

Piaget was primarily a structuralist, concerned with the *forms* of early speech rather than the motivation behind it (Zivin, 1979). For Piaget, egocentric speech was simply one of several manifestations of the child's immature cognitive structures. However, Piaget occasionally speculated about the child's communicative motives. For example, Piaget asserted that when the child speaks egocentrically,

> He does not bother to know to whom he is speaking nor whether he is being listened to. He talks either for himself or for the pleasure of associating anyone who happens to be there with the activity of the moment. This talk is egocentric, partly because the child speaks only about himself, but chiefly because he does not attempt to place himself at the point of view of his hearer . . . The child asks for no more than apparent interest, though he has the illusion . . . of being heard and understood. He feels no desire to influence his hearer nor to tell him anything. (Piaget, 1926, p. 9)

This quotation reveals that egocentric speech can result from a lack of either social *skill* or social *will*. Although Piaget clearly postulated a lack of social skill in the communication of young children, his position on the child's intent or will to communicate was ambiguous (Kohlberg, Yaeger, & Hjertholm, 1968; Zivin, 1979). Zivin (1979) attempted to clarify Piaget's speculations concerning communicative intent. She identified three motives for egocentric speech in Piaget's theory. Egocentric speech can be a "difficult-to-inhibit" accompaniment of the child's activity, a pleasure-producing use of sound play to evoke fantasized reality (in simple monologue or repetition), or a means for eliciting the verbal contact or interest of others (in collective monologue). Only the third of these three motives can be characterized as "social" in nature. Zivin (1979) also argued that these motives are only tangentially related to Piaget's main thesis. For Piaget, the defining aspect of egocentric speech was its socially unadapted *form*. In contrast, Vygotsky emphasized the communicative motives underlying egocentric speech.

B. VYGOTSKY'S ANALYSIS

According to Piaget, egocentric speech is unadapted to the needs of the listener and is primarily asocial in nature. Vygotsky (1962) had a very different view of egocentric speech. Vygotsky began with the assumption that the earliest speech of children is social in nature, although the social functions of early speech are very global. With development, the global functions of speech become differentiated into two major forms, communicative and egocentric speech. Communicative speech is, by definition, directed toward others and adapted to their needs and perspectives. Egocentric speech, in contrast, is self-directed and unadapted. However, self-directed speech in Vygotsky's analysis is still "social" in nature, because the child is *communicating* with himself or herself. In a sense, the child is playing both the "speaker" and "listener" roles in an effort to understand and regulate his or her own activity. In Piaget's analysis, the child's egocentric speech is undirected and not communicative. When Piaget argued that the young child speaks "for himself," he was commenting on the unadapted *structure* of egocentric speech rather than its social function (Zivin, 1979).

Vygotsky argued that as social and egocentric speech become more and more differentiated, egocentric speech begins to take on problem-solving and planning functions. In describing the planning functions of egocentric speech, Vygotsky drew heavily on Piaget's analysis of the motives underlying egocentric speech. Like Piaget, Vygotsky asserted that egocentric speech often is an uninhibited accompaniment to the child's activity. Occasionally, this incidental speech directs the child's subsequent activity. Vygotsky illustrated the planning function of egocentric speech in a well-known anecdote. According to the story, a young boy broke his pencil while drawing and exclaimed, "It's broken." Immediately following this exclamation, the boy drew a picture of a broken streetcar. According to Vygotsky, the semantic content of the child's utterance influenced his subsequent activity. Vygotsky also assigned "accidental" planning functions to egocentric speech that the child produced as an "emotional release." Finally, Vygotsky argued that more conscious planning could occur when the motive of egocentric speech was "social or emotional expression." For example, a child might say, "Now I'm going to draw a picture," before beginning the prescribed activity. Vygotsky attributed the "emotional release" and "expressive" motives for egocentric speech to Piaget (1926).

Although Vygotsky's extension of Piaget's work illustrates the common ground between the two theorists, several differences can also be identified. The most important of these differences involves the eventual fate of egocentric speech. Piaget argued that egocentric speech gradually atrophies and is replaced by socialized speech. As egocentric speech disappears, both its form and function remain constant. In contrast, Vygotsky asserted that egocentric speech is gradually internalized as the child becomes aware of its inappropriateness in social situations. As egocentric speech becomes "inner speech," it retains its planning function but becomes more abbreviated and incomprehensible to others in form.

A second major difference between the two theorists involves the influence of social context on egocentric speech. Piaget was not interested in situational variation in the occurrence of egocentric speech. Vygotsky, however, stated explicitly that, "Whether the child's talk is more egocentric or more social depends not only on his age but also on the surrounding conditions" (1962, p. 23). In a series of experiments, Vygotsky (1962) placed children in situations that made communication difficult. For example, in one study the child's utterances were "drowned out" by loud music and in another the child's audience consisted of deaf–mutes. When communication was difficult, the proportion of children's utterances that could be classified as egocentric declined relative to situations in which communication was fairly easy. On the basis of these results, Vygotsky argued that when the child's feeling of being understood declines, the proportion of speech that is egocentric also declines. Thus, egocentric speech can be seen as an intermediate step between social speech and inner speech. It has the *form* of social speech in that it occurs more often in social situations than in nonsocial ones, but it has the planning *function* of inner speech.

Other differences between the two theorists become apparent from Piaget's (1962) critique of Vygotsky's theory (Zivin, 1979). The third difference involves the social orientation of the child. Piaget described a developmental progression from subjective awareness of the world in early infancy to objective, socially appropriate comprehension of the world in middle childhood. In contrast, Vygotsky argued that a social orientation toward the world is present in early infancy, but social functions become more differentiated as the child matures. The fourth difference between the two theories involves the relationship between language and thought in development. Piaget argued that language follows and mirrors the intellectual development of the child whereas Vygotsky asserted that language actively contributes to intellectual growth.

We have briefly sketched four differences between the approaches of Piaget and Vygotsky, differences involving the fate of egocentric speech, the influence of social context on egocentric speech, the social orientation of the child, and the relationship between language and thought in development. These differences become even more acute when one considers that the "common ground" between the two theories exists in an area that was of little interest to Piaget—the motives underlying speech. Piaget readily accepted Vygotsky's extension of egocentric speech to include planning functions because this extension was irrelevant to Piaget's main thesis, that egocentric speech is symptomatic of an unadapted level of intelligence (Zivin, 1979). For Piaget, the social functions of egocentric speech warranted only brief speculation whereas for Vygotsky they were at the center of his theory of communicative development.

C. LIMITATIONS OF THE EARLY APPROACHES

Piaget and Vygotsky have had an enormous impact on the field of communicative development and there is a vast literature aimed at testing their hypotheses (e.g., Flavell, Botkin, Fry, Wright, & Jarvis, 1968; Glucksberg, Krauss, & Higgins, 1975; Kohlberg *et al.*, 1968; Miller, Shelton, & Flavell, 1970). However, serious limitations to both theories become apparent when one examines recent literature concerning communicative development. Most of these limitations are related to a tendency to describe communication in terms of simply egocentric or social speech. Utterances were placed in these categories on the basis of their structure and form. Piaget (1926) gave little attention to the motivation behind the utterances, the social or physical contexts of the utterances, or the degree to which the utterances were under the control of the child. Although Vygotsky considered motivation, context, and control more directly, his analyses were limited. We shall argue that these are precisely the factors that are crucial for interpreting communicative development.

Let us begin with the problem of communicative motives. We have already argued that Piaget was only tangentially interested in the motives underlying early speech. In contrast, Vygotsky gave communicative intent a central role in his theory. However, Vygotsky focused on only a few communicative motives, the most important of which were the desire to interact with others and the need to regulate one's own behavior. Recent theorists have discussed a wide range of communicative goals, such as sharing information with a listener, persuading, entertaining, or deceiving. In fact, some theorists have taken the diversity of communicative motives to its logical extreme and argued that every utterance should be evaluated in terms of its social intent as well as its semantic content (e.g., Dore, 1977). The justification for considering communicative motives in such detail is that motives serve as criteria for measuring communicative success or failure. By definition, communicative effectiveness depends on the effects that children are trying to achieve through their communicative attempts.

The problem of communicative motives is closely tied to the issue of how social context influences communication. To a large degree, situational factors will determine the child's communicative goals. For example, the goal of maintaining social contact will be rapidly abandoned if loud music is drowning out the child's utterances (Vygotsky, 1962). Vygotsky was concerned with the influence of social situations on communication. Similarly, recent researchers have argued that communication will be more effective in natural, familiar settings than in artificial, laboratory tasks (e.g., Maratsos, 1973; Menig-Peterson, 1975). However, Vygotsky and recent researchers have explored the effects of social context on very broad measures of communication, particularly the "egocentricity" of children's utterances. Little attempt has been made to examine the influence of specific contexts on specific aspects of verbal and nonverbal behavior. Notable exceptions to this rule will be identified when we turn to the recent literature concerning communicative development.

One final limitation of early approaches to communicative development involves the control that children exert over their communicative efforts. Although Piaget (1926) demonstrated little interest in the issue of communicative control, Vygotsky (1962) did discuss the planning functions of communication. However, Vygotsky was more concerned with children's control of problem-solving behavior than with their regulation of interpersonal exchanges. More recent theorists have asked how children select appropriate means for achieving their communicative purposes, how they deploy these means, how they evaluate the success of their communicative attempts, and how they modify their behavior when faced with communicative failure (e.g., Flavell, 1981; Markman, 1981; Robinson, 1981; Shatz, 1978). Examples of developmental changes in the planning and control of interpersonal communication will be provided in the literature review that follows. The planning component of communication will be given a central role in the model of communication proposed at the end of the article.

III. Representative Research Concerning the Development of Communicative Skills

This section presents a selective review of recent literature on four classes of communicative skills: (1) gaining and holding an audience, (2) adapting messages to the context of communication, (3) providing relevant responses to the listener's messages, and (4) providing feedback as a listener. The typology systematizes extensive research on communicative development and will help illustrate the development of children's goals, plans, and means for effective communication. Our selection of studies emphasized naturalistic investigations, often at the expense of experimental research. Our intent was to document the developing repertoire of skills available to children when task demands are minimal. In the model following the review, we shall consider factors determining the selection and use of these skills.

A. GAINING AND HOLDING AN AUDIENCE

Piaget (1926) argued that young children fail to direct their utterances toward others and are not concerned with obtaining relevant responses from their listeners. Similarly, Vygotsky (1962) believed that young children's utterances are often self-directed, although his position concerning the desire for acknowledgment from the listener was ambiguous. Presumably, Vygotsky attributed some desire for acknowledgment to the child because he predicted a decline in egocentric speech when communication was difficult. An initial examination of current research indicates that young children can secure a listener's attention and acknowledgment through a number of devices. Two year olds use vocatives (e.g., "Mommy, Mommy") and tag questions (e.g., "O.K.?") to ensure that others are listening to them (Bloom & Lahey, 1978). Also, the gestures that accompany the young child's actions often convey communicative intent to a listener, as well as conveying affective or cognitive meaning (Bruner, 1975; Dore, 1975). Finally, Keenan and Schieffelin (1976) observed that children's utterances often include an initial proposition that gains the listener's attention. We will review in detail first verbal and then nonverbal means of soliciting and maintaining the attention of the listener.

Although 2 and 3 year olds can elicit a listener's attention by calling the listener's name, using tag questions, gesturing, and highlighting propositions, how often do they display these behaviors in spontaneous speech to adults or peers? Mueller and his associates (Mueller, 1972; Mueller, Bleier, Krakow, Hegedus, & Cournoyer, 1977) have found that young children use attentional devices relatively infrequently. They recorded the spontaneous conversations of dyads between the ages of 2 and 5 in free-play situations. In the Mueller *et al.* (1977) study, only 9–15% of the utterances of 2 year olds included attention-getting devices. Similarly, Mueller (1972) found that children 3–5 years old used attention-getting devices in only 27% of their utterances. Further support for infrequent use of attentional devices by preschoolers can be found in a study by Wellman and Lempers (1977). Wellman and Lempers analyzed communicative interactions between 2 year olds in which the speaker tried to get the listener to look at a particular object and, even then, found that children used attentional devices in only 4% of their interactions.

Another method of addressing a listener is to look at the person. Wellman and Lempers (1977) found that 2 year olds visually attended to listeners during or immediately following 72% of their communicative interactions. Mueller *et al.* (1977) observed a lower frequency in their 2 year olds (53–55%) and Mueller

(1972) reported visual attention to the listener in only 42% of the interactions among children 3–5 years old. Even these frequencies are probably inflated, however, because speakers can attend to listeners as part of the environment in the absence of a specific motive to engage the listener in communication.

Nonverbal gestures can also be employed to engage and maintain the attention of a listener. Bates, Camaioni, and Volterra (1975) observed that infants show, give, and point to objects in order to elicit the other's attention and that the infant's first words usually accompany these actions. Wellman and Lempers (1977) found that 2 year olds pointed to objects during 45% of their interactions and showed objects to the listener 55% of the time. However, the evidence for the child's ability to direct communicative attempts toward others would be more convincing if it showed that the child visually attends to the listener while pointing to or showing an object. If pointing and showing are undirected or self-directed behaviors, one would expect the child to attend to the object rather than to potential listeners while manifesting these behaviors. Leung and Rheingold (1981) demonstrated that 38% of the points displayed by infants 10–16 months old were accompanied by visual attention to the child's mother. Furthermore, 87% of the infants' points were accompanied by vocalizations that were often "demonstrative" in tone. Leung and Rheingold concluded from these results that pointing is a "social" gesture from a very early age.

We have found that young children use both verbal and nonverbal means for soliciting the attention of a listener, although the frequency of attention-getting devices is low in their spontaneous interactions. Keenan and her associates (Keenan, 1974; Keenan & Klein, 1975) provided evidence that young children also seek appropriate responses from listeners. Keenan analyzed the early morning conversations of her 2-year-old twin boys in terms of speaker expectations and listener obligations. The comments, questions, and demands of each child seemed to impose certain obligations on the listener. The twins would repeat an utterance several times or use attention-getting devices in order to elicit a relevant response from the listener. Young speakers are apparently very successful at eliciting relevant responses, because less than 5% of the twins' utterances did not receive verbal acknowledgment.

However, the Keenan evidence can be questioned for several reasons. First, listener acknowledgment in the study included repetition of the speaker's utterance. Piaget (1926) classified repetition as an egocentric form of speech that is not adapted to the previous utterances of the listener. Second, repetition was also the means by which the speaker obtained a response from the listener. The speaker may have been repeating utterances for his own benefit and the observed listener "responses" may have been nothing more than interruptions of self-directed speech. Also, the use of attention-getting devices by the speaker is not necessarily evidence that the speaker expects a response from the listener. Finally, the generalizability of the Keenan results can be questioned on the grounds that her sample was limited to two subjects and the context of her observations was quite restricted.

Garvey and Hogan (1973) provided supporting evidence that slightly older children expect responses to their utterances. They observed the social speech of children $3\frac{1}{2}$ to 5 years old during dyadic interactions in a small playroom. Social speech was defined as speech adapted to the utterances or behavior of the other member of the dyad. Certain well-formed sequences of social speech were observed. For example, children often used the "summons–answer" routine to secure the involvement of the listener. The routine is a conventional gambit consisting of a summons by the speaker (e.g., "Guess what"), an answer by the listener ("What?"), and a reason provided by the speaker for the original summons ("I just got a new bike"). The 18 children in the Garvey and Hogan study produced a total of 23 instances of the summons–answer routine, instances that often led to the introduction of a new topic into the conversation and an extended dialogue. Clearly, the use of conventional gambits such as the summons–answer routine represents progress beyond the use of simple repetition to secure a listener's response. Thus, by age 5, the child occasionally expects a response from the listener and has fairly sophisticated means for obtaining that response.

The research reviewed above indicates that children between the ages of 1 and 5 years often exhibit social initiative and have diverse means available for gaining and holding the attention of an audience. However, the abilities to direct one's communicative efforts toward a listener and to solicit responses from that listener do not, by themselves, guarantee successful communication. Both Piaget and Vygotsky argued that adaptation of speech to the physical and social context is a crucial element of effective communication. In the following section, we shall examine developmental trends in this adaptation.

B. ADAPTING MESSAGES TO THE CONTEXT OF COMMUNICATION

The effects of contextual factors on children's communication have received a great deal of attention in recent years (e.g., Hall, Cole, Reder, & Dowley, 1977; Maratsos, 1973; Martlew, Connolly, & McLeod, 1978; Whitehurst & Sonnenschein, 1981). To facilitate our review of children's adaptation to the context of communication, three types of adaptation will be distinguished: adaptation to (1) the needs or characteristics of the listener, (2) the physical surroundings, and (3) the social setting. Children may need to adapt their messages to a variety of listener characteristics, including the listener's age, status, linguistic level, knowledge, and visual perspective. The physical surroundings of communication include potential referents and any physical obstructions to communication. The social setting consists of behavioral patterns that are expected or acceptable, given the general purpose of the social gathering. Different communicative goals will be pursued and different communicative means employed in a church, at a party, in a classroom, and so forth. Obviously, the three types of communicative adaptation we have specified are highly correlated. For example, we could change the physical surroundings of communication by introducing an opaque screen between the speaker and listener (Krauss & Glucksberg, 1969). By doing so, we have also changed the visual perspective of the listener, making nonverbal communicative attempts such as pointing to referents futile. We may even have changed the social setting from one in which the goal of transmitting information to the listener is perfectly understandable to one in which the same goal appears meaningless (Maratsos, 1973; Meissner & Apthorp, 1976).

Piaget (1926) was primarily interested in the child's adaptation to the characteristics of listeners and the bulk of recent research concerning contextual factors reflects this interest. Much of this research will be reviewed below. Adaptation to the physical surroundings of communication has also received some attention in the literature. For example, Greenfield and Smith (1976) and Greenfield (1978) have observed the effects of physical surroundings on the child's choice of the most "informative" words for describing ongoing activity. Similarly, Whitehurst and his colleagues (e.g., Whitehurst & Sonnenschein, 1981) have studied the processes by which children "compare" referents to other objects in an array in order to construct effective referential messages. Due to space constraints, adaptation to the physical surroundings of communication will not be reviewed in this article. Finally, only limited attention has been given to the effects of social setting on communication. As we discussed earlier, Vygotsky (1962) demonstrated that when the goal of conversing with others was difficult to pursue, egocentric speech was unlikely to occur. More recent researchers have also observed communication in different social settings, but the effects of social setting have rarely been the main focus of their investigations (e.g., Shatz & Gelman, 1973). We discuss two notable exceptions and then review the adaptation of children to the characteristics of the listener.

Martlew *et al.* examined the speech of a 5-year-old boy in three situations: play with the child's mother, play with a same-age friend, and play while alone. In all three settings, the child's utterances were tape-recorded and no observer was present. Many differences were observed between the child's speech while alone and his speech in the two social situations. He tended to engage in word play more often when alone than when he was with either his mother or his friend. Conversely, the child used the word "pretend" frequently and set the scene for fantasy play in the two social situations but never did so when he was alone. The Martlew *et al.* study, like the Vygotsky (1962) investigation, indicates that at least some young children vary their speech according to their opportunities for social interaction.

Hall *et al.* (1977) demonstrated that communication will vary across two settings even when both settings are clearly social in nature. They observed the spontaneous speech of children 3–4 years of age in a classroom setting and during a trip to the supermarket. The children used more words, paid greater attention to questions posed by adults, and were more verbal in their responses to those questions in the supermarket than in the classroom. Hall *et al.* proposed that differences in the formality of the two settings led to the observed differences in children's speech. However, they were not explicit in describing how situational formality influenced the communication of children. In the final section of this article, we propose that children pursue different communicative goals in different social settings. In the classroom, goals such as being quiet, doing what the teacher says to do, and sitting still may dominate the child's communicative attempts. In the supermarket, however, goals such as having a good time or talking with adults and peers may guide the child's behavior. At the end of the article, we illustrate how differences in communicative goals might lead to differences in communication such as those observed in the Hall *et al.* study.

1. Adaptation to Characteristics of the Listener in Spontaneous Interactions

Flavell *et al.* (1968) proposed that egocentric speakers code a cognized event for themselves and deliver this message to the listener. In socialized speech, however, speakers code the event for themselves, *recode* the event according to relevant needs of the listener, and then deliver the message. Do young children engage in this recoding process in their spontaneous interactions? Mueller (1972) reported that over 99% of the utterances of preschoolers ranging in age from $3\frac{1}{2}$ to $5\frac{1}{2}$ years were adapted to the perspective of the listener. Do these results necessarily indicate that nursery school children recode messages according to listener needs? One cannot infer that a recoding process has occurred simply because the messages of the child are appropriate from the perspective of the listener. Instead, one must establish the presence of discrepancies between speaker and listener perspectives and show that the child takes those discrepancies into account in communicating. In natural settings, common perspectives and shared presuppositions are probably the rule, not the exception (Higgins, 1976). Thus, the children in Mueller's study may have been producing socially adapted utterances because they did not have to recode their messages in order for them to be listener appropriate. In support of this interpretation, over 66% of children's utterances in the Mueller study were produced with the speaker and the listener less than 4 ft apart. Furthermore, the listener attended visually to what the speaker was saying 89% of the time and the listener's attention was one of the best predictors of communicative success. Close proximity and eye contact between young speakers and listeners may minimize discrepancies in visual perspectives and also help listeners to identify the referents of speakers' utterances. Perhaps with development, children encounter more and more communicative situations in which close proximity between the speaker and listener is not always possible and eye-to-eye contact is limited. In situations such as these, the recoding process may be a necessary prerequisite for communicative success.

However, the fact that early communicative situations may not require perspective taking does not rule out the possibility that young children could recode their messages if the situation so demanded. A large number of studies have placed young children in communicative situations involving discrepancies between the speaker and listener. The most prominent example is the standard referential communication task in which a speaker and listener are separated by an opaque screen and the speaker must communicate how to construct an array. Children below the age of 7 rarely consider the deprived perspective and information of the listener in such a task and therefore do not communicate effectively (see Glucksberg *et al.*, 1975, for a review). In the next section, we consider several other studies in which the speaker and listener did not share the same visual perspective and then we examine the child's adaptation to other discrepancies between the perspectives of the speaker and listener.

2. *Adaptation to Deprived Visual Perspectives*

Flavell *et al.* (1968) asked 8 and 14 year olds to describe the rules for playing a board game to both blindfolded and sighted peers. The 8 year olds gave the same message to both listeners, a message that was extremely inadequate for the blindfolded listener. Fourteen year olds, however, were more detailed and explicit in their game instructions when the listener was blindfolded than when the listener could see the game materials. Flavell *et al.* concluded that younger children were deficient in their abilities to take the blind listener's handicap into account in formulating their messages. In a study using the same stimulus materials, Pratt, Scribner, and Cole (1977) found that first and third graders (approximately 7 and 9 year olds) adapted their game description to the needs of same-age listeners who did not have access to game materials. When listeners could not see game materials, children provided more information, were more explicit, and tended to begin with a description of game materials more often than when listeners had access to materials. Pratt *et al.* reported listener adaptation at a somewhat earlier age than might be expected given the Flavell *et al.* results. In the Pratt *et al.* task the speakers and listeners in the no-access condition were separated by a low screen that permitted nonverbal communication whereas in the Flavell *et al.* study the listener in the no-access condition was blindfolded. Patterson, Cosgrove, and O'Brien (1980) have shown that young listeners display nonverbal indicators of noncomprehension in referential communication tasks. Perhaps the speakers in the Pratt *et al.* study benefited from nonverbal listener feedback and adapted their messages more easily than children at comparable age levels in the Flavell *et al.* study.

Pratt *et al.* found evidence for adaptation to listener needs in children as young as 6 years. A study by Maratsos (1973) indicates that even younger children are capable of overcoming differences in visual perspectives. Maratsos had preschoolers play a simple communication "game" with both blindfolded and sighted listeners. In the game, children were told to specify which of two toy passengers should be given a ride down a small hill. Children 3, 4, and 5 years old provided more adequate information in the blindfolded condition than in the sighted condition when adequacy was judged from the perspective of the blindfolded listener. However, developmental differences were observed in the means by which speakers adapted their messages. Three year olds took the listener's lack of sight into account by refraining from pointing in the blindfolded condition. Four and 5 year olds did not point to the referent in either the blindfolded or sighted conditions. Rather, these children adapted their messages by providing more information to the blindfolded listener than to the sighted listener.

The Maratsos study indicates that even preschool children can take listener needs into account in formulating messages. Why was this ability not manifested by much older children in the Flavell *et al.* (1968) study? Maratsos argued that the communicative situation in his study was more "natural" than the communicative situation in the Flavell *et al.* experiment. The goal of the Maratsos task involved playing a simple game and the means necessary for achieving this goal were fairly unsophisticated. The toys that the child had to describe differed on a limited number of readily identifiable attributes. To communicate successfully to the blindfolded listener, the child had only to refrain from pointing to the referent and to specify the relevant attributes of the referent. In contrast, the goals of the Flavell *et al.* task were highly complex and the means required for achieving these goals were quite sophisticated. The children had to describe materials that combined many stimulus attributes and game rules that had to be abstracted from concrete stimuli. When the listener was blind, an adequate message required an organized, well-sequenced presentation of information concerning multiple aspects of a complicated game. Not surprisingly, 8 year olds in the Flavell *et al.* study had difficulty providing adequate messages whereas preschoolers in the Maratsos study were able to adapt their messages to the needs of a blind listener.

3. *Adaptation to Age-Related Needs of the Listener*

The listeners in the studies reviewed above did not have access to the information the speaker was trying to convey. Access was blocked by the presence of concrete objects such as blindfolds (Flavell *et al.*, 1968; Maratsos, 1973) and opaque screens (Pratt *et al.*, 1977). What happens when speaker and listener perspectives are discrepant because the listener is significantly older or younger than the speaker? Can children take age-related needs of listeners into account in their communications?

Shatz and Gelman (1973) recorded the conversations of 4 year olds with 2 year olds, same-age peers, and adults. They found that the speech of the 4 year olds to 2 year olds tended to be shorter and simpler and to contain more attention-getting devices than their speech to peers and adults. This tendency was observed even in children who did not have younger siblings, suggesting that the children were not simply imitating the adult tendency to "talk down" to young children. Shatz and Gelman concluded that 4 year olds adapt their speech to the needs of younger listeners, although their study did not clearly indicate exactly which of the listener's characteristics elicit this adaptation. Age, size, linguistic level, cognitive or attentional capacity, status, or other age-related factors may contribute to listener adaptation.

Menig-Peterson (1975) challenged the Shatz and Gelman (1973) conclusion that 4 year olds adapt their messages to age-related needs of the listener. She suggested that the 4 year olds in the Shatz and Gelman study were simply imitating the shorter, simpler speech of the 2 year olds during their conversations. However, as Shatz and Gelman (1973) pointed out, the speech of the 4 year olds differed from the speech of the 2 year olds on several important dimensions. For example, the 4 year olds occasionally used complex constructions that one would not expect to find in the speech of 2 year olds. However, one should try to determine how much of an influence the younger child's speech can have on the 4 year old.

A study by Sachs and Devin (1976) indicated that speaker adaptation to age-related needs of the listener is more than simple imitation of immature speech forms. Sachs and Devin recorded the conversations of children 3–5 years old with four listeners: the child's mother, a baby just beginning to talk, a same-age peer, and a baby doll. They found that children's speech to either a baby or a baby doll was less complex and included more names and imperatives than speech to either the child's mother or a peer. Given that an inanimate object cannot provide linguistic feedback, the speech modifications to the baby doll may provide evidence for adaptation to listeners' needs that extends beyond immediate imitation of immature speech.

If the speech modifications in the Sachs and Devin study cannot be attributed entirely to immediate imitation, what factors can account for them? Should we credit the preschool speaker with sophisticated knowledge of the linguistic skills and needs of younger listeners? One alternate explanation of speech modifications is that young speakers engage in "delayed imitation" of immature speech. They may have an "immature" speech code that they use whenever talking to immature listeners, either animate or inanimate. The "delayed imitation" explanation seems unlikely, however, given additional data reported by Sachs and Devin. They recorded the speech of 4 year olds pretending to be babies "just learning to talk." Presumably, the children would use their immature codes in such a situation. Although the children had a firm grasp of the prosodic and phonological characteristics of baby talk, their imitations of the syntactic characteristics were highly inaccurate. Short of attributing sophisticated perspective taking to preschool speakers, how do we explain their tendency to produce shorter, simpler utterances to younger listeners than to peers or adults?

Shatz and Gelman (1977) presented an explanation of speech adaptation that depends neither on delayed imitation of immature speech nor on the speaker's appreciation of differences in the linguistic competence of listeners. They reanalyzed the data from the Shatz and Gelman (1973) study according to the situation in which speech had occurred. Shatz and Gelman (1973) had recorded the speech of 4 year olds in two situations, a structured task in which the child explained the use of a toy to the listener and an unstructured situation. In both situations, 4 year olds used less complex speech with 2 year olds than with adults. However, complex linguistic constructions did occur with 2-year-old listeners. To explain this occurrence, Shatz and Gelman (1977) argued that children choose not to talk about certain things to younger listeners rather than choosing not to use certain syntactic constructions. In other words, the selection of speech styles for various listeners takes place at the level of semantic function rather than at the level of syntactic complexity.

In support of this argument, Shatz and Gelman (1977) focused on the use by 4 year olds of one set of complex constructions: "wh" and "that" predicate complementizers. They noted that predicate complementizers were used to direct social interaction (e.g., "This is how we do it"), to talk about mental states (e.g., "Before, I thought that this was a crocodile"), and to modulate assertions (e.g., "I'm sure that this fits, too"). Shatz and Gelman (1977) found that both the age of the listener and the situation in which speech occurred determined which semantic function was served by the predicate complementizers. The age of the listener was an important determinant of the use of predicate complementizers to talk about mental states. Four year olds discussed mental states with adults much more often than they did with 2 year olds. The tendency to refrain from discussing mental states with 2 year olds may reflect some knowledge of the cognitive status of the young listener. Similarly, 4 year olds modulated assertions more frequently with adult listeners than with 2 year olds. Modulations with adults but not with 2 year olds may reflect recognition of the superior social status of the adult and the inferior status of the 2 year old. The situation in which speech occurs also was found to affect the use of complex constructions. In the unstructured situation, modulations with 2 year olds were more frequent than in the structured situation. This difference in frequency may reflect a shifting of goals from instructing a captive audience to attempting to maintain social interaction with an inattentive audience. Thus, the social context of speech and the social status of the listener may interact in determining use by 4 year olds of predicate complementizers to modulate assertions.

4. *Adaptation to the Knowledge and Abilities of the Listener*

The studies reviewed thus far have indicated that preschool children can recode messages to take into account both the visual perspective of the listener and the listener's age-related needs when task constraints are minimal. Speaker recodings have also been demonstrated as a function of the listener's knowledge and abilities. Speakers and listeners often have discrepant presuppositions and levels of knowledge about a topic. Several studies have indicated that young children are sensitive to these knowledge discrepancies. For example, Maratsos (1974) found that children 3 and 4 years old can use indefinite and definite articles (i.e., *a* and *the*) appropriately to specify new and old referents for a listener (but Warden, 1976, obtained contrary findings). This differential use of *a* and *the* would not be possible unless the child were at least partially sensitive to the listener's current knowledge regarding conversational topics.

A study by Menig-Peterson (1975) provides more convincing evidence for the young child's ability to take the knowledge of the listener into account in communicating. In her study, children 3 and 4 years old were interviewed by an adult about an event that the child had witnessed, the staged spilling of a cup of Kool-Aid. In one condition, the experimenter was "naive" in that she was not present during the event; and in the other condition, the experimenter was "knowledgeable" and had shared the event with the child. When the experimenter had not shared the experience with the child, the child introduced topics related to the experience more elaborately than when the experimenter was knowledgeable about the events. In other words, the child did not assume that the naive experimenter possessed information concerning the staged event. Furthermore, 4 year olds, but not 3 year olds, specified more referents in their speech concerning the events when the experimenter was naive than when the experimenter was knowledgeable. Thus, preschoolers were able to adapt their messages according to the amount of information they shared with the listener. Also, 4 year olds appeared to have more means at their disposal than 3 year olds for adapting their messages to the needs of the naive listener.

In addition to being able to adapt their messages to differences in listener knowledge, young children can recode messages according to the abilities of the listener. For example, Schiff (1976) observed that normal hearing children of deaf parents modified their speech according to whether they were speaking to their deaf mothers or a hearing adult. The children used longer utterances and fewer manual signs when speaking to the hearing adult. Other studies have shown that young children can adapt their speech to the cognitive and linguistic abilities of the listener (e.g., Guralnick & Paul-Brown, 1977; Masur, 1978). The Masur (1978) study is of particular interest because it suggests that the basis for adaptation to the listener's abilities may actually change during the course of a communicative interaction.

Masur asked 4 year olds to explain the use of a toy to 2 year olds at two linguistic levels. The linguistic level of the listener was defined in terms of the mean length of the listener's utterances. At the beginning of the experimental session, the mean length of the speaker's utterances was highly correlated with the mean length of the listener's utterances. In other words, the 4-year-old speakers shortened and simplified their speech according to the linguistic level of the listener. However, the magnitude of the correlation between the speaker's and listener's speech declined to near zero as the session proceeded. As the importance of the linguistic level of the listener declined, the importance of the listener's responsiveness increased. By the end of the session, 2 year olds who responded frequently to the utterances of 4 year olds received longer and more complex utterances than 2 year olds who were unresponsive.

The flexibility in the basis of adaptation to the listener demonstrated in the Masur study is important because, like the results of the Sachs and Devin (1976) study, it indicates that adaptation is more than simple imitation of immature speech forms. If 4 year olds were simply imitating the speech of 2 year olds in the Masur study, one would expect the correlation between their linguistic levels to increase as the session proceeded and the 4 year olds became more practiced at imitating. Instead, the correlation decreased and the responsiveness of the 2 year olds became important. Because the listener's responsiveness is a much better indicator of comprehension than the mean length of the listener's utterances, the switch in the basis of speech modifications in the Masur study seems highly adaptive. By focusing on listener responsiveness, the 4-year-old speakers may have been able to determine which types of speech were not being comprehended by the 2 year olds and to eliminate those types from their messages.

We have seen from our review of the literature that by age 4 children can adapt their communication to all of the following needs of the listener: lack of a common visual perspective (Maratsos, 1973), age (Sachs & Devin, 1976; Shatz & Gelman, 1973), social status (Shatz & Gelman, 1977), lack of common knowledge (Menig-Peterson, 1975), cognitive level (Guralnick & Paul-Brown, 1977; Shatz & Gelman, 1977), linguistic level (Masur, 1978), and communicative responsiveness (Masur, 1978). Furthermore, the studies reviewed have shown a variety of developmental differences in the means by which this adaptation is accomplished. In 3-year-old speakers, adaptation involves refraining from certain inappropriate actions (Maratsos, 1973) or providing appropriate introductions for topics that are new to the listener (Menig-Peterson, 1975). In 4-year-old speakers, adaptation involves providing more information or more specific information according to the needs of the listener. By age 4, children may also adapt their speech by refraining from discussing topics that are inappropriate for certain listeners (Shatz & Gelman, 1977) or from using syntactic constructions that are not comprehended by the listener (Masur, 1978). Finally, in the oldest children observed, adaptation involved complex processes such as sequencing messages in a manner appropriate to the informational needs of the listener (Pratt *et al.*, 1977).

Although it is clear that children adapt their speech to the characteristics of the listener from an early age, the processes underlying this adaptation remain unspecified. The results discussed above are consistent with the hypothesis that young children code messages for themselves, recode those messages according to the listener's needs, and then deliver the messages (see Flavell *et al.*, 1968). However, we do not have any direct evidence for the proposed recoding process. All we can safely conclude is that the messages of young children are often socially adapted even when discrepancies exist between the child's perspective and that of the listener. In the next section, we present evidence that young children adapt their speech to the content of the listener's utterances as well as to the listener's perspective.

C. PROVIDING RELEVANT RESPONSES TO THE LISTENER'S MESSAGES

One of the basic "rules" governing successful communication is that the participants in an exchange "be relevant" (Grice, 1968). In the present section, two ways in which young children can be relevant in responding to a listener will be discussed. First, children can achieve discourse coherence by saying something semantically or syntactically related to a previous utterance of the listener. Second, children can respond to direct requests for clarification of unclear messages by modifying those messages appropriately. Important developmental changes occur in the means by which children achieve discourse coherence and respond to feedback from the listener.

1. Achieving Discourse Coherence

The major obstacle to overcome in answering the question of how children of different ages achieve discourse coherence is determining what constitutes a "relevant" reply by the child. A disconcerting tendency on the part of researchers has been not to report the criteria by which children's responses were judged to be relevant. For example, Mueller (1972) reported that only 17% of preschoolers' utterances involved direct replies to the listener's utterances, but did not define what constituted a direct reply. Keenan (Keenan, 1974; Keenan & Klein, 1975) tackled the problem of defining response relevance directly. She suggested that relevance can be achieved by any of the following means, depending on the age of the child: (1) repeat all or part of the utterance without modification; (2) repeat part of the utterance in a modified form (e.g., respond to the utterance "big one" by saying "I got a big one"); (3) substitute a new word for one of the constituents of the listener's utterance (e.g., say "many moths" in response to "two moths"); or (4) produce a novel utterance that is semantically related to the listener's utterance. Keenan observed a developmental trend in the means by which her twin boys achieved relevance, from complete reliance on the *form* of the listener's utterance to reliance on the semantic *content* of the utterance. Before age 2 years and 10 months, the twins maintained discourse coherence by either repeating the listener's utterances or by modifying them slightly through propositional expansion. After 2 years and 10 months, the twins began substituting constituents in the listener's utterances and producing novel but semantically related utterances.

Several studies have corroborated this developmental trend from reliance on the form of previous utterances to reliance on semantic content. Most of these studies have indicated that prior to age 3 or 4, children rely on the form of the listener's utterances in achieving conversational coherence. Bloom *et al.* (1976) observed a sharp developmental increase between 2 and 3 years of age in the relative frequency of children's utterances that were linguistically related to prior utterances of adults. Children were learning to share the topic of a conversation by substituting, elaborating, or modifying constituents of the adults' utterances. Bloom and Lahey (1978) presented evidence that children between 2 and 4 years of age adapt their speech to the listener's remarks through the use of pronominal reference, deixis (appropriate use of terms such as "this" and "that," which depend on the situation for their interpretation), anaphoric reference, and grammatical ellipsis. Finally, Shugar (1976) found that 1- and 2-year-old children maintain discourse agreement by either reproducing previous utterances of their mothers with or without modification, substituting constituents in listeners' utterances, or conjoining utterances with new but related information. The children observed by Shugar had extreme difficulty introducing entirely new semantic content into their conversations with their mothers. When they attempted to introduce such information, discourse tended to break down.

Savic (1976) provided supporting evidence that young children often depend on the form of the listener's previous utterances in their early attempts at achieving conversational coherence. Savic looked at the strategies that 1- and 3-year-old children used for providing answers to adult questions. Three strategies were employed frequently by children. First, if children did not understand the question word in a question, they provided an answer that was appropriate for a question word that they did understand. For example, children answered "whose" questions as if they were "what" questions. Second, if children understood the question word but had not yet learned a wide range of appropriate answers for the question word, they would resort to "stereotypic" answers. For example, one child in the study always answered "tomorrow" when asked questions containing the word "when." Finally, if children understood the question word but did not understand the content of the question, they tended to repeat part of the question as a reply. The latter two strategies suggest that when children do not have an answer appropriate for the *content* of the adult's question, they provide an answer relevant to the *form* of the question. The first strategy, however, indicates that the form/content relationship in children's responses can be reversed. When children understand the content of the question but not the question word, they respond with content appropriate for another question form.

These studies indicate that almost as soon as children begin to speak they are capable of adapting their speech to the previous utterances of the listener. However, the means by which this adaptation is achieved undergoes rapid development. This development seems to reflect a trade-off between dependence on the linguistic form and the semantic content of the listener's utterance. In the Keenan (Keenan, 1974; Keenan & Klein, 1975) and Shugar (1976) studies, the earliest instances of adaptation involved either direct repetition or formal modification of the listener's utterance. With development, however, the semantic content of the listener's utterance can be conjoined with other information, partially substituted for by new information, or completely replaced by related information. Furthermore, the Savic (1976) investigation indicates that development is not simply a unidirectional progression from dependence on form to dependence on content of the listener's utterance. Rather, children at the same developmental level may switch from a focus on the form of an adult's utterance to a focus on content depending on their prior experience with similar utterances.

Horgan (1978) reported data indicating that concentration on one aspect of an utterance may be detrimental to the child's ability to deal with other aspects of the same utterance. Horgan recorded one child's answers to questions by adults over a period of several months. Before the child was $1\frac{1}{2}$ years old, she focused on the form of questions and responded to questions even when their content was not completely understood. For example, the child would answer yes/no questions even when they contained nonsense words. After age $1\frac{1}{2}$, the child began to concentrate on the content of questions. However, as her ability to provide content-appropriate answers improved, her ability to distinguish between question forms actually declined. The Horgan results have important implications for the relation between cognitive decentration and the young child's ability to adapt speech to previous utterances of the listener. Horgan's subject apparently centered her attention first on the form and then on the content of the listener's utterances, but had difficulty considering form and content simultaneously. With further development the child can decenter cognitively and deal with both the form and content of utterances in providing relevant responses. In fact, research by Garvey (1974) indicates that by age 5 children alternate turns in verbal interactions by attending to both the form and content of previous utterances by their peers.

We can see from this brief review of the literature concerning discourse coherence that children's utterances are related to previous utterances of the listener at a very young age. Furthermore, a developmental progression in the means by which coherence is achieved can be observed, from reliance on the form of previous utterances to reliance on content, and finally to a consideration of both form and content. However, the child's ability to say something formally or semantically related to the listener's utterances does not guarantee successful communication. Inevitably, the listener will fail to comprehend some of the speaker's messages. If the listener is an adult, he or she will typically request additional information to clarify inadequate messages (Rosenberg & Donner, 1968; Rosenberg & Markman, 1971). In the following section, we consider the child's tendency to avert communicative failure by responding appropriately to a listener's request for message clarification. Then, in Section III,D, we discuss the child's tendency to provide feedback as a listener when the speaker's message is inadequate.

2. *Responding to Requests for Clarification*

Wellman and Lempers (1977) found that 2-year-old speakers recommunicated their messages 54% of the time when they received no response from the listener, 3% of the time when they received an adequate response, and 100% of the time when they received either negative verbal feedback or visual attention. Recommunications tended to include either the same amount of information as was conveyed in the original message or less information. Thus, although 2 year olds did respond to listener feedback, their responses could hardly be considered adequate for repairing breakdowns in communication. The Wellman and Lempers (1977) study indicates, however, that the provision of feedback by the listener affects the likelihood that the speaker will recommunicate the message.

A study by Peterson, Danner, and Flavell (1972) indicates that young speakers are also influenced by the type of feedback given by the listener. Peterson *et al.* administered a referential communication task to preschoolers and first-graders. The purpose of the task was to construct messages that allowed a listener to pick a referent from an array. Children were given a pretest in which they were asked to describe stimuli similar to the test stimuli in as many ways as possible. If they did not provide spontaneously at least two descriptions of the pretest stimuli, the experimenter prompted them by saying, "What else does it look like? Is there anything else you can tell me about it?" During the test phase of the experiment, three types of feedback were given to the children: implicit nonverbal feedback (a facial expression of bewilderment), implicit verbal feedback ("I don't understand"), and explicit verbal feedback ("Look at it again. What else does it look like? Is there anything else you can tell me about it?"). Four year olds reformulated their messages only when explicit verbal feedback was provided, whereas 7 year olds modified their messages in response to both implicit and explicit verbal feedback. Implicit nonverbal feedback did not elicit new or modified referent descriptions at either age level, perhaps because the experimenter was a poor actor or because the type of nonverbal feedback presented was not appropriate for young speakers. Peterson *et al.* concluded that the explicitness of feedback is an important determinant of children's response to feedback.

However, explicitness per se may not be the effective variable in the Peterson *et al.* study. Perhaps the effect of explicitness can be attributed to the similarity between the explicit verbal feedback and pretest prompts to describe stimuli in as many ways as possible. In both, the child is told to look at the stimulus again and tell the experimenter more about it. Thus, in the explicit verbal feedback condition, children may perceive the goal of the task as providing multiple descriptions of the referent rather than as reformulating inadequate messages. In the two implicit feedback conditions, feedback did not resemble pretest prompts so the provision of additional descriptions of the referents in these conditions can be interpreted as message reformulations. Therefore, we may conclude that 7 year olds but not 4 year olds reformulate messages in response to verbal feedback from the listener.

A study by Spilton and Lee (1977) provides better evidence that the explicitness of feedback affects the speaker's response to feedback. Spilton and Lee recorded the conversations of dyads of 4 year olds in a free-play situation. They selected instances of "elaborated sequences" from the speech samples they obtained. Elaborated sequences consisted of a speaker utterance that was unclear either linguistically or semantically and included at least two listener and two speaker statements aimed at clarifying the original message. The investigators employed stringent criteria in identifying elaborated sequences because they were interested in the process by which children reached mutual understanding through a series of approximations and successive adaptations. Spilton and Lee analyzed the elaborated sequences in terms of the relationship between the type of listener feedback provided and the speaker's response to feedback. Twenty-five percent of listener's responses to unclear messages were specific questions about the messages, 24% were general questions (e.g., "What?"), 23% were replies, 9% were topic-relevant questions, and 9% were repetitions. The content of the remaining 10% of listener's responses was not specified. Overall, 66% of the speakers' responses to feedback were adaptive in that they provided additional information, confirmed or negated the listener's interpretation of the message, or expanded upon the original message. The majority of nonadaptive responses (81%) involved repetitions of the original message without modification. Furthermore, an orderly relationship between the type of listener feedback provided and the adaptiveness of the speaker's response to feedback was observed. The probability of obtaining an adaptive response from the speaker was much higher for specific questions than for any other type of listener feedback.

Thus, Peterson *et al.* appear to be correct in assuming that explicitness of feedback is a critical determinant of the speaker's response to feedback. What consequences does the importance of explicitness have for a theory of communicative development? Consider, first, that when feedback is not explicit (or when the speaker is quite young), the speaker tends to repeat the message without modification (Spilton & Lee, 1977; Wellman & Lempers, 1977). Message repetition may imply an awareness by the speaker that he or she has an obligation to reply to the listener's utterances but it does *not* necessarily imply an effort by the speaker to reformulate an ambiguous message according to listener needs. Now consider the situation in which feedback is explicit and the young speaker responds adequately to feedback. Does this ability reflect anything more than appropriate responding to direct requests for information by the listener? Presumably, when feedback is explicit, the child could provide an adequate response without any awareness of the relationship between the listener's request for information and a previous message by the speaker. Before we can credit the child with an ability to reformulate messages in response to listener feedback, we must show that children modify their messages when feedback is only implicit. When we adopt this stringent criterion for the speaker's response to feedback, we find that before age 6 or 7 children are usually unresponsive to feedback from the listener.

D. PROVIDING FEEDBACK AS A LISTENER

In the preceding section, we focused on the speaker's role in achieving conversational coherence and repairing breakdowns in communication. What about the listener's ability to provide adequate feedback when he or she does not understand the speaker's messages? In the Spilton and Lee (1977) study discussed in the preceding section, 4-year-old listeners provided both general and specific feedback to unclear utterances by the speaker. However, Spilton and Lee analyzed listener feedback in a very restricted sample of speech. They focused on elaborated sequences in which an intent to clarify messages was already apparent. One cannot extrapolate from the Spilton and Lee study the overall frequency with which 4 year olds provide feedback or when the ability to provide appropriate feedback develops.

Karabenick and Miller (1977) reported that the ability to provide appropriate feedback appears relatively late in development. They administered a referential communication task to 5, 6, and 7 year olds. Although almost all of the children provided at least one instance of listener feedback, the frequency of feedback in the study was quite low despite the fact that the average speaker message omitted critical information. More importantly, the appropriateness of feedback when it did occur was extremely limited. Only 57% of the *questions* listeners asked about speakers' messages were directed toward messages that were inadequate. Conversely, more than 60% of the listener's *acknowledgments* of comprehension of messages followed inadequate messages. Furthermore, no developmental improvements in the appropriateness of listener feedback were observed in the study.

The results of the Karabenick and Miller study indicate that the young listener does not provide feedback very often and when he or she does, this feedback tends to be inappropriate. However, in both studies only verbal feedback by the listener was considered. Patterson *et al.* (1980) have shown that young listeners are quite capable of providing nonverbal indicators of noncomprehension. Four year olds in their study displayed more eye contact with the speaker following uninformative messages than following informative ones, even though they did not differentiate between messages in their verbal feedback. Furthermore, a study by Cosgrove and Patterson (1977) suggests that even the tendency to provide *verbal* feedback can be enhanced in young children. In a referential communication task, Cosgrove and Patterson gave 4–10 year olds messages that were fully informative, partially informative, or uninformative. Half of the children at each age level also received a "plan" for providing listener feedback. The plan consisted of instructions to ask questions when unsure of the referent of the speaker's message. Overall, children asked more questions when the speaker's message was uninformative than when the message was partially or fully informative and sensitivity to message informativeness increased with age. The provision of a plan for feedback affected performance of all but the youngest children. When given a plan, children asked more questions, made more correct selections of the referent, and were more sensitive to message informativeness than when no plan was provided. The effect of providing a plan was most pronounced for the 6 year old who asked an average of .58 questions in the "no plan" condition and 8.83 questions in the "plan" condition. Ironsmith and Whitehurst (1978a) provided supporting evidence. When elementary school children, ranging in age from 5 to 12 years, are instructed to ask questions after unclear messages, they do ask more questions and the appropriateness of their questions improves with age.

The differences between the Cosgrove and Patterson (1977) and Karabenick and Miller (1977) studies are revealing. Karabenick and Miller found that listener feedback was infrequent and when it occurred it tended to be inappropriate. Cosgrove and Patterson found that when a plan for feedback was provided, 6, 8, and 10 year olds asked questions on almost every referential communication trial, and that these questions tended to be appropriate. Patterson and Kister (1981) have argued that discrepancies between the results may reflect the fact that speakers in the Karabenick and Miller study were naive peers and speakers in the Cosgrove and Patterson investigation were adult confederates. Perhaps the systematically varied message inadequacies of the adult confederates were easier to detect than the unsystematic (and presumably age-related) inadequacies of the speakers in the Karabenick and Miller study.

Alternatively, perhaps the children in the Karabenick and Miller study were aware that speakers' messages were inadequate but did not know how to deal with message inadequacy. Unlike the children in the "plan" condition in the Cosgrove and Patterson study, they did not employ appropriate means for repairing communicative breakdowns. A particularly relevant point is that the Karabenick and Miller subjects did have the means available for correcting message inadequacies—they could and did ask questions—they just did not often coordinate their question-asking behavior with the goal of disambiguating the speaker's messages. Therefore, the plan for feedback in the Cosgrove and Patterson study may have provided two kinds of information. The plan told the children *what* they should do (i.e., ask questions), and it told them *when* they should do it (i.e., when they were unsure of which referent to pick). Related studies by Cosgrove and Patterson (1978) and Ironsmith and Whitehurst (1978b) indicate that "what" and "when" information can also be acquired through exposure to a model who provides appropriate feedback. We shall return to the issue of the link between communicative goals and behavior in the final sections of the article.

The studies reviewed above reveal important age-related trends in the child's tendency to provide feedback as a listener. Preschoolers have difficulty providing verbal feedback even when they are given a plan for doing so (Cosgrove & Patterson, 1977), although they display nonverbal indicators of confusion spontaneously (Patterson *et al.*, 1980). Kindergarteners can provide appropriate verbal feedback when exposed to a plan or model demonstrating when and how feedback should be provided (Cosgrove & Patterson, 1977; Karabenick & Miller, 1977). Finally, children in late elementary school years provide verbal feedback in the absence of plans or modeling procedures (Cosgrove & Patterson, 1977).

E. SUMMARY: BEYOND UNIDIMENSIONAL CONCEPTIONS OF COMMUNICATION

In our selective review of the literature on children's communication we identified the following skills of social speech: (1) gaining and holding an audience, (2) adapting messages to the context of communication, (3) providing relevant responses to the listener's messages, and (4) providing feedback as a listener. From our review of the research concerning each skill, we can conclude that children engage in dyadic communication from a very young age and make considerable progress in communicative effectiveness during the preschool years. By 3 or 4 years of age, children can solicit the attention of a listener by verbal or nonverbal means, expect and secure a response from the listener, adapt messages to the needs of the listener, achieve discourse coherence by saying something either formally *or* semantically related to the listener's utterances, and display nonverbal indicators of noncomprehension when the speaker's messages are inadequate. Between 5 and 7 years of age, children begin to adapt messages to the social context of communication, adapt their messages formally *and* semantically to previous utterances of the listener, respond to feedback from the listener even when it is implicit, and provide verbal feedback if they have been told when and how to do so. Only children's tendencies to provide verbal feedback in the absence of plans or modeling procedures remain infrequent until middle childhood.

Our review of the literature served several purposes. It showed that children's speech during the preschool years is not as egocentric as one might have expected, given the early communicative analyses of Piaget (1926) and Vygotsky (1962). More importantly, the review illustrated that macrolevel constructs such as "egocentric speech" cannot capture the diverse developmental changes that occur during early childhood. By identifying four different classes of communicative skills, we have shown how communication is a *multi*dimensional phenomenon. The multifaceted nature of communication becomes even more apparent when one considers that our taxonomy of skills could be extended to include nonverbal signals, written communication, and so forth.

Although we have shown that preschoolers have a variety of communicative skills available by 2 or 3 years of age under ideal conditions, constraints on communication continue well into middle childhood when children communicate in novel or complex contexts such as experimental settings (e.g., Glucksberg *et al.*, 1975; Patterson & Kister, 1981; Shatz, 1978). Clearly, we must distinguish between the child's repertoire of skills and the processes by which these skills are selected and used in the service of social goals. Central to this skill/will distinction are the issues of communicative motivation, the influence of contextual factors on communication, and the child's control of his or her communicative efforts. In the following section, we discuss some recent theoretical attempts to deal with these issues and then propose a new framework for interpreting communicative development that integrates and extends these attempts.

IV. Toward a Model of Communicative Development

The past decade has been marked by a shift away from a Piagetian emphasis on the form of children's speech toward a concern for communicative motives, contextual factors, and communicative control. In the case of communicative motivation, this shift was fostered by methods for identifying the communicative intentions of very young children. Recent researchers have argued that communicative intent can be inferred when the child's behavior is "directed" toward some desired goal, end state, or "perlocutionary effect" (e.g., Bruner, 1974; Dore, Gearhart, & Newman, 1978; Greenfield, 1977). The desired end state can be identified when the listener finds an acceptable interpretation of the child's actions or verbalizations. For example, an adult might suggest successive interpretations of the child's communicative attempts until the child finally "accepts" one of these interpretations by repeating or assenting to the adult's utterance (Greenfield, 1977). Given that the child's communicative intentions can be identified, at least indirectly, what can be said about early communicative motives? Many researchers have argued that young children's behavior is guided by two general communicative purposes, referential and interpersonal motives (Moerk, 1977; Olson, 1977a; Trevarthen, 1977). Referential motives encompass efforts to share some object or event in the environment with a listener whereas interpersonal motives include attempts to coordinate behavior with the listener, express human feelings, engage in reciprocal exchanges, and so forth (Trevarthen, 1977). In the model of communicative development we propose, the development of a wide variety of referential and interpersonal motives for communicating will be discussed under the heading of "communicative goals."

The recent emphasis on communicative intentions has been tied closely to an interest in the influence of contextual factors on communication. The physical or social context of communication can affect the child's behavior in several ways. First, contextual factors can influence the child's communicative goals, as we suggested in discussing the Hall *et al.* (1977) and Shatz and Gelman (1977) studies concerning speech in structured and unstructured settings. Second, both the physical and social setting can have an impact on children's *control* of their communicative efforts. Olson (Olson, 1977b; Olson & Hilyard, 1981) has asserted that young children depend more on the *context* of messages (the "utterance") than on their veridical *content* (the "text") in regulating their communication with others. As a result, the fine semantic discriminations among messages often required in experimental settings may not be possible for the young child (e.g., Krauss & Glucksberg, 1969; Robinson, 1981; Whitehurst & Sonnenschein, 1981). Finally, contextual factors may influence the means that children employ in achieving their communicative goals by imposing physical or social constraints on the child's verbal and nonverbal behavior (e.g., Greenfield & Smith, 1976; Moerk, 1977; Mueller & Lucas, 1975). The model of communicative development to be proposed will reflect the widespread influence of contextual factors on children's communication. Contextual factors will be considered when we discuss children's communicative goals, their regulation of communication, and the means by which they achieve their communicative purposes.

Although recent theorists have emphasized both intentions and contextual factors in discussing communicative development, even more emphasis has been given to children's control of their communicative efforts. Several theorists have made similar distinctions between the communicative skills children have available and the control they exert over these skills. For example, Ammon (1981) distinguished between "knowing how" to employ a communicative skill and "knowing about" the skill and when it should be employed. Similarly, Whitehurst and Sonnenschein (1981) distinguished between "novel" skills that require learning new component routines and "accustomed" skills for which the child has all the necessary components but lacks knowledge concerning how to organize and deploy these components. Finally, Flavell (1981) and Markman (1981) discussed the child's metacognitive awareness in controlling and monitoring communicative behavior. Recent theorists appear to agree that children learn *how* to employ communicative skills through extensive practice in communicative settings. However, they learn *about* these skills through reflection on their communicative performance, exposure to models, direct instruction, and so forth. Therefore, mature communicators can play a major role in teaching children how to control their communicative efforts. We shall discuss the development of children's control of communication and the role others can play in this development in Section IV,C, on "communicative plans."

A. OVERVIEW OF THE MODEL

Our proposal is an attempt to synthesize and extend new conceptualizations of the social and cognitive factors involved in communicative development. Our concern is with the development of communicative *skills*. By "skill" we mean a set of behavioral responses selected and controlled to accomplish particular purposes in particular settings (see Fischer, 1980). In our view, skills include motivational, social, and cognitive components such as "metacognitive experiences" (Flavell, 1981), attributions for success and failure (Robinson, 1981), and beliefs about the listener and the value of communicating. We have illustrated how children's selection and use of particular goals, plans, and means facilitates effective communication in our literature review. Now we would like to sketch the goals/plans/means framework in more detail in order to show its value for interpreting developmental changes in communicative skills.

Our model emphasizes how children learn to coordinate intentions and communicative strategies selectively and shares similarities with several other interpretations of children's learning and deliberate problem-solving behavior (e.g., Brown, 1981; Paris, 1978; Paris & Lindauer, 1982; Vygotsky, 1978). We begin with the assumption that most conversations require that communicators make a series of choices regarding their communicative goals, plans, and means. Communicative goals answer the question of *why* the child is communicating in the first place. These goals might include maintaining social interaction, persuading others, entertaining, being entertained, and so forth. Communicative goals may be imposed on the child by others, dictated by environmental constraints (e.g., Mueller & Lucas, 1975), or consciously selected and pursued. Once a communicative goal has been defined, a plan for achieving the goal must be instituted. Communicative plans answer the question of *what* must be done to fulfill a communicative goal. Communicative plans are the rules that govern the child's deployment of behavioral means. They may be provided for the child by others (e.g., Cosgrove & Patterson, 1977) or they may follow more or less automatically from a specific communicative goal. Being polite, taking the listener into account, providing or responding to feedback, and taking turns could all be examples of communicative plans. Once the communicator has adopted a plan for achieving a communicative goal, he or she must choose the best combination of communicative means for carrying out that plan. Communicative

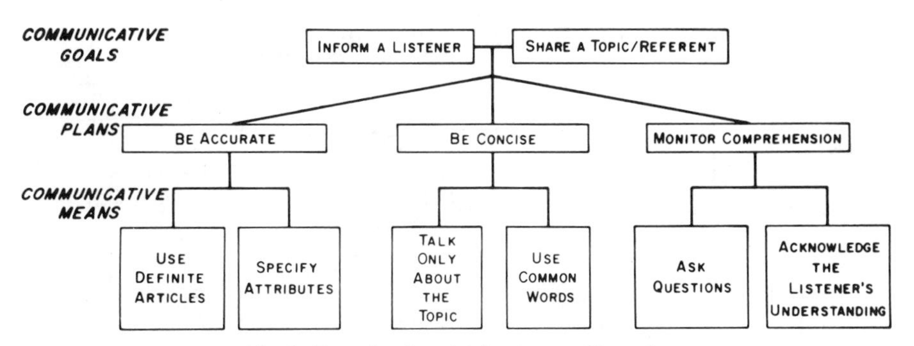

Fig. 1. Example of goals/plans/means hierarchy.

means answer the question of *how* plans are implemented. They consist of concrete, observable behaviors such as saying "please" and "thank you" or pausing to let a listener contribute to a conversation. Thus, the links among goals, plans, and means represent a translation of thought into action in communicative exchanges.

Figure 1 provides a graphic example of the goals/plans/means hierarchy. It is not possible to provide a simple list of goals, plans, and means comprising the repertoire of communicative skills because these depend on the participants, setting, and purposes. What functions as a goal in one setting may be a plan in another interaction. Our model allows variable "slot filling" so that the goals, plans, and means can be specified differently for various individuals and contexts. One must assess the purpose, participants, and behavior of particular conversations in order to derive situational goals, plans, and means, a procedure similar to the "task analysis" advocated by Fischer (1980). The perceived goals, plans, and means of the participants can also be compared to their actual behavior to determine the functional relationships among cognitive purposes and plans and communicative behavior.

The successful coordination of goals, plans, and means in our framework depends on many cognitive processes. Figure 2 illustrates communicative interchanges in a flow chart where cognitive generation, selection, evaluation, and monitoring are evident. Our framework permits recursive repair during communication as well as construction of new goals, plans, and means for interaction. Figure 2 also illustrates how attributions, affect, and metacognition can easily be incorporated into the goals/plans/means framework.

The goals/plans/means framework is not offered as a "panacea" explanation for all communication. Instead, it is a heuristic approach that permits simultaneous consideration of social and cognitive processes. The model provides a synthesis of the cognitive *skill* required to assume speaker and listener roles appropriately with the motivational *will* to communicate in a particular manner. For example, choosing a communicative goal requires sensitivity to the listener's status and goals. Planning how to accomplish a goal involves forethought, hy-

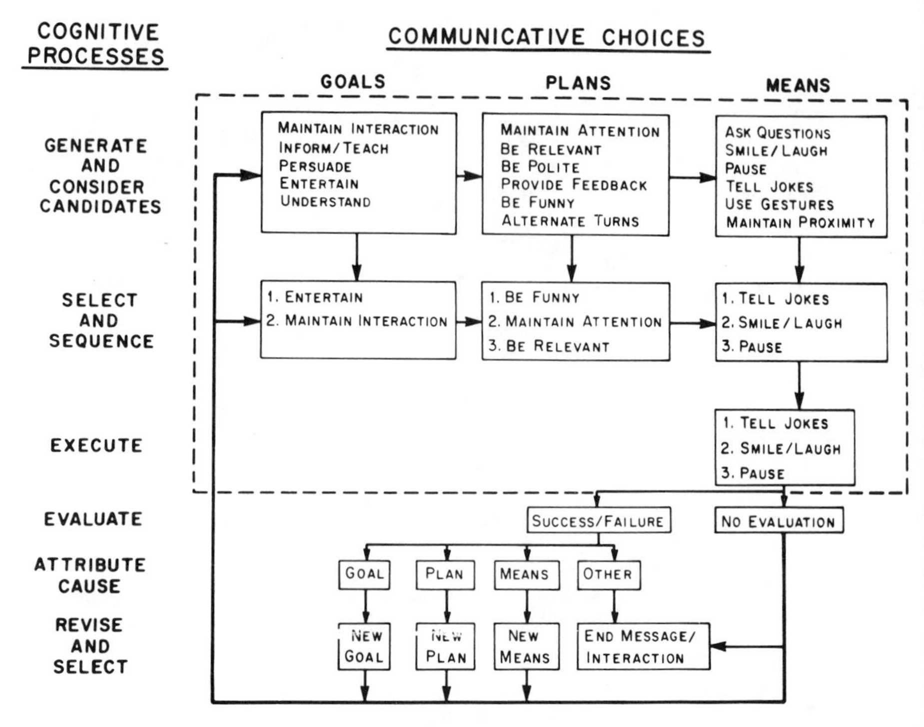

Fig. 2. An illustration of cognitive generation, evaluation, monitoring, and revision for coordinating goals, plans, and means in communication.

pothesis testing, and decisions based on expectancies and incentives. Using a particular means for communicating may require monitoring and regulation during the conversation and reflective analysis afterward. The *developmental* aspects of how children acquire, use, select, and coordinate goals, plans, and means have not been investigated systematically, although some initial speculations concerning these skills have been offered (cf. Dickson, 1981). We might also add that communicative skills are often quite specific to a task, audience, or setting and children's communications are probably not equally effective or "normative" across settings.

B. COMMUNICATIVE GOALS

Participants enter and remain in conversations for particular purposes. Communicative goals are the intentions of speakers and listeners that guide their interactions. Several theorists have compiled "lists" of referential and interpersonal goals that direct communication in children and adults. For example,

Higgins, Fondacaro, and McCann (1981) proposed a list of goals including the maintenance of social relationships, the transmission of social reality, face goals (i.e., impression management), task goals such as problem solving, and entertainment goals. Unfortunately, few theorists have discussed communicative goals from a *developmental* perspective. Higgins *et al.*, Olson and Hilyard (1981), Trevarthen (1977), and others speculated briefly concerning the development of communicative goals, but their speculations were not supported by data and uncertainty remains concerning how such data might be obtained. Expanding on the work of recent theorists, we would like to identify four potential developmental changes in communicative goals and illustrate, where appropriate, how these changes might be studied. We shall argue that developmental differences may be observed in the specific goals that children adopt, children's metacognitive awareness and control over these goals, the degree to which children can pursue multiple goals simultaneously, and children's awareness of the reciprocal nature of speaker and listener goals.

The nature of children's communicative goals probably changes dramatically with development. One would hardly expect a 1 or 2 year old to be concerned with making a good impression on a listener, nor would one expect the goal of mutually attending to an object to be a primary motivator in adolescent communication. We believe that a gradual differentiation of specific goals can be observed from very general interpersonal and referential goals as children mature. Trevarthen (1977) specified the nature of these general communicative goals. He argued that dyadic interactions between mothers and infants in the first months of life are characterized by "primary intersubjectivity." The young infant is motivated innately to coordinate his or her behavior with that of the mother. The infant is oriented toward the face, voice, and hands of the mother and produces facial expressions, postural cues, movement, and vocalizations in response to maternal stimuli. During the first few years of life, primary intersubjectivity is gradually replaced by "secondary intersubjectivity" as objects and events in the world play an increasingly important role in dyadic interactions. A developmental shift can be observed from the primarily interpersonal goal of coordinating behavior with others to the more "referential" goal of jointly experiencing objects or events with the listener.

The early goals Trevarthen proposed are precisely those that require the most social and environmental support for their fulfillment. This support compensates for a lack of awareness or control of communicative intent on the part of the child. Social support for children's goals takes the form of mature communicators who actively interpret the child's communicative intent and take primary responsibility for regulating interactions (e.g., Brazelton & Tronick, 1977; Greenfield, 1977). In mature communication, metacognitive evaluations may help the speaker delineate appropriate communicative goals. Such thoughtful reflections are probably beyond the capacity of the young child (Wertsch, 1978;

Wood, 1977). However, adults can compensate for the child's lack of awareness and control by providing explicit goals for the child or by suggesting acceptable interpretations of the child's vague interpersonal or referential goals. Gradually, however, children gain control of their own communicative intentions, first in familiar, naturalistic settings (Maratsos, 1973; Meissner & Apthrop, 1976; Menig-Peterson, 1975) and then in more artificial experimental settings (Flavell *et al.*, 1968; Krauss & Glucksberg, 1969).

Social support for the child's communicative goals can be facilitated by the presence of close proximity between speaker and listener, plenty of eye contact, and shared perspectives and presuppositions. Recall that in the Mueller (1972) study, the majority of young children's utterances occurred when the speaker and listener were less than 4 ft apart. This finding makes sense when one considers that the communicative skills of the young child are particularly well suited for sharing focus on an object or event with a *nearby* listener. Pointing and showing behaviors appear quite frequently in the communications of 1 and 2 year olds and are often accompanied by visual attention to the listener (Leung & Rheingold, 1981; Wellman & Lempers, 1977). Furthermore, even the words the young child selects tend to be ones that reduce the most uncertainty concerning the referent of the child's speech (Greenfield, 1978; Greenfield & Smith, 1976). Referential and interpersonal goals are differentiated, including goals that involve nonpresent objects and past and future events. Eventually, the child can communicate about abstract topics and overcome physical barriers that prevent eye contact and shared perspectives (e.g., Flavell *et al.*, 1968; Krauss & Glucksberg, 1969).

We have proposed that developmental changes occur in the types of goals children pursue and in their awareness and control of communicative intentions. As more and more communicative goals are differentiated by the child, we believe the child becomes better able to fulfill multiple goals simultaneously and to modify goals during the course of an interaction. These skills are important when one considers that speakers and listeners may approach the same communicative situation with different goals. Higgins *et al.* (1981) characterized communication as a "social game" in which the speaker and listener have different social roles and follow different communicative rules. Conflicts between the speaker and listener inevitably arise and successful communication requires reciprocal "tuning" to resolve these conflicts. For example, one child might approach a situation with the goal of persuading the other child to perform some action whereas the other child may simply want to be entertained. The would-be persuader in this situation may be successful only to the extent that his or her goals can be modified to include the goal of entertaining the other child. Similarly, the other child may not find the persuader very entertaining unless he or she is willing to acquiesce to the persuader's request.

Higgins *et al.* suggested that young children may have difficulty coordinating their communicative goals with others, but did not elaborate on developmental differences in cognitive "tuning" skills. We believe that the communicative means available to the young child may not be efficient or well practiced enough to permit the pursuit of simultaneous, and perhaps contradictory, communicative goals. We agree with Shatz (1978) that an important mechanism of communicative development is "the acquisition and routinization of new techniques that make efficient use of [the] limited processing capacity" (p. 42) of the communicator. In other words, young children might fail to persuade the listener in our hypothetical situation because they have fewer and less practiced means available than do older children for achieving the competing communicative goals and may therefore focus only on their own goal of persuasion.

The hypothesis that there are developmental improvements in the tendency to follow multiple goals simultaneously could be easily tested. Speakers of different ages could be asked to persuade a listener to perform some action. The listener's goal could be either to agree with the speaker's suggestions, to try to have a good time and laugh a lot, or could remain unspecified. We would predict that the speaker's communicative behaviors would remain relatively constant across the three situations for younger children but vary widely for older children. Furthermore, younger children should be much more likely to succeed at persuading the listener when the listener has a complementary goal than when the listener has a different or unspecified goal. However, communicative success should vary less across situations for the older children. The specific behaviors one might observe in such an experiment will become clearer after we discuss the development of communicative plans and means.

In discussing a possible developmental trend toward pursuing simultaneous communicative goals, we hinted that the adoption of goals that are complementary to listener goals might be beneficial. Thus, if the listener's goal is to "be entertained," a good communicator might adopt the goal "to entertain." Developmental changes in the child's awareness of the reciprocal nature of many speaker and listener goals may also occur. Research on children's turn-taking skills has shown a developmental progression from "role-rigid" turn-taking exchanges to "role-complementary" exchanges (Mueller & Lucas, 1975). In role-rigid turn taking, each participant in an exchange adopts a fixed role and does not appear to be aware of the reciprocal relation that exists between his or her role and the role of the other participant. For example, young infants often engage in games of "give and take" with their mothers, but their role is always that of the recipient (Bruner, 1975). With development, however, children become capable of reversing roles with the other participant in an exchange (Bruner, 1975; Garvey, 1974; Mueller & Lucas, 1975). Because a child's role in an exchange is probably determined to some degree by his or her communicative goals, the progression toward role-complementary exchanges may well be accompanied by an increasing awareness of the reciprocity that can exist between speaker and listener goals. This hypothesis could be tested by instructing children of different ages to pursue first one goal in a conversation and then another. The first goal would either be a complement of the second goal or unrelated to it. If young children have difficulty dealing with goal reciprocity, their success at achieving the second goal should be greater when it is unrelated to the first goal than when it complements the first goal.

We believe that many developmental trends in children's communication reflect changes in goals. As children acquire richer language and more social experience, they differentiate new communicative goals, gain more control over their goals, begin to pursue multiple goals simultaneously, and become more knowledgeable about the complementary, reciprocal nature of the purposes of speakers and listeners. These accomplishments are important for communicative success and require both role taking and metacognitive evaluation of the task and the self–other relationship. The important linkage in our approach is between intent and skill. The development of this relationship in communication is fostered by the acquisition of cognitive strategies, increased memory and processing capabilities, and reflective monitoring during conversations. These cognitive resources permit the child to consider alternative goals, establish subgoals and modify, discard, or replace communicative goals. However, communicative intentions must be selected and adapted to particular settings and constraints. Planning involves decisions about how to choose specific behaviors to maximize one's purposes. In the next section we shall discuss possible developmental changes in children's communicative plans.

C. COMMUNICATIVE PLANS

Communicative plans control the child's selection and sequencing of particular communicative means. Planning can be seen as a two-stage process involving the "predetermination of a course of action aimed at achieving some goal" and the control and guidance of that course of action as the plan is executed (Hayes-Roth & Hayes-Roth, 1979). Drawing heavily on the work of Higgins *et al.* (1981), we have identified 11 plans for effective communication. These plans concern communication of accurate information, because that has been the common purpose of the studies we have reviewed. The reader is invited to generate additional plans for other communicative goals such as entertainment or deception. The plans include the following: (1) maintain mutual attention, (2) be relevant, (3) monitor comprehension of the listener and speaker, (4) consider the needs and perspective of the listener, (5) provide feedback to the listener, (6) respond to feedback from the listener, (7) be concise, (8) be polite, (9) convey only the truth, (10) alternate turns with the listener, and (11) consider the communicative goals of the listener.

Similar listings have been made by numerous sociolinguists and philosophers (e.g., Grice, 1968; Searle, 1969). For our purposes, the specific plans included are much less important than the proposed relations between the plans and the child's communicative goals and means. We propose that the goals a communicator chooses to emphasize will have a profound effect on the plans that are adopted and the means by which the communicator implements these plans. If the goal of a communicative task was to transmit a certain message to a listener, a speaker might emphasize plans such as conveying the truth, making himself or herself understood, and being concise. If, however, the goal was to maintain social contact, plans such as being relevant, trying to understand the listener, or alternating turns might take precedence.

An example of the influence of communicative goals on the plans followed by the communicator can be found in the Shatz and Gelman (1977) study. In the study, 4 year olds modulated their assertions to 2 year olds in an unstructured situation but not in a toy description task. If we assume that modulation is a means for adhering to the communicative plan "be polite," then the study provides support for the relationship between communicative goals and plans. In the toy description task, the goal of the communicator was probably to transmit information to the listener. Plans such as "make yourself understood" should take precedence over being polite in achieving this goal. However, in the unstructured situation, the goal may have been to maintain social interaction with the listener. The communicative plan "be polite" might be given high priority by the child in selecting a means for achieving this goal.

If plans are influenced by communicative goals even at a very young age, what can be said about developmental changes in communicative plans? We believe that two major developmental changes occur. First, the nature of children's plans may change from simple plans tied very closely to concrete behaviors, to more complex and fully elaborated plans, to cognitively "abbreviated" plans. Second, a developmental trend from dependence on external support for communicative plans to internally controlled planfulness may also occur. Both of these proposed trends will be discussed briefly below.

Some evidence is already available that the nature of children's spontaneously adopted plans changes with development. Mischel and Mischel (1977) noted that when children are asked to describe their plans for resisting temptation, children 9 and 10 years old describe elaborated plans and older children rely on a cognitive "short-hand" in discussing their plans. According to Mischel and Mischel, children develop plans that become more "automatic, abbreviated, and rapid, without requiring extensive or explicit self-instructions for each step" (p. 53). Further support for the proposed trend in communicative plans comes from a study by Carter, Patterson, and Quasebarth (1979). Carter *et al.* measured persistence in game playing and demonstrated that fully elaborated plans were necessary to sustain goal-directed work in preschoolers but more general plans could be used by older children.

In addition to proposing a trend from elaborated to abbreviated plans that occurs during middle childhood, we would like to suggest that in early childhood plans tend to be very simple and tied closely to concrete behaviors. For example, a young child's plan to maintain social contact might be to look frequently at the listener during an exchange. A somewhat older child might have a more complex plan involving eye contact, verbal and nonverbal attention-getting devices, questions, and contingent behaviors for averting communication breakdowns. An even older child might also plan to use all of these communicative means, but his or her plan might be abstract and abbreviated, consisting of self-instructions to "maintain mutual attention" with the listener. If the proposed developmental progression is accurate, then the communicative means of older children with complex plans should vary more widely with varying communicative goals than the means of young children with simple plans. Some preliminary evidence reported by Schmidt (1980) indicates that this is indeed the case. Schmidt videotaped the communicative interactions of same-age, same-sex dyads of 6 and 9 year olds. The speaker in each dyad pursued one of two communicative goals: Maintain a conversation with the listener or teach the listener how to play a simple board game. When asked to maintain a conversation, kindergarteners displayed more eye contact than when asked to explain the game to the listener, suggesting that in the former situation their communicative plan may have been to "look at the listener." Older children also displayed more eye contact in the conversation situation than in the game situation but, in addition, they asked more questions to introduce new topics and to keep alive already introduced topics. Thus, older children may have had a fairly complex and abstract plan such as "maintain mutual attention" that they implemented through a variety of communicative means. Younger children, however, may have generated limited plans that were virtually identical with one behavior, visual regard.

We have suggested that the communicative plans of very young children tend to be simple and tied to concrete behaviors. It is also possible that young children will fail to adopt any plan for achieving a particular communicative goal. As reported earlier, researchers have found that young children are often capable of implementing plans when given explicit directions, but fail to invoke these plans spontaneously (e.g., Cosgrove & Patterson, 1977). Wertsch (1978) has argued that children depend on the external support of adults in regulating their behavior. He suggests that in adult–child interactions, the adult supplies the metacognitive awareness and planfulness that the child lacks. In problem-solving situations, for example, the adult leads the child through the task by asking regulative questions aimed at reminding the child of the goal of the task, revealing overall strategies, and identifying relevant stimulus properties. Adults who are particularly successful at this regulative "scaffolding" vary their level of intervention from nonspecific encouragement to explicit demonstrations according to the child's level of performance (Wood, 1977). Adults may also decrease the amount of scaffolding they provide as the child matures (e.g., Bruner, 1975; Holmberg, 1980; Moerk, 1975).

Although adults may gradually relinquish their control of the child's communication, peer interaction may be necessary for the development of self-regulation and planfulness. The communicative failures that are fairly abundant in child–child exchanges but which occur more rarely in adult–child interactions may force the child to consider communicative goals, plans, and means. Robinson and Robinson (1977) found that children between 6 and 7 years old are more likely to detect message inadequacies when they lead to communicative failure than when they are associated with successful communication. Similarly, Sonnenschein and Whitehurst (1980) demonstrated that the messages of 6 year olds improved more after exposure to incompetent peer models than after exposure to incompetent adults. Apparently, the authority and prestige of adult communicators is so high that children cannot detect adult incompetence even when it leads to communicative failure. If communicative failures and exposure to incompetent peers have a similar effect on the tendency to adopt communicative plans, then peer interaction may be essential in the development of planfulness.

Research concerning the development of communicative plans has been extremely limited. However, we can draw some tentative conclusions from the research we reviewed concerning children's planning and control in problem-solving situations (Wertsch, 1978; Wood, 1977) while resisting temptation (Mischel & Mischel, 1977) and while persisting at assigned tasks (Carter *et al.*, 1979). First, young children tend not to invoke plans spontaneously, although they can follow plans provided by adults. Young children may lack the social decentering and hypothesis-testing skills required for choosing appropriate plans and means to meet specific goals. Alternately, they may have these skills available but may not consider planning necessary or worthwhile. Second, when young children do adopt plans spontaneously, their plans become increasingly complex and abstract with development (Carter *et al.*, 1979; Mischel & Mischel, 1977). Finally, the development of planfulness may involve a gradual relinquishing of control by adults coupled with exposure to communicative failures in peer interaction (Robinson & Robinson, 1977; Sonnenschein & Whitehurst, 1980).

Further research concerning children's control of their communication is clearly needed. Two methods of approaching this issue could be employed. First, researchers could assign plans to children of different ages and see how these plans affect their communicative behavior (e.g., Cosgrove & Patterson, 1977). This method would be particularly fruitful if researchers included tests of children's *evaluation* of their plans and flexibility in choosing among alternate plans. For example, an experimenter might assign the goal of maintaining a conversation with a listener to the child. The experimenter might suggest several "plans" for achieving this goal, plans that are operationalized in terms of specific communicative behaviors. The success of these plans could be manipulated by having the responsiveness of a confederate listener vary with the child's communicative behavior. The measure of interest in such a study would be the degree to which the child retains successful plans and modifies unsuccessful ones, with "success" defined in terms of the listener's responsiveness. A second method of studying planfulness would be to assign a goal to the child and then interview the child concerning his or her spontaneous plans for fulfilling that goal (e.g., Mischel & Mischel, 1977). The major drawback of the "interview" method is that reported plans may not correlate well with the child's actual communicative behavior. For example, Schmidt (1980) found that 9 year olds planned to engage a listener in a conversation by relying on nonverbal attention-getting devices (e.g., tugging on the listener's arm), but actually employed these devices infrequently. However, when reported plans do reflect communicative behavior, the interview method may yield useful information concerning children's planfulness and control of communication. Even when reported plans and behavior are discrepant, interviews may reveal developmental changes in communicative competence that are not always apparent when actual performance is assessed.

D. COMMUNICATIVE MEANS

We have discussed possible developmental changes in the goals children bring to communicative tasks and in the plans they adopt for achieving these goals. We found in the review of the literature that developmental changes also occur in children's communicative means. During early and middle childhood, children acquire a repertoire of skills to solve communicative problems and meet diverse communicative goals. We found, for instance, that children press their claim for the listener's understanding first by repeating utterances that do not receive a response from the listener (Keenan, 1974; Keenan & Klein, 1975; Wellman & Lempers, 1977) and then by employing sophisticated gambits such as the summons–answer routine (Garvey & Hogan, 1973). We also found that children take the needs of the listener into account first by refraining from inappropriate actions (Maratsos, 1973) and later by being more explicit or sequencing information in a logical manner (Maratsos, 1973; Pratt *et al.*, 1977). Further, we found a developmental trend in the child's ability to adapt utterances to previous speech of the listener from prior adaptation to one aspect of the utterance (Horgan, 1978; Savic, 1976; Shugar, 1976) to adaptation to multiple aspects (Garvey, 1974). Finally, we observed that children respond to feedback first by repeating messages unchanged (Wellman & Lempers, 1977) and then by modifying their messages or presenting additional information (Peterson *et al.*, 1972; Spilton & Lee, 1977).

Simple acquisition of communicative means is not enough, however, to ensure communicative effectiveness. Children must learn to coordinate particular means with particular goals. In examining the child's provision of feedback as a listener, we found that although 5 year olds do not provide feedback spontaneously

(Karabenick & Miller, 1977), they can provide it when given a plan telling them when and how to do so (Cosgrove & Patterson, 1977, 1978; Ironsmith & Whitehurst, 1978b). The plan apparently alerts children to the appropriate means for achieving the communicative goal of understanding the speaker's messages. As we noted earlier, the appropriate means—asking questions—was already in the child's repertoire, it simply had to be linked with the child's communicative goals. In this fashion, a means becomes coordinated with a goal to develop a communicative skill that can be exercised and generalized.

We have seen from our review of the literature that young children do not have many means available for implementing communicative plans. We can assume that the means they do have available are not well practiced and require a good deal of cognitive capacity for their implementation. With development, the child acquires new means and becomes more practiced at employing old ones. What consequences do the acquisition and routinization of communicative means have for the child's implementation of plans and selection of goals? As communicative means become more efficient, the child will become more successful at following high priority communicative plans. The child will also have more capacity to spare for adhering to communicative plans with lower priorities. Thus, in a situation demanding accurate transmissions of information, older children might be "polite" or "alternate turns" whereas younger children will have to use all available capacity to make themselves understood. Another consequence of the freeing up of cognitive resources is one that was discussed previously. As the child acquires new capacity-stretching techniques for communicating, he or she will become increasingly able to fulfill multiple communicative goals simultaneously and become increasingly flexible in the selection and pursuit of these goals.

We argued that with development children acquire new means for fulfilling communicative goals. The means that are appropriate for implementing a given communicative plan will change dramatically depending on the amount of external support that is available for the child's communications. For example, the plan "maintain mutual attention" could be easily fulfilled by engaging in eye-to-eye contact and maintaining close proximity to the listener in situations in which a lot of external support is present. However, in situations in which external support is limited—for example, if the child was talking on a telephone—communicative means such as the use of attention-getting devices or the summons–answer routine would be more appropriate. The shift from external to internal control of communication requires that new means be developed for following previously existing communicative plans and goals.

E. THE GOALS/PLANS/MEANS FRAMEWORK IN RETROSPECT

Our purpose in this section has been to describe a three-level hierarchical model for communication and to identify potential developmental changes at each level in the hierarchy. Basically, we are arguing that communication involves the coordination of communicative goals and behavioral means available for accomplishing these goals. The connecting link between goals and means is the communicative plan. In any communicative situation, the communicator must first define the purpose of the interaction, then choose a plan for achieving that purpose, and, finally, employ a means for carrying out that plan. We do not mean to imply that these decisions are always deliberate or conscious. Our guess is that the deliberate coordination of means and goals via planfulness is most frequent and crucial during initial learning and practice in a given communicative task. Whether the coordination of goals and means is directed and supported by adults or discovered by the child, we believe that the realization of the need for considering goals, plans, and means is vital to self-directed use of communicative skills. Beyond initial learning of a skill, practice and feedback are required to ensure continued discovery of the instrumental value and appropriate application of the skill.

Our model is compatible with many theories of children's learning although it may be most similar to a functional, sociocognitive perspective espoused by Soviet researchers. In essence, the Soviets emphasize how children select and control their own behavior to accomplish particular purposes. Actions are rudimentary, goal-directed behaviors that become consciously subordinated to new and diverse goals. When these initial behaviors become intentional strategies directed toward new goals, they are referred to as operations. Social forces help to mediate the development of intentionality and strategic control through prescription and support of "leading activities," a term roughly similar to motives. Parents, teachers, peers, and children themselves contribute to developmental changes in motives that give rise to new actions and operations. This kind of pragmatic and social coordination of goals with behavioral means provides a theoretical perspective that is very consistent with our developmental model of communicative goals, plans, and means. Similar applications of the Soviet view to children's learning (Reese, 1977) and memory (Meacham, 1977; Paris, 1978) illustrate the heuristic value of this framework.

In our proposal, we have illustrated the goals/plans/means framework by including numerous examples from previous studies of communicative development. None of these studies was based on our framework and our reinterpretations may be debatable by the original authors. However, the heuristic value of the goals/plans/means framework is that it allows reinterpretations of a vast, disorganized literature on children's communication and begins to shape recent findings into a coherent view of communicative development. We discussed ample data demonstrating that (1) very young children can engage in reciprocal, socially adaptive exchanges; (2) macrolevel constructs such as egocentric speech do not provide adequate explanations of communicative development; and (3) the child's communicative motives, contextual factors, and communicative control must be considered in any model of communicative development. We believe that the goals/plans/means framework is a beginning step toward a synthesis of these data. We have cast the approach in general terms to illustrate its power in capturing a diversity of developmental changes in communication, but the approach can be made more precise by filling in each ''slot'' in the hierarchy with particular instances of communicative skills. Although we have not presented a comprehensive ''theory'' of communicative development subject to falsifiability, we have made specific predictions about goals, plans, and means and suggested how they might be tested. Ultimately, the framework must be judged on the basis of the quality and fruitfulness of the research it generates and explains.

V. Summary and Conclusions

At the beginning of the article, a controversy concerning children's communicative skills was identified. On one side of this controversy, the young child is seen as an egocentric communicator, incapable of taking the needs of the listener into account (Piaget, 1926; Vygotsky, 1962). On the other side, recent investigators have argued that the child is a sociocentric communicator almost from birth onward. We suggested that this controversy stems from an oversimplified dichotomization of speech into egocentric and socialized categories and from a failure to consider communicative motives, contextual influences, and the child's control of communication. We illustrated in the literature review that communication is a multidimensional phenomenon and that the development of communication involves changes in communicative *will* as well as changes in *skill*. At the end of the review, we discussed some recent theoretical attempts to deal with the issues of motivation, context, and control. Then we introduced a new framework for interpreting communicative development that integrates and extends these conceptualizations. In our framework, children's communication is described in terms of communicative goals, plans, and means. Developmental changes are proposed at each level of the hierarchy. We believe that the goals/plans/means framework affords a heuristic interpretation of children's communication and provides testable hypotheses concerning the cognitive skills underlying communicative development.

ACKNOWLEDGMENTS

This project was supported by a National Science Foundation predoctoral fellowship to C. R. Schmidt at Purdue University and a University of Michigan Rackham Graduate Faculty Fellowship to S. G. Paris. We appreciate the helpful comments of Marilyn Shatz, Bruce Carter, Dave Cross, Evelyn Oka, Russ Whitehurst, and Rob Kail on earlier drafts of this article. We would like to thank Charlotte Patterson especially for her thought-provoking, meticulous, and erudite suggestions about children's communication.

REFERENCES

Ammon, P. Communication skills and communicative competence: A neo-Piagetian process-structural view. In W. P. Dickson (Ed.), *Children's oral communication skills.* New York: Academic Press, 1981.

Bates, E., Camaioni, L., & Volterra, V. The acquisition of performatives prior to speech. *Merrill-Palmer Quarterly,* 1975, **21,** 205–226.

Bloom, L., & Lahey, M. *Language development and language disorders.* New York: Wiley, 1978.

Bloom, L., Rocissano, L., & Hood, L. Adult-child discourse: Developmental interaction between information processing and linguistic knowledge. *Cognitive Psychology,* 1976, **8,** 521–552.

Brazelton, T. B., & Tronick, E. Preverbal communication between mothers and infants. In D. R. Olson (Ed.), *The social foundations of thought and language.* New York: Norton, 1977.

Brown, A. L. Learning and development: The problems of compatability, access, and induction. *Human Development,* 1981, **25.**

Bruner, J. S. The organization of early skilled action. In M. P. M. Richards (Ed.), *The integration of a child into a social world.* London and New York: Cambridge Univ. Press, 1974.

Bruner, J. S. The ontogenesis of speech acts. *Journal of Child Language,* 1975, **2,** 1–21.

Carter, D. B., Patterson, C. J., & Quasebarth, S. J. Development of children's use of plans for self-control. *Cognitive Therapy and Research,* 1979, **3,** 407–413.

Cosgrove, J. M., & Patterson, C. J. Plans and the development of listener skills. *Developmental Psychology,* 1977, **13,** 557–564.

Cosgrove, J. M., & Patterson, C. J. Generalization of training for children's listener skills. *Child Development,* 1978, **49,** 513–516.

Dickson, W. P. (Ed.). *Children's oral communication skills.* New York: Academic Press, 1981.

Dore, J. Holophrases, speech acts, and language universals. *Journal of Child Language,* 1975, **2,** 21–40.

Dore, J. Children's illocutionary acts. In R. O. Freedle (Ed.), *Discourse processes: Advances in research and theory* (Vol. 1). Norwood, New Jersey: Ablex, 1977.

Dore, J., Gearhart, M., & Newman, D. The structure of nursery school conversation. In K. E. Nelson (Ed.), *Children's language.* New York: Gardner, 1978.

Fischer, K. W. A theory of cognitive development: The control and construction of hierarchies of skills. *Psychological Review,* 1980, **87,** 477–531.

Flavell, J. H. Cognitive monitoring. In W. P. Dickson (Ed.), *Children's oral communication skills.* New York: Academic Press, 1981.

Flavell, J. H., Botkin, P. T., Fry, C. L., Wright, J. C., & Jarvis, P. E. *The development of role-taking and communication skills in children.* New York: Wiley, 1968.

Ford, M. E. The construct validity of egocentrism. *Psychological Bulletin,* 1979, **86,** 1169–1187.

Garvey, C. Some properties of social play. *Merrill-Palmer Quarterly,* 1974, **20,** 163–180.

Garvey, C., & Hogan, R. Social speech and social interaction: Egocentrism revisited. *Child Development,* 1973, **44,** 562–568.

Glucksberg, S., Krauss, R., & Higgins, E. T. The development of referential communication skills. In F. D. Horowitz (Ed.), *Child development research* (Vol. 4). Chicago, Illinois: Univ. of Chicago Press, 1975.

Greenfield, P. M. Toward an operational and logical analysis of intentionality: The use of discourse in early child language. In D. R. Olson (Ed.), *The social foundations of thought and language.* New York: Norton, 1977.

Greenfield, P. M. Informativeness, presupposition, and semantic choice in single-word utterances. In N. Waterson & C. Snow (Eds.), *The development of communication.* New York: Wiley, 1978.

Greenfield, P. M., & Smith, J. H. *The structure of communication in early language development.* New York: Academic Press, 1976.

Grice, P. *Logic and conversation.* Unpublished manuscript, 1968.

Guralnick, M. J., & Paul-Brown, D. The nature of verbal interactions among handicapped and nonhandicapped preschool children. *Child Development,* 1977, **48,** 254–260.

Hall, W. S., Cole, M., Reder, S., & Dowley, G. Variations in young children's use of language: Some effects of setting and dialect. In R. O. Freedle (Ed.), *Discourse processes: Advances in research and theory* (Vol. 1). Norwood, New Jersey: Ablex, 1977.

Hayes-Roth, B., & Hayes-Roth, F. A cognitive model of planning. *Cognitive Science,* 1979, **3,** 275–310.

Higgins, E. T. Social class differences in verbal communicative accuracy: A question of which question? *Pyschological Bulletin,* 1976, **83,** 695–714.

Higgins, E. T., Fondacaro, R., & McCann, D. Rules and roles: The "communication game" and speaker-listener processes. In W. P. Dickson (Ed.), *Children's oral communication skills.* New York: Academic Press, 1981.

Holmberg, M. C. The development of social interchange patterns from 12 to 42 months. *Child Development,* 1980, **51,** 448–456.

Horgan, D. How to answer questions when you've got nothing to say. *Journal of Child Language,* 1978, **5,** 159–165.

Ironsmith, M., & Whitehurst, G. J. The development of listener abilities in communication: How children deal with ambiguous information. *Child Development,* 1978, **49,** 348–352. (a)

Ironsmith, M., & Whitehurst, G. J. How children learn to listen: The effects of modeling and feedback styles on children's performance in referential communication. *Developmental Psychology,* 1978, **14,** 546–554. (b)

Karabenick, J. D., & Miller, S. A. The effects of age, sex, and listener feedback on grade school children's referential communication. *Child Development,* 1977, **48,** 678–683.

Keenan, E. O. Conversational competence in children. *Journal of Child Language,* 1974, **1,** 163–183.

Keenan, E. O., & Klein, E. Coherency in children's discourse. *Journal of Psycholinguistic Research,* 1975, **4,** 365–380.

Keenan, E. O., & Schieffelin, B. Topic as a discourse notion: A study of topic in the conversations of children and adults. In C. Li (Ed.), *Subject and topic.* New York: Academic Press, 1976.

Kohlberg, L., Yaeger, J., & Hjertholm, E. Private speech: Four studies and a review of theories. *Child Development,* 1968, **39,** 691–736.

Krauss, R. M., & Glucksberg, S. The development of communication: Competence as a function of age. *Child Development,* 1969, **40,** 255–266.

Leung, E. H. L., & Rheingold, H. L. Development of pointing as a social gesture. *Developmental Psychology,* 1981, **17,** 215–220.

Maratsos, M. P. Nonegocentric communication abilities in preschool children. *Child Development,* 1973, **44,** 697–700.

Maratsos, M. P. Preschool children's use of definite and indefinite articles. *Child Development,* 1974, **45,** 446–455.

Markman, E. M. Comprehension monitoring. In W. P. Dickson (Ed.), *Children's oral communication skills.* New York: Academic Press, 1981.

Martlew, M., Connolly, K., & McLeod, C. Language use, role and context in a five year old. *Journal of Child Language,* 1978, **5,** 81–99.

Masur, E. F. Preschool boy's speech modification: The effect of listeners' linguistic levels and conversational responsiveness. *Child Development,* 1978, **49,** 924–927.

Meacham, J. A. Soviet investigations of memory development. In R. V. Kail & J. W. Hagen (Eds.), *Perspectives on the development of memory and cognition.* Hillsdale, New Jersey: Erlbaum, 1977.

Meissner, J. A., & Apthorp, H. Nonegocentrism and communication mode switching in black preschool children. *Developmental Psychology,* 1976, **12,** 245–249.

Menig-Peterson, C. L. The modification of communicative behavior in preschool-aged children as a function of the listener's perspective. *Child Development*, 1975, **46,** 1015–1018.

Miller, S. A., Shelton, J., & Flavell, J. H. A test of Luria's hypotheses concerning the development of verbal self-regulation. *Child Development*, 1970, **41,** 651–665.

Mischel, W., & Mischel, H. N. Self-control and the self. In T. Mischel (Ed.), *The self: Philosophical and psychological issues*. Oxford: Blackwell, 1977.

Moerk, E. L. Verbal interactions between children and their mothers during the preschool years. *Developmental Psychology*, 1975, **11,** 788–794.

Moerk, E. L. *Pragmatic and semantic aspects of early language development*. Baltimore, Maryland: Univ. Park Press, 1977.

Mueller, E. The maintenance of verbal exchanges between young children. *Child Development*, 1972, **43,** 930–938.

Mueller, E., Bleier, M., Krakow, J., Hegedus, K., & Cournoyer, P. The development of peer verbal interaction among two-year-old boys. *Child Development*, 1977, **48,** 284–287.

Mueller, E., & Lucas, T. A developmental analysis of peer interaction among toddlers. In M. Lewis & L. A. Rosenblum (Eds.), *Friendship and peer relations*. New York: Wiley, 1975.

Olson, D. R. Some social aspects of meaning in oral and written language. In D. R. Olson (Ed.), *The social foundations of language and thought*. New York: Norton, 1977. (a)

Olson, D. R. From utterance to text: The bias of language in speech and writing. *Harvard Educational Review*, 1977, **47,** 257–281. (b)

Olson, D. R., & Hilyard, A. Assent and compliance in children's language. In W. P. Dickson (Ed.), *Children's oral communication skills*. New York: Academic Press, 1981.

Paris, S. G. Coordination of means and goals in the development of mnemonic skills. In P. Ornstein (Ed.), *Memory development in children*. Hillsdale, New Jersey: Erlbaum, 1978.

Paris, S. G., & Lindauer, B. K. The development of cognitive skills during childhood. In B. Wolman (Ed.), *Handbook of developmental psychology*. New York: Prentice-Hall, 1982.

Patterson, C. J., Cosgrove, J. M., & O'Brien, R. G. Nonverbal indicants of comprehension and noncomprehension in children. *Developmental Psychology*, 1980, **16,** 38–48.

Patterson, C. J., & Kister, M. C. The development of listener skills for referential communication. In W. P. Dickson (Ed.), *Children's oral communication skills*. New York: Academic Press, 1981.

Peterson, C. L., Danner, F. W., & Flavell, J. H. Developmental changes in children's response to three indications of communicative failure. *Child Development*, 1972, **43,** 1463–1468.

Piaget, J. *The language and thought of the child*. New York: Harcourt, 1926. (Reprinted by Humanities Press, Atlantic Heights, New Jersey, 1955).

Piaget, J. *The psychology of intelligence*. New York: Harcourt, 1950.

Piaget, J. Comments on Vygotsky's critical remarks. Cambridge, Massachusetts: MIT Press, 1962. (Pamphlet published in conjunction with Vygotsky's *Thought and language*.)

Pratt, M. W., Scribner, S., & Cole, M. Children as teachers: Developmental studies of instructional communication. *Child Development*, 1977, **48,** 1475–1481.

Reese, H. W. Discriminative learning and transfer: Dialectical perspectives. In N. Datan & H. W. Reese (Eds.), *Life-span developmental psychology*. New York: Academic Press, 1977.

Robinson, E. J. The child's understanding of inadequate messages and communication failure: A problem of ignorance or egocentrism? In W. P. Dickson (Ed.), *Children's oral communication skills*. New York: Academic Press, 1981.

Robinson, E. J., & Robinson, E. P. Children's explanations of communication failure and the inadequacy of the misunderstood message. *Developmental Psychology*, 1977, **13,** 156–161.

Rosenberg, S., & Donner, L. Choice behavior in a verbal recognition task as a function of individual associative strength. *Journal of Experimental Psychology*, 1968, **76,** 341–347.

Rosenberg, S., & Markman, B. Choice behavior in a referentially ambiguous task. *Journal of Personality and Social Psychology*, 1971, **17,** 99–105.

Sachs, J., & Devin, J. Young children's use of age-appropriate speech styles. *Journal of Child Language,* 1976, **3,** 81–98.

Savic, S. Strategies children use to answer questions posed by adults (Serbo-Croatian-speaking children from 1 to 3). In N. Waterson & C. Snow (Eds.), *The development of communication: Social and pragmatic factors in language acquisition.* New York: Wiley, 1976.

Schiff, N. *The development of form and meaning in the language of hearing children of deaf parents.* Unpublished doctoral dissertation, Columbia University, 1976.

Schmidt, C. R. *Goals, plans, means and the development of communication.* Unpublished doctoral dissertation, Purdue University, 1980.

Searle, J. *Speech acts.* London and New York: Cambridge Univ. Press, 1969.

Shatz, M. The relationship between cognitive processes and the development of communication skills. In B. Keasey (Ed.), *Nebraska symposium on motivation.* Lincoln, Nebraska: Univ. of Nebraska Press, 1978.

Shatz, M., & Gelman, R. The development of communication skills: Modifications in the speech of young children as a function of the listener. *Monographs of the Society for Research in Child Development,* 1973, **38,** (5, Serial No. 152), 1–38.

Shatz, M., & Gelman, R. Beyond syntax: The influence of conversation constraints on speech modifications. In C. Snow & C. A. Ferguson (Eds.), *Talking to children.* London and New York: Cambridge Univ. Press, 1977.

Shugar, G. W. Text analysis as an approach to the study of early linguistic operations. In N. Waterson & C. Snow (Eds.), *The development of communication: Social and pragmatic factors in language acquisition.* New York: Wiley, 1976.

Sonnenschein, S., & Whitehurst, G. J. The development of communication: When a bad model makes a good teacher. *Journal of Experimental Child Psychology,* 1980, **3,** 371–390.

Spilton, D., & Lee, L. C. Some determinants of effective communication in 4-year-olds. *Child Development,* 1977, **48,** 968–977.

Trevarthen, C. The foundations of intersubjectivity: Development of interpersonal and cooperative understanding in infants. In D. R. Olson (Ed.), *The social foundations of language and thought.* New York: Norton, 1977.

Vygotsky, L. S. *Thought and language.* Cambridge, Massachusetts: MIT Press, 1962.

Vygotsky, L. S. *Mind in society.* Cambridge, Massachusetts: Harvard Univ. Press, 1978.

Warden, D. The influence of context on children's use of identifying expressions and references. *British Journal of Psychology,* 1976, **67,** 101–112.

Wellman, H. M., & Lempers, J. D. The naturalistic communicative abilities of two-year-olds. *Child Development,* 1977, **48,** 1052–1057.

Wertsch, J. V. Adult-child interaction and the roots of metacognition. *Quarterly Newsletter of the Institute for Comparative Human Development,* 1978, **2,** 15–18.

Whitehurst, G. J., & Sonnenschein, S. The development of informative messages in referential communication: Knowing when versus knowing how. In W. P. Dickson (Ed.), *Children's oral communication skills.* New York: Academic Press, 1981.

Wood, D. J. Teaching the young child: Some relationships between social interaction, language, and thought. In D. R. Olson (Ed.), *The social foundations of thought and language.* New York: Norton, 1977.

Zivin, G. Removing common confusions about egocentric speech, private speech, and self-regulation. In G. Zivin (Ed.), *The development of self-regulation through private speech.* New York: Wiley, 1979.

AUDITORY FEEDBACK AND SPEECH DEVELOPMENT

Gerald M. Siegel, Herbert L. Pick, Jr., and Sharon R. Garber
CENTER FOR RESEARCH IN HUMAN LEARNING
UNIVERSITY OF MINNESOTA
MINNEAPOLIS, MINNESOTA

I. Introduction

During the course of normal speech development, children have access to two important sources of auditory information. The speech of persons around them defines the repertoire of sounds to be mastered. The fact that children from

ADVANCES IN CHILD DEVELOPMENT
AND BEHAVIOR, VOL. 18

ISBN 0-12-009718-4

different linguistic cultures learn the languages of these cultures is evidence that environmental stimulation is crucial for speech development. The children also receive auditory feedback. That is, they hear their own attempts at production as they explore the surfaces and spaces of the oral cavity and experiment with the vocal apparatus. This article is concerned with the role of this second source of stimulation, auditory feedback, on the development of speech.

The deaf child has great difficulty learning to talk, and yet vocal activity during the first few months seems to be essentially normal (Fry, 1966; Lewis, 1936; Mavilya, 1970). According to Lenneberg (1964):

> Neither deafness nor deaf parents reduces the sound activity during the first six months to any appreciable extent. Qualitatively, the sounds of the first three months are virtually identical among deaf and hearing children. From the fourth to the 12th month there can be no question that a great number of sounds emitted by deaf children are very much like the sounds of hearing children; however, after the sixth month of life the total range of babbling sounds heard in the deaf appeared to be somewhat more restricted than those of hearing children. (p. 120)

Lenneberg's observation suggests that auditory experience does not influence early vocal behaviors. In virtually all theories of speech development, however, auditory feedback is attributed an important role in the first year of life. In his circular reflex theory, Allport (1924) posited a link between the experience of performing the motor speech act and hearing its auditory consequences. Lewis (1936) stated that an important criterion for babbling is that babbling children appear to be attending to and enjoying their own sounds. In his "autism" theory of speech development, Mowrer (1952, 1958) assumed that the infant is intrinsically reinforced for producing sounds reminiscent of those heard during primary reinforcement with the parent or caretaker. Staats and Staats (1964) offered much the same account of early infant vocal behavior. According to Fry (1966), "Motor learning in speech is very largely dependent on hearing; the child must be able to hear the results of his own speech movements if he is ever to acquire normal speech or something approaching normal speech" (p. 193).

Once speech is mastered, auditory feedback may not be necessary for moment-to-moment regulation. Fry (1966) stated that auditory feedback becomes less important as speech habits are established, and that as auditory feedback control wanes, tactile feedback becomes more important. Van Riper and Irwin (1958) also posited a shift in control from auditory to tactile feedback. They mentioned the possibility that certain speech disorders of puzzling origins may have arisen because of a temporary hearing loss during the speech-learning period.

Simner (1971) found that the more closely an auditory stimulus approximated a newborn infant's own vocalizations, the more likely it was to induce the child to cry. A newborn cry was more effective than the cry of a $5\frac{1}{2}$ month old, and the infant's own cry was more effective yet. Infants do appear to note the properties of environmental auditory stimuli, and to have a special reaction to their own vocalizations. These data suggest that the mechanisms for feedback monitoring and regulation are available very early in the child's life.

The relative contribution of auditory versus tactile–kinesthetic feedback to speech development has not been studied directly, but Siegenthaler and Bianchi's (1968) data add to the plausibility that auditory may give way to tactile feedback during speech development. Children between $4\frac{1}{2}$ and $11\frac{1}{2}$ years were tested for simple reaction time to above-threshold presentations of an auditory and a tactile stimulus. From about $6\frac{1}{2}$ years onward, reaction time to the tactile stimulus became progressively faster, whereas response to the auditory stimulus remained stable until about 10 years of age. Extrapolating from the data of Van Riper and Irwin (1958), normal children may take advantage of this changing efficiency by switching from auditory to tactile feedback control, whereas speech-defective children persist in relying on the auditory feedback mode.

As was noted earlier, not all authors agree that feedback is required for ongoing speech. Peterson and Shoup (1966), for example, suggested that speech gradually becomes freed from any feedback control. They cited the persistence of accurate speech in loud noise as support for their claim that auditory feedback is not crucial once speech has been learned, and they argued further that tactile or proprioceptive paths are unlikely to be necessary to maintain speech. Zimmerman and Rettaliata (1981) also indicated that constant feedback monitoring is probably unnecessary in speech production.

In his influential servo system model of the speech mechanism, Fairbanks (1954) did not deal with developmental issues, but he clearly emphasized auditory over tactile–kinesthetic feedback loops for speech production, even in adults. More recent model builders, such as Sanders (1976), show a similar tendency to include a closed-loop auditory feedback component in characterizing adult speech.

MacNeilage (1970) presented a more balanced view concerning the potential contribution of feedback control for speech regulation:

> Although there appears to be closed-loop control of some aspects of the initiation of speech, it is not known at present whether closed-loop control operates within utterances. However, one is encouraged to continue to search for evidence of closed-loop control because of the enormous amount of a priori information the brain appears to require for open-loop control, and because of the considerable indirect neurophysiological evidence that possibilities for closed-loop control exist. (p. 192)

In summary, the finding reported by Lenneberg and others, that the vocalizations of deaf and normal hearing infants are indistinguishable during the early months of life, has been interpreted to signify that auditory feedback is not important in production at this age. Once the child has begun to master the sound system, however, as indicated by babbling at about 3 to 5 months, auditory feedback is considered crucial for the developing child, and deaf and normal-hearing children presumably begin to sound noticeably different. Still later, when speech has become highly automatic, control may shift from auditory to tactile–kinesthetic feedback control, or all forms of feedback regulation may become unnecessary.

Thus far we have been concerned primarily with descriptive studies and with models and theoretical positions. In succeeding sections greater attention will be given to the experimental literature. First, however, certain methodological issues will be considered.

II. Methodological Issues

In most perception experiments, considerable control can be exercised over the stimuli that lead to the subject's responses. Loudness, brightness, texture, etc., can be systematically manipulated by the experimenter. Auditory feedback, however, is not directly under experimental control because it is a self-generated perceptual event. The fact that feedback is self-generated creates a rather special set of problems for those who would examine its role in human behavior. Despite the difficulties, feedback defines a most interesting domain where sensation and motor performance intersect, and where important insights concerning speech control and speech disorder may reside.

A. MONITORING AND REGULATION

A distinction should be made between feedback as a source of information concerning one's own behavior and as a component in the regulation of that behavior (Marteniuk, 1976; Shelton & McReynolds, 1979). In the Fairbanks (1954) feedback model, monitoring leads automatically to regulation of speech. Fairbanks took as his analogy a device such as a thermostat, which both records the temperature in some environment and controls the heating or cooling units that are responsible for maintaining a certain temperature. Monitoring need not always lead to regulation, however. For example, a thermometer does not affect temperature. In the area of speech, Rockler (1976) had college students read difficult tongue twisters in quiet and against a background of loud noise. The reduced feedback under the noise did not cause an increase in the number of speech errors, but it did interfere with the tendency of the speakers to notice when they had made an error.

B. STIMULUS CONTROL IN FEEDBACK STUDIES

Three primary research strategies are used to gain experimental control over the feedback stimulus. One is to intercept and alter the speech before it is fed back; a second is to mask the feedback signal; and a third is to block its transmission.

1. Intercept and Alter the Subject's Speech

In delayed auditory feedback, which is perhaps the most familiar manipulation, the subject's speech is intercepted at the lips by a microphone that shunts the signal into a delaying device (usually a tape recorder with separate play and record heads) before passing it on to the subject's earphones. When the delay falls within some critical range, usually reported to center around 200 msec, the effect is a disruption in the ongoing flow of speech—"artificial stutter," as Lee (1951) first termed it. In order to obtain this effect, the experimenter must amplify, as well as delay, the air-conducted message, so that it can effectively compete with bone-conducted feedback, which is not subject to direct experimental control. Thus, the procedure involves delay plus amplification of the airborne feedback.

Another application of this basic procedure is in the method of sidetone amplification. Here the subject's speech is fed back without delay, but only after it has been amplified. This is an effective means of studying the accommodations speakers make when their voice is made to sound too loud, but the process is not symmetrical. That is, it can be used to study the effects of amplifying the voice, but not the effects of attenuating it. When the attenuated speech falls below the level of the bone-conducted signal, the experimenter effectively loses control of the stimulus. The process is much like testing various levels of hearing, all of which fall below the subject's threshold. Thus, feedback can be amplified, but not directly attenuated. Considerations such as these led to the investigation of analog systems involving auditory feedback without bone conduction. The electric guitar, for example, has no significant bone-conduction component and thus allows much greater control over the acoustic stimulus reaching the player's earphones.

The method of intercepting speech can be used to study other aspects of the signal, such as the quality or pitch of the feedback. Garber and Moller (1979) found that speakers spontaneously alter their nasality in response to selective filtering of their feedback. Theoretically, the effects of intricate transformations of feedback could be studied so that, for example, speakers would hear themselves producing one vowel while actually uttering another. Of course, even in ordinary conversation a quality transformation occurs. One does not hear one's own voice as others hear it. The speaker's feedback is always a combination of air and bone conduction. Listeners receive the signal directly through the air. Most individuals are startled at the sound of their voice when heard for the first time from a tape recorder—that is, as an entirely air-conducted signal.

2. Interfere with the Signal

A second experimental strategy is to add a signal, such as a loud noise, that interferes with feedback. In interpreting the effect of this procedure, two factors have to be considered: Does speech change because the noise interferes with self-perception (a feedback explanation), or because the noise itself affects speech?

For purposes of studying feedback, we would hope that interference with feedback is the important factor, and data by Garber, Siegel, Pick, and Alcorn (1976) suggest that interference with feedback is, indeed, the crucial factor.

3. *Block the Signal*

A more radical way to gain control over the speaker's feedback is to leave the signal intact but to block its transmission through the nervous system. Black (1951) introduced auditory fatigue by exposing subjects to intense noise for extended periods. This procedure induced a temporary hearing loss, and thereby caused a shift in the subjects' threshold for their own speech, as well as for environmentally produced sounds.

The method of blocking transmission has been used more extensively in the realm of tactile–kinesthetic feedback, generally by injecting anesthesia into the sensory nerves of the oral cavity (Ringel, 1970). An assumption underlying the procedure is that interference with sensory transmission can be produced without affecting other aspects of neural transmission. Borden, Harris, and Catena (1973) have questioned the plausibility of this assumption. The problem is that in order to reduce sensation, anesthesia must be added, and the effects of this intrusion cannot be entirely controlled.

Rather than resort to the desensitization procedure, some alteration in tactile sensation can be accomplished by placing a palatal plate in the oral cavity, thus distorting cues from the palatal (although not the lingual) surface (Garber, Speidel, & Siegel, 1980). Another possibility might be to create an equivalence to auditory masking by presenting random vibratory sensation to the oral structures in such a way as to mask normal tactile sensation. If feasible, this might prove an acceptable alternative to the more confounded and noxious nerve block procedure.

4. *Analog Studies*

Another alternative, already alluded to, is to do analog studies in other domains that involve auditory feedback. Some of the constraints on the feasible manipulations for auditory feedback in speech can be avoided by using a musical instrument. The study of other organisms provides another kind of analog. Many extremely important questions simply cannot be addressed directly with human subjects. In particular, crucial questions concerning the importance of an intact feedback system for the initial development of speech cannot be studied directly. Deaf children do, of course, have profound difficulty in developing speech. But they are cut off both from feedback and from environmental sounds, and these sources of deprivation cannot be untangled.

Marler (1970) has suggested that the development of speech in humans has important parallels in the development of bird song in certain species. The role of feedback has been studied extensively in white-crowned sparrows and these song birds respond to manipulations of their auditory experience in a way that seems close to that of human children. For example, if these birds are deafened early in life, they do vocalize, but in a highly abnormal manner (Marler, 1975). They also develop abnormal song if they are raised in total isolation and are thereby deprived of all external stimulation, although they can hear their own vocalizations. Similarly, white-crowned sparrows do not develop normal song even if they are allowed to hear the species song during the usual critical learning period, but are then deafened just before they begin their own vocalizing. For these birds, both external auditory stimulation and self-perception seem necessary for normal song to develop. Studies of this sort have important implications for speech acquisition although, as always, the appropriateness of the analog must be considered.

III. The Logic of Feedback Studies

All of the strategies for studying feedback processes in speech share one problematic feature. In every case inferences about normal function are drawn from the effects of introducing some abnormality into feedback functioning. In order to study its role, the normal feedback system must be tampered with. The problems are, perhaps, obvious. For example, delayed auditory feedback creates a condition of anomalous feedback that is very disruptive to speech, but one cannot conclude from this finding that intact feedback is necessary for normal speech. Other procedures, such as the addition of very loud masking noise, also interfere with feedback but have virtually none of the disruptive effects found under delayed auditory feedback. Indeed, even sudden deafness in adults, which results in the total elimination of auditory feedback, is far less disruptive than the delay procedure. One would, of course, prefer to study the operation of feedback loops directly during normal performance, but until such procedures are possible, inferences about normal control mechanisms must be based on the effects of experimentally induced perturbations.

IV. Feedback Research with Children

In almost all of the experimental studies of speech and feedback processes in children, delayed auditory feedback has been the only experimental manipulation. One exception was an experiment by Tingley and Allen (1975), who studied variations in timing of repeated phrases in children between 5 and 11 years old. The children were asked to repeat a simple phrase (''Twinkle, twinkle . . .'') in the same way as many as 30 times, and also to perform a repetitive tapping task. Timing control, as indicated by reduced temporal variability, increased with age in a similar fashion for both tasks. On the basis of a complex statistical analysis, Tingley and Allen concluded that auditory feedback was not a source of variation in the children's vocal performance. That is, temporal stability did not depend on feedback. A possible interpretation is, again, that by age 5 years the kind of speech used in this experiment has become so automatic that it is free of feedback control. The authors noted, however, that the performance of one 5 year old who had to be taught the phrase was similar to that of the other children. Unfortunately, data were not collected on younger children who are in the midst of speech mastery.

The dominant approach to studying feedback processes in children has been to study the effects of delayed auditory feedback on some aspect of vocalization. The logic of the studies has been roughly the following: Delayed auditory feedback can severely disrupt the speech of normal adults; speakers differ in their susceptibility, however, and a general assumption has been that the extent of the disturbance is a direct reflection of the speaker's dependence on intact feedback for normal speech (Yates, 1963). The question of developmental interest has been whether delay effects vary systematically with age. If children rely most on auditory feedback when they are developing speech, delay should have greater disruptive effects on younger children than on older ones, assuming that the delay procedure provides a sensitive indicator of feedback control and that no distinction need be made among various parameters of speech such as articulation, intensity, quality, and pitch.

A. RESEARCH AT JOHNS HOPKINS

The most extensive developmental work appears in a series of papers from the Johns Hopkins University School of Medicine. These studies included children ranging in age from 24 hours to 9 years. All of the experiments involved a delay interval of 200 msec, the delay time that has been reported to be maximally disruptive to adults. Because of the wide range of ages and verbal abilities, a variety of speech tasks and dependent measures were used.

Cullen, Fargo, Chase, and Baker (1968) studied the effect of delayed feedback on infants who were between 24 and 168 hours at the time of testing. Vocal behavior (crying) was induced by snapping a rubber band against the sole of the child's foot. The bursts of crying were significantly longer under delay. Cullen *et al.* noted that the changes in the cry might have been obtained with other forms of auditory stimulation and suggested that an interesting procedure would be to use several different delay times in order to determine more precisely the relation between infant crying and the experimental procedure.

Belmore, Kewley-Port, Mobley, and Goodman (1973) extended the research to children between 6 and 10 months old and between 12 and 19 months old. Subjects who used identifiable words at any time during the sessions were classified as the advanced language group, regardless of chronological age. Subjects for whom fewer than 25% of the utterances were consonant–vowel combinations involving consonants other than /h/ or a glottal stop were arbitrarily considered to be in the least advanced language group. These classifications were derived after the experiment was completed. Delayed feedback caused 46.7% of the children to show some difference in either duration or intensity of vocalization. However, the differences were not always in the same direction. That is, some children responded to the delay with increased intensity, and others with reduced intensity of vocalization. Age was not significantly related to the child's response, but language level was. Children in the advanced language classification were more likely to respond in some fashion to the delayed feedback than were the subjects in the lowest language group.

Yeni-Kimshian, Chase, and Mobley (1968) also found considerable variability in response to delayed feedback in children between 1 year, 9 months and 2 years, 2 months. They concluded that speech is not strongly affected by delayed feedback in children at this age level. Another group of children, between 2 and 3 years of age, showed stable and significant increases in phonation time when delayed feedback was introduced.

The last study to be discussed in this series was the first to be published. Chase, Sutton, First, and Zubin (1961) studied the effects of delayed auditory feedback with young (4–6 years) and older (7–9 years) children. The subjects were asked to draw a person and then to tell a story about the drawing under normal and under delayed feedback. The delay condition was disruptive to both groups, but the effects were more marked among the older children, especially on measures of word rate and syllable prolongation.

In the Johns Hopkins studies, the disruptive effects of delay were most clearly found among the oldest subjects. The results with infants were generally unstable and variable. A simple developmental interpretation placed upon the findings would be that the effects of delay become larger and more reliable with age (or language maturity), suggesting that feedback control of speech becomes more important as the child matures. This is not the developmental pattern suggested by the theories of Allport, Fry, Mowrer, Staats and Staats, etc.

B. CONFLICTING DATA

Several studies call into question the developmental generalizations in the Johns Hopkins research. Ratner, Gawronski, and Rice (1964) studied the effects of delay on four age groups between 6 years, 9 months and 13 years, 6 months. The children repeated a brief sentence six times with normal and delayed feedback. The delay interval selected was 630 msec because in pilot work this interval seemed maximally disruptive. At first encounter with the delay, all age groups increased vocal intensity and articulation errors. Over a number of trials, however, the oldest children decreased intensity and errors whereas the younger children became more disrupted by the delay. The authors concluded that delayed feedback is more disturbing to younger than to older children, a finding at variance with the pattern in the Johns Hopkins studies.

A second breach in the previous pattern of results came from a systematic exploration of the interaction between delay interval and age of subjects reported by MacKay (1968). Five year olds, 8 year olds, and college students repeated a set of standard sentences, with instructions to speak as rapidly as possible. The delay intervals used with the children were 0, 100, 250, 375, 524, and 750 msec. The adults spoke under these same delay intervals, except that a 263-msec delay was added and the 524-msec delay was deleted. In addition, subjects repeated a set of sentences while hearing another voice in their earphones reading an entirely different text. This "irrelevant voice" procedure provided a check on whether the basis for speech disruption was the delayed feedback or a competing voice. MacKay found that delayed feedback caused a reduction in speech rate in all age groups, but the most disruptive interval for the younger children was 524 msec, 375 msec for the older children, and 200 msec for the adults. Thus, the younger the children, the greater the delay interval that produced maximum interference with rate. Moreover, at the maximally disruptive interval, the youngest children were much more disrupted than the older children or adults. A similar pattern was found for the number of speech errors. The irrelevant voice procedure had only minor effects on speech rate or errors.

A possible explanation of the relationship between age and maximally disruptive interval seemed to be that younger children typically speak more slowly and have longer syllable durations than do older children and adults. MacKay included a condition in which his adults were asked to repeat a set of sentences at a "medium slow" and a "very slow" rate, in addition to the maximum rate. The slowing of rate was to be accomplished by prolonging sounds rather than by inserting pauses. Only two delay intervals were used, 200 and 263 msec. Slowing of rate by prolonging the syllables reduced the delayed feedback effect, but the critical interval did not shift from 200 to 263 msec. That is, 200 msec remained more disruptive regardless of rate of speech.

Waters (1968) studied subjects between 10 and 18 years old. The delay interval was 200 msec and speakers read passages in normal voice and whispering. In general, disturbance was greater during the whispering condition than during the phonated reading. For both whispering and reading, older subjects were less affected by the delay than were the youngest subjects. Thus, a developmental change in susceptibility appears even among subjects in their teens, with greater response to the delayed feedback among younger subjects. Waters' study appeared in the wake of the first of the Johns Hopkins experiments (Chase *et al.*, 1961) and prompted him to postulate a bow-shaped function in which the effects of delayed auditory feedback initially increase with age and subsequently decrease.

Timmons and Boudreau (1976) studied the effects of intervals between 113 and 520 msec in girls and boys aged 5, 7, 9, 11, and 13 years. The children recited a familiar nursery rhyme. The effects of delayed feedback were evaluated by means of difference scores for speaking time and number of disfluencies, comparing each delay interval with performance under simultaneous feedback. Unfortunately, the raw scores from which the differences were computed were not reported. Age and interval differences were obtained. The 5 year olds reacted with greater rate change at 520 msec than did the older subjects. Five and 7 year olds were more disfluent at 413- and 520-msec delays than were the older subjects. The results support the impression that young children are more affected by the experimental procedure than older ones, and that the younger the subject the greater the delay interval that is required for maximum perturbation of speech. Timmons and Boudreau (1978) reported the same pattern of results in a later study comparing stuttering and normal children.

Siegel, Fehst, Garber, and Pick (1980) attempted a systematic replication of MacKay's study with special attention to the critical interval hypothesis and the possible effect of MacKay's instruction to speak as rapidly as possible. The subjects were 5 year olds, 8 year olds, and adult speakers who performed MacKay's sentence repetition task under 0-, 250-, 375-, 500-, and 625-msec delays. All subjects performed the task under normal rate instructions and under instructions to speak as rapidly as possible. The results partially corroborated the developmental pattern reported by MacKay, Waters, and Timmons and Boudreau. The youngest children were more affected by delay than were the older children and adults on sentence duration, syllable rate, and nonfluencies. The critical interval hypothesis did not fare so well. For the most part, the different delay intervals were equally disruptive for all age groups. Finally, instructions to speak as rapidly as possible were not uniformly successful. In particular, the youngest children did not change rate when so instructed, although the adults did increase syllable rate by an average of 24% when so instructed. Furthermore, increasing rate did not accentuate the experimental effects. If anything, the curves are somewhat flatter during the maximum rate conditions.

C. SUMMARY OF DELAYED AUDITORY FEEDBACK EXPERIMENTS WITH CHILDREN

The Johns Hopkins research seemed to point to a rather clear developmental picture, in which effects of delayed speech are small and unstable in very young children but are increasingly reliable and pronounced with increasing age and verbal maturity. Later experiments failed to replicate this pattern. The preponderance of results now indicates that, contrary to the Johns Hopkins reports, younger children are more susceptible to delayed auditory feedback than older children. The reason for the discrepancy between the earlier and later data is unclear. Devising procedures that are appropriate over a wide age range is very difficult, and variable success in doing so may account for some of the difficulty. Is the cry of pain induced by a rubber band snapped against the foot akin to the chatterings of a preschool child? In addition, factors such as microphone placement, earphone placement, experimental environment, and amplification of the feedback varied widely from study to study, even within the Johns Hopkins series.

From our own laboratory experience and from our reading of the data, we suggest that the pattern of decreasing delay effects with age is correct, but that the critical interval hypothesis is not. Some support for both of these conclusions has been obtained in a number of other experiments that may be considered as analogs to the speech development studies. These are experiments in which degree of speech deficiency or mastery of a second language take the place of age or linguistic development in the first language.

V. Analog Experiments

Goldfarb and Braunstein (1958) compared the response of normal and "confirmed schizophrenic" children to delayed auditory feedback of 160 msec. The mean age for both groups was approximately 9 years. Subjective judgments of the effects were informally collected. Goldfarb and Braunstein reported smaller effects with the disturbed children than were observed in the normal children, suggesting that the disturbed children are less attentive to their own feedback than are their normal age-mates. Ossip (1971) compared the effects of 200 msec of delay on five normal children and five who had articulation errors. The data again were primarily subjective, but Ossip concluded that the misarticulating children were less disrupted by delay than were the normal children, and therefore were less attuned to their own speech productions. Ossip conjectured that reduced attention to feedback might account for articulation problems.

A second analog approach has been to study adults who are speaking in a first versus a second language. The second language is presumed to represent a lower level of mastery and therefore to be comparable to the skill in a young, language-learning child. Rouse and Tucker (1966) studied three groups of college students who read under normal or delayed (225-msec) feedback. Group 1 consisted of Americans reading in English. Group 2 consisted of a conglomeration of foreign students who also read in English, although it was their second language. Group 3 students were Americans who had studied French for almost 5 years. In the experiment, Group 3 read in French. Although all groups were affected by delayed feedback, the disruption was greatest for the American subjects speaking in their native English (Group 1), and the difference between the two nonnative-speaking groups (Groups 2 and 3) was not significant. Rouse and Tucker did not include a group reading in a native language other than English. Including such a group would have helped establish the point that native versus nonnative language determines susceptibility to the delayed feedback.

MacKay (1970) was unconvinced by the Rouse and Tucker experiment on two grounds. He objected to the fact that each speaker was not used as his own control, speaking in both his native and second language under delay; and, as might be expected, he objected to Rouse and Tucker's use of only a single delay interval. Based on his earlier work with children (MacKay, 1968), he suggested that the critical interval may vary with language mastery, as it does with age.

In checking these possibilities, he introduced a series of ingenious control procedures. The subjects were 21 college students. A native English group consisted of six speakers who had approximately 4 years of experience with German, at least part of it in Germany. A native German group included 15 subjects with approximately 6 years of exposure to English, some of it in the United States. All subjects read sentences in English and German under delays between 150 and 300 msec. The subjects also read a list of sentences in Congolese, a language none of them knew.

MacKay's results differed systematically from those of Rouse and Tucker. Under delay, the rate of speech was faster and "stutterings" fewer in the native language than in the acquired language and in the totally unfamiliar Congolese. Furthermore, the maximally disruptive delay was always 200 msec, indicating that the most disruptive delay interval was not determined either by the particular languages studied, or by the degree of familiarity the subjects had with the languages.

Additional research is necessary before the differences can be reconciled between the findings reported by MacKay and by Rouse and Tucker. These analog studies offer interesting opportunities to pose questions concerning the role of feedback in language acquisition and language production. Many issues have not been addressed. Should language maturity be defined in terms of comprehension or production? Are effects comparable across all languages? Would they differ, for example, in tonal languages? Do students of a second language change in their susceptibility to delayed feedback as they proceed through their language studies? Similar questions can be raised concerning individuals with speech disturbance. Another area that has been barely explored is the effect of delay on students at varying levels of skill as they progress through mastery of a musical instrument. These studies are interesting not only in their own right, but also as they might contribute to an understanding of feedback processes in normal speech development.

VI. Other Manipulations of Auditory Feedback

Feedback can be affected by adding noise, or by filtering, interrupting, or amplifying the feedback signal. Delayed feedback is dramatic in its effects but is created and experienced primarily in a laboratory. Other feedback modifications result from natural variations in environmental conditions. We speak in varying conditions of noise. Pitch and quality change naturally when one wears a helmet or has a bad head cold. Various feedback modifications affect different aspects of the speech stream. Delay interferes with temporal aspects. Filtering and loudness modifications interfere with more steady-state aspects of speech. Siegel, Schork, Pick, and Garber (1982) found virtually no correlation in the extent to which subjects reacted to sidetone amplification, masking noise, and delayed auditory feedback. The procedures did not produce equivalent results. In the present section we review the few developmental studies that involved feedback manipulations other than delay.

Siegel, Pick, Olsen, and Sawin (1976) asked 3- and 4-year-old children to tell stories about familiar picture books. During sidetone amplification, the child's voice was fed back through earphones without delay at three levels of amplification: 0, +10, and +20 dB (SPL) of sidetone gain. During all three gain conditions, 80 dB (SPL) of speech spectrum background noise was mixed with the feedback in the child's earphones. Each condition lasted for 2 minutes and was tape-recorded. The tape recordings were later analyzed to provide data concerning the average intensity level of the child's voice at each of the gain levels. The results for the two age groups were compared with data obtained in a previous experiment with college adults. For each of the groups, sidetone amplification had a significant effect. That is, as feedback was amplified, the subjects compensated by lowering vocal intensity. The degree of compensation, however, differed for the three groups. The adults reduced vocal intensity between the 0 and +20 dB conditions by about 35%, the 4 year olds by 26%, and the 3 year olds by 17%. The difference between the 3 year olds and the other groups was statistically significant, but the difference between 4 year olds and adults was not significant. Thus, with respect to sidetone amplification, evidence for a developmental trend emerged, with the youngest children less responsive to the intensity manipulations than were the older subjects.

After a brief rest, a feedback-masking procedure was also carried out for a sample of the 3 and 4 year olds. During this procedure no feedback was given through the earphones, but the subjects spoke for 2 minutes in each of three noise conditions: quiet, 60, and 80 dB (SPL) of speech spectrum noise. A group of 11 adult subjects was also included for comparison purposes. A significant effect was obtained for all three groups. As the noise level increased, the subjects increased vocal intensity. In order to have an estimate of the extent of the effect, the percentage change between the 60 and 80 dB noise conditions was computed.

The percentage change was 22% for the 3 year olds, 12% for the 4 year olds, and 18% for the adults. These scores were not significantly different. In contrast to sidetone amplification, the masking data do not reveal any developmental progression. Finally, the percentages of change for the masking and the sidetone amplification procedures were correlated for each age group. The correlation obtained for the 4 year olds was a significant $r = .52$; the correlation for the adults ($r = .10$) and the 3 year olds ($r = .08$) did not reach significance.

Sidetone amplification and masking effects were also explored in young children by Kennard (1980), but she extended the analysis to include a group of children that misarticulated the /r/ sound, and added instructions designed to tap a possible difference between performance and competence in reacting to the loudness manipulations. The /r/ misarticulation group consisted of 12 children between 7 and 10 years old who were referred by their school clinicians. They were matched with age-mates selected from the same classroom. The task and procedures were similar to those used by Siegel *et al.* (1976). During sidetone amplification, the gain levels were 0 and +20 dB. In the masking procedure, the two noise levels were 60 dB (SPL) and 90 dB (SPL) of speech spectrum noise. Half of the children in each group went through these two procedures twice. The other half went through the procedures once, and were then given instructions designed to maximize the effects. For the masking procedure, the children were instructed to speak louder when the noise came on in order to hear themselves better. The instruction under sidetone amplification was to speak more softly when the child's voice sounded unnaturally loud. After being instructed, these subjects went through the masking and sidetone amplification procedures a second time.

Both groups demonstrated significant masking and sidetone amplification effects without instructions, and even greater effects after receiving the maximizing instructions. For some reason, the instructions were more effective in maximizing the sidetone amplification effect rather than the masking effect, for the clinical speakers as well as for the normal speakers. The magnitude of the children's response to sidetone amplification was less than had been found previously with adults, again suggesting that the sidetone amplification procedure becomes more effective with age. Kennard found no evidence for a developmental trend in the masking procedure, however, a finding that accords with the results reported by Siegel *et al.* (1976). Why the masking and sidetone amplification effects should differ in these respects is unclear, but the data do indicate in still another way a lack of equivalence between the two procedures. This lack of equivalence is noteworthy in light of Lane and Tranel's (1971) claim that the phenomena are two sides of the same coin.

Costley, Siegel, and Olsen (1978) asked 3 year olds, 5 year olds, and college adults to match the loudness of an externally produced vowel. The subjects listened to the vowel /a/ presented at four intensity levels through earphones: 60,

70, 80, and 90 dB (SPL). After hearing the vowel, the subject was required to vocalize an /a/ of the same loudness. The subjects heard their own voice fed back at unity gain. That is, vocalization of 80 dB at the microphone resulted in 80 dB in the speaker's earphones.

Costley *et al.* adduced three hypotheses to explain why the children had flatter functions than did the adults when using their own voices to match external loudness, and this led Costley (1981) to conduct three additional experiments. One hypothesis is that children hear external sounds as growing in loudness less rapidly than adults. In order to test this possibility, Costley designed a cross-modality matching study, in which 12 subjects in each of 3 age groups (3 year olds, 4 year olds, and adults) viewed stick figures of varying lengths (between 1.25 and 60 cm) and instructed the experimenter to manipulate an attenuator until they judged that loudness of an externally produced /a/ matched the length of the stick. The task required no vocalization on the part of the subject. The growth-of-loudness functions were very similar for the three groups, indicating that the children were as capable as the adults in making loudness judgments concerning externally produced sounds. Thus, the first hypothesis was rejected. Children do not hear external sounds as growing less rapidly in loudness than do adults.

A second hypothesis is that children perceive their own voices as growing in loudness more rapidly than do adults. This hypothesis pertains more directly than does the first to self-perception. In a second experiment, the same children and adults were again shown the sticks, and were asked to vocalize a vowel sound at loudness levels that matched the stick lengths. Once again, the three groups performed the task in a comparable manner, except that the youngest children were more variable, especially for the low intensity levels required to match the shortest stick lengths. The second hypothesis was also rejected. The children did not significantly differ from adults with respect to the loudness growth of their own voices.

The final hypothesis focuses on motor production rather than perception. In the last experiment, the same subjects faced a television monitor on which vocal intensity was represented as a "bouncing ball" that moved between two horizontal lines on the screen (Garber, Burzynski, Vale, & Nelson, 1979). The speaker's task was to keep the ball between the lines while vocalizing. The separation between the lines was equivalent to 1 dB. The subjects had to maintain the ball between the lines at 70, 80, and 90 dB (SPL). Three trials were given at each target intensity. The subjects were instructed to sustain a phonation for several seconds at each target intensity. The adults and the 7 year olds were very successful on this production task, but the 3 year olds were systematically too loud at the 70-dB target and they had difficulty sustaining their vocalizations. Rather than prolong the vowel, the youngest children made many staccato attempts to hit the target intensity. These young children were also more variable than were the other subjects in their intensity peaks around the target intensities.

In summary, the children and adults in Costley's experiments produced essentially the same growth of loudness functions, both for self-generated and for externally generated vowels. The greatest disparities occurred in the production study, suggesting that precise regulation of vocal intensity may be a gradually learned skill. The youngest children found the task most difficult. They did not sustain the vowel and they were more variable around the target intensity. The difficulty was especially marked at the lower end of the continuum. The children tended to speak too loudly. Reasoning from these data, we would suggest that the reduced sidetone amplification effect in young children, found in earlier studies, may result from this same lack of precision in motor control. Still remaining, however, is the question of why a similar developmental trend is not obtained in the masking effect and why the progression of development is the opposite under delayed auditory feedback. These topics will be considered later, in Section VII.

Garber *et al.* (1980) examined the interaction between masking and interference with tactile feedback in normal 5-year-old children. Palatal inserts (1.5 mm thick) were individually fashioned and fitted to the oral cavity of each child. In the masking noise condition, the child heard 90 dB (SPL) of speech noise through earphones. The children named pictures in noise, with the palatal inserts in place, with noise and palates combined, and in control conditions. The effects of the various combinations of noise and palatal appliance were analyzed in terms of articulation scores and vocal intensity. The articulation data testify to the robustness of articulatory skills in children as young as 5 years. Very few errors were induced, even when the appliance and noise conditions were combined. Large changes were observed, however, in vocal intensity under the noise. The children increased vocal intensity by 12 dB under noise. This result is important, because in a similarly designed earlier study (Garber, Speidel, Siegel, Miller, & Glass, 1980) adults increased intensity by only 6 dB.

The role of task variables in determining the size of the masking effect was studied in 5 year olds and adults by Amazi and Garber (1982). The subjects were divided into groups that either labeled pictures or told stories about the pictures in quiet and in 90 dB (SPL) of noise. An interaction between task and age emerged. The children responded to both tasks with approximately the same magnitude of the masking effect (again between 11 and 12 dB). The adults made a distinction between tasks, increasing by 12 dB in story telling and only 9 dB in the labeling task. Amazi and Garber suggested that the adults are sensitive both to the noise and to the communication requirements. Uttering single words does not place a high premium on intelligibility (Lane & Tranel, 1971), and so the adults react less to noise than when the task becomes more communicative, as in story telling. Children, however, may not be as sensitive to communicative aspects of the situation, and so respond only to the noise, regardless of the communicative aspects.

All of the experimental procedures reviewed thus far involve some modification of feedback at the subject's own ears. One naturally occurring situation, however, combines visual information with feedback. Adult speakers increase loudness in order to maintain communication when speaking to a distant or retreating listener. In this case, the speaker clearly is not attempting to maintain loudness, but is using self-perception to help regulate the signal that will fall on the listener's ears. It is possible, of course, that the cues that determine vocal intensity over distance are entirely related to the distance, and do not involve self-perception at all. Deaf speakers may respond to listeners at varying distances in the same way as do hearing speakers. Speaking to a listener who is vanishing into a quiet sunset may be no different from shouting to a friend as a noisy train pulls out of the station. These interactions have not been studied, but they offer some interesting possibilities for studying the interplay between feedback regulation and the development of communication skills.

Johnson, Pick, Siegel, Cicciarelli, and Garber (1981) asked 3 year olds, 5 year olds, and college adults to instruct an artist in what to draw when the artist was positioned 6, 12, and 24 ft from the subject. Each increase in distance represents a doubling of the preceding distance. According to the inverse square law, when distance from the sound source is doubled, the intensity of the sound decreases by 6 dB. The dependent measure was vocal intensity at each of the listener distances. A significant distance effect was obtained, with no age difference or age-by-distance interaction. Even the youngest children seemed to understand the need to increase intensity as the listener moved farther away. Rather than 6 dB for each doubling, however, the changes were more in the order of 1 or 2 dB, a value similar to the results reported by Markel, Prebor, and Brandt (1972). Although adults and children did not differ, some evidence indicated that the children were responding to absolute distance but the adults were attentive to the doublings. In future experiments, the effects of combining background noise with distance should be studied. Adults may reason that only minor changes are usually necessary in order to maintain communication with a listener over small distances in quiet. Under noise, however, adults may be more aware than are children of the additional penalty in communication that occurs when the listener moves away.

A. MASKING AND ARTICULATION

The studies of masking with normal adults and children indicate that accuracy of articulation is scarcely affected by interference with auditory feedback, even when the masking is combined with the insertion of palatal appliances that interfere with oral tactile sensation. As will be apparent, a similar conclusion can be drawn concerning the effects of oral anesthesia, and even the combination of anesthetization of the oral cavity plus masking noise. Clearly, articulation is very resistant to breakdown due to interference with feedback channels. The only exception might be the effects of delayed auditory feedback, but the changes that occur under delay, the prolongations, repetitions, hesitations—even the struggle behaviors—seem less articulatory responses than attempts to restore temporal aspects of the speech. Furthermore, the misarticulating children studied by Kennard (1980) were similar to normal speakers in their response to masking and sidetone procedures, and to the instructions to maximize these procedures. A general defect in auditory feedback processes in children with articulation disorders is not supported by the literature. Masking does have an effect, however, on articulation skills of an important subgroup of these children.

Manning and his colleagues have conducted a series of studies on the effects of masking on children who have just been or are about to be dismissed from articulation therapy. Manning reasoned that during the acquisition of a sound, the child passes through several stages of mastery until the production becomes highly automatic. Initially, correct production requires careful monitoring of auditory feedback; later, control may switch to kinesthetic feedback or perhaps become fully preprogrammed, with greatly reduced attention to feedback. Manning, Keappock, and Stick (1976) administered the McDonald Deep Test of Articulation to 71 elementary school children who were about to be dismissed from articulation therapy. The test was given in quiet and in 86 dB (SPL) of noise. When the children were retested in quiet after a summer vacation with no intervening therapy, those children whose articulation had broken down during testing under noise tended to relapse over the summer, but those who had been unaffected by the noise retained their newly acquired articulatory skill. The effects of masking on a newly mastered sound were replicated with /r/- and /s/-defective children (Campbell, Manning, Robertson, & DiSalvo, 1976), using different kinds of masking noise (Manning, Ortman, & Scheer, 1977), as well as competing speech (Campbell *et al.*, 1976), and with different sound pressure levels of masking (Manning, Scheer, & Louko, 1977).

Manning and Ortman (1980) and Manning, Louko, and DiSalvo (1978) suggested that the response to masking may be an indicator of the extent to which the speaker is still relying on auditory feedback for correct production. Fully competent speakers do not require auditory feedback for correct articulation and are therefore unaffected by disturbance of that feedback; speakers who do not yet have mastery of the sounds cannot forego auditory feedback, and so deteriorate in production when auditory feedback is disturbed. Presumably, the same could be said of normal children who are in the process of articulation development, or even of adults who are attempting to learn a second language.

Although Manning's findings are quite reliable and are certainly useful for making predictions concerning dismissal from therapy, the data are not entirely consistent with a feedback hypothesis. Manning and Ortman (1980) found no difference in the effects of competing speech, backward speech, time-compressed speech, and a combination of sawtooth plus white noise masking, although these various sound sources should differ in their ability to mask self-perception of speech, and therefore in the extent to which they disrupt articulation. Similarly, Manning and Scheer (1978) found no differences when the masking noise (competing speech) was presented at 50, 60, 70, or 80 dB. Campbell *et al.* (1976) obtained similar results for masking presented either at 65 or 85 dB (SPL). If speech breaks down because of interference with auditory feedback, higher masking levels should be more interfering. Indeed, why 50 dB of masking should have any effect on articulation at all is puzzling, given that it interferes so little with self-perception.

Rather than interfering with auditory self-perception, masking may disrupt articulation because it is a novel stimulus that distracts the speaker's attention while the speaker is producing a sound over which he or she still has only tenuous mastery. Yanez, Siegel, Garber, and Wellen (1982) designed an experiment to test this alternative hypothesis. The subjects were 30 elementary school children who had been in therapy for either the /s/ or the /r/ sound, but now performed at 90% or better on the target phoneme during testing in quiet. The children were administered either the /s/ or the /r/ portion of the McDonald Deep Test of Articulation, in quiet and under two noises.

The noises were selected so that each would be a potential masker for one group of children and a potential distractor for the second group. The s-noise was produced by filtering a white noise so that only the energy above 2000 Hz was passed, thus creating a high-pitched noise with energy concentrated in the region usually associated with the /s/ sound. To create the r-noise, the filters were set to pass all of the energy up to a cutoff frequency of 1250 Hz, thereby creating a low frequency noise concentrating in the region usually associated with /r/.

Each child was tested individually in three conditions. Depending on the articulation error, the child was administered either the /s/ or the /r/ portion of the articulation test in quiet. The test was then administered two more times, once under the s-noise, and once under r-noise. The noises were presented binaurally through earphones at 80 dB (SPL). The results for the children in the /s/ group were fairly straightforward and seemed to favor a feedback explanation. These children made virtually no errors in quiet or under r-noise, but had a significant increase in errors under the s-noise. The /r/-defective children also had few errors in quiet but showed significant and equal increases under both noises.

Several possible explanations may be offered for the fact that the /r/ children were equally disrupted by both noises, whereas the /s/ children showed a more selective response. One possibility is simply that these are very different sorts of children who suffer different underlying problems. Because tactile information is so hard to obtain during production of /r/, some clinicians characterize it as a more "auditory" sound than /s/. Children with an /r/ problem may be vulnerable to auditory interference. Possibly, the s-noise was not as neutral as had been intended with respect to /r/. The sound most often substituted for /r/ is /w/, and the acoustic difference between /r/ and /w/ is primarily in the region of the third formant, between 1200 and 2500 Hz—the region of the s-noise. The design of the study may not have succeeded in creating a potential masker versus a distractor for the /r/ children; perhaps both sounds ended up in the region that could interfere with auditory feedback.

Although a clear choice is not possible between a distraction and a feedback explanation for the results of the Yanez *et al.* study, this experiment and the earlier ones by Manning and colleagues are important in that they all make a clear distinction between normal and misarticulating children. The significant difference is that masking does interfere with the production of sounds that are in the process of being mastered by articulatory defective children but masking is virtually never found to interfere with articulation in normal speakers. A major variable may be level of mastery. Perhaps children with normal articulatory development would demonstrate the same effect for sounds they have not yet fully acquired. The same pattern might apply for adults who are learning the sound system of a second language. These interpretations suggest that speech-defective children do not have a generalized disturbance of feedback processing but are vulnerable to disrupted feedback for the particular sounds they are attempting to learn, and at certain stages of the learning process. Once the sound is fully mastered, children who had articulation defects are not different from normals. Indeed, even within subjects, the noise does not cause all sounds to degenerate, only those that were previously in error.

B. TACTILE–KINESTHETIC FEEDBACK

Although this article is devoted primarily to a consideration of auditory feedback, studies of tactile–kinesthetic variables are also relevant. MacNeilage, Rootes, and Chase (1967) described the speech production and perception of a 17-year-old girl with an unusual disability. She was significantly impaired in her ability to perform all but the most simple types of voluntary movement. Her deficit, however, was not due to primary damage to the motor system. Rather, she was unable to obtain or to process somesthetic information. The patient was significantly impaired in stereognosis, sensitivity to painful stimuli, tactile localization, and two-point discrimination, although the specific locus of damage in the nervous system could not be identified.

Although her speech perception and understanding of language were close to normal, her speech production was grossly deficient. To MacNeilage *et al.*, this pattern suggested that somesthetic information is essential for the learning of speech, although the skilled speaker may not use somesthetic correlates to regulate moment-to-moment output.

The importance of somesthetic information, or, as it is more usually called, tactile and kinesthetic feedback, in speech production of adults has generally been examined via procedures that anesthetize the oral cavity, either through topical application or nerve block injections. It is generally conceded that these procedures more effectively perturb speech articulation than does interference with auditory feedback through loud noise, but even so, the speech generally remains quite intelligible (Ringel, 1970). Obviously, speech control cannot be entirely determined by tactile–kinesthetic feedback in adult speakers.

Quite understandably, these aversive procedures have not been widely attempted with children. Borden (1976) described the pre- and postinjection speech performance of seven 4-year-old boys who were patients at a dental clinic. The children were given bilateral mandibular injections and were recorded in a variety of speech tasks. The recordings were then phonetically transcribed. Overall, the nerve blocks significantly disturbed the speech of only four of the children, and even then the effects were limited to a small portion of the total utterances, usually fricatives and consonant clusters. The results were marked by great variation among the subjects and the errors that occurred were often farther off target than has typically been observed among adults. Nonetheless, the children managed the speech task quite well despite the anesthetization. Borden did not speculate about the support provided by auditory feedback in these children and made no attempt to combine masking with the oral anesthetization. We are left to wonder whether combined tactile anesthetization and auditory masking would have had a more profound effect on the children than has generally been reported with adults (Gammon, Smith, Daniloff, & Kim, 1971; McCroskey, 1958; Ringel & Steer, 1963; Schliesser & Coleman, 1968).

Weiss (1969a,b) obtained results very similar to those of Borden in two experiments involving 11-year-old children. Anesthetic was administered topically, rather than through injections, to the surfaces of the tongue, the alveolar ridge, and the back of the hard palate. The children were given a number of speech tasks before and after the anesthetic was administered (Weiss, 1969a). In a second article, the results of various physiological measures were reported (Weiss, 1969b). The changes induced by the anesthesia, as indicated both by articulation and physiological measures, were minimal and generally nonsignificant.

A number of research directions in the auditory feedback literature might also be applicable to the study of tactile–kinesthetic feedback. For example, a feasible alternative to the use of nerve block with children might be to study adult second language learners employing the logic suggested by Belmore *et al.* (1973), MacKay (1970), and Rouse and Tucker (1966), that the degree of language familiarity or skill, rather than age, is causally related to the effects of feedback disturbance. Siegel, Gunderson, Speaks, Rockler, and Niccum (1977) examined the effects of nerve block on the learning of unfamiliar Swedish sounds in a single adult subject. The subject attempted to imitate five of these unfamiliar sounds both before and after extensive nerve blocks, and five additional sounds only after the injections. Listeners were later asked to rate each of the talker's attempts to match the Swedish model. The listeners judged that imitation had deteriorated after the nerve block procedure for each of the five sounds that was produced both pre- and postinjection. Furthermore, the sounds that were attempted only postinjection were rated as even poorer attempts at imitation. Siegel *et al.* (1977) suggested that acquisition of new articulatory skills may be particularly impaired by anesthetization. The data are based on only a small set of comparisons, however, for a single subject, and the two sets of sounds were not necessarily equally difficult for an English speaker at the outset. The findings of this study are consistent with the report by MacNeilage *et al.* (1967) of their somesthetically impaired subject, and also with Locke's (1968) finding that accuracy in oral stereognosis is positively related to ability to learn new phonemes in children 6–8 years old.

Another experiment that might be of critical interest would be to study the effects of oral anesthetic on adventitiously deaf subjects. Speech is sometimes presumed to remain intelligible among these subjects because of the control provided by tactile monitoring. We might assume then, that oral anesthetization would have profound effects, rendering deaf speakers almost or totally unintelligible. If, however, speech is not regulated by either tactile or auditory feedback, the effect of the anesthesia on deaf subjects should be no more disruptive than occurs when tactile feedback is blocked in normal speakers. On the basis of the few experiments in which oral anesthetic has been combined with auditory masking, we would predict that nerve blocks would not be especially disruptive for the adventitiously deaf adult.

VII. Summary and Conclusions

The purpose of this article has been to evaluate the role of feedback, particularly auditory feedback, in the development of speech in children. We have approached speech as a complex motor skill. In the recent enthusiasm for exploring rule-governed bases of linguistic competence, the fact that speech is a highly coordinated motor skill has been almost ignored. Competence theories have ruled the imagination of researchers whereas performance data have been grudgingly accepted as the imperfect source from which competence theories are derived. As important as linguistic considerations are, they inevitably take form through an expressive system such as speech, writing, or signing, and such a system could scarcely function without the contribution of feedback, at least during certain stages of development.

The findings of the studies we have reviewed do not lend themselves to tidy integration, at least partly because the data are in conflict. The impressively large and programmatic studies done by the Johns Hopkins group are in conflict with studies by MacKay, Ratner *et al.*, Siegel *et al.*, and Timmons and Boudreau. Many methodological differences existed among the various studies, having to do with the kinds of speech samples, the physical conditions in which the children were tested, the intensity level and microphone placement in the various studies, and the kinds of responses that were analyzed. Our own view is that the preponderance of evidence argues that susceptibility to delayed feedback decreases with age, an interpretation that fits with theories in which auditory feedback is assumed to be especially important during acquisition of speech.

MacKay's critical interval hypothesis is also subject to question. One reason, of course, is our failure to replicate it. A second is based on MacKay's own findings of no shift in critical interval for second languages. Finally, the statistical significance of MacKay's own data with children was never tested, and therefore the reliability of the patterns he observed is unknown. As with so much of the work on delayed auditory feedback, the data base is inadequate. One could design an extensive set of experiments simply following the leads suggested by MacKay with children and adults, in first and second languages, and exploring further the effects of slowing and speeding speech rate through changes in syllable duration.

According to Lenneberg, no perceptible differences occurred in the vocalizations of very young deaf children, normal children with deaf parents, and normal children with normal parents. This finding would indicate that vocal behavior is scarcely influenced by environmental stimulation or self-perception during the first months of life. Weir (1966) reported a confirming observation. She remarked that not until babies were 6 months old could listeners distinguish among the vocalizations from infants born into American, Russian, or Chinese linguistic environments. Apparently, auditory stimulation does not leave an observable mark on infant vocal behavior until the child is "babbling," presumably beyond the fifth or sixth month. This is a curious finding, because a wealth of information attests to the remarkable sensitivity of newborns to very subtle acoustic stimulation. The speech perception work shows that 4-week-old children distinguish among sounds that differ on a scale of tens of milliseconds (e.g., Cutting & Eimas, 1975). Simner's work suggests that newborns less than 3 days old respond differently to recordings of their own voice in contrast to the voice of another infant. Infants come into the world well equipped to perceive differences among speech sounds, but this remarkable sensitivity works its way into the child's speech production in an observable way much later. Other experiments show that 3-month-old infants can be differentially conditioned to produce either vowels or consonants (Routh, 1969), indicating that infants must be able to hear this distinction to note the differential reinforcement and, of course, to produce both classes of sounds.

Perhaps the gap between perceptual ability and motor performance in infants' vocalizations lies at the motor end. Perhaps the infants register the relationship between what they produce and what they hear, but do not yet have the motor control to reflect these perceptions vocally. Conceivably, auditory feedback in the first months allows the infant to explore the oral cavity in terms of its acoustic possibilities, but this information must lie in wait until the requisite motor control finally develops. Somewhat the same point of view was expressed by Palermo (1975).

Other evidence for the same sort of discrepancy between skill in perception versus production can be found in the response of children to sidetone amplification. Studies by Siegel *et al.*, Kennard, and Costley indicate that children respond less to sidetone amplification than do adults, but the difference seems to be attributable to skill in production, rather than to differences in either external perception or self-perception of loudness. The difference in developmental pattern between sidetone amplification and delayed feedback may also be relevant. Young children are more disrupted by delay but are less responsive to sidetone amplification than are adults. The greater response to delay may indicate their greater vulnerability to a procedure that disrupts performance. The response to sidetone amplification, in contrast, is more in the form of a skilled compensation. It involves an adjustment in vocal intensity and may therefore be a skill that is not yet entirely available to the younger children.

Similarly, the articulation of normal children and adults is difficult to disrupt. Children who are in the process of correcting an articulation error, however, do break down under masking, presumably because the motor control (program) for the difficult sound is relatively fragile. The same child who is learning /r/, however, and whose production of /r/ suffers under noise, has no difficulty with any other speech sound under noise. In these cases, even though it is an interference with auditory feedback that induces the disruption, the root cause seems to lie in lack of motor control or skill development. During acquisition, the speaker needs all the supportive cues that are available. These notions could be tested with adults learning novel sounds. Is there a stage in which pronunciation of these unfamiliar sounds would pass as adequate but would deteriorate under masking? The adult in this instance already has a well-established repertoire of sounds in the first language, and that fact might alter the role of auditory feedback in the acquisition of novel sounds.

The masking data for children did not display the same pattern as did the sidetone amplification results. In spontaneous speech tasks, children had essentially the same magnitude of response to noise as did adults. When speaking single words, however, the children maintained the same reaction to noise, but the adults showed a lesser effect. Amazi and Garber suggested that the difference lies in how the adults interpret the two situations. Uttering single words is much less communicative than telling stories, and therefore requires less accommodation to noise. Adults may be much more sensitive to the interaction between communicative variables and the desire to maintain optimal levels of self-perception. Adults and children also responded similarly to a situation in which the listener was positioned at varying distances from the speaker. For adults as well as children, the increase in vocal intensity with distance was minimal. The factor of communicative awareness may again emerge when the situation is made more complex by the addition of background noise in addition to distance, or by placing the source of noise at varying distances from speaker versus listener.

Another reason that masking and sidetone amplification effects may not be entirely comparable is that children find it easier to increase than to maintain reduced vocal intensity levels. According to Costley's study, the children had the greatest difficulty maintaining the low vocal levels, an observation that is consistent with the reports of distraught parents. Children seen for voice therapy almost always display excessive vocal level and vocal abuse, rather than speech that is too soft. Thus, the masking procedure may simply not require as much skill as the sidetone amplification procedure.

We have been concerned in this article with the contribution of auditory feedback to the development of speech in children. Under normal circumstances, speech clearly is multiply determined. Speakers acquire the language to which they have been exposed in the presence of different kinds of listeners and in a variety of social and physical situations. Although it is a motor skill, speech is the expression of linguistic codes and communication needs. Speakers talk louder in noise and also to impress a listener with their determination. Choice of words, speech rate, and inflectional pattern are all multiply determined, reflecting the contributions of social and physical variables, as well as the physiological constraints of the speech system.

We have dealt with only a narrow slice of the determinants that influence speech. Even while treating speech as primarily a motor skill, we have necessarily incorporated communication variables. Perhaps the most important questions are those that rest at the interstices. Children respond to noise and to distance from a listener. At least the second of these variables seems to tap the child's perception of speech as a social behavior that, to be successful, must take the listener into account. Persons may talk louder to hear themselves better in noise, but this is not the reason they talk louder when addressing someone distant. Children acquire mastery of the motor skills involved in speech production at the same time they are learning to deal with social conventions and complex linguistic rule systems, and all of this learning occurs at a time when the sheer physical dimensions of the vocal system are changing as the child matures.

Although it clearly contributes to speech development, auditory feedback should also clearly not imply a single experimental procedure. Delays and sidetone amplification show very different developmental patterns, for understandable reasons. Treating the various experimental procedures as though they were simply different models of the same measuring instrument has led to contradictory data and confusion.

Speech has also been treated in a unitary fashion, without regard for its parameters. Prosodic and articulatory aspects of speech may develop very differently, however, especially as they relate to feedback systems. At first glance it seems paradoxical that articulation, which requires such elaborate timing control and synchrony, should be scarcely affected by noise, deafness, or nerve blocks, although vocal intensity, which seems much less intricate, is highly responsive to feedback manipulations. Articulation, however, is too fleeting to be under the control of immediate feedback. By the time one senses that one's articulation is fractionally off target, the vocal system will have moved on to another utterance, and the feedback will be of little use. Intensity, pitch, or quality, however, are more stable and can therefore take greater advantage of feedback. Furthermore, the significance of these speech attributes may change with development. Very young children may need to concentrate on articulatory aspects. They speak more slowly and less precisely than older children, and may be highly tuned to feedback for the sounds they are learning. The steady-state variables, like intensity, are less crucial, and less under control. With maturity, the child may need to devote less attention to articulation and may become more skilled in modulating other aspects of speech production. In fact, even for adults, the simplest and often the most effective strategy to improve communication in a difficult situation is to talk louder. Thus, once articulation has been mastered, monitoring of loudness may be very adaptive for effective communication.

The relationship between forms of feedback and the various parameters of speech production are well worth exploring in future research. The area is an exciting one, as it pertains both to normal and deviant speech development. The literature concerning the speech production skills and the sensory capabilities of very young children is now substantial. Studies that concentrate on the contribution of feedback to speech development stand at the intersection of sensation and production, a unique perspective from which to consider speech and language acquisition.

ACKNOWLEDGMENTS

Preparation of this article was supported by grants from the National Science Foundation (NSF/BNS 77-22075) and the National Institute of Child Health and Human Development (5-P01 HD01136) to the Center for Research in Human Learning of the University of Minnesota, and by Program Project Grant 5-P01-0507 from the National Institute of Child Health and Human Development to the Institute of Child Development of the University of Minnesota. We are very grateful to W. Manning and A. Pick for helpful criticism of an earlier draft of this article.

REFERENCES

Allport, F. H. *Social psychology.* Boston, Massachusetts: Houghton-Mifflin, 1924.

Amazi, D. K., & Garber, S. R. The Lombard sign as a function of age and task. *Journal of Speech and Hearing Research,* 1982, **25,** 581–585.

Belmore, N. F., Kewley-Port, D., Mobley, R. L., & Goodman, V. E. The development of auditory feedback monitoring: Delayed auditory feedback studies on the vocalizations of children aged six months to 19 months. *Journal of Speech and Hearing Research,* 1973, **16,** 709–720.

Black, J. W. The effect of noise induced temporary deafness upon vocal intensity. *Speech Monographs,* 1951, **18,** 74–77.

Borden, G. The effect of mandibular nerve block upon the speech of four-year-old boys. *Language and Speech,* 1976, **19,** 173–178.

Borden, G. B., Harris, K. S., & Catena, L. Oral feedback. II. An electromyographic study of speech under nerve-block anesthesia. *Journal of Phonetics,* 1973, **1,** 197–308.

Campbell, T., Manning, W., Robertson, P., & DiSalvo, V. The use of competing speech for making dismissal decisions in articulation therapy. *Journal of Human Communication,* 1976, **1,** 37–45.

Chase, R. A., Sutton, S., First, D., & Zubin, J. A developmental study of changes in behavior under delayed auditory feedback. *Journal of Genetic Psychology,* 1961, **99,** 101–112.

Costley, M. S. *The perception and production of loudness by children.* Unpublished doctoral dissertation, University of Minnesota, 1981.

Costley, M. S., Siegel, G. M., & Olsen, M. G. *Self-perception of loudness in children.* Paper presented to the American Speech and Hearing Association, San Francisco, 1978.

Cullen, J. K., Fargo, N., Chase, R. A., & Baker, P. The development of auditory feedback monitoring. I. Delayed auditory feedback studies on infant cry. *Journal of Speech and Hearing Research,* 1968, **11,** 85–93.

Cutting, J. E., & Eimas, P. D. Phonetic feature analyzers and the processing of speech in infants. In J. F. Kavanaugh & J. E. Cutting (Eds.), *The role of speech in language.* Cambridge, Massachusetts: MIT Press, 1975.

Fairbanks, G. Systematic research in experimental phonetics. A theory of the speech mechanism as a servosystem. *Journal of Speech and Hearing Disorders,* 1954, **19,** 133–139.

Fry, D. B. The development of the phonological system in the normal and the deaf child. In F. Smith & G. A. Miller (Eds.), *The genesis of language.* Cambridge, Massachusetts: MIT Press, 1966.

Gammon, A., Smith, P. J., Daniloff, R. G., & Kim, C. W. Articulation and stress/juncture production under oral anesthetization and masking. *Journal of Speech and Hearing Research,* 1971, **14,** 271–282.

Garber, S. R., Burzynski, C. M., Vale, C., & Nelson, R. The use of visual feedback to control vocal intensity and nasalization. *Journal of Communication Disorders,* 1979, **12,** 399–410.

Garber, S. R., & Moller, K. The effects of feedback filtering on nasalization in normal and hypernasal speakers. *Journal of Speech and Hearing Research,* 1979, **22,** 321–333.

Garber, S. R., Siegel, G. M., Pick, H. L., Jr., & Alcorn, S. The influence of selected masking noises on Lombard and sidetone amplification effects. *Journal of Speech and Hearing Research,* 1976, **19,** 523–535.

Garber, S. R., Speidel, T. M., & Siegel, G. M. The effects of noise and palatal appliances on the speech of five-year-old children. *Journal of Speech and Hearing Research,* 1980, **23,** 853–863.

Garber, S. R., Speidel, T. M., Siegel, G. M., Miller, E., & Glass, L. The effects of presentation of noise and dental appliances on speech. *Journal of Speech and Hearing Research,* 1980, **23,** 838–852.

Goldfarb, W., & Braunstein, P. Reactions to delayed auditory feedback in schizophrenic children. In P. H. Hock & J. Zubin (Eds.), *Psychopathology of communication.* New York: Grune & Stratton, 1958.

Johnson, C. J., Pick, H. L., Jr., Siegel, G. M., Cicciarelli, A. W., & Garber, S. R. Effects of interpersonal distance on children's vocal intensity. *Child Development,* 1981, **52,** 721–723.

Kennard, K. L. *The effects of sidetone amplification and Lombard feedback manipulations in children with articulation defects.* Unpublished Master's thesis, University of Minnesota, 1980.

Lane, H. L., & Tranel, B. The Lombard sign and the role of hearing in speech. *Journal of Speech and Hearing Research,* 1971, **14,** 677–709.

Lee, B. S. Artificial stutter. *Journal of Speech and Hearing Disorders,* 1951, **16,** 53–55.

Lenneberg, E. H. Speech as a motor skill with special reference to nonaphasic disorders. In U. Belugi and R. Brown (Eds.), *The acquisition of language. Monographs of the Society for Research in Child Development,* 1964, **29,** 115–127.

Lewis, M. M. *Infant speech: A study of the beginnings of language.* New York: Harcourt, 1936. (Reprinted New York: Arno Press, 1975.)

Locke, J. L. Oral perception and articulation learning. *Perceptual and Motor Skills,* 1968, **26,** 1259–1264.

MacKay, D. G. Metamorphosis of critical interval: Age-linked changes in the delay in auditory feedback that produces maximal disruption of speech. *Journal of the Acoustical Society of America,* 1968, **43,** 811–821.

MacKay, D. G. How does language familiarity influence stuttering under delayed auditory feedback? *Perceptual and Motor Skills,* 1970, **30,** 655–669.

MacNeilage, P. F. Motor control of serial ordering of speech. *Psychological Review,* 1970, **77,** 182–196.

MacNeilage, P. F., Rootes, T. P., & Chase, R. A. Speech production and perception in a patient with severe impairment of somasthetic perception and motor control. *Journal of Speech and Hearing Research,* 1967, **10,** 449–467.

Manning, W. H., Keappock, N. E., & Stick, S. L. The use of auditory masking to estimate automatization of correct articulatory production. *Journal of Speech and Hearing Disorders,* 1976, **41,** 143–149.

Manning, W. H., Louko, L. J., & DiSalvo, V. C. A right ear effect for auditory feedback control of children's newly-acquired phonemes. *Journal of Speech and Hearing Research,* 1978, **21,** 580–588.

Manning, W. H., & Ortman, K. J. Use of auditory masking to estimate automatization of correct articulation in children. *Folia Phoniatrika,* 1980, **32,** 29–38.

Manning, W., Ortman, K., & Scheer, R. *Using masking to estimate automatization: Effect of four masking types.* Paper presented to the American Speech and Hearing Association, Chicago, 1977.

Manning, W., & Sheer, B. Using competing speech to estimate articulatory automatization in children: The possible effect of masking level and subject grade. *Journal of Communication Disorders,* 1978, **11,** 391–397.

Manning, W. H., Scheer, R. R., & Louko, L. J. *Using competing speech to estimate articulatory automatization in children: The effect of masking level and subject grade.* Paper presented to the American Speech and Hearing Association, Chicago, 1977.

Markel, N. N., Prebor, L. D., & Brandt, J. F. Biosocial factors in dyadic communication: Sex and speaking intensity. *Journal of Personality and Social Psychology,* 1972, **23,** 11–13.

Marler, P. Birdsong and speech development: Could there be parallels? *American Scientist,* 1970, **58,** 669–673.

Marler, P. On the origin of speech from animal sounds. In J. F. Kavanaugh & J. E. Cutting (Eds.), *The role of speech in language.* Cambridge, Massachusetts: MIT Press, 1975.

Marteniuk, R. G. *Information processing in motor skills.* New York: Holt, 1976.

Mavilya, M. Spontaneous vocalization and babbling in hearing impaired infants. *Proceedings of the International Congress on Education of the Deaf, Stockholm,* 1970, 73–80.

McCroskey, R. L., Jr. The relative contribution of auditory and tactile cues to certain aspects of speech. *Southern Speech Journal,* 1958, **24,** 84–90.

Mowrer, O. H. Speech development in the young child. I. The autism theory of speech development and some clinical applications. *Journal of Speech and Hearing Disorders,* 1952, **17,** 263–268.

Mowrer, O. H. Hearing and speaking: An analysis of language learning. *Journal of Speech and Hearing Disorders,* 1958, **23,** 143–152.

Ossip, S. Operation of the auditory feedback monitoring loop in children with articulatory defects. *Journal of the South African Speech and Hearing Association,* 1971, **13,** 48–56.

Palermo, D. S. Developmental aspects of speech perception: Problems for a motor theory. In J. F. Kavanaugh & J. E. Cutting (Eds.), *The role of speech in language.* Cambridge, Massachusetts: MIT Press, 1975.

Peterson, G. E., & Shoup, J. E. A physiological theory of phonetics. *Journal of Speech and Hearing Research,* 1966, **9,** 5–67.

Ratner, S. C., Gawronski, J. J., & Rice, F. E. The variable of concurrent action in the language of children: Effects of delayed speech feedback. *Psychological Record,* 1964, **14,** 47–56.

Ringel, R. L. Oral sensation and perception: A selective review. *Speech and the dentofacial complex: The state of the art.* Rockville, Maryland: American Speech and Hearing Association, Report No. 5, 1970, 188–206.

Ringel, R. L., & Steer, M. D. Some effects of tactile and auditory alterations on speech output. *Journal of Speech and Hearing Research,* 1963, **6,** 369–378.

Rockler, J. L. *The role of auditory feedback in speech monitoring.* Unpublished Master's thesis, University of Minnesota, 1976.

Rouse, R. O., & Tucker, G. R. An effect of delayed auditory feedback on speech in American and foreign students. *Journal of Speech and Hearing Research,* 1966, **9,** 456–460.

Routh, D. K. Conditioning of vocal response differentiation in infants. *Developmental Psychology,* 1969, **1,** 219–226.

Sanders, D. A. A model for communication. In L. Lloyd (Ed.), *Communication assessment and intervention strategies.* Baltimore, Maryland: Univ. Park Press, 1976.

Schliesser, H. F., & Coleman, R. O. Effectiveness of certain procedures of alteration of auditory and oral tactile sensations for speech. *Perceptual and Motor Skills,* 1968, **26,** 275–281.

Shelton, R. L., & McReynolds, L. V. Functional articulation disorders: Preliminaries to treatment. In N. J. Lass (Ed.), *Speech and language: Advances in basic research and practice.* New York: Academic Press, 1979.

Siegel, G. M., Fehst, C. A., Garber, S. R., & Pick, H. L., Jr. Delayed auditory feedback with children. *Journal of Speech and Hearing Research,* 1980, **23,** 802–813.

Siegel, G. M., Gunderson, D., Speaks, C. E., Rockler, J., & Niccum, N. The effects of task variables on speech during oral anesthesia. *Journal of Communication Disorders,* 1977, **10,** 253–265.

Siegel, G. M., Pick, H. L., Jr., Olsen, M. G., & Sawin, L. Auditory feedback in the regulation of vocal intensity of preschool children. *Developmental Psychology,* 1976, **12,** 255–261.

Siegel, G. M., Schork, E. J., Pick, H. L., Jr., & Garber, S. R. Parameters of auditory feedback. *Journal of Speech and Hearing Research,* 1982, **25,** 473–475.

Siegenthaler, B. M., & Bianchi, P. Reaction time of jaw movement to auditory and tactile stimulation in children. *Perceptual and Motor Skills,* 1968, **27,** 583–588.

Simner, M. L. Newborn's response to the cry of another infant. *Developmental Psychology,* 1971, **5,** 136–150.

Staats, A. W., & Staats, C. K. *Complex human behavior.* New York: Holt, 1964.

Timmons, B., & Boudreau, J. Age, sex and delay time as factors affecting reaction to delayed auditory feedback. *Perceptual and Motor Skills,* 1976, **43,** 27–30.

Timmons, B., & Boudreau, J. Delayed auditory feedback and the speech of stuttering and non-stuttering children. *Perceptual and Motor Skills,* 1978, **46,** 551–555.

Tingley, B. M., & Allen, G. D. Development of speech timing control in children. *Child Development,* 1975, **46,** 186–194.

Van Riper, C., & Irwin, J. V. *Voice and articulation.* New York: Prentice-Hall, 1958.

Waters, J. E. A theoretical and developmental investigation of delayed speech feedback. *Genetic Psychology Monographs,* 1968, **78,** 3–54.

Weir, R. H. Some questions on the child's learning of phonology. In F. Smith & G. A. Miller (Eds.), *The genesis of language.* Cambridge, Massachusetts: MIT Press, 1966.

Weiss, C. E. The effects of disrupted linguapalatal taction on articulation. *Journal of Communication Disorders,* 1969, **2,** 14–19. (a)

Weiss, C. E. The effects of disrupted linguapalatal taction on physiologic parameters of articulation. *Journal of Communication Disorders,* 1969, **2,** 312–321. (b)

Yanez, E. A., Siegel, G. M., Garber, S. R., & Wellen, C. J. The effects of different masking noises on children with /s/ or /r/ errors. *Journal of Speech and Hearing Disorders,* 1982, **47,** 150–153.

Yates, A. J. Delayed auditory feedback. *Psychological Bulletin,* 1963, **60,** 213–232.

Yeni-Kimshian, G., Chase, R. A., & Mobley, R. L. The development of auditory feedback monitoring. II. Delayed auditory feedback studies on the speech of children between two and three years of age. *Journal of Speech and Hearing Research,* 1968, **11,** 307–315.

Zimmerman, G., & Rettaliata, P. Articulatory patterns of an adventitiously deaf speaker. *Journal of Speech and Hearing Research,* 1981, **24,** 169–178.

BODY SIZE OF INFANTS AND CHILDREN AROUND THE WORLD IN RELATION TO SOCIOECONOMIC STATUS

Howard V. Meredith
DEPARTMENT OF PHYSICAL EDUCATION
UNIVERSITY OF SOUTH CAROLINA
COLUMBIA, SOUTH CAROLINA

I. Purpose and Method

The purpose of this article is to assemble, order, and systematize findings from different parts of the world on body size of infants and children in relation to socioeconomic status. Socioeconomic comparisons were colligated for body

ADVANCES IN CHILD DEVELOPMENT
AND BEHAVIOR, VOL. 18

ISBN 0-12-009718-4

weight, stature (vertex–soles length in infancy, vertex–soles height in childhood), and several somatic measures of the head, trunk, and limbs. The ontogenetic span investigated extended from birth to age 9 years.

Socioeconomic comparisons were obtained for the sexes and pooled. Sex differences in body size throughout the segment of human ontogeny between birth and age 9 years are small and, for the variables considered, consistent in direction. Therefore, separate tables for girls and boys were not necessary. Socioeconomic comparisons for the sexes combined, in the present project, are parsimonious and satisfactory.

As documented in an earlier report (Meredith, 1951), socioeconomic status is "neither a precisely defined concept nor a variable described from study to study by means of a single standardized scale" (p. 702). Different investigators have characterized socioeconomic status through information on variables such as parental occupation; parental education; family income; per capita income; postdelivery hospitalization in free ward, pay ward, or private room; home health provisions and practices; parental access to pediatric services and nutritional advice on infant and child care; type of neighborhood; and attendance at free or tuition schools.

Information on these variables has been used in several ways. The range of parental occupations has been partitioned into two categories (MacDonald, 1899; Roberts, 1876), three categories (van Wering, 1978; van Wieringen, 1972), four categories (Banik, Krishna, Mane, Raj, & Taskar, 1970b), and five categories (Goldstein, 1971; Weinberg, Dietz, Penick, & McAlister, 1974). Similarly, the family income continuum has been partitioned into categories varying from 3 (Nekisheva, 1974), through 7 (Indian Council of Medical Research, 1972), to 10 (Hamill, Johnston, & Lemeshow, 1972). Penchaszadeh, Hardy, Mellits, Cohen, and McKusick (1972) used a nine-category scale taking account of family income, parental occupation, and parental education. Garn, Shaw, and McCabe (1978) compared magnitudes of somatic difference from successively using, on the same sample, three socioeconomic indicators, namely, family income, maternal education, and a multivariable socioeconomic index.

Neighborhood comparisons have pertained typically to children living in slum or exclusive residential sections of a city (Enačhescu, Grintescu-Pop, & Glavce, 1971; Janes, 1974; Neyzi & Gürson, 1966). School studies have in some instances compared children attending schools in the poorest and best districts of a city (Hopkins, 1947; Mackenzie & Foster, 1907; Weisman, 1935) and in other instances compared children attending schools in urban poverty zones with those attending elite private schools (Hammond, 1953; Raghavan, Singh, & Swaminathan, 1971).

For each study used in this article, care has been taken to describe the socioeconomic groups sampled. These descriptions are pertinent for sound understanding and interpretation of the text. An example will suffice. In respect to any somatic variable, smaller differences should be expected from bipartition of the socioeconomic continuum (comparing children from families of unskilled, semi-skilled, and skilled workers with peers in clerical, mercantile, and professional families) than from multipartitioning and comparing children in families of unskilled workers with peers in major executive and professional families.

II. Socioeconomic Comparisons for Body Weight

A. INFANCY

1. Birth

Assembled in Table I are comparisons for body weight at birth. The statistics in columns 3 and 4 represent lower socioeconomic groups than do those in columns 5 and 6. Columns 7 and 8 show the absolute and relative amounts by which the averages in column 6 exceed (or are smaller than) those in column 4. Particulars complementing those shown in each row of the table are as follows:

Tag I-1: Offspring of the ''poorest'' and ''best'' socioeconomic groups living in Bombay in about 1960 (Udani, 1963).

Tag I-2: Comparison of neonates born in 1962 into ''lower'' socioeconomic families, and between 1947 and 1961 into families of ''the upper social stratum'' (Jayant, 1964).

Tag I-3: Newborn progeny of parents in the ''poorest'' and ''well-to-do'' economic classes (Varkki, Venkatachalam, Srikantia, & Gopalan, 1955).

Tag I-4: Data collected between 1956 and 1959 at Hyderabad, Madras, and Coonoor; means represent south Indian urban newborns of ''low income'' and ''wealthy'' classes (Venkatachalam, 1962).

Tag I-5: Male neonates born between 1950 and 1951 into ''the most unfavorable milieu'' and ''the most favorable milieu'' of this city (Enačhescu *et al.*, 1971).

Tag I-6: Infants born between 1950 and 1959 into ''poor'' and ''upper'' socioeconomic families (Hollingsworth, 1965).

Tag I-7: Progeny of the ''lowest'' and ''highest'' socioeconomic classes in this city (Luna-Jaspe, Ariza, Rueda-Williamson, Mora, & Pardo, 1970).

Tag I-8: Offspring born between 1962 and 1963 to parents in the ''unskilled'' and ''professional major managerial'' occupational categories (Banik *et al.*, 1970b).

Tag I-9: Neonates born at Nashville between 1951 and 1956; comparison of those in the lowest and highest categories of a four-category socioeconomic classification (Crump, Horton, Masuoka, & Ryan, 1957).

Tag I-10: Records amassed between 1954 and 1958 on progeny of ''indigent'' and ''well-to-do'' parents (Timmer, 1961).

Tag I-11: Live-born, singleton offspring of Bengali-speaking parents; born in 1976 at Ramakrishna Mission Seva Pratisthan and weighed ''within a few min-

TABLE I

Body Weight (kg) at Birth: Means for Both Sexes Pooled in Relation to Socioeconomic Status

Tag	Group	Low status		High status		High heavier than low by	
		Sample size	Mean weight	Sample size	Mean weight	(kg)	(%)
Comparisons for terminal segments of the socioeconomic continuum							
I-1	Indian, Bombay	~1000	2.58	~270	3.25	.67[a]	26.0
I-2	Hindu, Bombay	2279	2.53	3822	2.91	.38	15.0
I-3	Indian, Coonoor	500	2.73	200	3.11	.38	13.9
I-4	Indian, three towns	2777	2.81	1753	3.18	.37	13.2
I-5	Romanian, Bucharest[b]	30	3.07	30	3.46	.39	12.7
I-6	Ghanaian, Accra	917	2.88	201	3.18	.30	10.4
I-7	Colombian, Bogotá	69	2.85	63	3.13	.28	9.8
I-8	Indian, Delhi	730	2.75	79	3.00	.25	9.1
I-9	United States Black	382	2.96[c]	137	3.19	.23	7.8
I-10	Javanese, Jogjakarta	1618	2.81	894	3.02	.21	7.5
I-11	Bengali, Calcutta	1396	2.53	288	2.70	.17	6.7
I-12	Bengali, Calcutta	60	2.79	50	2.96	.17	6.1
I-13	Indian, Bombay	8381	2.61	278	2.77	.16	6.1
I-14	Iranian, Teheran	824	3.18	340	3.37	.19	6.0
I-15	Uruguayan, Montevideo	48	3.29	255	3.48	.19	5.8
I-16	United States White	38	3.10	46	3.29	.19	5.8
I-17	United States White	67	3.20	599	3.38	.18	5.6
I-18	Brazilian	1068	3.12	792	3.28	.16[d]	5.1[d]
I-19	Iranian, Shiraz	1802	2.98	557	3.10	.12	4.0
I-20	United States Black	100	3.17	100	3.29	.12	3.8
I-21	United States Black	333	2.89	182	3.00	.11	3.8
I-22	Lebanese, Beirut	247	3.35	254	3.40	.05	1.5
I-23	Peruvian, Cuzco	433	3.14	138	3.18	.04	1.3

(*continued*)

utes after birth'' (Pakrasi, Sil, & Dasgupta, 1982). Grouped by hospital accomodation of mother: free bed (''poor'') and pay bed (''well-off'').

Tag I-12: Infants born in 1971, one group into ''low income'' and the other into ''high income'' families (Bandyopadhyay, Pakrasi, Banerjee, & Banerjee, 1981).

Tag I-13: Data gathered between 1954 and 1957 on live-born offspring of parents in the ''unskilled'' and ''professional'' socioeconomic strata (Basavarajappa, Deshpande, & Ramachandran, 1962).

Tag I-14: Viable, singleton neonates born between 1967 and 1970 and weighed ''within a few minutes'' after birth; comparison of the terminal subgroups from four-category classification by family income (Hedayat, Koohestani, Ghassemi, & Kamali, 1971).

TABLE I (*Continued*)

Tag	Group	Low status: Sample size	Low status: Mean weight	High status: Sample size	High status: Mean weight	High heavier than low by (kg)	High heavier than low by (%)
	Comparisons involving wider segments of the socioeconomic continuum						
I-24	Indian, Singapore	5166	2.82	138	3.10	.28	9.9
I-25	Tamilian, Madras	5176	2.74	448	2.99	.25	9.1
I-26	Indian, Kuala Lumpur	4696	2.64	2783	2.88	.24	9.1
I-27	Italian, Bologna	100	3.10	100	3.37	.27	8.7
I-28	Indian, Calcutta	878	2.66	160	2.85	.19	7.1
I-29	United States White	508	3.22	1487	3.40	.18	5.6
I-30	Chinese, Singapore	46,750	3.02	298	3.15	.13	4.3
I-31	Burmese	3970	2.74	~1200	2.83	.09	3.3
I-32	United States White	886	3.39	454	3.44	.05	1.5
I-33	English, N.E. town	137	3.42	43	3.41	−.01	−.3
I-34	United States White	3928	3.40	905	3.38	−.02	−.6

[a]Using .55 kg as population standard deviations (Fraccaro, 1958) and estimating at $p = .01$, one can infer in 23 instances that the paired socioeconomic groups differed significantly in body weight at birth. Comparisons not yielding this level of confidence are those in rows I-12, I-15 through I-17, I-20 through I-23, and I-32 through I-34.

[b]Males only.

[c]Cherry (1968) reported a mean of 3.11 kg for 200 United States black neonates born between 1960 and 1962 in Charity Hospital, New Orleans, into economically "underprivileged" homes. See also rows I-20 and I-21.

[d]These differences, obtained between 1959 and 1960 on live-born infants delivered at Bello Horizonte, are somewhat smaller than those obtained in Campinas from 1970–1971 data on live-born, full-term, physically normal neonates of the "indigent" and "private patient" classes (Martins-Filho, Aristodemo-Pinotti, Carvalho, Bueno, Paes de Freitas, Carvalho, & Moraes, 1974). Specifics, in row form, are as follows: Brazilian, Campinas: 752, 3.17, 507, 3.38, .21, 6.6%.

Tag I-15: Data gathered between 1972 and 1974 on full-term offspring of "employed working" parents (Martell, Falkner, Bertolini, Diaz, Nieto, Tenzer, & Belitzky, 1978) compared with 1943–1949 data on full-term births to parents of "high socioeconomic status" (Ramón-Guerra, 1950).

Tags I-16 and I-21: Viable, singleton infants born in Baltimore in about 1970 and rated on a nine-category scale taking account of parental education, occupation, and income; comparison of infants in categories 1 and 2 with those in categories 8 and 9 (Penchaszadeh *et al.*, 1972).

Tag I-17: Comparison of two groups of full-term neonates of northwest European ancestry born between 1955 and 1962—a "low socioeconomic" group delivered in Massachusetts (Rueda-Williamson & Rose, 1962) and a private practice "well-born" group delivered in Missouri (Jackson, Westerfeld, Flynn, Kimball, & Lewis, 1964).

Tag I-18: Live-born offspring of the lower and upper economic classes delivered in Bello Horizonte between 1959 and 1960 (Machado & Memōria, 1966).

Tag I-19: Infants born in 1963 to "indigent" mothers delivered in the Red Lion and Sun Hospital and "private patients" delivered in Nemazee Hospital. Members of both groups weighed more than 1.0 kg at birth and "were weighed immediately after birth" (Sarram & Saadatnejadi, 1967).

Tag I-20: Physically normal, singleton neonates of indigent (free ward) and upper income (private patient) families born in the District of Columbia between 1948 and 1949 and weighing 2.2 kg or more at birth (Kessler & Scott, 1950).

Tag I-22: Full-term neonates of "Arab stock"—one group from "the low socioeconomic stratum" studied from 1960–62 (Harfouche, 1966) and the other group from the high stratum studied from 1965–67 (Hasan, Najjar, & Asfour, 1969).

Tag I-23: Hospital data for 1965 on full-term progeny of "largely Quechua-speaking" Amerind parents from lower and upper socioeconomic groups (McClung, 1969).

Tags I-24 and I-30: Neonates studied in Singapore between 1950 and 1953; for each ethnic group, one subgroup born into low income families (Millis, 1958) and the other into families of middle and upper income (Millis, 1952).

Tag I-25: Neonates born between 1954 and 1955 into Tamilian and Telugu families of "poor and lower middle class" and "well-to-do class" (Achar & Yankauer, 1962).

Tag I-26: Infants of Indian descent from "the poorer classes" born between 1951 and 1953 (Llewellyn-Jones, 1955) compared with Tamilian infants born between 1953 and 1959 in three Kuala Lumpur hospitals, one "a special hospital for wealthy patients" (Thomson, 1962).

Tag I-27: Data collected between 1962 and 1963 on illegitimate newborns (social level not specified) and legitimate newborns in families of above-average socioeconomic status (Grandi, 1965).

Tag I-28: Data collected in 1957 at deliveries of "non-paying" (low economic status) and "paying" (largely middle class) mothers (Mukherjee & Biswas, 1959).

Tag I-29: Infants born into South Carolina families of "below average" and "above average" socioeconomic status (Underwood, Hester, Laffitte, & Gregg, 1965).

Tag I-31: Offspring of "poor class" mothers largely unsupervised during pregnancy compared with those of poor and middle class mothers receiving pregnancy guidance and supplied regularly with skimmed milk powder (Postmus, 1958).

Tag I-32: Records amassed in New York City between 1930 and 1931 on infants of "poor homes" and "homes of moderate income" (Bakwin, Bakwin, & Milgram, 1934).

Tag I-33: Neonates born in 1947 in Newcastle upon Tyne, one group having parents in occupational categories "unskilled and skilled," and the other group having parents in the "clerical and professional" categories (Miller, Billewicz, & Thomson, 1972).

Tag I-34: "Minneapolis General Hospital" and "private" deliveries of viable, first-born infants between 1927 and 1932 (Gunstad & Treloar, 1936).

Examples of the findings in Table I are as follows:

1. Twenty-three comparisons of paired averages for body weight showed that offspring of parents near the upper terminus of the social class distribution weighed more at birth than did offspring of parents near the lower terminus by absolute amounts greater than .03 kg and relative amounts greater than 1.0%. Typical (median) absolute and relative differences were .19 kg and 6.1%, respectively.

2. Among 11 paired comparisons involving broader sections of the social class distribution, two gave differences slightly larger for the poorer of the paired socioeconomic subgroups. Both were studies on white neonates (I-33, I-34). Neither of these differences allows rejection of the null hypothesis at the .05 level of confidence.

3. Combining statistics on the neonates of Indian ancestry from rows I-2, I-3, I-4, I-8, I-11, I-12, and I-13 gave means of 2.64 kg for 16,123 infants of low socioeconomic status and 2.98 kg for 6470 infants of high socioeconomic status, thereby yielding an average birth weight greater for the latter than the former by .34 kg, or 12.9%. Smaller differences in the same direction were .30 kg or 10.4% for Ghanaian neonates in Accra (I-6), .21 kg or 7.5% for Javanese neonates in Jogjakarta (I-10), .16 kg or 5.3% for Iranian urban neonates (I-14, I-19), .16 kg or 5.1% for Brazilian neonates in Bello Horizonte (I-18), .13 kg or 4.3% from pooled samples of United States black neonates in Baltimore, Nashville, and Washington D.C. (I-9, I-20, I-21), and .05 kg or 1.5% for Lebanese neonates in Beirut (I-22).

4. Average body weight at birth for infants of economically prosperous parents differed widely among ethnic groups. Specific averages were 2.70 kg for Indian offspring of "well-off" families in Calcutta (I-11), 3.02 kg for Javanese infants of "well-to-do" parents in Jogjakarta (I-10), 3.18 kg for Ghanaian infants of "upper class" families in Accra (I-6), 3.38 kg for United States white neonates delivered in private pediatric practice in Missouri (I-17), and 3.48 for Uruguayan neonates of "high status" parents in Montevideo (I-15). The Uruguayan average surpassed the preceding averages (taken in reverse order) by 3.0, 9.4, 15.2, and 28.9%.

5. For infants at the lower end of the socioeconomic distribution, averages for body weight at birth varied from 2.53 (I-2) to 3.42 kg (I-33). Averages among the "lower" groups were below 2.85 kg for the Burmese, Javanese, and each of

the 12 Indian samples; between 2.85 and 3.15 kg for the Brazilian, Colombian, Ghanaian, composite Iranian, Peruvian, Romanian, Singapore Chinese, and composite United States Black samples; and above 3.20 kg for the English, Lebanese, and Uruguayan samples.

2. *Age 1 Year*

Socioeconomic comparisons for body weight at age 1 year are displayed in Table II. Sources and sample details pertaining to rows with the tag prefix "I" have been given (Section III,A,1). Comparable particulars for other rows are as follows:

Tag II-1: Infants reared during the 1960s in "a poor quarter of Baghdad" and given no other food than mother's milk (Jager, 1961) compared with peers of "the highest socioeconomic class at Shiraz" reared between 1969 and 1972 under superior home and pediatric care (Amirhakimi, 1974).

Tag II-2: Infants born in New York City during the early 1930s, reared in "poverty stricken homes," and lacking pediatric care (Bakwin *et al.*, 1934) compared with contemporary peers born in Cleveland, reared largely in homes of professional and managerial status, and receiving regular pediatric supervision (Simmons & Todd, 1938).

Tag II-3: Data collected between 1963 and 1965 on offspring of parents in the "unskilled" and "professional and managerial" occupational categories (Rea, 1971).

Tag II-4: Individuals born between 1963 and 1964 into homes of "bajo" (low) and "alto" (high) socioeconomic status (Barja, La Fuente, Ballester, Mönckeberg, & Donoso, 1965).

Tag II-5: Children born in Singapore during the early 1950s into homes of "semiskilled and unskilled" workers (Millis, 1958) compared with peers born in Hyderabad in the early 1970s into families of "well-to-do executives" (Indian National Institute of Nutrition, 1975).

Tag II-6: Infants studied between 1958 and 1959, one group in Tlaltizapan in homes mainly of "day laborers" (Navarrete, Franco, Vilchis, Arrieta, Santibáñez, Rivera, & Cravioto, 1960) and the other in Mexico City in homes mainly of professional parents and "good hygienic conditions" (Faulhaber, 1976).

Tag II-7: Individuals reared in "underprivileged" and "privileged" homes (H. B. Young, personal communication, 1979).

Tag II-8: Full-term infants of "low socioeconomic stock" born in 1959 in Boston and receiving health guidance (Rueda-Williamson & Rose, 1962) compared with New York City infants born during the 1910s, weighed in private pediatric practice, and reared "under good control so far as diet, rest, and exercise" were concerned (Freeman, 1914).

TABLE II
Body Weight (kg) at Age 1 Year: Means for Both Sexes Together in Relation to Socioeconomic Status

Tag	Group	Low status		High status		High heavier than low by	
		Sample size	Mean weight	Sample size	Mean weight	(kg)	(%)
	Comparisons for terminal segments of the socioeconomic continuum						
I-12	Bengali, Calcutta	60	6.48	50	8.57	1.79[a]	26.4
II-1	Iraqi and Iranian	1601	7.84	115	9.90	2.06	26.3
II-2	United States White	52	8.28	302	10.40	2.12	25.6
II-3	Nigerian, Lagos	37	8.05	26	9.85	1.80	22.4
II-4	Chilean, Santiago	~120	8.70	~35	10.50	1.80	20.7
I-8	Indian, Delhi	399	7.51	47	8.82	1.31	17.4
II-5	Indian, two states	106	7.88	>25	8.97	1.09[b]	13.8[b]
I-7	Colombian, Bogotá	72	8.50	64	9.51	1.01	11.9
II-6	Mexican, two towns	36	7.82	249	8.75	.93	11.9
I-22	Lebanese, Beirut	197	9.32	53	10.30	.98	10.5
II-7	Tunisian, Tunis	35	8.97	39	9.64	.67	7.5
II-8	United States White	67	9.86	120	10.52	.66[c]	6.7[c]
	Comparisons involving wider segments of the socioeconomic continuum						
II-9	Chinese, two towns	103	8.34	104	9.94	1.60	19.2
II-10	East German	>100	8.85	>200	10.10	1.25	14.1
II-11	United States Black	582	9.30[d]	95	10.26	.96[c]	10.3[c]
II-12	United States White	249	9.82	90	10.35	.53	5.4
II-13	Swiss, Zurich	22	9.98	39	9.55	.43	4.3
II-14	Swedish, Stockholm	73	9.90	46	10.27	.37	3.7
II-15	French, Paris	67	9.41	28	9.70	.29	3.1
II-16	English, London	69	9.81	19	9.88	.07	.7
II-17	Belgian, Brussels	32	10.29	43	10.27	−.02	−.2

[a]Using 1.10 kg as population standard deviations (Goldfeld, Merkova, & Tseimlina, 1965), and estimating at $p = .01$, one can infer that the socioeconomic groups paired in each row except rows II-7 and II-13 through II-17 differed dependably in body weight at age 1 year.

[b]Adjustment for secular change would decrease these differences to about .80 kg and 10.5% (Meredith, 1963).

[c]Adjustment for secular change would increase the tag II-8 differences to about 1.25 kg and 12.7%, and the tag II-11 differences to about 1.25 kg and 13.4%.

[d]A mean of 9.48 kg was obtained by Cherry (1968) from data collected between 1961 and 1963 on 180 United States black infants living in New Orleans in "underprivileged" homes.

Tag II-9: Comparison of two groups of infants studied between 1952 and 1955, one group from "lower income sections" of Singapore (Millis, 1958) and the other representing a socioeconomic cross-section in Peking (Ch'in & Sui, 1956).

Tag II-10: Records made between 1958 and 1959 on children living in orphanages compared with those on peers living with their parents (Sälzler, 1960).

Tag II-11: Data on "poverty area children" gathered during 1968 in 36 projects having a "large geographic spread" (Systems Development Project Staff, 1968) compared with data collected in New York City during the 1940s on children in "moderate income families" receiving health care and nutritional advice in private pediatric practice (Bakwin & Patrick, 1944).

Tag II-12: Detroit infants of "the indigent and near-indigent class" given regular pediatric examinations and mother advised on feeding by visiting nurses (Kelly & Reynolds, 1947) compared with New York City infants in "homes of moderate income" supervised from birth through periodic attendance at a well-baby clinic (Bakwin & Bakwin, 1936).

Tags II-13 through II-17: Data collected mainly during the late 1950s and early 1960s in coordinated longitudinal studies (Graffar & Corbier, 1972). Socioeconomic classification was based on "profession, educational level, parents' chief source of income, and kind of living quarters." Predominantly, the groups compared in each city were progeny of semiskilled workers and progeny of moderately well-paid business employees.

At age 1 year, Table II and its supporting text showed, for example:

1. Average body weight of infants in families near the upper end of the socioeconomic distribution exceeded that of infants near the lower end by absolute amounts spread between .65 and 2.15 kg. Statistical testing revealed a difference between terminal groups significant in 11 of the 12 comparisons at or above $p = .01$, and in the Tunisian comparison significant between $p = .05$ and $p = .01$. Relative differences were 7.5% from the Tunisian comparison, between 10.0 and 12.0% from the Colombian, Mexican, and Lebanese comparisons, between 20.0 and 23.0% from the Chilean and Nigerian comparisons, and near 26.0% from the Iraqi–Iranian comparison.
2. For United States white infants, small and large absolute differences were .53 and 2.12 kg. Comparison of infant groups in low and moderate income families, both receiving pediatric supervision, gave the smaller difference (Tag II-12). The larger difference (II-2) resulted from an infant group lacking pediatric care and living under poverty conditions compared with a peer group receiving pediatric care and living in professional and managerial homes.
3. Average body weight of infants belonging to families classified in the upper tail of the socioeconomic distribution varied from less than 9.0 kg for Indian and Mexican groups (I-8, II-5, II-6) to more than 10.0 kg for Chilean,

Lebanese, and United States white groups (I-22, II-2, II-4). Variation among low status groups was from less than 7.0 to more than 9.0 kg.

B. EARLY CHILDHOOD

1. Age 3 Years

Presented in Table III are socioeconomic comparisons for mean body weight of children age 3 years. Section III,A provided research references and sample particulars regarding rows with tag prefixes I and II. Corresponding specifics for other rows are as follows:

Tag III-1: Comparison of two groups of children measured between 1970 and 1975, one group living in an area near Hyderabad City where drainage was lacking and malnutrition prevalent (Mathur, Gupta, & Rao, 1972), and the other group from homes of "well-to-do executives" living in Hyderabad communities (Indian National Institute of Nutrition, 1975).

Tag III-2: Measures taken in 1958 on children in the "low" and "high" categories of a threefold classification based on family income (Caasi, Bulato-Jayme, Alego, Peralta, & Pascual, 1964).

Tag III-3: Progeny of unskilled factory workers measured during 1965 in the Murat district compared with age peers of the highly privileged class measured between 1955 and 1965 in the Nisantasi district (Neyzi, Tanman, & Saner, 1965; Neyzi & Gurson, 1966).

Tag III-4: Children "mainly of Arab ancestry" born in Baghdad, one group from families of "low and irregular income" living in slum areas, and the other group from well-to-do families living in "fashionable residential areas" (Shakir & Zaini, 1974).

Tag III-5: Data from an Indian national sample measured between 1956 and 1965 were sorted into seven categories of family "per capita income" (Indian Council of Medical Research, 1972). The statistics shown represent children in the lowest and highest categories.

Tag III-6: Yoruba children measured between 1962 and 1971 in "the poorest section" of the city, and in "well-to-do residential areas" (Janes, 1974; also M. D. Janes, personal communication, 1975).

Tag III-7: Statistics from data collected at Petropavlovak in 1971 on children in the lowest and highest categories of a threefold rating on living conditions (Nekisheva, 1974).

Tag III-8: Data collected between 1936 and 1946 in Johannesburg on children in families of "the semiskilled, unskilled, and unemployed classes" and between 1943 and 1949 in Capetown, Durban, and Johannesburg on children in families of "the professional, industrial, and managerial classes" (Phillips, 1953).

TABLE III

Body Weight (kg) at Age 3 Years: Means for Children of Both Sexes in Relation to Socioeconomic Status

Tag	Group	Low status: Sample size	Low status: Mean weight	High status: Sample size	High status: Mean weight	High heavier than low by (kg)	High heavier than low by (%)
	Comparisons for terminal segments of the socioeconomic continuum						
I-1	Indian, Bombay	~150	10.7	~35	15.2	4.5[a]	42.1
III-1	Indian, Hyderabad	300	9.8	~50	13.1	3.3	33.7
III-2	Filipino, Manila[b]	17	10.7	12	13.5	2.8	26.2
II-3	Nigerian, Lagos	34	12.2	19	14.8	2.6	21.3
II-4	Chilean, Santiago	~120	12.4	~35	14.9	2.5	20.2
III-3	Turkish, Istanbul	78	12.1	~70	14.2	2.1	17.4
I-8	Indian, Delhi	206	10.9	19	12.7	1.8	16.5
III-4	Iraqi, Baghdad	45	12.8	87	14.8	2.0	15.6
III-5	Indian, national	323	10.3	207	11.9	1.6	15.5
I-7	Colombian, Bogotá	66	12.1	62	13.9	1.8	14.9
III-6	Nigerian, Ibadan	291	12.4	224	14.2	1.8	14.5
III-7	Russian, Asian town	77	14.4	92	15.7	1.3	9.0
III-8	South African White	109	13.8	72	15.0	1.2	8.7
III-9	Tunisian, Tunis	48	13.3	45	14.4	1.1	8.3
III-10	United States White	265	14.1[c]	351	14.8[d]	.7	5.0
III-11	English, N.E. town	212	14.4	66	14.8	.4	2.8
III-12	Dutch, Netherlands	1596	15.2	32	15.5	.3	2.0
	Comparisons involving wider segments of the socioeconomic continuum						
III-13	Nigerian, two sites	~35	11.4	ns[e]	14.6	3.2	28.1
III-14	Indian, Agra	40	10.1	39	12.8	2.7	26.7
II-9	Chinese, two towns	~90	12.4	112	14.3	1.9	15.3
II-13	Swiss, Zurich	22	13.7	39	15.1	1.4	10.2
II-14	Swedish, Stockholm	73	14.3	46	15.2	.9	6.3
II-10	East German	>100	13.7	>200	14.3	.6	4.4
II-16	English, London	69	14.0	19	14.6	.6	4.3
II-15	French, Paris	67	13.7	28	14.1	.4	2.9
II-17	Belgian, Brussels	32	14.6	43	14.8	.2	1.4

[a]Using 1.7 kg as population standard deviations (Yanev, 1965) and estimating at $p = .01$, one can infer that the socioeconomic groups paired in each row except rows III-11, III-12, and II-15 through II-17 differed dependably in body weight at age 3 years.

[b]Interpolated values from statistics at ages 2 and 4 years.

[c]A mean of 13.9 kg was obtained on 198 white children of the unskilled and semiskilled classes measured between 1968 and 1970 in widely scattered urban and rural regions of the United States (Owen, Kram, Garry, Lowe, & Lubin, 1974).

[d]To adjust for weight of clothing, .2 kg was deducted. Adjustment for secular change increased the difference to about 1.4 kg (9.9%).

[e]Sample size not specified (ns).

Tag III-9: Members of socioeconomically ''underprivileged'' and ''privileged'' families, measured between 1968 and 1972 (H. B. Young, personal communication, 1980).

Tag III-10: Comparison of records obtained on ''poverty area children'' during 1968 in surveys yielding a ''large geographic spread'' (Systems Development Project Staff, 1968) and between 1931 and 1937 on children born in Cleveland, reared largely in homes of professional and managerial status, and receiving sustained pediatric care (Simmons & Todd, 1938).

Tag III-11: Measures taken in 1950 at Newcastle upon Tyne on offspring of parents in the occupational categories ''unskilled or semiskilled'' and ''major managerial or professional'' (Miller, Court, Walton, & Knox, 1960).

Tag III-12: Comparison of children in the ''lower'' and ''higher'' categories from tripartite classification by parental occupation; the children were measured between 1964 and 1966 at ''toddler health centres'' and preschools (van Wieringen, 1972).

Tag III-13: Data collected between 1960 and 1962 on village children of the Jos Plateau whose diets were ''above FAO requirements . . . for calorie and protein intake,'' and on peers of well-to-do families residing in Ibadan (Collis, Dema, & Lesi, 1962).

Tag III-14: A group of homes of below average income compared with another from homes of above average income (Prasad, Kumar, & Dayal, 1971).

Given below are selected findings at age 3 years yielded by Table III and the complemental text:

1. Absolute differences in average body weight of children in homes of low and high socioeconomic status were less than 1.0 kg for groups studied in England, the Netherlands, and the United States; between 1.5 and 2.0 kg for groups in Colombia, India (national sample), Iraq, and Nigeria (Ibadan); and more than 2.0 kg for groups in Hyderabad, Istanbul, and Santiago.
2. Relative differences within the span from 14.0 to 16.0% characterized average amounts by which children of upper class homes in Baghdad, Bogotá, Ibadan, and India (national sample) were heavier than peers in lower class families. Corresponding values were below 10% for white groups in England, South Africa, and the United States, and above 20% for Indian children in Bombay and Hyderabad.
3. Among children in homes of high socioeconomic status, means for body weight were near 12.0 kg for Indian children (national sample), near 14.0 kg for Nigerian children in Ibadan, 15.0 kg for South African white children, and near 15.5 kg for Russian children in Petropavlovsk. Compared with the Hyderabad mean for children of ''well-to-do executives'' (13.1 kg), the Russian mean for children in upper class families was higher by 2.6 kg (almost 20.0%). The mean

TABLE IV
Body Weight (kg) at Age 5 Years: Means for Children of Both Sexes in Relation to Socioeconomic Status

		Low status		High status		High heavier than low by	
Tag	Group	Sample size	Mean weight	Sample size	Mean weight	(kg)	(%)
	Comparisons for terminal segments of the socioeconomic continuum						
I-1	Indian, Bombay	~150	12.4	~35	20.5	8.1[a]	65.3
III-2	Filipino, Manila	12	13.4	10	17.7	4.3	32.1
IV-1	Indian, Bombay	87	14.3	23	18.3	4.0	28.0
IV-2	Guatemalan[b]	42	15.6	49	19.9	4.3	27.6
II-3	Nigerian, Lagos	30	15.2	11	19.0	3.8	25.0
II-5	Indian, two states	~100	14.4	>25	17.2	2.8	19.4
III-6	Nigerian, Ibadan	243	15.4	192	18.3	2.9	18.8
II-4	Chilean, Santiago	~120	15.9	~35	18.8	2.9	18.2
III-3	Turkish, Istanbul	113	15.4	~70	18.2	2.8	18.2
IV-3	Jamaican Black[b]	143	16.8	25	19.4	2.6	15.5
I-7	Colombian, Bogotá	66	15.3	64	17.4	2.1	13.7
III-5	Indian, national	343	13.5	333	15.3	1.8	13.3
IV-4	Polish, Breslau	71	16.4	21	18.5	2.1	12.8
IV-5	Indian, Delhi	61	14.1	46	15.8	1.7	12.1
III-4	Iraqi, Baghdad	30	16.6	85	18.3	1.7	10.2
III-8	South African White	178	17.7	88	19.4	1.7	9.6
III-7	Russian, Asian town	143	17.9	186	19.3	1.4	7.8
IV-6	English, Birmingham	>100	15.1	>100	16.2	1.1	7.3
III-12	Dutch, Netherlands	1319	19.1	95	20.0	.9	4.7
III-9	Tunisian, Tunis	52	17.1	48	17.9	.8	4.7
IV-7	Aruba Islander	81	18.4	27	18.9	.5	2.7
	Comparisons involving wider segments of the socioeconomic continuum						
IV-8	Chilean, Santiago	111	16.0	141	19.0	3.0	18.8
III-13	Nigerian, two sites	~35	15.5	ns[c]	18.3	2.8	18.1
II-9	Chinese, two towns	~80	14.9	188	17.6	2.7	18.1
IV-9	Armenian, Beirut	151	17.2	207	19.7	2.5	14.5
IV-10	United States White[b]	202	18.1[d]	500	20.5[d]	2.4	13.3
II-13	Swiss, Zurich	22	17.7	39	19.6	1.9	10.7
IV-11	United States Black[b]	385	19.2[d]	120	20.8[d]	1.6	8.3
II-14	Swedish, Stockholm	67	18.2	43	19.3	1.1	6.0
IV-12	English, N.E. town[e]	123	19.0	29	20.0	1.0	5.3
II-16	English, London	69	17.8	19	18.7	.9	5.1
IV-13	United States White	1738	17.9	1493	18.7	.8	4.5
IV-14	East German	121	17.4	1985	18.1	.7	4.0
IV-15	English, Birmingham[b]	>40	19.9	~30	20.6	.7	3.5

TABLE IV (*Continued*)

Tag	Group	Low status		High status		High heavier than low by	
		Sample size	Mean weight	Sample size	Mean weight	(kg)	(%)
	Comparisons involving wider segments of the socioeconomic continuum						
II-15	French, Paris	67	17.2	28	17.8	.6	3.5
II-17	Belgian, Brussels	32	18.7	43	19.1	.4	2.1
IV-16	U.S. Black and White	88	18.1[f]	215	18.4	.3	1.7

[a]Using 2.4 kg as population standard deviations (O'Brien *et al.*, 1941) and estimating at $p = .01$, one can infer that the socioeconomic groups paired in each row except rows II-14 through II-17, III-9, IV-7, IV-12, IV-15, and IV-16 differed dependably in body weight at age 5 years.

[b]Age 5.5 years.

[c]Sample size not specified (ns).

[d]Median.

[e]5.7 years.

[f]Complementing this ethnically joint average for United States children below the poverty level measured between 1970 and 1971 are separate averages for United States black and white children of the unskilled and semiskilled classes measured during 1968–1970—averages of 18.1 kg for 184 white children and 18.5 kg for 65 black children (Owen *et al.*, 1974).

in Newcastle upon Tyne for English progeny of "unskilled and semiskilled" workers (14.4 kg) was 3.5 kg (32.1%) higher than that in Delhi for Indian progeny of "unskilled" workers, and 2.5 kg (21.0%) higher than that from a national sample of Indian children in homes of high socioeconomic status (III-5).

2. *Age 5 Years*

Socioeconomic comparisons for body weight of children age 5 years are brought together and ordered in Table IV. Source identifications and sample notations for 21 of the rows have been supplied in Sections III,A and III,B,1. Similar specifics for other rows are as follows:

Tag IV-1: Data collected in 1952 on offspring of "the poor classes" and "the privileged classes" in Bombay (Currimbhoy, 1963).

Tag IV-2: Comparison of children studied in the 1970s in villages "where malnutrition was prevalent" (Blanco, Acheson, Canosa, & Salomon, 1974) and children studied in the 1950s in a private school in Guatemala City drawing from upper class homes (Johnston, Borden, & MacVean, 1973).

Tag IV-3: Economically "poor" and "well-to-do" groups of children "predominantly of West African ancestry" measured between 1963 and 1964 (Ashcroft, Heneage, & Lovell, 1966).

Tag IV-4: Records obtained during the early 1920s on offspring of parents in the occupational categories "unskilled or semiskilled" and "professional or managerial" (Zellner, 1926).

Tag IV-5: Statistics from 1969–1970 data on children in the lowest and highest categories of a four-category family income classification (Banik, Nayar, Krishna, Raj, & Taskar, 1970c).

Tag IV-6: Data collected in about 1910 in the lower class St. Bartholomew's ward and the Edgbaston residential ward in England (Auden, 1910).

Tag IV-7: Comparison of "low" and "high" groups after applying tripartite family income classification to data gathered between 1973 and 1974 (van Wering, 1978).

Tag IV-8: Measures taken in 1963 on children in "lower class" and "upper middle class" families (Montoya & Ipinza, 1964).

Tag IV-9: Lebanese–Armenian children measured in Beirut in the early 1970s, one group from "lower and middle" class families, and the other from "well-to-do" families (S. J. Karayan, personal communication, 1975).

Tags IV-10 and IV-11: Data collected between 1967 and 1970 on a "large geographic spread" of "poverty area children" (Systems Development Project Staff, 1968) and on San Francisco children from "a wide range of socioeconomic households," but including few "unemployed or recipients of financial assistance" (Barr, Allen, & Shinefield, 1972; G. D. Barr, personal communication, 1973).

Tag IV-12: Records gathered from a follow-up study of the infant groups described in I-31 (Miller *et al.*, 1972).

Tag IV-13: Findings from bipartite division of the socioeconomic continuum, using data amassed between 1937 and 1939 in 16 states and the District of Columbia (O'Brien, Girshick, & Hunt, 1941).

Tag IV-14: Data collected between 1956 and 1958 on orphanage and kindergarten children (Marcusson, 1961).

Tag IV-15: Children measured in 1947, one group from families in the "unskilled and semiskilled" occupational categories and the other from families with moderately high income (Clements, 1953).

Tag IV-16: Records taken in 23 states on children representative of the noninstitutionalized 1971–1972 United States black and white population, subgrouping for "below poverty level" and "above poverty level" (Abraham, Lowenstein, & O'Connell, 1975).

Examining Table IV revealed the following illustrative findings at age 5 years:

1. Average body weight for children of high socioeconomic status surpassed that for peers of low status by absolute amounts varying from .5 to 8.1 kg, and by relative amounts varying from 2.7 to 65.3%. Typical values from the 21

terminal segment comparisons were near 2.0 kg and 14.0%.

2. Differences less than 1.5 kg and 8.0% were obtained on Dutch children in the Netherlands, children of Dutch and Spanish descent on Aruba Island, English children in Birmingham, Russian children in Petropavlovsk, and Tunisian children in Tunis.

3. Differences greater than 2.5 kg and 15.0% were found for Chilean children in Santiago, Indian children in Bombay, Nigerian children in Ibadan, Turkish children in Istanbul, and in other comparisons for Guatemalan, Jamaican black, and Nigerian children. In two instances (IV-2, IV-3), differences may have been smaller had intracity groups been compared rather than rural poor with urban wealthy.

4. From data gathered during the 1960s, average body weight was 15.8 kg for children in high income families at Delhi (IV-5) and 20.0 kg for Netherland peers in professional and managerial families (III-12). For these upper class groups, the Dutch children were heavier than the Indian children by 4.2 kg, or 26.6%. Averages near 18.0 kg were obtained for well-to-do groups in Baghdad, Ibadan, and Istanbul. Similar variation was found among the low status values; averages from data collected in India (III-5) and the Netherlands (III-12) were 13.5 and 19.1 kg, the latter exceeding the former by 5.6 kg, or 41.5%. Sample size for the averages cited in this paragraph was between 46 and 1319.

Studies providing statistics at age 6 years, but not at ages earlier or later, were made on German children in Halle (Schmid-Monnard, 1901) and United States white children in Philadelphia (Hundley, Mickelsen, Mantel, Weaver, & Taber, 1955). At Halle, measures were taken on 56 children in families of the "laboring and poorer classes" and 96 peers in middle class families of "skilled workers, merchants, and officials"; corresponding means were 17.3 and 18.4 kg, indicating heavier average weight of the middle class group by 1.1 kg, or 4.4%. In Philadelphia, data were collected between 1925 and 1949 in areas "underprivileged economically" and "economically favored." Means were 20.0 kg for 1674 underprivileged children and 21.3 kg for 2571 privileged children, indicating the privileged group had the higher average body weight by 1.3 kg, or 6.5%.

C. LATER CHILDHOOD

1. Age 7 Years

Compiled in Table V are socioeconomic comparisons for body weight of children age 7 years. Particulars for the 14 rows with tag prefixes I, III, or IV were given in conjunction with Tables I, III, and IV. The sources and samples drawn upon for other rows were as follows:

Tag V-1: Children in "lower income" families living in Hyderabad City

TABLE V
Body Weight (kg) at Age 7 Years: Means for Children of Both Sexes in Relation to Socioeconomic Status

Tag	Group	Low status		High status		High heavier than low by	
		Sample size	Mean weight	Sample size	Mean weight	(kg)	(%)
	Comparisons for terminal segments of the socioeconomic continuum						
V-1	Indian, several sites	165	15.6	262	23.2	7.6[a]	48.7
I-1	Indian, Bombay	~150	14.9	~35	21.2	6.3	42.3
V-2	Ghanaian, Accra	~70	18.1	~50	24.4	6.3	34.8
V-3	Guatemalan	35	18.4	95	24.0	5.6	30.4
III-6	Nigerian, Ibadan	165	18.5	119	22.5	4.0	21.6
V-4	Colombian, two towns	71	18.5	~60	22.1	3.6	19.5
III-3	Turkish, Istanbul	114	18.7	~70	21.9	3.2	17.1
IV-3	Jamaican Black	812	20.1	28	23.4	3.3	16.4
V-5	United States White	84	20.4	23	23.5	3.1	15.2
V-6	Haitian, Port au Prince	208	21.8	234	25.0	3.2	14.7
III-5	Indian, national	386	16.5	345	18.8	2.3	13.9
V-7	English, several sites	105	21.2	71	23.9	2.7	12.7
V-8	United States White	130	21.8	168	24.0	2.2	10.1
III-7	Russian, Asian town	80	21.6	131	23.7	2.1	9.7
III-9	Tunisian, Tunis	46	19.8	38	21.6	1.8	9.1
IV-6	English, Birmingham[b]	>100	19.5	>100	21.1	1.6	8.2
V-9	Chinese, Peking[c]	ns[d]	19.0	21	20.5	1.5	7.9
IV-5	Indian, Delhi	56	17.2	59	18.5	1.3	7.6
V-10	Scottish, Glasgow	2759	19.8	966	21.0	1.2	6.1
V-11	Chinese, Hong Kong	851	18.5[e]	197	19.5[e]	1.0	5.4
V-12	United States White[c]	51	23.3	55	24.5	1.2	5.2
V-13	United States White	146	22.0	273	23.0	1.0	4.5
V-14	Australian, Queensland	212	23.4	57	24.3	.9	3.8
III-12	Dutch, Netherlands	1331	23.4	85	24.1	.7	3.0
V-15	Danish, Copenhagen	880	21.7	613	22.1	.4	1.8
V-16	United States White	147	21.0	74	21.3	.3	1.4
V-17	English, London[f]	~1000	21.2	~800	21.4	.2	.9
	Comparisons involving wider segments of the socioeconomic continuum						
IV-11	United States Black	227	22.0[e]	139	26.6[e]	4.6	20.9
V-18	Mexican, two sites	50	19.2	166	22.1	2.9	15.1
V-19	Czechoslovakian, Prague	206	23.5	281	24.6	1.1	4.7
IV-15	English, Birmingham	>40	22.7	~30	23.6	.9	4.0
IV-13	United States White	4829	22.1[e]	4617	22.9[e]	.8	3.6
IV-16	United States Black and White	59	22.3	115	22.9	.6	2.7

TABLE V (*Continued*)

Tag	Group	Low status: Sample size	Low status: Mean weight	High status: Sample size	High status: Mean weight	High heavier than low by (kg)	High heavier than low by (%)
	Comparisons involving wider segments of the socioeconomic continuum						
V-20	Scottish, Glasgow	233	20.1	71	20.6	.5	2.5
V-21	Canadian, Ottawa	~140	21.1	~140	21.6	.5	2.4
V-22	Danish, Copenhagen	100	20.4	123	20.8	.4	2.0
V-23	United States White[g]	604	20.7	148	20.6	−.1	−.5
V-24	United States White	412	21.2	367	21.1	−.1	−.5

[a]Using 3.2 kg as population standard deviations (O'Brien *et al.*, 1941) and estimating at $p = .01$, one can infer in 23 instances that the paired socioeconomic groups differed significantly in body weight at age 7 years. Comparisons not reaching this level of dependability are those in rows III-9, III-12, IV-5, IV-15, IV-16, V-12, V-14 through V-17, and V-20 through V-24.

[b]Age 7.5 years.

[c]Males only.

[d]Sample size not specified (ns).

[e]Median.

[f]Age 7.1 years.

[g]Females only.

compared with children attending elite residential schools in various parts of India (Raghavan *et al.*, 1971).

Tag V-2: Measures taken between 1966 and 1968 on children in "wage-earner" families living under "the minimum of social amenities" and on age peers in "wealthy or highly educated" families (Faiwoo, 1973).

Tag V-3: Data obtained in rural villages on Mayan Amerind children of low socioeconomic status (Méndez & Behrhorst, 1963; Sabharwal, Morales, & Méndez, 1966) and in Guatemala City on white private school children considered as highly privileged as any in the country (Johnston *et al.*, 1973). Explicit in this description is the confounding of ethnic, locale, and economic variables.

Tag V-4: Children in families of "low economic status" measured in 1967 in San Jacinto (Mora, 1969) and age peers in "upper class" families measured between 1965 and 1968 in Bogotá (Rueda-Williamson, Luna-Jaspe, Ariza, Pardo, & Mora, 1969).

Tag V-5: Measures taken at an orphanage on children "from among the poor" compared with peers reared in wealthy families "under the most favorable conditions" (Hellman, 1923).

Tag V-6: Children in "poor" families living in Port au Prince compared with peers attending private schools in Port au Prince and Petionville (King, Foucauld, Fougere, & Severinghaus, 1963).

Tag V-7: Records obtained between 1945 and 1952 in slum areas of industrial towns and in private schools (Hammond, 1953).

Tag V-8: Subgroups selected from a probability sampling of "noninstitutionalized" children between 1963 and 1965, one subgroup from families with an annual income below $3000, the other from families having an annual income of $10,000 or more (Hamill *et al.*, 1972).

Tag V-9: Data collected in about 1924 on "orphans and waifs" (Hammond & Sheng, 1925) and in 1926 on private school boys of well-to-do families (Hsu & Liang, 1930).

Tag V-10: Records amassed between 1905 and 1906 in the "poorest" and "best residential" districts of Glasgow (Mackenzie & Foster, 1907; Elderton, 1914).

Tag V-11: Measures accumulated between 1961 and 1963 on children of south Chinese descent, one subgroup drawn from families of unskilled laborers and the other from families in the "major managerial and professional" category (Low, 1971).

Tag V-12: Boys of northwest European ancestry measured in 1950 in Eugene, Oregon; subgroups with parents in the "unskilled and semiskilled" and the "managerial and professional" categories (Meredith, 1951).

Tag V-13: Data obtained in the early 1930s in schools in the "poorest" and "best" districts of Minneapolis (Weisman, 1935).

Tag V-14: White children attending Queensland schools in 1976, from families classified as "unskilled and unemployed" or "professional and managerial" (May, O'Hara, & Dugdale, 1979).

Tag V-15: Children attending schools between 1926 and 1928 in the "poorest" and "socially better off" districts of Copenhagen (Døssing, 1950).

Tag V-16: Data gathered between 1923 and 1926 in Massachusetts (in Beverly, Medford, and Revere) on children of northwest European ancestry in families of "unskilled and semiskilled" status, and families of "major managerial and professional" status (Dearborn, Rothney, & Shuttleworth, 1938; Meredith, 1951).

Tag V-17: Measures obtained during 1938 in schools in the "poorer" and "better residential" districts of the County of London (Menzies, 1940).

Tag V-18: Data collected in the 1970s on children of low socioeconomic status living in a suburban community southwest of Oaxaca de Juarez (R. M. Malina, personal communication, 1979) and between 1964 and 1965 in Mexico City on children in middle and upper class families reared with superior diet and health care (Faulhaber, 1976).

Tag V-19: Measures amassed in 1951 on a group of children "whose fathers were industrial workers'' and a peer group whose fathers were ''employed as clerks or in similar (white-collar) occupations'' (Prokopec, 1970).

Tag V-20: Records made between 1921 and 1922 on offspring of parents largely in the unskilled and mercantile socioeconomic categories; one group included ''children of dockers and unskilled labourers,'' the other ''children of boarding-house keepers, tradesmen, and theatrical artistes'' (Tully, 1924 to 1925). Predominantly, the unskilled group was of Irish ancestry and the mercantile group of Scottish ancestry.

Tag V-21: Measures taken between 1933 and 1945 in schools attended predominantly by ''children of artisans, tradespeople, and government employees of the clerical grades'' and in schools in ''better-class residential districts'' drawing from ''business, professional and administrative'' families (Hopkins, 1947).

Tag V-22: Comparison of children enrolled during 1909 in public and private (tuition) schools (Hertz, 1912).

Tag V-23: Measures taken in St. Louis in 1892 on girls predominantly from lower middle class (''manual trade'') and upper middle class families (Porter, 1894).

Tag V-24: Statistics from a bipartite classification of data gathered between 1896 and 1898 on District of Columbia school children in ''laboring'' (unskilled through skilled) and ''nonlaboring'' (mercantile through professional) families (MacDonald, 1899).

The following illustrative findings on body weight at age 7 years were extracted from Table V:

1. In 33 of 38 rows, the higher of the paired socioeconomic groups exceeded the lower by relative amounts between 2.0 and 48.7%. The small positive value of .9% for English children in London (V-17) was associated with higher values of 4.0, 8.2, and 12.7% from other English studies (IV-6, IV-15, V-7). The slightly negative values obtained for United States white children studied in St. Louis and the District of Columbia (V-23, V-24) were at the low end of 8 comparative values, 5 yielding positive results within the limits of 3.5 and 15.2% (IV-13, V-5, V-8, V-12, V-13).

2. Absolute differences fell between .4 and .9 kg for Australian children in Queensland, Canadian children in Ottawa, Danish children in Copenhagen, Dutch children in the Netherlands, English children in Birmingham, and Scottish children in Glasgow; from significance tests at 99% probability, none of these outcomes allowed acceptance of the hypothesis that socioeconomic subgroups differed in body weight at age 7 years. Absolute differences fell between 3.0 and 7.0 kg for Ghanaian children in Accra, Haitian children in Port au Prince, Indian children in Bombay, Nigerian children in Ibadan, Turkish children in Istanbul,

and United States black children. Each of these comparisons permitted acceptance of a difference between the subgroups at 99% probability.

3. From studies made in the 1960s on samples of 50 or more, groups representing upper class homes varied in average body weight from 18.5 kg for Indian children in Delhi, through 22.5 kg for Nigerian children in Ibadan, to 25.0 kg for Haitian children in Port au Prince and Petionville (IV-5, III-6, V-6). The highest of these averages surpassed the lowest by 6.5 kg, or near 35.0%.

2. *Age 9 Years*

Socioeconomic comparisons for body weight at age 9 years are itemized in Table VI. Group descriptions and references not included in Sections III,A or III,B are as follows:

Tag VI-1: "Khatri and Arora Panjabi" children measured in 1970, one sample drawn from the "lower classes" and the other from "private schools" (Sikri, 1972).

Tag VI-2: Girls of "low" and "high" socioeconomic status measured in 1969 (Swaminathan, 1971; M. C. Swaminathan, personal communication, 1975).

Tag VI-3: Data collected in the early 187Os at an orphanage and on offspring of well-to-do parents (Pagliani, 1876).

Tag VI-4: Spanish-speaking children measured in Guatemala City between 1964 and 1971, 46 from "poor" families, and 46 attending "expensive private schools" (Bogin & MacVean, 1983).

Tag VI-5: Measures taken during the early 1910s in a "poor industrial district" and a "wealthy residential section" of Oakland, California (Robertson, 1916).

Tag VI-6: Records obtained between 1967 and 1969 on children of "unskilled and semiskilled" workers, and peers of "professional and managerial" families (Neyzi, Yalçindağ, & Alp, 1973).

Tag VI-7: Missouri boys "attending three St. Louis City and four St. Louis County regular schools," one group members of unskilled and semiskilled families, the other group members of professional and major managerial families (Weinberg *et al.*, 1974).

Tag VI-8: Data amassed between 1965 and 1968 on children of "unskilled and skilled laborers" and members of "professional and managerial" families (Camcam, 1969).

Tag VI-9: Measures taken between 1944 and 1945 on boys of "poor" and "upper middle class" families (Prevosti, 1949).

Tag VI-10: Records secured in 1920 in public schools and "higher schools" (Schiøtz, 1923).

Tag VI-11: Data collected during 1974 in Knoxville, Tennessee, on girls in

TABLE VI
Body Weight (kg) at Age 9 Years: Means for Children of Both Sexes in Relation to Socioeconomic Status

Tag	Group	Low status		High status		High heavier than low by	
		Sample size	Mean weight	Sample size	Mean weight	(kg)	(%)
	Comparisons for terminal segments of the socioeconomic continuum						
V-1	Indian, several sites	176	19.3	436	28.1	8.8[a]	45.6
V-2	Ghanaian, Accra	~70	22.2	~50	30.4	8.2	36.9
I-1	Indian, Bombay	~150	17.7	~35	23.6	5.9	33.3
V-3	Guatemalan	68	22.0	134	29.0	7.0	31.8
VI-1	Punjabi, Delhi	61	21.7	48	27.6	5.9	27.2
III-6	Yoruba, Ibadan	57	22.0	51	27.3	5.3	24.1
V-4	Colombian, two towns	118	22.4	~60	27.6	5.2	23.2
IV-3	Jamaican Black	1625	24.1	35	29.6	5.5	22.8
VI-2	Indian, Hyderabad[b]	55	19.2	246	23.2	4.0	20.8
VI-3	Italian, Turino	79	20.4	24	24.4	4.0	19.6
V-6	Haitian, Port au Prince	222	23.2	221	27.7	4.5	19.4
VI-4	Guatemalan, Spanish	46	25.3	46	30.0	4.7	18.6
III-5	Indian, national	377	19.6	336	23.0	3.4	17.3
V-7	English, several sites	130	25.6	115	29.8	4.2	16.4
IV-7	Aruba Islander[c]	73	26.8	13	30.4	3.6	13.4
V-5	United States White	132	25.4	68	28.5	3.1	12.2
VI-5	United States White[d]	100	23.8	100	26.7	2.9	12.2
VI-6	Turkish, Istanbul	110	26.3	104	29.2	2.9	11.0
III-9	Tunisian, Tunis	45	24.7	38	26.9	2.2	8.9
V-8	United States White	138	28.1	192	30.3	2.2	7.8
V-10	Scottish, Glasgow	2716	23.3	1032	25.1	1.8	7.7
V-11	Chinese, Hong Kong	1129	22.0	415	23.5	1.5	6.8
V-13	United States White	287	26.8	296	28.5	1.7	6.3
IV-5	Indian, Delhi	55	20.8	43	21.9[e]	1.1	5.3
V-9	Chinese, Peking[c]	ns[f]	23.0	46	24.1	1.1	4.8
VI-7	United States White, Missouri[g]	68	28.4	64	29.7	1.3	4.6
VI-8	Filipino, Manila	960	20.5	124	21.4	.9	4.4
III-12	Dutch, Netherlands	1149	29.0	88	29.7	.7	2.4
V-14	Australian, Queensland	231	29.0	64	29.6	.6	2.1
V-15	Danish, Copenhagen	1350	26.3	912	26.8	.5	1.9
V-16	United States White	193	23.0	98	23.4	.4	1.7
V-17	English, London[h]	~1000	25.9	~800	26.2	.3	1.2

(*continued*)

TABLE VI (*Continued*)

Tag	Group	Low status		High status		High heavier than low by	
		Sample size	Mean weight	Sample size	Mean weight	(kg)	(%)
	Comparisons involving wider segments of the socioeconomic continuum						
V-18	Mexican, two sites	72	22.9	136	27.8	4.9	21.4
VI-9	Spanish, Barcelona[c]	100	25.1	100	29.8	4.7	18.7
VI-10	Norwegian, Oslo	3098	24.9	83	28.2	3.3	13.3
IV-10	United States White	132	26.9[i]	643	30.1[i]	3.2	11.9
VI-11	United States Black[b]	29	30.6	30	34.2	3.6	11.8
IV-11	United States Black	201	27.9[i]	154	30.7[i]	2.8	10.0
IV-12	English, N.E. town	134	26.4	42	28.6	2.2	8.3
VI-12	Dutch, Netherlands	174	26.6	166	28.6	2.0	7.5
IV-16	United States Black and White	50	27.9	114	29.7	1.8	6.5
VI-13	Swedish, Stockholm[b]	~400	25.2	~200	26.8	1.6	6.3
IV-13	United States White	6097	27.0	5716	28.1	1.1	4.1
V-20	Scottish, Glasgow	277	23.3	78	24.2	.9	3.9
V-21	Canadian, Ottawa	~140	22.9	~140	23.5	.6	2.6
VI-14	English, several towns	864	24.9	154	25.5	.6	2.4
V-24	United States White	703	24.7	613	25.1	.4	1.6
V-23	United States White[b]	688	25.1	152	25.5	.4	1.6
V-22	Danish, Copenhagen	191	24.2	169	24.5	.3	1.2
IV-15	English, Birmingham	>40	27.2	~30	26.8	−.4	−1.5

[a]Using 4.3 kg as population standard deviations (O'Brien *et al.*, 1941) and estimating at $p = .01$, one can infer in 35 instances that the paired socioeconomic groups differed significantly in body weight at age 9 years. Comparisons not reaching this level of dependability are those in rows III-9, IV-5, IV-15, V-9, V-14, V-16, V-17, V-20 through V-23, VI-7, VI-8, and VI-14.

[b]Females only.

[c]Males only.

[d]Age 8.5 years.

[e]Interpolated value using means at ages 8 and 10 years.

[f]Sample size not specified (ns).

[g]Age 8.9 years.

[h]Age 9.1 years.

[i]Median.

"low income" and "middle income" families (Wakefield, Disney, Mason, & Beauchene, 1980).

Tag VI-12: Measures taken in large cities between 1952 and 1956 on children in the "lower social group" and "upper social group" (de Wijn & de Haas, 1960).

Tag VI-13: Girls attending public and private schools (Key, 1889).

Tag VI-14: Records amassed between 1880 and 1883 in several English towns on children of unskilled and semiskilled workers, and children of "clerks and shopkeepers" (Galton, 1883–1884).

Six Indian studies were among the materials assembled in Table VI. Five of these studies (I-1, III-5, V-1, VI-1, VI-2) showed that, on average, children in families of high socioeconomic status were heavier than those in families of low status by amounts between 17.3 and 45.6%. One study (IV-5) yielded 5.3% as the amount by which average body weight was more for children in the highest than lowest category of a four-category family income classification. Rajalakshmi and Chandrasekaran (1967) indicated by graph that at all childhood ages averages for body weight of Indian children from high income families living in "residential areas of Baroda City" exceeded those of peers living in "poor localities" of Gujarat.

Chinese comparisons in Table VI showed average body weight was greater by 6.8% for Hong Kong children of upper than lower classes (V-11), and by 4.8% for Peking children of upper than lower classes (V-9). In another analysis of Hong Kong data, 12.3% was obtained as the average amount by which 138 children in professional and managerial families were heavier than 358 children in families of unskilled laborers (Chang, Lee, Low, & Kvan, 1963).

Among the 10 comparisons in Table VI for United Stated white children, 6 pertained to terminal segments of the socioeconomic continuum (V-5, V-8, V-13, V-16, VI-5, VI-7). For these 6 studies combined, average body weight of 818 children in high income families (28.2 kg) surpassed that of 918 peers in low income families (25.8 kg) by 2.4 kg, or 9.3%.

D. SUMMARY

A row count including the "terminal segment" and "wider segment" sections of Tables I through VI summed to 206 rows of comparative statistics for body weight. Average body weight of the higher socioeconomic group in each pairing was greater than that of the lower socioeconomic group by 1.0% or more in 199 (97%) of the pairings. The higher socioeconomic group was heavier than its lower counterpart by 2.0% or more in 185 (90%) of the comparisons, and by 3.0% or more in 172 (83%) of the entire series.

Tables I through VI contained 132 rows in which infants and children in low status families (described as poor, indigent, slum area, underprivileged, unskilled and semiskilled, or low income) were compared with children in families of high status (described as well to do, wealthy, living in an expensive residential area, privileged, managerial and professional, or educationally favored). Typically, the high status infants and children exceeded their low status peers in average body weight by amounts near 6.0% at birth, 15.0% at ages 1 and 3 years, and between 10.0 and 14.0% at ages 5 to 9 years. Composite analysis of the 151 relative differences for ages between 3 and 9 years gave a median near 10%, the central one-half of the distribution clustered between 4 and 18%, and the central four-fifths of the values scattered from near 2 to 28%.

III. Socioeconomic Comparisons for Stature

A. INFANCY

1. Statement on Stature

Stature is defined as maximum distance from vertex to soles. Vertex is the topmost point on the head when the head is positioned so that the lowest point on the border of the bone below the left eye and the highest point on the anterior border of the tragus of each ear lie in a plane at right angles to the long axis of the trunk.

In determining stature, the head is positioned to obtain vertex, the lower limbs are parallel and fully extended, and the feet are at right angles with the long axes of the lower limbs. Stature is measured during infancy with the body supine (recumbent length) and, during childhood, usually with the body erect (standing height). Research bearing on the measurement of stature has been reviewed elsewhere (Meredith, 1960).

2. Birth

Socioeconomic comparisons for stature at birth are presented in Table VII. Sources and sample notations relating to nine rows of the table were supplied in Section II,A. Similar particulars for other rows are as follows:

Tag VII-1: Data collected in Baroda City in the early 1970s on normal, singleton offspring of parents in "the unskilled labour class" (Sharma, Sapra, & Mainigi, 1975) and in Bombay in about 1960 on progeny of "the best socioeconomic group" at that place and time (Udani, 1963).

Tag VII-2: Comparison of children born into urban families of low and high socioeconomic status, measures taken between 1962 and 1973 (Banik, 1982).

Tag VII-3: White, full-term neonates measured within 48 hours after birth, one group of low socioeconomic status born in 1933 in Iowa City, Iowa (Stebbins, 1933) compared with a group from "the better class" born in about 1920 in Minneapolis, Minnesota (Adair & Scammon, 1921).

Tag VII-4: Full-term, singleton infants of Chinese ancestry born during 1951 in Singapore into "lower income" families (Millis, 1954) compared with full-term Chinese infants born between 1932 and 1936 in Shantung and "considered as typical" (King & T'ang, 1937).

Tag VII-5: These "two groups represent roughly non-manual (professional to

TABLE VII
Recumbent Body Length (cm) at Birth: Means for Neonates of Both Sexes in Relation to Socioeconomic Status

Tag	Group	Low status		High status		High longer than low by	
		Sample size	Mean length	Sample size	Mean length	(cm)	(%)
	Comparisons for terminal segments of the socioeconomic continuum						
VII-1	Indian, two towns	122	47.4	270	50.8	3.4[a]	7.2
VII-2	Indian, Delhi	450	48.7	164	50.8	2.1	4.3
I-15	Uruguayan, Montevideo	48	49.4	255	50.8	1.4	2.8
I-12	Bengali, Calcutta	60	48.2	50	49.4	1.2	2.5
I-5	Romanian, Bucharest[b]	30	49.9	30	50.8	.9	1.8
I-18	Brazilian	1068	49.3	792	50.0	.7	1.4
I-20	United States Black	100	49.4[c]	100	50.1	.7	1.4
VII-3	United States White	100	49.7	100	50.3	.6	1.2
I-7	Colombian, Bogotá	69	48.5	63	48.9	.4	.8
I-22	Lebanese, Beirut	247	49.9	36	50.0	.1	.2
	Comparisons involving wider segments of the socioeconomic continuum						
VII-4	Chinese, two towns	9474	48.6	1000	49.5	.9	1.9
I-32	United States White	886	50.1	454	50.8	.7	1.4
I-34	United States White	862	50.4	905	50.5	.1	.2
VII-5	Danish, Odense	155	50.7	156	50.7	.0	.0

[a]Using 2.0 cm as population standard deviations (Bakwin & Bakwin, 1936), and estimating at $p = .01$, one can infer that the socioeconomic groups paired in each row except rows I-5, I-7, I-20, I-22, I-34, VII-3, and VII-5 differed dependably in body length at birth.

[b]Males only.

[c]Cherry (1968) obtained a mean of 49.2 cm for 200 United States black neonates born in New Orleans into economically "underprivileged" homes. See Table I, footnote *c*.

clerical) versus manual (skilled through unskilled) types of employment" (Ulrich, 1982).

Table VII showed, for example:

1. Averages for body length at birth were 47.4 cm for Indian neonates of "unskilled" parents in Baroda City (VII-1), 49.9 cm for Lebanese–Arab neonates of "the low socioeconomic stratum" in Beirut (I-22), 48.9 cm for Colombian offspring of the "highest socioeconomic classes" in Bogotá (I-7), and 50.8 cm for Uruguayan newborns in families of "high socioeconomic status" in Montevideo (I-15). Variation in average body length among ethnic groups was evident within each social class and across social classes.
2. Typically, average body length was greater for newborns in high status

families than for those in low status families by absolute and relative amounts near .8 cm and 1.6%. In four instances differences exceeded 1.0 cm and 2.5%, and in three instances differences were no larger than .6 cm and 1.2%.

3. On average, compared with neonates in families of low social status those in families of high status were longer by absolute amounts of 2.1 cm at Delhi, 1.4 cm at Montevideo, .7 cm in the District of Columbia (I-20), and .4 cm at Bogotá. Corresponding relative values were 4.3, 2.8, 1.4, and .8%. Low and high socioeconomic groups in Beirut were practically alike in average body length.

Obtaining close approximations to valid measures of body length at birth is difficult (Meredith & Goodman, 1941); in some measurement programs satisfactory data have not been obtained due to inadequacy of equipment, insufficient training of personnel in positioning infants for measurement, or slackening as time passes in maintenance of high standards. Studies such as those drawn upon in rows I-22, I-34, VII-1, and VII-5 should be augmented with well-controlled replications.

3. *Age 1 Year*

Assembled in Table VIII are socioeconomic comparisons for body length at age 1 year. Reference citations and sample descriptions for rows commencing with the tag prefix VIII are as follows:

Tag VIII-1: Infants born in the 1930s in New York City, reared in "poverty stricken" homes, and lacking pediatric care (Bakwin *et al.*, 1934) compared with contemporary peers born in Iowa City and reared in homes of "the professional and managerial classes" (Meredith, 1943).

Tag VIII-2: Data collected in the Saint Gilles area between 1955 and 1958, one sample from the "unskilled and semiskilled" strata and the other from "professional and managerial" strata (Graffar, Asiel, & Emery-Hauzeur, 1961).

Tag VIII-3: Comparison of data on "poverty area children" gathered during 1968 in 36 projects having a "large geographic spread" (Systems Development Project Staff, 1968) with data gathered on singleton infants born in Philadelphia and measured between 1947 and 1952 at a well-baby clinic where mothers received "diet instructions and vitamin supplements for their babies" (Kasius, Randall, Tompkins, & Wiehl, 1957).

Tag VIII-4: Measures taken between 1963 and 1967 on children in families of "low" and "middle" socioeconomic status (Low, 1971).

Tag VIII-5: Comparison of records obtained in the 1930s on Detroit infants of "indigent or near indigent parents" supervised by trained visiting nurses who "kept the mothers supplied with essential materials for formulas" and with formula supplements (Hamil, Reynolds, Poole, & Macy, 1938; Kelly & Reynolds, 1947) and on Connecticut and New York infants of upper middle and upper

TABLE VIII
Vertex–Soles Length (cm) at Age 1 Year: Means for Infants of Both Sexes in Relation to Socioeconomic Status

Tag	Group	Low status		High status		High longer than low by	
		Sample size	Mean length	Sample size	Mean length	(cm)	(%)
	Comparisons for terminal segments of the socioeconomic continuum						
I-12	Bengali, Calcutta	60	66.7	50	71.1	4.4[a]	6.6
II-3	Nigerian, Lagos	36	70.9	26	75.6	4.7	6.6
I-8	Indian, Delhi	399	69.7	47	73.4	3.7	5.3[b]
II-8	United States White	67	74.4	120	78.2	3.8[c]	5.1[c]
I-7	Colombian, Bogotá	72	71.1	64	74.1	3.0	4.2
VIII-1	United States White	52	73.4	207	76.1	2.7	3.7
II-6	Mexican, two towns	36	70.8	255	72.8	2.0	2.8
I-22	Lebanese, Beirut	197	73.9	49	75.4	1.5	2.0
II-7	Tunisian, Tunis	35	71.4	38	72.6	1.2	1.7
VIII-2	Belgian, Brussels	49	74.5	61	75.3	0.8	1.1
	Comparisons involving wider segments of the socioeconomic continuum						
II-13	Swiss, Zurich	22	73.6	39	76.2	2.6	3.5
VIII-3	United States Black	562	74.3[d]	173	76.3	2.0[c]	2.7[c]
II-9	Chinese, two towns	103	72.8	104	74.4	1.6	2.2
II-15	French, Paris	67	72.9	28	74.5	1.6	2.2
VIII-4	Chinese, Hong Kong	257	73.6	47	74.8	1.2	1.6
II-10	East German	>100	74.3	>200	75.5	1.2	1.6
II-14	Swedish, Stockholm	73	75.6	46	76.3	.7	.9
II-16	English, London	69	74.4	19	74.6	.2	.3
VIII-5	United States White	249	75.6	296	75.6	.0	.0

[a]Using 2.9 cm as population standard deviations (Meredith, 1943) and estimating at $p = .01$, one can infer that the socioeconomic groups paired in each row except rows II-7, II-14 through II-16, VIII-2, and VIII-5 were dependably different in body length at age 1 year.

[b]In a later report using larger samples, Banik (1982) obtained a mean of 70.4 cm for 540 children living in "poor residential areas" of Delhi, and a mean 1.6 cm (2.3%) higher for 156 peers living in "better residential quarters" of Delhi.

[c]Adjustment for secular change would increase this difference (Meredith, 1943, 1963).

[d]A mean of 73.0 cm was obtained by Cherry (1968) for 180 New Orleans black children born between 1960 and 1962 into "underprivileged" families.

class parents receiving dietary and health care in private pediatric practice (Peatman & Higgons, 1938).

Table VIII and its complementary text revealed these exemplary findings:

1. From measures taken between 1968 and 1972 on low status groups, average body length at age 1 year was 66.7 cm for Indian infants in ''low income'' families in Calcutta (I-12) and 7.6 cm (11.4%) higher for infants of United States black parents living in poverty areas (VIII-3).

2. Average stature of infants age 1 year in families of high socioeconomic status surpassed that of age peers in families of low status by an absolute amount centering near 3.0 cm. Specific study values were 4.7 cm for Nigerian infants in Lagos, 3.7 cm for Indian infants in Delhi, 3.0 cm for Colombian infants in Bogotá, 1.5 cm for Lebanese infants in Beirut, and .8 cm for Belgian infants in Brussels. Matching relative differences were 6.6, 5.3, 4.2, 2.0, and 1.1%.

3. In one comparison (VIII-5), no difference in average body length was found between infants in ''indigent and near-indigent'' families and infants in upper middle and upper class families. Both of these groups received exceptional postnatal supervision, one group through a superior home visiting program and the other through what was characterized as ''optimal pediatric and home care.''

Measures of body length were taken at birth in 1940 and at age 1 year in 1941 on Iowa City white infants; average increments during the first postnatal year were 24.7 cm for 8 offspring of parents in the ''unskilled and semiskilled'' category, and 25.4 cm for 10 offspring of parents in the ''professional and managerial'' category (Meredith, 1943). The difference, while not significant statistically, was suggestive for further increment research on larger socioeconomic samples.

B. EARLY CHILDHOOD

1. Age 3 Years

Statistics on stature of socioeconomic groups of children age 3 years were brought together in Table IX. Except for the row designated IX-1, the populations sampled were described previously.

Tag IX-1: Indian children in Delhi living in ''poor residential areas'' compared with peers in homes of ''professors, doctors, lawyers, engineers, and military officers'' (Banik, 1982). The records were accumulated between 1962 and 1973.

The following comparative findings were extracted from Table IX:

1. Children in families of high socioeconomic status, on average, were taller than those in families of low status by absolute amounts between 1.4 and 11.4

TABLE IX
Standing Height (cm) at Age 3 Years: Means for Children of Both Sexes in Relation to Socioeconomic Status

Tag	Group	Low status		High status		High taller than low by	
		Sample size	Mean height	Sample size	Mean height	(cm)	(%)
	Comparisons for terminal segments of the socioeconomic continuum						
I-1	Indian, Bombay	~150	82.6	~35	94.0	11.4[a]	13.8
III-3	Turkish, Istanbul	76	84.1	~70	95.0	10.9	13.0
III-1	Indian, Hyderabad	300	83.2	~50	93.4	10.2	12.3
II-3	Nigerian, Lagos	33	87.6	19	96.7	9.1	10.4
II-4	Chilean, Santiago	~120	87.1	~35	96.0	8.9	10.2
I-7	Colombian, Bogotá	66	87.4	62	94.3	6.9	7.9
III-6	Yoruba, Ibadan	89	89.9	114	96.5	6.6	7.3
III-5	Indian, national	323	83.6	207	88.5	4.9	5.9
II-5	Indian, two states	~100	88.2	>25	93.4	5.2	5.9
III-8	South African White	108	91.6	68	96.5	4.9	5.3
III-9	Tunisian, Tunis	48	89.1	45	93.6	4.5	5.1
IX-1	Indian, Delhi	531	88.5	150	91.6	3.1	3.5
III-10	United States White	261	93.0[b]	351	95.8	2.8[c]	3.0[c]
III-4	Iraqi, Baghdad	45	89.8	87	92.3	2.5	2.8
III-11	English, N.E. town	207	91.8	64	94.4	2.6	2.8
III-7	Russian, Asian town	77	94.9	92	96.8	1.9	2.0
III-12	Dutch, Netherlands	1596	96.7	32	98.1	1.4	1.4
	Comparisons involving wider segments of the socioeconomic continuum						
III-13	Nigerian, two sites	~35	85.1	ns[d]	92.4	7.3	8.6
III-14	Indian, Agra	40	87.4	39	92.3	4.9	5.6
II-13	Swiss, Zurich	22	93.6[e]	39	97.7[e]	4.1	4.4
II-9	Chinese, two towns	~90	90.0	112	93.4	3.4	3.8
VIII-4	Chinese, Hong Kong	185	91.5	24	94.6	3.1	3.4
II-10	East German	>100	91.5	>200	94.4	2.9	3.2
II-14	Swedish, Stockholm	73	96.0[e]	46	98.7[e]	2.7	2.8
II-15	French, Paris	67	92.7[e]	28	94.7[e]	2.0	2.2
II-16	English, London	69	93.9[e]	19	95.1[e]	1.2	1.3
II-17	Belgian, Brussels	32	95.7[e]	43	96.2[e]	.5	.5

[a]Using 4.5 cm as population standard deviations (Meredith, 1978a) and estimating at $p = .01$, one can infer that the socioeconomic groups paired in each row except rows II-15 through II-17 and III-12 were dependably different in stature at age 3 years.

[b]Median. A mean of 93.9 cm was obtained on 198 United States white children of the unskilled and semiskilled classes measured between 1968 and 1970 in widely scattered urban and rural locations; for 66 United States black children, comparable geographically, secularly, and socioeconomically, the mean was 95.6 cm (Owen *et al.*, 1974).

[c]Adjustment for secular change would increase these differences to about 3.8 cm and 4.1%.

[d]Sample size not specified (ns).

[e]Recumbent vertex–soles length.

cm. Differences exceeded 6.0 cm in a comparison of Chilean groups in Santiago, Colombian groups in Bogotá, Indian groups in Bombay and Hyderabad, Nigerian groups in Ibadan and Lagos, and Turkish groups in Istanbul. Differences were between 2.5 and 5.0 cm in comparisons of English children in Newcastle upon Tyne, Indian children in Delhi, Iraqi children in Baghdad, Tunisian children in Tunis, South African white children in Johannesburg, and United States white children living in scattered poverty areas and an upper class residential area of Cleveland.

2. Average standing height of children in well-to-do families surpassed that of cohorts in low income families by relative amounts between 3.5 and 13.8% in Indian comparisons (I-1, II-5, III-1, III-5, IX-1), between 7.3 and 10.4% in Nigerian comparisons (II-3, III-6), and between 2.8 and 5.3% in a comparison of white groups in England, South Africa, and the United States (III-8, III-10, III-11). Relative differences were large (13.0%) in the Turkish comparison and small (2.8%) in the Iraqi comparison.

3. From data collected in the early 1970s, means for standing height were 92.3 cm for 87 Iraqi children living in "fashionable residential areas" of Baghdad and 4.5 cm higher for 92 Russian children living under superior conditions at Petropavlovsk. From measures of stature taken during the period 1956–1966, means were 83.6 cm for 323 progeny of low income families in India (III-5) and 13.1 cm higher on 1596 progeny of unskilled and semiskilled workers in the Netherlands (III-12).

2. *Age 5 Years*

In Table X, 38 socioeconomic comparisons were aggregated for stature at ages between 5 and 5.7 years. Sources and sample descriptions not provided earlier were as follows:

Tags X-1 and X-2: Statistics based on measures taken during 1972 in 6 areas of Scotland (X-1) and 22 areas of England (X-2); children in the "Low status" category were offspring of "semiskilled and unskilled" workers and those in the "High status" category were members of "professional and managerial" families (Rona, Swan, & Altman, 1978; R. J. Rona, personal communication, 1981).

Table X revealed, for example:

1. Differences in average standing height of children belonging to families of low and high socioeconomic status were in one direction consistently. For 31 of the 38 rows, the inference was tenable that the "High status" population, on average, was taller than the "Low status" population.

2. Absolute and relative differences for the ordered "terminal segment" comparisons varied from 1.6 to 20.8 cm, and from 1.5 to 23.4%. Differences greater

TABLE X
Standing Height (cm) at Age 5 Years: Means for Children of Both Sexes in Relation to Socioeconomic Status

Tag	Group	Low status		High status		High taller than low by	
		Sample size	Mean height	Sample size	Mean height	(cm)	(%)
	Comparisons for terminal segments of the socioeconomic continuum						
I-1	Indian, Bombay	~150	88.9	~35	109.7	20.8[a]	23.4
III-3	Turkish, Istanbul	113	97.1	~70	109.5	12.4	12.8
IV-2	Guatemalan[b]	42	100.4	49	111.5	11.1	11.1
IV-1	Indian, Bombay	87	100.9	23	112.0	11.1	11.0
II-3	Nigerian, Lagos	29	101.2	11	110.6	9.4	9.3
II-4	Chilean, Santiago	~120	99.8	~35	109.0	9.2	9.2
III-6	Nigerian, Ibadan	236	102.0	185	110.2	8.2	8.0
I-7	Colombian, Bogotá	66	99.5	64	107.5	8.0	8.0
IV-4	Polish, Breslau	70	102.1	19	108.9	6.8	6.7
III-5	Indian, national	343	97.1	333	103.0	5.9	6.1
II-5	Indian, two states	~100	102.1	>25	108.0	5.9	5.8
IV-6	English, Birmingham	>100	96.7	>100	101.8	5.1	5.3
IV-3	Jamaican Black[b]	143	107.6	25	112.4	4.8	4.5
III-8	South African White	176	105.8	88	110.6	4.8	4.5
III-9	Tunisian, Tunis	52	103.8	48	107.2	3.4	3.3
IX-1	Indian, Delhi	534	103.0	146	105.9	2.9	2.8
III-4	Iraqi, Baghdad	30	103.2	85	105.7	2.5	2.4
X-1	British, Scotland[c]	38	106.5	20	108.7	2.2	2.1
X-2	British, England[c]	112	108.2	113	110.0	1.8	1.7
III-12	Dutch, Netherlands	1319	110.7	95	112.4	1.7	1.5
III-7	Russian, Asian town	143	107.8	186	109.4	1.6	1.5
IV-7	Aruba Islander	81	108.5	27	110.1	1.6	1.5
	Comparisons involving wider segments of the socioeconomic continuum						
IV-8	Chilean, Santiago	111	101.8	141	107.6	5.8	5.7
IV-10	United States White[b]	202	108.5[d]	498	113.6[d]	5.1	4.7
II-13	Swiss, Zurich	22	107.2[e]	39	112.2[e]	5.0	4.7
II-9	Chinese, two towns	~80	101.7	188	106.4	4.7	4.6
III-13	Nigerian, two sites	~35	101.1	ns[f]	105.8	4.7	4.6
IV-12	English, N.E. town[g]	123	108.7	28	112.0	3.3	3.0
IV-15	English, Birmingham[b]	>40	109.2	~30	112.5	3.3	3.0
IV-11	United States Black[b]	384	111.6[d]	119	114.7[d]	3.1	2.8
II-14	Swedish, Stockholm	67	110.0[e]	43	112.9[e]	2.9	2.6
II-15	French, Paris	67	106.4[e]	28	108.6[e]	2.2	2.1
IV-9	Armenian, Beirut	151	107.2	207	109.3	2.1	2.0

(continued)

TABLE X (*Continued*)

Tag	Group	Low status: Sample size	Low status: Mean height	High status: Sample size	High status: Mean height	High taller than low by (cm)	High taller than low by (%)
	Comparisons involving wider segments of the socioeconomic continuum						
IV-13	United States White	1738	107.2	1493	109.1	1.9	1.8
IV-16	United States Black and White	88	107.8[h]	215	109.7	1.9	1.8
IV-14	East German	121	105.8	1985	107.6	1.8	1.7
II-16	English, London	69	108.4[e]	19	109.8[e]	1.4	1.3
II-17	Belgian, Brussels	32	109.7[e]	43	110.6[e]	.9	.8

[a]Using 5.0 cm as population standard deviations and estimating at $p = .01$, one can infer that the paired socioeconomic groups in all rows except II-15, II-16, II-17, III-4, III-13, IV-7, and X-1 were dependably different in stature at age 5 years (Meredith, 1978a).

[b]Age 5.5 years.

[c]Age 5.1 years.

[d]Median.

[e]Recumbent vertex–soles length.

[f]Sample size not specified (ns).

[g]Age 5.7 years.

[h]Means were 107.9 cm for 186 "underprivileged" black children in New Orleans (Cherry, 1968) and, for 184 white and 65 black children of the unskilled and semiskilled classes, 108.3 and 109.7 cm, respectively (Owen *et al.*, 1974).

than 3.0 cm and 3.0% were obtained for Chilean children in Santiago, Colombian children in Bogotá, English children in Birmingham, Indian children in Bombay, Nigerian children in Ibadan, Tunisian children in Tunis, Turkish children in Istanbul, and white South African children in Johannesburg.

3. Among analyses of data gathered during the decade of 1956 to 1965 on children in families of low socioeconomic status, averages for stature at age 5 years were 97.1 cm in Istanbul (III-3) and 110.7 cm in the Netherlands (III-12). The Turkish subgroup was 13.6 cm, or 12.3%, shorter than the Dutch subgroup. Similarly, a national sample of Indian children in lower class families (III-5) averaged 13.6 cm (12.3%) shorter than the large sample of Dutch peers.

4. Averages for stature were 96.7 cm at age 5 years for English children measured in about 1910 in a poor district of Birmingham (IV-6) and 108.7 cm at age 5.7 years for English children measured during 1952 in low income families at Newcastle upon Tyne (IV-12). Reducing the 108.7-cm average by 4.0 cm as an estimated adjustment to age 5 years gave a probable secular increase near 8.0 cm for a period of about 40 years.

Socioeconomic comparisons for standing height at age 6 years—but not at either 5 or 7 years—were reported by Ewart (1912), Hundley *et al.* (1955), Schmid-Monnard (1901), and Topp, Cook, Holland, and Elliott (1970). Schmid-Monnard, using data collected at Halle, obtained means of 105.4 cm for 56 children of the "laboring and poorer classes" and 110.4 cm (4.7% higher) for 96 children of the middle (skilled, mercantile, clerical) classes. From measures taken in 1911 in Middlesbrough, Ewart obtained means of 102.4 cm for 267 "inhabitants of slum property" and 105.4 cm (2.9% higher) for 281 children of the "superior artizen class."

Records on white children in Philadelphia measured between 1925 and 1949 gave means of 112.2 cm for 1674 pupils attending schools in areas "underprivileged economically" and 115.8 cm (3.2% higher) for 2571 pupils at schools in "economically favored" areas (Hundley *et al.*, 1955). Means from data collected between 1964 and 1965 "in four areas of Kent" (Topp *et al.*, 1970) were 109.4 cm for 941 progeny of "unskilled and semiskilled" workers, and 110.7 cm (1.2% higher) for 988 members of "professional and managerial" families. Each of these comparisons at age 6 years yielded differences statistically significant at the $p = .01$ level.

C. LATER CHILDHOOD

1. Age 7 Years

Socioeconomic comparisons for standing height at age 7 years were assembled in Table XI. Except for the following, the row samples and sources were identified earlier:

Tag XI-1: Measures taken by Freeman (1914) on New York "orphanage" children and "well-cared-for" children supervised in private pediatric practice.

Tag XI-2: Records amassed during 1965 in England, Scotland, and Wales on offspring of parents in the "unskilled" and "professional and managerial" categories (Goldstein, 1971).

Tag XI-3: Data collected in Boston between 1875 and 1876 on children of parents in the occupational categories "unskilled" and "professional" (Bowditch, 1879).

Tag XI-4: Data collected in Guatemala City on children of "low socioeconomic families" completing primary school—many of the poor did not complete primary school (Bogin & MacVean, 1978)—and on peers of "the highest socioeconomic levels of the country . . . whose parents were native born and each possessed a Spanish surname" (Johnston, Wainer, Thissen, & MacVean, 1976).

Tag XI-5: Measures taken in 1953 on children of parents in the "lower manual" and "upper middle" socioeconomic categories (Douglas & Simpson, 1964).

TABLE XI
Standing Height (cm) at Age 7 Years: Means for Children of Both Sexes in Relation to Socioeconomic Status

Tag	Group	Low status		High status		High taller than low by	
		Sample size	Mean height	Sample size	Mean height	(cm)	(%)
	Comparisons for terminal segments of the socioeconomic continuum						
I-1	Indian, Bombay	~150	101.6	~35	117.6	16.0[a]	15.7
V-1	Indian, several sites	165	107.3	262	120.6	13.3	12.4
III-3	Turkish, Istanbul	113	109.4	~70	121.0	11.6	10.6
V-2	Ghanaian, Accra	~70	113.3	~50	122.2	8.9	7.9
V-5	United States White	84	112.5	23	121.4	8.9	7.9
V-7	British, several sites	105	115.4	71	124.1	8.7	7.5
III-6	Yoruba, Ibadan	165	113.5	118	121.9	8.4	7.4
XI-1	United States White	~70	116.3	~20	123.7	7.4	6.4
V-4	Colombian, two towns	71	111.7	~60	118.4	6.7	6.0
IX-1	Indian, Delhi	548	113.5	152	118.8	5.3	4.7
III-5	Indian, national	386	109.6	345	114.8	5.2	4.7
IV-6	English, Birmingham[b]	>100	112.0	>100	117.0	5.0	4.5
IV-3	Jamaican Black	812	116.5	28	121.7	5.2	4.5
V-10	Scottish, Glasgow	2759	109.1	966	113.8	4.7	4.3
V-9	Chinese, Peking[c]	ns[d]	113.0	21	117.1	4.1	3.6
V-11	Chinese, Hong Kong	851	114.6	197	118.4	3.8	3.3
III-9	Tunisian, Tunis	46	114.9	38	118.3	3.4	3.0
V-8	United States White	130	118.9	168	122.2	3.3	2.8
XI-2	British, Great Britain[b]	>2000	118.3	>500	121.6	3.3	2.8
V-13	United States White	183	119.8	285	123.0	3.2	2.7
X-12	British, Scotland	46	118.1	31	120.9	2.8	2.4
IV-5	Indian, Delhi	56	112.7	59	115.1	2.4	2.1
V-12	United States White[c]	51	121.4	55	123.6	2.2	1.8
X-2	British, England	191	119.5	174	121.4	1.9	1.6
III-12	Dutch, Netherlands	1331	122.7	85	124.4	1.7	1.4
V-14	Australian, Queensland	212	119.6	57	121.3	1.7	1.4
V-16	United States White	147	117.6	74	119.2	1.6	1.4
V-15	Danish, Copenhagen	880	119.0	613	120.5	1.5	1.3
V-6	Haitian, Port au Prince	208	119.5	234	121.0	1.5	1.3
XI-3	United States White	123	113.3	43	114.8	1.5	1.3
III-7	Russian, Asian town	80	118.9	131	120.4	1.5	1.3
V-17	English, London[e]	>1000	114.0	>800	115.3	1.3	1.1
	Comparisons involving wider segments of the socioeconomic continuum						
XI-4	Guatemalan, capital[b]	70	116.3	35	123.2	6.9	5.9
V-18	Mexican, two sites	50	111.7	166	118.0	6.3	5.6

TABLE XI (*Continued*)

Tag	Group	Low status: Sample size	Low status: Mean height	High status: Sample size	High status: Mean height	High taller than low by (cm)	High taller than low by (%)
	Comparisons involving wider segments of the socioeconomic continuum						
V-20	Scottish, Glasgow	233	108.7	71	113.8	5.1	4.7
VI-9	Spanish, Barcelona[c]	100	116.4	62	121.2	4.8	4.1
IV-10	United States White	137	118.2[f]	624	121.9[f]	3.7	3.1
IV-11	United States Black	224	121.0[f]	136	124.4[f]	3.4	2.8
XI-5	British, Great Britain	>600	118.7	>400	121.7	3.0	2.5
V-21	Canadian, Ottawa	~140	118.0	~140	120.8	2.8	2.4
IV-15	English, Birmingham	>40	118.4	~30	121.3	2.9	2.4
XI-6	French, several cities	>1000	118.3	>150	120.7	2.4	2.0
V-22	Danish, Copenhagen	100	113.5	123	115.8	2.3	2.0
IV-13	United States White	4829	119.3	4617	120.7	1.4	1.2
IV-16	United States Black and White	59	120.5	115	121.9	1.4	1.2
V-24	United States White	412	115.1	367	116.2	1.1	1.0

[a]Using 5.6 cm as population standard deviations (O'Brien *et al.*,1941) and estimating at $p = .01$, one can infer in 36 instances that the paired socioeconomic groups differed significantly in stature at age 7 years. Comparisons not allowing this level of confidence are those in rows III-9, IV-5, IV-15, IV-16, V-9, V-12, V-14, V-16, X-1, and XI-3.

[b]Age 7.5 years.

[c]Males only.

[d]Sample size not specified (ns).

[e]Age 7.1 years.

[f]Median.

Tag XI-6: Materials gathered in 1955 in urban centers with more than 50,000 inhabitants; offspring of "skilled and unskilled laborers" compared with peers in "professional and major managerial" families (Aubenque & Desabie, 1957).

Table XI showed, for example:

1. Average standing height was greater for children represented in the "High status" column than those in the "Low status" column with whom they were aligned by absolute amounts from 1.1 to 16.0 cm, and relative amounts from 1.0 to 15.7%. In comparisons for terminal segments of the socioeconomic continuum, 62% of the averages for children in professional and major managerial families exceeded those for progeny of unskilled and semiskilled workers by not less than 3.0 cm, or 2.5%.
2. From comparisons in which the number of children in each socioeconomic

subgroup was at least 50, absolute differences in stature were 6.0 cm or more for British (V-7), Colombian (V-4), Ghanaian (V-2), Indian (V-1), Mexican (V-18), Nigerian (III-6), and Turkish (III-3) children. Differences were between 3.0 and 6.0 cm in other comparisons for British (IV-6, V-10, V-20, XI-2, XI-5), Chinese (V-11), Indian (III-5, IX-1), Spanish (VI-9), United States black (IV-11), and United States white (IV-10, V-8, V-13) children. Each of these comparisons allowed the inference of a highly likely difference between the subgroup populations.

3. Stature averages from measures taken during the 1960s on children in high income families were 114.8 cm in India (III-5), 118.4 cm in Bogotá and Hong Kong (V-4, V-11), 121.0 cm in Port au Prince (V-6), and 124.4 cm in the Netherlands (III-12). Dutch children, on average, were taller than the Haitian children by 2.8%, the Chinese and Colombian children by 5.1%, and the Indian children by 8.4%.

4. Means based on stature data collected in the 1970s showed progeny in ''lower income'' families in Hyderabad City (V-1) were shorter than English progeny of ''semiskilled and unskilled'' laborers (X-2) by 12.2 cm, or 10.2%. An intermediate ''Low status'' Mexican subgroup (V-18) was shorter than the English subgroup by 7.8 cm, or 6.5%.

5. Stature averages evincing large secular increase were 113.8 cm for children measured between 1905 and 1906 in the ''best residential'' districts of Glasgow (V-10) and 4.3 cm (3.8%) *higher* for Scottish offspring of ''semiskilled and unskilled'' workers measured in 1972 (X-1). Similarly for United States white children, stature averages were 114.8 cm from measures of members of the ''professional'' class taken between 1875 and 1876 in Boston (XI-3) and 4.1 cm (3.6%) *higher* from data collected between 1963 and 1965 on a wide sampling of children in ''low income'' families (V-8).

2. *Age 9 Years*

Sample descriptions and references for 55 of the comparative rows in Table XII were supplied in conjunction with earlier tables. Three other rows pertain to:

Tag XII-1: Measures taken in 1932 on children of northwest European ancestry and low economic status attending schools ''in the mountains of eastern Tennessee'' (Wheeler, 1933) compared with contemporary peers attending private schools in Illinois and New York (Gray & Fraley, 1926; Gray & Gower, 1928).

Tag XII-2: Data collected between 1955 and 1956 on progeny of ''unskilled'' and ''professional and managerial'' parents (Craig, 1963).

Tag XII-3: Records on English boys assembled from several sources and sorted by parental occupation into ''labouring'' and ''non-labouring'' categories (Roberts, 1876).

TABLE XII
Standing Height (cm) at Age 9 Years: Means for Children of Both Sexes in Relation to Socioeconomic Status

Tag	Group	Low status		High status		High taller than low by	
		Sample size	Mean height	Sample size	Mean height	(cm)	(%)
	Comparisons for terminal segments of the socioeconomic continuum						
I-1	Indian, Bombay	~150	110.5	~35	124.0	13.5[a]	12.2
V-1	Indian, several sites	176	119.0	436	130.4	11.4	9.6
V-2	Ghanaian, Accra	~70	123.0	~50	133.4	10.4	8.5
IV-1	Punjabi, Delhi	61	120.4	48	130.6	10.2	8.5
XI-1	United States White	~70	125.2	~20	134.6	9.4	7.5
V-7	British, several sites	130	125.7	115	134.1	8.4	6.7
VI-2	Indian, Hyderabad[b]	55	118.9	246	126.8	7.9	6.6
III-6	Yoruba, Ibadan	58	124.3	51	132.4	8.1	6.5
V-4	Colombian, two towns	118	121.3	~60	128.8	7.5	6.2
VI-3	Italian, Turino	79	116.2	24	123.3	7.1	6.1
VI-4	Guatemalan, Spanish	46	124.6	46	131.9[c]	7.3	5.9
V-5	United States White[d]	132	123.1	68	130.3	7.2	5.8
XII-1	United States White	152	127.1	167	134.3	7.2	5.7
III-5	Indian, national	377	118.9	336	125.5	6.6	5.6
VI-11	United States White[e]	>100	122.9	>100	129.0	6.1	5.0
IV-3	Jamaican Black	1625	126.6	35	132.6	6.0	4.7
IX-1	Indian, Delhi	535	125.8	138	131.3	5.5	4.4
V-10	Scottish, Glasgow	2716	118.9	1032	124.0	5.1	4.3
XII-2	Scottish, Glasgow[f]	1528	128.7	86	134.0	5.3	4.1
V-9	Chinese, Peking[g]	ns[h]	121.0	46	125.5	4.5	3.7
V-13	United States White	267	129.8	310	134.5	4.7	3.6
VI-6	Turkish, Istanbul	110	127.2	104	131.4	4.2	3.3
V-11	Chinese, Hong Kong	1129	124.6	415	128.4	3.8	3.0
III-9	Tunisian, Tunis	45	126.5	41	130.1	3.6	2.8
VI-8	Filipino, Manila	960	119.4	124	122.5	3.1	2.6
V-8	United States White	138	130.6	192	133.7	3.1	2.4
IV-7	Aruba Islander[g]	73	130.4	13	133.5	3.1	2.4
VI-7	United States White, Missouri[i]	68	130.6	64	133.5	2.9	2.2
V-6	Haitian, Port au Prince	222	129.5	221	131.8	2.3	1.8
IV-5	Indian, Delhi	55	121.9	43	124.1	2.2	1.8
III-12	Dutch, Netherlands	1149	134.5	88	136.8	2.3	1.7
V-16	United States White	193	128.7	98	130.8	2.1	1.6
X-1	British, Scotland	54	129.5	21	131.2	1.7	1.3
V-15	Danish, Copenhagen	1350	128.8	912	130.4	1.6	1.2
X-2	British, England	199	130.9	180	132.5	1.6	1.2
V-17	English, London[j]	~1000	125.1	~800	126.6	1.5	1.2
V-14	Australian, Queensland	231	131.3	64	131.5	.2	.2

(continued)

TABLE XII (*Continued*)

Tag	Group	Low status		High status		High taller than low by	
		Sample size	Mean height	Sample size	Mean height	(cm)	(%)
	Comparisons involving wider segments of the socioeconomic continuum						
V-18	Mexican, two sites	72	120.4	136	128.9	8.5	7.1
XI-4	Guatemalan, capital	144	123.2	134	130.1	6.9	5.6
VI-10	Norwegian, Oslo	3098	125.7	83	131.5	5.8	4.6
V-20	Scottish, Glasgow	277	117.6	78	122.7	5.1	4.3
VI-9	Spanish, Barcelona	100	124.1	100	129.2	5.1	4.1
VI-12	Dutch, Netherlands	174	129.7	166	134.2	4.5	3.5
VI-14	English, several towns	1637	119.5	166	123.6	4.1	3.4
IV-10	United States White	130	129.3[k]	639	133.3[k]	4.0	3.1
XII-3	English, several sites[f]	1252	124.0	62	127.9	3.9	3.1
IV-11	United States Black	198	131.2[k]	152	135.1[k]	3.9	3.0
VI-11	United States Black	29	133.4	30	137.1	3.7	2.8
VI-13	Swedish, Stockholm	~400	123.3	~200	126.7	3.4	2.8
IV-12	English, N.E. town	134	126.8	42	130.2	3.4	2.7
V-21	Canadian, Ottawa	~140	128.3	~140	131.5	3.2	2.5
XI-6	French, several cities	>1000	128.6	>150	131.5	2.9	2.3
IV-16	United States Black and White	50	130.0	114	132.9	2.9	2.2
XI-5	United States White	121	124.0	39	126.4	2.4	1.9
V-22	Danish, Copenhagen	191	123.4	169	124.9	1.5	1.2
IV-15	English, Birmingham	>40	128.0	~30	129.5	1.5	1.2
IV-13	United States White	6097	130.0	5716	131.5	1.5	1.2
V-24	United States White	703	125.4	613	126.2	.8	.6

[a]Using 6.2 cm as population standard deviations (Jones, Hemphill, & Meyers, 1973) and estimating at $p = .01$, one can infer in 47 instances that the paired socioeconomic groups differed significantly in stature at age 9 years. Comparisons not allowing this level of confidence were those in rows IV-5, IV-7, IV-15, V-9, V-14, V-22, V-24, VI-9, X-1, X-2, and XI-5.

[b]Females only.

[c]A mean of 131.5 cm was obtained for 62 Bolivian Spanish children living in La Paz in families of "doctors, lawyers, engineers, accountants, architects" and others in the professional stratum; over 80% of the children had resided since birth at "altitudes between 3200 and 3600 meters" (Stinson, 1982).

[d]Jewish children living in New York City (V-5 and Boas, 1923).

[e]Age 8.5 years.

[f]Age 9.5 years.

[g]Males only.

[h]Sample size not specified (ns).

[i]Age 8.9 years.

[j]Age 9.1 years.

[k]Median.

Table XII revealed, for example:

1. Averages for stature during the 1960s in upper class families were 122.5 cm for Filipino children in Manila (VI-8), 128.4 cm for Chinese children in Hong Kong (V-11), and 132.4 cm for Nigerian children in Ibadan (III-6). The Nigerian children were taller than their Chinese and Filipino age peers by 3.1 and 8.1%, respectively.
2. Other comparisons for average stature in the 1960s showed that United States black children of "poverty area" families (IV-11) were taller than age peers of *upper class* Filipino families by 8.7 cm, or 7.1%. Similarly, United States white children of "low income" families (V-8) exceeded age peers in upper class Filipino families by 8.1 cm, or 6.6%.
3. From subgroup samples of 50 or more children, obtained differences in stature between terminal segments of the socioeconomic continuum were above 8.0 cm and 6.5% for British (V-7), Ghanaian (V-2), Indian (V-1, VI-2), and Nigerian (III-6) comparisons. Differences near 1.5 cm and 1.2% were obtained from Danish (V-15) and English (V-17) comparisons. Intermediate absolute values were 5.1 cm for Scottish children in Glasgow (V-10), 4.2 cm for Turkish children in Istanbul (IV-6), and 2.3 cm for Haitian children in Port au Prince (V-6). In each of these 10 instances, rejection of the null hypothesis was tenable at a high level of confidence.

In a study on English children of different socioeconomic groups, Hammond (1957) analyzed data for increase in height during several annual periods. Between ages 8 and 9 years, average increments were 4.4 cm for 140 children in working class families and 5.5 cm for 76 age peers in professional and executive families. Comparable findings for the period between ages 9 and 10 years were 4.1 and 5.5 cm for samples of 184 and 94, respectively.

Data collected in "a semi-urban area of Cairo" by Hafez, Salem, Cole, Galal, and Massoud (1981) indicated that at age 9.5 years averages for standing height, body weight, and arm girth were smaller for 17 boys in families of unskilled workers than for 8 boys with parents in the professional, managerial, or civil service categories.

Rajalakshmi and Chandrasekaran (1967) showed graphically that at all ages from 2 to 10 years Indian children in Baroda City were shorter in "poor localities" than in "residential areas."

Across the age period between 6 and 10 years, Prokopec, Titlbachová, Zlámalová, and Padevětová (1979) reported that average stature was near 3.5 cm higher for Czechoslovakian sons of fathers with university education than those of fathers with basic education only.

On about 200 Quechua and 300 mestizo children between ages 6 and 11 years living at Lamas, Peru, "skinfold thickness and upper arm muscle" were used by

Frisancho, Guire, Babler, Borkan, and Way (1980) to derive estimates of nutritional adequacy. The "poor nutrition" groups, on average, were 5.8 and 5.2 cm shorter than the "good nutrition" groups.

D. SUMMARY

Overall, more than 200 socioeconomic comparisons for stature in infancy and childhood were brought together by means of Tables VII through XII and additional text citations. The entire series pertained to "terminal segments" and "wider segments" of the socioeconomic continuum. Comparisons for terminal social class groups numbered 128. Of these 128, 105 (82%) allowed rejection of the null hypothesis and made tenable the inference of taller upper than lower class childhood populations.

IV. Socioeconomic Comparisons for Head, Trunk, and Limbs

A. INFANCY

Socioeconomic differences at birth and age 1 year were itemized in Tables XIII and XIV for head girth, chest girth, hip width, arm girth, and calf girth. In addition, Table XIII included comparisons for shoulder width and stem (head, neck, and trunk) length. Sources for the studies represented in several rows were as follows:

Tag XIII-1: Infants born between 1962 and 1967 into families of the "unskilled" and "professional or major managerial" classes (Banik, Krishna, Mane, & Raj, 1970a).

Tag XIII-2: Male infants born into "very poor homes" compared with peers of the same sex born into homes of "moderate income" (Bakwin & Bakwin, 1936).

Tag XIV-1: Detroit infants of "the indigent and near-indigent class" receiving regular pediatric examinations, the mothers advised on feeding by visiting nurses (Kelly & Reynolds, 1947), compared with Boston infants "in homes of low to middle economic circumstances," the mothers given "periodic health and nutritional advice" (Vickers & Stuart, 1943).

Examples of findings extractable from Tables XIII and XIV were the following:

1. Among the 24 infancy comparisons, none showed a somatic average for infants of low socioeconomic status to equal (or exceed) that for comparable groups of middle or upper socioeconomic status.

TABLE XIII
Head, Trunk, and Limb Dimensions (cm) at Birth: Means for Both Sexes, or Males only, in Relation to Socioeconomic Class

		Lower class		Higher class		Higher larger by	
Tag	Group	Number	Mean	Number	Mean	(cm)	(%)
		Head girth					
I-5	Romanian, Bucharest[a]	30	34.1	30	35.0	.9[b]	2.6
XIII-1	Indian, Delhi	730	33.7[c]	79	34.3	.6[b]	1.8
VII-5	Danish, Odense	155	34.7	156	34.9	.2	.6
		Chest girth					
I-5	Romanian, Bucharest[a]	30	32.0	30	33.1	1.1	3.4
XIII-1	Indian, Delhi	730	32.1	79	33.0	.9[b]	2.8
I-12	Bengali, Calcutta	60	30.4	50	31.2	.8	2.6
XIII-2	United States White[a]	470	31.4[d]	205	31.9	.5[b]	1.6
VII-5	Danish, Odense	155	31.4	156	31.6	.2	.6
		Shoulder width					
XIII-2	United States White[a]	470	11.4	205	11.5	.1	.9
		Hip width					
XIII-1	Indian, Delhi	730	8.3	79	8.6	.3[b]	3.6
XIII-2	United States White[a]	470	7.6	205	7.7	.1	1.3
		Stem (vertex–subischia) length					
I-5	Romanian, Bucharest[a]	30	33.2	30	34.2	1.0	3.0
		Arm girth					
XIII-1	Indian, Delhi	730	9.1	79	9.5	.4[b]	4.4
		Calf girth					
XIII-1	Indian, Delhi	730	9.9	79	10.3	.4[b]	4.0

[a]Males only.

[b]Using as population standard deviations 1.3 cm for head girth, 1.7 cm for chest girth, .8 cm for shoulder width, .6 cm for hip width, 1.6 cm for stem length, .7 cm for arm girth, and .9 cm for calf girth (Kasius *et al.*, 1957) and estimating at $p = .01$, one can infer that where the superscript *b* appears the paired socioeconomic groups differed significantly.

[c]An identical mean was obtained for a contemporary group of 200 United States black neonates born in New Orleans into "underprivileged" homes (Cherry, 1968).

[d]This average for United States white male infants born into "very poor homes" in New York City in the early 1930s is similar to the average of 31.5 cm reported for 99 United States black peers born into "underprivileged" homes in New Orleans in the early 1960s (Cherry, 1968).

TABLE XIV
Head, Trunk, and Limb Dimensions (cm) at Age 1 Year: Means for Both Sexes Together in Relation to Socioeconomic Class

Tag	Group	Lower class		Higher class		Higher larger by	
		Number	Mean	Number	Mean	(cm)	(%)
			Head girth				
XIII-1	Indian, Delhi	399	43.6	47	45.0	1.4[a]	3.2
III-6	Yoruba, Ibadan	299	45.0	198	46.2	1.2	2.7
XIV-1	United States White	249	45.7[b]	234	46.5	.8	1.8
			Chest girth				
I-12	Bengali, Calcutta	60	43.7	50	47.8	4.1	9.4
XIII-1	Indian, Delhi	399	42.6	47	45.3	2.7	6.3
XIV-1	United States White	249	45.5	232	47.5	2.0	4.4
			Hip width				
XIII-1	Indian, Delhi	399	11.5	47	12.3	.8	7.0
			Arm girth				
III-6	Yoruba, Ibadan	319	13.7	203	15.3	1.6	11.7
XIII-1	Indian, Delhi	399	13.0	47	14.1	1.1	8.5
			Calf girth				
XIII-1	Indian, Delhi	399	15.1	47	17.1	2.0	13.2

[a]Using as population standard deviations 1.4 cm for head girth, 2.2 cm for chest girth, .8 cm for hip width, 1.2 cm for arm girth, and 1.4 cm for calf girth (Kasius *et al.*, 1957; Meredith and Boynton, 1937) and estimating at $p = .01$, one can infer the two socioeconomic groups represented in each row differed dependably in the somatic variable specified.

[b]This average for United States white infants of the "indigent and near-indigent class" at Detroit is identical with the average obtained for United States black infants of the "underprivileged" class in New Orleans (Cherry, 1968).

2. At birth, offspring of parents of low economic status at Bucharest, Calcutta, and Delhi were smaller than ethnic peers of high economic status by average amounts between .4 and 1.1 cm for head girth, chest girth, arm girth, and calf girth. At age 1 year, socioeconomically similar comparisons at Calcutta, Delhi, and Ibadan yielded differences between 1.1 and 4.1 cm.

3. Relative differences from data collected in Delhi showed that upper class

neonates surpassed lower class neonates by 1.8% in head girth, 2.8% in chest girth, 3.6% in hip width, and 4.4% in arm girth. At age 1 year, corresponding differences were 3.2, 6.3, 7.0, and 8.5%, respectively. Similarly, comparisons for chest girth on United States white infants of low and middle social classes registered greater relative differences at age 1 year (4.4%) than at birth (1.6%).

B. EARLY CHILDHOOD

Statistics for head, trunk, and limb dimensions of socioeconomic subgroups were ordered in Table XV at age 3 years, and Table XVI at age 5 years. Studies drawn upon in preparing several rows of these tables were as follows:

Tag XV-1: Girls "predominantly from low socioeconomic groups" living in or near Birmingham, Alabama; 63% of the fathers were unskilled workers or on relief (Wise & Meredith, 1942) compared with girls living in Boston in homes of "low to middle" economic status and participating in a normal development study providing "periodic health and nutritional advice" (Vickers & Stuart, 1943).

Tag XV-2: Comparison of boys living in areas where "protein-calorie malnutrition" was common (Vijayaraghavan & Sastry, 1976) and in "well-to-do" families (Indian National Institute of Nutrition, 1975).

Among the 43 comparative rows in Tables XV and XVI, 38 showed children in the upper part of the socioeconomic continuum to surpass age peers of low socioeconomic status by absolute amounts between .5 and 4.2 cm, and relative amounts between .9 and 17.8%. The row pertaining to chest girth of East German children age 5 years registered no difference between an orphanage sample and a kindergarten sample.

From the Indian national study of 1956–1965 (III-5), "high" status groups exceeded "low" status cohorts at ages 3 and 5 years by amounts near 3.0 cm in sitting height, and within the limits of .6 and 1.1 cm for head girth, chest girth, and hip width. Absolute differences at these ages on Yoruba children in Ibadan were between .9 and 1.5 cm for head girth and arm girth, relative differences being near 3.0% for head girth and above 5.0% for arm girth. At age 5 years, absolute and relative differences on Russian children in Petropavlovsk were 1.3 cm and 2.3%, respectively. In each of these comparisons, the number of subjects per subgroup exceeded 100.

Comparisons at age 5 years for United States white children of below and above average socioeconomic status, the number in each subgroup surpassing 1000, gave absolute differences of .3 cm for arm girth, .4 cm for hip width and calf girth, .5 cm for chest girth, and .7 cm for upper limb length. Relative differences for these dimensions were between .9 and 2.0%.

TABLE XV

Head, Trunk, and Limb Dimensions (cm) at Age 3 Years: Means for Both Sexes Together in Relation to Socioeconomic Class

Tag	Group	Lower class		Higher class		Higher larger by	
		Number	Mean	Number	Mean	(cm)	(%)
			Head Girth				
III-1	Indian, Hyderabad	300	45.7	~50	48.0	2.3[a]	5.0
XIII-1	Indian, Delhi	206	47.1	19	48.7	1.6	3.4
III-6	Yoruba, Ibadan	281	48.2[b]	194	49.7	1.5	3.1
III-5	Indian, national	254	45.9	174	47.0	1.1	2.4
III-14	Indian, Agra	40	47.4	39	47.9	.5	1.1
			Chest girth				
III-1	Indian, Hyderabad	300	46.2	~50	50.0	3.8	8.2
XIII-1	Indian, Delhi	206	47.3	19	49.1	1.8	3.8
III-7	Russian, Asian town	77	52.5	92	54.1	1.6	3.0
III-14	Indian, Agra	40	48.6	39	49.8	1.2	2.5
III-5	Indian, national	264	46.5	173	47.6	1.1	2.4
XV-1	United States White[c]	20	51.0	103	52.1	1.1	2.2
			Hip width				
XIII-1	Indian, Delhi	206	14.1	19	15.3	1.2	8.5
III-5	Indian, national	323	13.8	207	14.6	.8	5.8
XV-1	United States White[c]	20	15.8	30	16.4	.6	3.8
			Stem length: Sitting height				
III-5	Indian, national	323	48.7	207	51.7	3.0	6.2
			Arm girth				
XV-2	Indian, Hyderabad[d]	153	13.5	~35	15.9	2.4	17.8
XIII-1	Indian, Delhi	206	14.6	19	15.5	.9	6.2
III-6	Yoruba, Ibadan	299	15.4	220	16.3	.9	5.8
			Calf girth				
XIII-1	Indian, Delhi	206	17.5	19	19.4	1.9	10.9

[a]Using as population standard deviations 1.5 cm for head girth, 2.4 cm for chest girth, 1.3 cm for hip width, 1.2 cm for arm girth, and 1.4 cm for calf girth (Banik *et al.*, 1970a; Yanev, 1965) and estimating at $p = .01$, one can infer that the two socioeconomic groups represented in each row except rows III-14 (head girth and chest girth) and XV-1 (chest girth and hip width) differed significantly.

[b]A larger head girth mean (49.6 cm) was obtained from 1960–1962 data for 118 United States black children of the "underprivileged" class (Cherry, 1968).

[c]Females only.

[d]Males only.

TABLE XVI
Head, Trunk, and Limb Dimensions (cm) at Age 5 Years: Means for Both Sexes Together in Relation to Socioeconomic Class

Tag	Group	Lower class		Higher class		Higher larger by	
		Number	Mean	Number	Mean	(cm)	(%)
		Head girth					
XIII-1	Indian, Delhi	52	48.8	9	50.9	2.1[a]	4.3
III-6	Yoruba, Ibadan	233	49.5	180	50.8	1.3	2.6
IV-1	Indian, Bombay	87	49.6	23	50.7	1.1	2.2
III-5	Indian, national	201	47.9	203	48.5	.6	1.3
		Chest girth					
XIII-1	Indian, Delhi	52	49.3	9	51.2	1.9	3.9
IV-1	Indian, Bombay	87	53.1	23	54.7	1.6	3.0
III-7	Russian, Asian town	143	55.6	186	56.9	1.3	2.3
XV-1	United States White[b]	23	53.4[c]	87	54.6	1.2	2.2
III-5	Indian, national	247	50.0	184	50.7	.7	1.4
IV-13	United States White	1738	56.7	1493	57.2	.5	.9
IV-14	East German	121	55.1	1985	55.1	.0	.0
		Hip width					
XV-1	United States White[b]	23	17.2	87	18.2	1.0	5.8
III-5	Indian, national	343	15.7	333	16.5	.8	5.1
XIII-1	Indian, Delhi	52	15.8	9	16.2	.4	2.5
IV-13	United States White	1738	19.9[d]	1493	20.3	.4	2.0
		Stem length: Sitting height[e]					
IV-1	Indian, Bombay	87	52.1	23	56.3	4.2	8.1
III-5	Indian, national	343	54.2	333	57.4	3.2	5.9
XV-1	United States White[b]	23	59.6	86	60.4	.8	1.3
		Upper limb length					
IV-13	United States White	1738	37.3	1493	38.0	.7	1.9
		Arm girth					
III-6	Yoruba, Ibadan	241	15.8	187	17.2	1.4	8.9
XIII-1	Indian, Delhi	52	15.5	9	16.3	.8	5.2
IV-13	United States White	1738	16.6	1493	16.9	.3	1.8

(*continued*)

TABLE XVI (*Continued*)

Tag	Group	Lower class		Higher class		Higher larger by	
		Number	Mean	Number	Mean	(cm)	(%)
		Calf girth					
XIII-1	Indian, Delhi	52	18.9	9	20.8	1.9	10.1
IV-13	United States White	1738	22.1	1493	22.5	.4	1.8

[a]Using as population standard deviations 1.5 cm for head girth, 2.5 cm for chest girth, 1.3 cm for hip width, 2.9 cm for stem length, 2.3 cm for upper limb length, 1.3 cm for arm girth, and 1.5 cm for calf girth (Banik *et al.*, 1970c; Boynton, 1936; O'Brien *et al.*, 1941) and estimating at $p = .01$, one can infer that the two socioeconomic groups represented in each row except rows IV-13 (chest girth), IV-14 (chest girth), XV-1 (chest girth and stem length), and XIII-1 (chest girth, hip width, and arm girth) were dependably different in the body dimension indicated.

[b]Females only.

[c]This average for United States white girls "predominantly from low socioeconomic groups" measured in Birmingham, Alabama is similar to the average of 53.2 cm obtained for 94 United States black girls of the "indigent" class measured in New Orleans (Cherry, 1968).

[d]Bitrochanteric diameter. In the preceding three studies of hip width the biiliocristal diameter was measured.

[e]Row IV-1, length from vertex to pubis.

C. LATER CHILDHOOD

1. *Age 7 Years*

Socioeconomic comparisons pertaining to four somatic girths, two transverse dimensions, sitting height, and upper limb length were assembled in Table XVII. One row was assigned the following tag number:

Tag XVII-1: Measures of arm girth taken in 1976 in Guatemala City on "socioeconomically impoverished" children and age peers in the "wealthiest" families (Bogin & MacVean, 1981).

For the dimensions in Table XVII, and some additional dimensions measured at age 7 years, illustrative findings follow:

1. United States white children measured between 1937 and 1939 and grouped by sectioning the socioeconomic continuum into two parts (IV-13) gave means higher from the upper part than the lower by .3 cm in hip width and arm girth, .4 cm in calf girth, .5 cm in upper limb length, .6 cm in chest girth, .8 cm

TABLE XVII
Head, Trunk, and Limb Dimensions (cm) at Age 7 Years: Means for Both Sexes Together in Relation to Socioeconomic Class

		Lower class		Higher class		Higher larger by	
Tag	Group	Number	Mean	Number	Mean	(cm)	(%)
		Head girth					
III-6	Yoruba, Ibadan	154	50.1	113	51.6	1.5[a]	3.0
VI-9	Spanish, Barcelona[b]	100	51.6	62	52.4	.8	1.6
III-5	Indian, national	226	48.9	212	49.5	.6	1.2
V-24	United States White	408	51.1	363	51.4	.3	.6
		Chest girth					
III-7	Russian, Asian town	80	58.8	131	60.7	1.9	3.2
V-12	United States White[c]	51	57.8	55	58.6	.8	1.4
IV-13	United States White	4829	60.3	4617	60.9	.6	1.0
VI-9	Spanish, Barcelona[b]	100	60.1	62	60.7	.6	1.0
V-7	British, several sites	105	56.4	71	56.9	.5	.9
III-5	Indian, national	286	53.5	200	53.8	.3	.6
		Shoulder width					
V-7	British, several sites	105	25.0	71	26.3	1.3	5.2
VI-9	Spanish, Barcelona[b]	100	25.5	62	26.6	1.1	4.3
V-12	United States White[c]	51	26.7	55	27.2	.5	1.9
		Hip width[d]					
III-5	Indian, national	386	17.2	345	17.9	.7	4.1
VI-9	Spanish, Barcelona[b]	100	19.7	62	20.4	.7	3.6
V-7	British, several sites	105	20.7	71	21.3	.6	2.9
V-12	United States White[c]	51	19.2	55	19.5	.3	1.6
IV-13	United States White	4829	21.6	4617	21.9	.3	1.4
		Sitting height					
V-7	British, several sites	105	64.5	71	68.1	3.6	5.6
III-5	Indian, national	386	59.0	345	61.8	2.8	4.7
VI-9	Spanish, Barcelona[b]	100	62.9	62	65.8	2.9	4.6
V-20	Scottish, Glasgow	233	59.7	71	61.1	1.4	2.3
V-12	United States White	51	67.2	55	68.0	.8	1.2

(*continued*)

TABLE XVII (*Continued*)

Tag	Group	Lower class		Higher class		Higher larger by	
		Number	Mean	Number	Mean	(cm)	(%)
		Upper limb length					
VI-9	Spanish, Barcelona[b]	100	50.9	62	54.0	3.1	6.1
V-7	British, several sites	105	48.4	71	49.8	1.4	2.9
V-12	United States White[c]	51	51.3	55	52.4	1.1	2.1
IV-13	United States White	4829	41.9	4617	42.4	.5	1.2
		Arm girth					
XVII-1	Guatemalan, capital[e]	42	17.6	88	19.8	2.2	12.5
V-18	Mexican, two sites	50	16.8	166	18.6	1.8	10.7
III-6	Yoruba, Ibadan	164	16.2	118	17.9	1.7	10.5
V-7	British, several sites	105	16.4	71	16.8	.4	2.4
IV-13	United States White	4829	17.4	4617	17.7	.3	1.7
V-12	United States White[c]	51	18.2	55	18.5	.3	1.6
		Calf girth					
IV-13	United States White	4829	23.8	4617	24.2	.4	1.7
V-12	United States White[c]	51	24.5	55	24.9	.4	1.6

[a]Using as population standard deviations 1.5 cm for head girth, 3.2 cm for chest girth, 1.8 cm for shoulder width, 1.5 cm for hip width, 2.9 cm for sitting height, 2.5 cm for upper limb length, 1.7 cm for arm girth, and 1.9 cm for calf girth (Meredith & Boynton, 1937; O'Brien *et al.*, 1941; Yanev, 1965) and estimating at $p = .01$, one can infer that the two socioeconomic groups in each row except rows III-5 (chest girth), V-7 (chest girth and arm girth), V-12 (chest girth, shoulder width, hip width, sitting height, upper limb length, arm girth, calf girth), and VI-9 (chest girth) represent different somatic populations.

[b]Age 7.5 years, males only.

[c]Males only.

[d]Rows III-5, VI-9, and V-12, biiliocristal diameter; rows IV-13 and V-7, bitrochanteric diameter.

[e]Age 7.5 years.

in thigh girth, and .9 cm in lower limb length. Relative differences were between 1.0 and 2.2%. From a 1950 study on United States white boys (V-12), means were higher for those in the "professional and managerial" category than for peers in the "unskilled and semiskilled" category by .3 cm in hip width and arm girth, .4 cm in calf girth, .5 cm in shoulder width, .8 cm in chest girth and sitting height, .9 cm in abdomen girth, 1.1 cm in upper limb length, and 1.4 cm in lower limb length. Relative differences were between 1.4 and 2.6%. A

1945–1952 study on British children (V-7) gave means higher for "private school" pupils than "slum area" peers by .4 cm in arm girth, .5 cm in chest girth, .6 cm in hip width, 1.0 cm in foot length, 1.3 cm in shoulder width, 1.4 cm in upper limb length, 3.6 cm in sitting height, and 4.7 cm in lower limb length. Relative differences were 2.4, .9, 2.9, 5.5, 5.2, 2.9, 5.6, and 8.2%, respectively.

2. Yoruba children living in "well-to-do residential areas" of Ibadan during the 1960s, on average, were larger than contemporary peers living in "the poorest section" of the city by 1.5 cm (3.0%) in head girth and 1.7 cm (10.5%) in arm girth. Average arm girth of children in "wealthy" families in Guatemala City was 2.2 cm (12.5%) larger than that of Guatemalan peers in "impoverished" families. Absolute differences between means from "poor" and "upper middle class" Spanish boys measured at Barcelona between 1944 and 1945 were .6 cm for chest girth, .7 cm for hip width, .8 cm for head girth, 1.1 cm for shoulder width, 2.9 cm for sitting height, 3.1 cm for upper limb length, and 3.4 cm for lower limb length. Relative differences were between 1.0 and 6.1%.

2. *Age 9 Years*

Twenty-nine socioeconomic comparisons at age 9 years were ordered in Table XVIII. Examination of this table in conjunction with Table XVII revealed, for example:

1. Absolute differences from the large samples of United States white children age 9 years (IV-13) were .4 cm for hip width, .5 cm for arm and calf girths, .6 cm for upper limb length, .8 cm for chest girth, .9 cm for lower limb length, and 1.1 cm for thigh girth. Relative differences were between 1.2 and 2.9%. For each dimension, the differences were slightly larger at 9 than at 7 years. These differences were from bipartition of the economic continuum.

2. As in Table XVII, relative differences for arm girth in Table XVIII were more than 10.0% higher for socially privileged children in Guatemala City, Mexico City, and Ibadan than for the underprivileged peers with whom they were compared.

3. At age 7 years, averages for sitting height were 59.7 cm for Scottish children of "dockers and unskilled labourers" measured between 1921 and 1922 (V-20), and 4.8 cm higher for English children measured between 1945 and 1952 in slum areas of industrial towns (V-7). The corresponding difference obtained at age 9 years was 6.7 cm. Possibly as much as 50% of each difference was due to secular change (Meredith, 1978b); plausibly, the remainder arose from sources including variation in measurement procedure, ethnic composition, and social milieu.

TABLE XVIII
Head, Trunk, and Limb Dimensions (cm) at Age 9 Years: Means for Both Sexes Together in Relation to Socioeconomic Class

		Lower class		Higher class		Higher larger by	
Tag	Group	Number	Mean	Number	Mean	(cm)	(%)
		Head girth					
VI-7	United States White	68	51.8	64	53.2	1.4[a]	2.7
VI-9	Spanish, Barcelona[b]	100	52.2	100	52.9	.7	1.3
III-5	Indian, national	205	49.7	198	50.3	.6	1.2
V-24	United States White	696	51.8	604	52.0	.2	.4
		Chest girth					
VI-9	Spanish, Barcelona[b]	100	62.0	100	64.0	2.0	3.2
III-5	Indian, national	261	56.2	186	57.0	.8	1.4
V-7	British, several sites	130	59.5	115	60.3	.8	1.3
IV-13	United States White	6097	64.5	5716	65.3	.8	1.2
		Shoulder width					
V-7	British, several sites	130	26.6	115	28.5	1.9	7.1
VI-9	Spanish, Barcelona[b]	100	26.8	100	28.0	1.2	4.5
		Hip width[c]					
III-5	Indian, national	377	18.3	336	19.3	1.0	5.5
VI-9	Spanish, Barcelona[b]	100	20.5	100	21.6	1.1	5.4
V-7	British, several sites	130	22.3	115	23.2	.9	4.0
IV-13	United States White	6097	23.4	5716	23.8	.4	1.7
		Sitting height					
III-5	Indian, national	377	62.8	336	66.0	3.2	5.1
VI-9	Spanish, Barcelona[b]	100	66.4	100	69.4	3.0	4.5
V-7	British, several sites	130	69.1	115	71.5	2.4	3.5
V-20	Scottish, Glasgow	277	62.4	78	64.5	2.1	3.4
VI-8	Filipino, Manila	960	64.8	124	65.4	.6	.9
		Upper limb length					
VI-9	Spanish, Barcelona[b]	100	54.6	100	57.4	2.8	5.1
IV-13	United States White	6097	46.2	5716	46.8	.6	1.3
V-7	British, several sites	130	55.0	115	55.6	.6	1.1

TABLE XVIII (*Continued*)

Tag	Group	Lower class		Higher class		Higher larger by	
		Number	Mean	Number	Mean	(cm)	(%)
		Arm girth					
V-18	Mexican, two sites	72	17.8	136	20.2	2.4	13.5
XVII-1	Guatemalan, capital	55	18.5	96	20.7	2.2	11.9
III-6	Yoruba, Ibadan	58	17.1	51	19.0	1.9	11.1
V-7	British, several sites	130	17.3	115	18.3	1.0	5.8
VI-2	Indian, Hyderabad[d]	55	16.1	246	17.0	.9	5.6
IV-13	United States White	6097	18.5	5716	19.0	.5	2.7
		Calf girth					
IV-13	United States White	6097	25.6	5716	26.1	.5	2.0

[a]Using as population standard deviations 1.5 cm for head girth, 3.9 cm for chest girth, 2.0 cm for shoulder width, 1.7 cm for hip width, 3.1 cm for sitting height, 2.7 cm for upper limb length, 2.1 cm for arm girth, and 2.2 cm for calf girth (see footnote *a*, Table XVII) and estimating at $p = .01$, one can infer that the two socioeconomic groups in each row except rows III-5 (chest girth), V-24 (head girth), V-7 (chest girth, upper limb length), and VI-8 (sitting height) represent different somatic populations.

[b]Males only.

[c]See Table XVII, footnote *d*.

[d]Females only.

V. Summary

More than 500 socioeconomic comparisons of body size of infants and children were aggregated, arranged in tables, and discussed. The studies drawn upon were made in Africa (Ghana, Nigeria, South Africa, Tunisia), Asia (China, Burma, India, Iran, Iraq, Lebanon, Singapore, USSR), Australasia (Australia, Java), Central and North America (Canada, Guatemala, Mexico, United States), Europe (Belgium, British Isles, Czechoslovakia, Denmark, German Democratic Republic, France, Italy, the Netherlands, Romania, Scandinavia, Spain, Switzerland, Turkey, Federal Republic of Germany), the Philippines, South America (Brazil, Chile, Colombia, Peru, Uruguay), and the West Indies (Aruba, Haiti, Jamaica). Differences between somatic means were predominantly in the direction of higher socioeconomic groups—those from "above average" to "expensive residential" homes—exceeding those from "below average" to "slum area" homes. Statistical testing showed that for 74% of 539 comparisons the null hypothesis could be rejected at the 1% confidence level. Differences in the direction of low economic groups surpassing high economic groups were found in six instances only; these were all small differences in body weight, and none was significant statistically at or above the 5% level of confidence.

Primary attention was given to comparing offspring of parents at or near the lower end of the socioeconomic continuum (indigent, low income, underprivileged, unskilled, or semiskilled) with offspring of parents at or near the upper end of the continuum (professional or major executive, well to do, wealthy). The 343 obtained differences of this type were all in the direction of paired means being higher for children in upper than lower class families. In 272 instances (79% of 343), a dependable difference in body size of the paired terminal populations could be inferred at $p = .01$.

Summary statements were formulated for the social class comparisons described in the preceding paragraph. Those on body weight were as follows:

1. From 23 pairs of means at birth, typical absolute and relative differences were near .2 kg and 6.0%. Composite averages from eight studies on Indian neonates in Bombay, Calcutta, Coonoor, Delhi, Hyderabad, and Madras gave an absolute difference of .35 kg (the lower and upper class means were 2.63 and 2.99 kg, respectively) and a relative difference of 13.4%. Smaller relative differences were near 7.5% for Javanese neonates in Jogjakarta, 5.0% for Iranian neonates in Shiraz and Teheran, and 4.0% for United States black neonates in Baltimore and Washington D.C., and 1.5% for Arab neonates in Beirut.

2. Typical absolute and relative differences in body weight from 12 pairs of means at age 1 year were near 1.1 kg and 14.0%. Absolute differences varied from .7 kg for Tunisian infants in Tunis to 2.1 kg for United States white infants in New York and Cleveland. Variation among relative differences was from near 7.5% for Tunisian infants in Tunis, through 12.0% for Colombian infants in Bogotá, and 21.0% for Chilean infants in Santiago, to 26.0% for Bengali infants in Calcutta.

3. Typical differences were near 1.9 kg (15.0%) in 17 pair of means at age 3 years, and 2.1 kg (14.0%) in 21 pair of means at age 5 years. Where sample sizes exceeded 30, differences greater than 2.5 kg were obtained for children age 3 years in Bombay and Hyderabad, and for children age 5 years in Bombay, Ibadan, Istanbul, and Santiago (Chile). Corresponding differences between 1.0 and 2.0 kg were obtained for children age 3 years in Baghdad, Bogotá, Ibadan, Johannesburg (white), Petropavlovsk, and Tunis and for children age 5 years in Birmingham (England), Delhi, Johannesburg (white), and Petropavlovsk.

4. From *combined* ordering of 27 paired comparisons at age 7 years and 32 at age 9 years, typical absolute and relative differences were near 2.3 kg and 11.0%. At both ages, relative differences were between 19.0 and 49.0% for

Colombian, Ghanaian, Indian, and Nigerian children, and between 1.0 and 4.0% for Australian children in Queensland, Danish children in Copenhagen, and Dutch children in the Netherlands. The typical relative difference from 10 comparisons of United States white children was near 7.0%.

For stature, statements derived from aligning averages on infants and children in the "low" and "high" tails of the socioeconomic distribution were as follows:

1. Among paired means for body length of neonates, typical absolute and relative differences were .9 cm and 1.8% for Romanian males in Bucharest. Differences were larger for Uruguayan neonates in Montevideo, and Indian neonates in Baroda, Bombay, and Calcutta; they were smaller for Brazilian neonates in Bello Horizonte, Colombian neonates in Bogotá, Lebanese neonates in Beirut, and United States black neonates in Washington D.C.
2. Typical differences in body length from 10 pairs of means at age 1 year were near 2.9 cm and 4.0%. Relative differences were between 1.0 and 2.0% for infants in Beirut, Brussels, and Turin and between 5.0 and 7.0% for infants in Calcutta, Delhi, and Lagos.
3. Pooling and ordering absolute differences from 17 and 22 comparisons at ages 3 and 5 years, respectively, gave a distribution with a median of 5.2 cm. Values were between 1.4 and 2.0 cm for Russian children in Petropavlovsk and Dutch children in the Netherlands, and above 10.0 cm for Indian children in Bombay and Turkish children in Istanbul. The companion distribution from relative differences had a median of 5.8%, with values between 1.0 and 2.0% for Dutch children in the Netherlands and between 11.0 and 24.0% for Indian children in Bombay and Turkish children in Istanbul.
4. Averages for stature of children in professional and executive families exceeded those for progeny of unskilled and semiskilled workers by more than 2.0 cm in 69% of 32 comparisons at age 7 years, and 86% of 37 comparisons at age 9 years. Upper class groups were taller than corresponding lower class peers by more than 2.0% in 22 (69%) of the comparisons at age 7 years, and 28 (76%) of those at age 9 years.
5. From data collected in upper class families during the 1960s, averages for stature at age 7 years were near 115 cm for Indian children in Delhi, 118 cm for Chinese children in Hong Kong, 122 cm for Yoruba children in Ibadan, and 124 cm for Dutch children in the Netherlands. At age 9 years, variation among stature averages of upper class groups extended from near 123 cm for Filipino children in Manila to fully 136 cm for Dutch children in the Netherlands, and yielded a statistically dependable spread among upper class populations of more than 10 cm.

For dimensions of the head, trunk, and limbs, the following generalizations were formulated from paired averages on infants and children near the termini of the socioeconomic distribution:

1. Averages for head girth were consistently smaller from lower class groups than from the upper class groups with which they were fitly aligned. Twenty-two (96%) of the 23 paired comparisons gave a difference statistically significant at the $p = .01$ level of confidence. Hip width—a second dimension qualifying as primarily "skeletal"—gave similarly consistent differences at ages from late infancy through late childhood.
2. Arm girth—qualifying as a largely "soft tissue" dimension—produced averages consistently larger for children of the upper classes than for lower class peers of the same age and racial stock. In 18 of 21 comparisons, statistical tests at $p = .01$ allowed the inference of dependably different arm girth populations.
3. Other comparisons for chest girth, shoulder width, sitting height, upper limb length, and calf girth revealed no instance where a group of children of low socioeconomic status, on average, equaled or exceeded a comparable group of high status.

For any social class (e.g., executive or unskilled) the average size of a somatic variable arises from multiple interactions among components of the gene pool, physical environment, and social milieu. Lower and upper socioeconomic groups differ substantially in social milieu. Do lower and upper social classes differ in respect to genetic potential for somatic growth? If so, to the extent persons reared in slum areas select marriage mates reared in similarly underprivileged neighborhoods, and persons reared in upper class settings select marriage mates reared in similarly privileged settings, progeny of the two social classes—besides differing from influences relating to sanitation, nutrition, and health supervision—will differ from influences relating to genetic structure and function. In short, the effort to explain social class differences in human body size requires attention to facets of both heredity and nurture, as does formulation of comprehensive programs directed toward elimination of social class differences in body size.

ACKNOWLEDGMENTS

Gratitude is expressed to the following persons who assisted with literature search, reference procurement, provision of unpublished material, language translation, verification of statistics, and manuscript criticism: G. D. Barr, L. Finger, M. D. Janes, S. J. Karayan, V. B. Knott, R. M. Malina, E. M. Meredith, F. J. Miller, O. Neyzi, H. Oglesbee, H. W. Reese, R. J. Rona, M. C. Swaminathan, J. H. Spurgeon, and H. B. Young.

REFERENCES

Abraham, S., Lowenstein, F. W., & O'Connell, D. E. *Preliminary findings of the first health and nutrition examination survey, United States, 1971–1972: Anthropometric and clinical findings.* (National Center for Health Statistics Publ. No. HRA 75-1229). Washington, D.C.: U.S. Govt. Printing Office, 1975.

Achar, S. T., & Yankauer, A. Studies on the birth weight of South Indian infants. *Indian Journal of Child Health,* 1962, **11,** 157–167.

Adair, F. L., & Scammon, R. E. A study of the ossification centers of the wrist, knee, and ankle at birth, with particular reference to the physical development and maturity of the newborn. *American Journal of Obstetrics,* 1921, **2,** 35–60.

Amirhakimi, G. H. Growth from birth to two years of rich urban and poor rural Iranian children compared with Western norms. *Annals of Human Biology,* 1974, **1,** 427–442.

Ashcroft, M. T., Heneage, P., & Lovell, H. G. Heights and weights of Jamaican schoolchildren of various ethnic groups. *American Journal of Physical Anthropology,* 1966, **24,** 35–44.

Aubenque, M., & Desabie, M. Enquête sur la taille et sur le poids des écoliers en 1955. *Société Parisienne d'Imprimerie,* 1957, **1,** 1–12.

Auden, G. A. Heights and weights of Birmingham school children in relation to infant mortality. *School Hygiene,* 1910, **1,** 290–291.

Bakwin, H., & Bakwin, R. M. Growth of thirty-two external dimensions during the first year of life. *Journal of Pediatrics,* 1936, **8,** 177–183.

Bakwin, H., Bakwin, R. M., & Milgram, L. Body build in infants. IV. The influence of retarded growth. *American Journal of Diseases of Children,* 1934, **48,** 1030–1040.

Bakwin, H., & Patrick, T. W. The weight of Negro infants. *Journal of Pediatrics,* 1944, **24,** 405–407.

Bandyopadhyay, S., Pakrasi, K., Banerjee, A. R., & Banerjee, J. Growth of Bengali infants by feeding habit from birth to age twelve months. *Anthropologiai Közelmenyek,* 1981, **25,** 61–80.

Banik, N. D. D. Semilongitudinal growth evaluation of children from birth to 14 years in different socioeconomic groups. *Indian Pediatrics,* 1982, **19,** 353–359.

Banik, N. D. D., Krishna, R., Mane, S. I. S., & Raj, L. Longitudinal growth pattern of children during pre-school age and its relationship with different socio-economic classes. *Indian Journal of Pediatrics,* 1970, **37,** 438–447. (a)

Banik, N. D. D., Krishna, R., Mane, S. I. S., Raj, L., & Taskar, A. D. A longitudinal study of physical growth of children from birth up to 5 years of age in Delhi. *Indian Journal of Medical Research,* 1970, **58,** 135–142. (b)

Banik, N. D. D., Nayar, S., Krishna, R., Raj, L., & Taskar, A. D. A semilongitudinal study of physical growth of primary school children in Delhi. *Indian Journal of Pediatrics,* 1970, **37,** 453–459. (c)

Barja, I., LaFuente, M. E., Ballester, D., Mönckeberg, F., & Donoso, G. Peso y talla de pre-escolares chilenos urbanos de tres niveles de vida. *Revista Chilena de Pediatria,* 1965, **36,** 525–529.

Barr, G. D., Allen, C. M., & Shinefield, H. R. Height and weight of 7,500 children of three skin colors. *American Journal of Diseases of Children,* 1972, **124,** 866–872.

Basavarajappa, K. G., Deshpande, V. A., & Ramachandran, K. V. Effect of sex, maternal age, birth order, and socio-economic status on the birth weight of live born infants. *Indian Journal of Public Health,* 1962, **1,** 18–27.

Blanco, R. A., Acheson, R. M., Canosa, C., & Salomon, J. B. Height, weight, and lines of arrested growth in young Guatemalan children. *American Journal of Physical Anthropology,* 1974, **40,** 39–47.

Boas, F. The growth of children as influenced by environmental and hereditary conditions. *School and Society,* 1923, **17,** 305–308.

Bogin, B. A., & MacVean, R. B. Growth in height and weight of urban Guatemalan primary school children of low and high socioeconomic class. *Human Biology,* 1978, **50,** 477–487.

Bogin, B., & MacVean, R. B. Body composition and nutritional status of urban Guatemalan children of high and low socioeconomic status. *American Journal of Physical Anthropology,* 1981, **55,** 543–551.

Bogin, B., & MacVean, R. B. The relationship of socioeconomic status and sex to body size, skeletal maturation, and cognitive status of Guatemala City schoolchildren. *Child Development,* 1983, **54,** 115–128.

Bowditch, H. P. The growth of children: A supplementary investigation. *Tenth Annual Report, Massachusetts State Board of Health,* 1879, 35–62.

Boynton, B. The physical growth of girls: A study of the rhythm of physical growth from anthropometric measurement of girls. *University of Iowa Studies in Child Welfare,* 1936, **12,** No. 4.

Caasi, P. I., Bulato-Jayme, J., Alego, L. G., Peralta, F. L., & Pascual, C. R. Evaluation of the protein intake of 200 preschool children in metropolitan Manila. *Philippine Journal of Science,* 1964, **93,** 1–36.

Camcam, G. A. The heights and weights of school children in relation to socio-economic status. *Philippine Journal of Nutrition,* 1969, **22,** 11–24.

Chang, K. S. F., Lee, M. M. C., Low, W. D., & Kvan, E. Height and weight of Southern Chinese children. *American Journal of Physical Anthropology,* 1963, **21,** 497–509.

Cherry, F. F. Growth from birth to five years of New Orleans underprivileged Negro children. *Bulletin, Tulane University Medical Faculty,* 1968, **24,** 233–240.

Ch'in, C. T., & Sui, T. C. Physical measurements of children under 7 years of age in Peking after liberation. *Zhonghua erke Zazhi,* 1956, **7,** 336–344.

Clements, E. M. B. Changes in the mean stature and weight of British children over the last seventy years. *British Medical Journal,* 1953, Oct. 24, 897–902.

Collis, W. R. F., Dema, I., & Lesi, F. E. A. Transverse survey of health and nutrition, Pankshin Division, Northern Nigeria. *West African Medical Journal,* 1962, **11,** 131–154.

Craig, J. O. The heights of Glasgow boys: Secular and social influences. *Human Biology,* 1963, **35,** 524–539.

Crump, E. P., Horton, C. P., Masuoka, J., & Ryan, D. Growth and development. I. Relation of birth weight in Negro infants to sex, maternal age, parity, prenatal care, and socioeconomic status. *Journal of Pediatrics,* 1957, **51,** 678–697.

Currimbhoy, Z. Growth and development of Bombay children. *Indian Journal of Child Health,* 1963, **12,** 627–651.

Dearborn, W. F., Rothney, J. W. M., & Shuttleworth, F. K. Data on the growth of public school children. *Monographs of the Society for Research in Child Development,* 1938, **3,** Serial No. 14.

Døssing, J. Gennemsnitsvaerdier for vaegt-højde-alder forhold hos drenge og piger i skolealderen. *Ugeskrift f. Laeger,* 1950, **34,** 1171–1181.

Douglas, J. W. B., & Simpson, H. R. Height in relation to puberty, family size, and social class: A longitudinal study. *Milbank Memorial Fund Quarterly,* 1964, **42,** 20–35.

Elderton, E. M. Height and weight of school children in Glasgow. *Biometrika,* 1914, **10,** 288–339.

Enačhescu, T., Grintescu-Pop, S., & Glavce, C. The ontogenetic specificity of the acceleration in the newborn's physical development. *Annuaire Roumain D'Anthropologie,* 1971, **8,** 27–31.

Ewart, R. J. The influence of parental age on offspring. *Eugenics Review,* 1912, **3,** 201–232.

Faiwoo, D. K. *Physical growth and the social environment: A West African example.* Paper distributed at the Ninth International Congress of Anthropological and Ethnological Sciences, 1973.

Faulhaber, J. *Investigacion longitudinal del crecimiento*. Mexico D.F.: Instituto Nacional de Antropologia e Historia, 1976.

Fraccaro, M. Data for quantitative genetics in man: Birth weight in official statistics. *Human Biology*, 1958, **30,** 142–149.

Freeman, R. G. Weights and measurements of infants and children in private practice compared with institution children and schoolchildren. *American Journal of Diseases of Children*, 1914, **8,** 321–326.

Frisancho, A. R., Guire, K., Babler, W., Borkan, G., & Way, A. Nutritional influence on childhood development and genetic control of adolescent growth of Quechuas and Mestizos from the Peruvian lowlands. *American Journal of Physical Anthropology*, 1980, **52,** 367–375.

Galton, F. Final report of the anthropometric committee, 1883. *British Association of Advancement of Science Reports*, 1883–1884, 253–306.

Garn, S. M., Shaw, H. A., & McCabe, K. D. Effect of socioeconomic status on early growth as measured by three different indicators. *Ecology of Food and Nutrition*, 1978, **7,** 51–55.

Goldfeld, A. Y., Merkova, A. A., & Tseimlina, A. G. *Materials on the physical development of children and adolescents in cities and rural locations of the USSR*. Leningrad: Meditsina, 1965.

Goldstein, H. Factors influencing the height of seven year old children: Results from the National Child Development Study. *Human Biology*, 1971, **43,** 92–111.

Graffar, M., Asiel, M., & Emery-Hauzeur, C. La taille et le périmètre céphalique pendant la première année de la vie. *Acta Paediatrica Belgica*, 1961, **15,** 61–74.

Graffar, M., & Corbier, J. Contribution to the study of the influence of socio-economic conditions on the growth and development of the child. *Early Childhood Development and Care*, 1972, **1,** 141–179.

Grandi, F. Confronto fra l'accrescimento nel primo anno di vita del bambino allevato in istituto (I.P.I. di Bologna) a del bambino di privata consultazione, su di una base di eguale condotta dietologica e terapeutica. *Minerva Pediatrica Monograph Series*, 1965, 178–182.

Gray, H., & Fraley, F. Growth standards: Height, chest girth and weight of private school boys. *American Journal of Diseases of Children*, 1926, **32,** 554–555.

Gray, H., & Gower, C. Growth standards: Height and weight of girls in private schools. *American Journal of Diseases of Children*, 1928, **35,** 411–413.

Gunstad, B., & Treloar, A. E. The relationship between the length and weight of the new-born infant and the height and weight of the mother. *Human Biology*, 1936, **8,** 565–580.

Hafez, A. S., Salem, S. I., Cole, T. J., Galal, O. M., & Massoud, A. Sexual maturation and growth pattern in Egyptian boys. *Annals of Human Biology*, 1981, **8,** 461–467.

Hamil, B. M., Reynolds, L., Poole, M. W., & Macy, I. G. Mineral vitamin C requirements of artificially fed infants: A study of four hundred and twenty-seven children under a controlled dietary regimen. *American Journal of Diseases of Children*, 1938, **56,** 561–583.

Hamill, P. V. V., Johnston, F. E., & Lemeshow, S. *Height and weight of children: Socioeconomic status*. (Vital and Health Statistics, Series 11, No. 119, United States National Center for Health Statistics). Washington, D.C.: U.S. Govt. Printing Office, 1972.

Hammond, J., & Sheng, H. The development and diet of Chinese children. *American Journal of Diseases of Children*, 1925, **29,** 728–742.

Hammond, W. H. Physique and development of boys and girls from different types of school. *British Journal of Preventive and Social Medicine*, 1953, **7,** 231–239.

Hammond, W. H. Some aspects of growth, with norms from birth to 18 years. *British Journal of Preventive and Social Medicine*, 1957, **11,** 131–141.

Harfouche, J. K. *The growth and illness patterns of Lebanese infants: Birth to 18 months*. Beirut: Khayats, 1966.

Hasan, F., Najjar, S. S., & Asfour, R. Y. Growth of Lebanese infants in the first year of life. *Archives of Disease in Childhood,* 1969, **44,** 131–133.

Hedayat, S., Koohestani, P. A., Ghassemi, H., & Kamali, D. Birth weight in relation to economic status and certain maternal factors, based on an Iranian sample. *Tropical and Geographical Medicine,* 1971, **23,** 355–364.

Hellman, M. Nutrition, growth and dentition. *Dental Cosmos,* 1923, **65,** 34–49.

Hertz, P. Investigations on the growth of children in the Copenhagen elementary schools. *School Hygiene,* 1912, **3,** 175–178.

Hollingsworth, M. J. Observations on the birth weights and survival of African babies: Single births. *Annals of Human Genetics,* 1965, **28,** 291–300.

Hopkins, J. W. Height and weight of Ottawa elementary school children of two socioeconomic strata. *Human Biology,* 1947, **19,** 68–82.

Hsu, K. L., & Liang, I. W. A study of the growth development of school children in Peiping. *National Medical Journal of China,* 1930, **16,** 195–214.

Hundley, J. M., Mickelsen, O., Mantel, N., Weaver, R. N., & Taber, R. C. Height and weight of first-grade children as a potential index of nutritional status. *American Journal of Public Health,* 1955, **45,** 1454–1461.

Indian Council of Medical Research. *Growth and physical development of Indian infants and children.* New Delhi: Indian Council of Medical Research, 1972.

Indian National Institute of Nutrition. Growth status of pre-school children of well-to-do communities in Hyderabad. *Annual Report, Indian National Institute of Nutrition,* 1975, 162–167.

Jackson, R. L., Westerfeld, R., Flynn, M. A., Kimball, E. R., & Lewis, R. R. Growth of "well-born" American infants fed human and cow's milk. *Pediatrics,* 1964, **33,** 642–652.

Jager, S. Statistical information from a welfare clinic in Baghdad, Iraq. *Journal of Tropical Medicine and Hygiene,* 1961, **64,** 212–216.

Janes, M. D. Physical growth of Nigerian Yoruba children. *Tropical and Geographical Medicine,* 1974, **26,** 389–398.

Jayant, K. Birth weight and some other factors in relation to infant survival: A study on an Indian sample. *Annals of Human Genetics,* 1964, **27,** 261–270.

Johnston, F. E., Borden, M., & MacVean, R. B. Height, weight, and their growth velocities in Guatemalan private school children of high socioeconomic class. *Human Biology,* 1973, **45,** 627–641.

Johnston, F. E., Wainer, H., Thissen, D., & MacVean, R. B. Hereditary and environmental determinants of growth in height in a longitudinal sample of children and youth of Guatemalan and European ancestry. *American Journal of Physical Anthropology,* 1976, **44,** 469–476.

Jones, D. L., Hemphill, W., & Meyers, E. S. A. *Height, weight and other physical characteristics of New South Wales children. I. Children aged five years and over.* Sydney: New South Wales Dept. of Health, 1973.

Kasius, R. V., Randall, A., Tompkins, W. T., & Wiehl, D. G. Maternal and newborn nutrition studies at Philadelphia Lying-In Hospital: Newborn studies. V. Size and growth of babies during the first year of life. *Milbank Memorial Fund Quarterly,* 1957, **35,** 323–372.

Kelly, H. J., & Reynolds, L. Appearance and growth of ossification centers and increase in the body dimensions of White and Negro infants. *American Journal of Roentgenology and Radium Therapy,* 1947, **57,** 477–516.

Kessler, A., & Scott, R. B. Growth and development of Negro infants. II. Relation of birth weight, body length and epiphyseal maturation to economic status. *American Journal of Diseases of Children,* 1950, **80,** 370–378.

Key, A. *Schulhygienische Untersuchungen.* Leipzig: Bürgerstein, 1889.

King, G., & T'ang, Y. T. Obstetrical criteria in North China. II. The weights and measurements of the mature new-born child. *Chinese Medical Journal,* 1937, **52,** 501–506.

King, K. W., Foucauld, J., Fougere, W., & Severinghaus, E. L. Height and weight of Haitian children. *American Journal of Clinical Nutrition,* 1963, **13,** 106–109.

Llewellyn-Jones, D. Premature babies in the tropics. *Journal of Obstetrics and Gynecology of the British Empire,* 1955, **62,** 275–279.

Low, W. D. Stature and body weight of Southern Chinese children. *Zeitschrift für Morphologie und Anthropologie,* 1971, **63,** 11–45.

Luna-Jaspe, H., Ariza, J., Rueda-Williamson, R., Mora, J. O., & Pardo, F. Estudio seccional de crecimiento, desarrollo y nutricion en 12,138 niños de Bogotá, Colombia. *Archivos Latino-Americanos de Nutricion,* 1970, **20,** 151–165.

MacDonald, A. Experimental study of children. *Annual Report, United States Commissioner of Education,* 1899, **1,** 985–1204.

Machado, J. P., & Memõria, J. M. P. Pêso de recém-nascidos em hospitais de Belo Horizonte. *O Hospital,* 1966, **69,** 393–402.

Mackenzie, W. L., & Foster, C. A. *Report of the physical condition of children attending the public schools of the School Board of Glasgow, 1907.* Glasgow: Wyman, 1907.

Marcusson, H. *Das Wachstum von Kindern und Jugendlichen in der deutschen demokratischen Republik: Grösse, Gewicht und Brustumfang nach Untersuchungen in den Jahren 1956–1958.* Berlin: Akademie-Verlag, 1961.

Martell, M., Falkner, F., Bertolini, L. B., Diaz, J. L., Nieto, F., Tenzer, S. M., & Belitzky, R. Early postnatal growth evaluation in full-term, preterm, and small-for-dates infants. *Early Human Development,* 1978, **1,** 313–323.

Martins-Filho, J., Aristodemo-Pinotti, J., Carvalho, J. F., Bueno, R. D., Paes de Freitas, N. A., Carvalho, M. B., & Moraes, L. P. Dénutrition intra-uterine, variation du poids a la naissance en function de la classe socio-economique dans une maternité de la Ville de Campinas S. P. Bresil. *Courrier,* 1974, **24,** 122–129.

Mathur, Y. C., Gupta, K. B., & Rao, N. P. Study of growth pattern in pre-school children of low socio-economic status in a rural area near Hyderabad. *Indian Pediatrics,* 1972, **9,** 411–414.

May, G. M. S., O'Hara, V. M., & Dugdale, A. E. Patterns of growth in Queensland schoolchildren, 1911 to 1976. *Medical Journal of Australia,* 1979, **2,** 610–614.

McClung, J. *Effects of high altitude on human birth.* London and New York: Harvard Univ. Press, 1969.

Méndez, J., & Behrhorst, C. The anthropometric characteristics of Indian and rural Guatemalans. *Human Biology,* 1963, **35,** 457–469.

Menzies, F. *Report on the average heights and weights of elementary school children in the County of London in 1938.* London County Council, 1940.

Meredith, H. V. Physical growth from birth to two years: Stature. *University of Iowa Studies in Child Welfare,* 1943, **19,** 185–190.

Meredith, H. V. Relation between socioeconomic status and body size in boys seven to ten years of age. *American Journal of Diseases of Children,* 1951, **82,** 702–709.

Meredith, H. V. Methods of studying physical growth. In P. H. Mussen (Ed.), *Handbook of research methods in child development.* New York: Wiley, 1960.

Meredith, H. V. Change in the stature and body weight of North American boys during the last 80 years. In L. P. Lipsitt & C. C. Spiker (Eds.), *Advances in child development and behavior.* New York: Academic Press, 1963.

Meredith, H. V. Research between 1960 and 1970 on the standing height of young children in different parts of the world. In H. W. Reese & L. P. Lipsitt (Eds.), *Advances in child development and behavior.* New York: Academic Press, 1978. (a)

Meredith, H. V. Secular change in sitting height and lower limb height of children, youths, and young adults of Afro-Black, European, and Japanese ancestry. *Growth,* 1978, **42,** 37–41. (b)

Meredith, H. V., & Boynton, B. The transverse growth of the extremities: An analysis of girth measurements for arm, forearm, thigh, and leg. *Human Biology,* 1937, **9,** 366–403.

Meredith, H. V., & Goodman, J. L. A comparison of routine hospital records of birth stature with measurements of birth stature obtained for longitudinal research. *Child Development,* 1941, **12,** 175–181.

Miller, F. J. W., Billewicz, W. Z., & Thomson, A. M. Growth from birth to adult life of 442 Newcastle-upon-Tyne children. *British Journal of Preventive and Social Medicine,* 1972, **26,** 224–230.

Miller, F. J. W., Court, S. D. M., Walton, W. S., & Knox, E. G. *Growing up in Newcastle-upon-Tyne.* London: Oxford Univ. Press, 1960.

Millis, J. A study of the effect of nutrition on fertility and the outcome of pregnancy in Singapore in 1947 and 1950. *Medical Journal of Malaya,* 1952, **6,** 157–177.

Millis, J. Gain in weight and length in the first year of life of Chinese infants born in Singapore in 1951. *Medical Journal of Australia,* 1954, **1,** 283–285.

Millis, J. Distribution of birth weights of Chinese and Indian infants born in Singapore: Birth weight as an index of maturity. *Annals of Human Genetics,* 1958, **23,** 164–170.

Montoya, C., & Ipinza, M. Peso y estatura de pre-escolares santiaguinos pertenecientes a dos estratos sociales diferentes. *Revista Chilena de Pediatria,* 1964, **35,** 269–277.

Mora, J. O. Somatometria en niños de clas socio-economica baja. *Archivos Latinoamericanos de Nutricion,* 1969, **19,** 17–33.

Mukherjee, S., & Biswas, S. Birth weight and its relationship to gestation period, sex, maternal age, parity and socio-economic status. *Journal of the Indian Medical Association,* 1959, **32,** 389–398.

Navarrete, J. L. P., Franco, L. V., Vilchis, A., Arrieta, R., Santibáñez, E., Rivera, L., & Cravioto, J. Operación Zacatepec. V. Estudio longitudinal de un grupo de niños a los que se les singuió durante su primer año de vida en la Villa de Tlaltizapán del Estado de Morelos, República Mexicana. *Boletin Medico del Hospital Infantil de Mexico,* 1960, **17,** 283–296.

Nekisheva, Z. I. Effect of certain social factors on the physical development of preschool children attending kindergartens. *Gigiena Sanitariya,* 1974, **2,** 58–61.

Neyzi, O., & Gürson, C. T. *Physical measurements on two groups of Istanbul children: Normal and undernourished.* Stockholm: Swedish Medical Research Council, 1966.

Neyzi, O., Tanman, F., & Saner, G. *Preliminary results of a child health survey in an under-developed area of Istanbul.* Mimeographed Report, University of Istanbul, 1965.

Neyzi, O., Yalçindağ, A., & Alp, H. Heights and weights of Turkish children. *Environmental Child Health,* 1973, **19,** 5–13.

O'Brien, R., Girshick, M. A., & Hunt, E. P. *Body measurements of American boys and girls for garment and pattern construction* (Bureau of Home Economics, U.S. Dept. of Agriculture, Publ. No. 366). Washington, D.C.: U.S. Govt. Printing Office, 1941.

Owen, G. M., Kram, K. M., Garry, P. J., Lowe, J. E., & Lubin, A. H. A study of nutritional status of preschool children in the United States, 1968–1970. *Pediatrics,* 1974, **53,** 597–646.

Pagliani, L. Sopra alcuni fattori dello sviluppo umano-richerche anthropometriche. *Archivio per l'Antropologia e l'Etnologia Italiana,* 1876, **6,** 129–183.

Pakrasi, K., Sil, S., & Dasgupta, P. *Body weight at birth and incidence of low-weight babies in Calcutta.* Calcutta: Biological Science Division, Indian Statistical Institute, 1982.

Peatman, J. G., & Higgons, R. A. Growth norms from birth to the age of five years: A study of children reared with optimal pediatric and home care. *American Journal of Diseases of Children,* 1938, **55,** 1233–1247.

Penchaszadeh, V. B., Hardy, J. B., Mellits, E. D., Cohen, B. H., & McKusick, V. A. Growth and development in an "inner city" population: An assessment of possible biological and environmental influences. *Johns Hopkins Medical Journal,* 1972, **131,** 11–23.

Phillips, H. T. Some social and ethnic variations in the physique of South African nursery school children. *Archives of Disease in Childhood,* 1953, **28,** 226–231.

Porter, W. T. The growth of St. Louis children. *Transactions, Academy of Science of St. Louis,* 1894, **6,** 265–369.

Postmus, S. Beriberi of mother and child in Burma. *Tropical and Geographical Medicine,* 1958, **10,** 363–370.

Prasad, R., Kumar, R., & Dayal, R. S. Physical growth and development from one to five years. *Indian Pediatrics,* 1971, **8,** 105–119.

Prevosti, A. Estudio del crecimiento en escolares Barceloneses. *Trabajos del Instituto Bernardino de Sahagun de Antropologia y Etnologia,* 1949, **8,** 1–335.

Prokopec, M. Growth and socioeconomic environment. *Monographs, Society for Research in Child Development,* 1970, **35,** Series No. 140, 55–60.

Prokopec, M., Titlbachová, S., Zlámalová, H., & Padevětová, D. Odraz životního prostředi na tělesný a duševní vývoj děti. *Československá Hygiena,* 1979, **24,** 280–300.

Raghavan, K. V., Singh, D., & Swaminathan, M. C. Heights and weights of well-nourished Indian school children. *Indian Journal of Medical Research,* 1971, **59,** 648–654.

Rajalakshmi, R., & Chandrasekaran, K. N. Comparative data on the heights and weights of subjects in low and high income groups in Gujarat. *Problems of World Nutrition,* 1967, **4,** 125–131.

Ramón-Guerra, A. U. Peso y talla de nuestros recien nacidos y lactantes hasta el año de edad. *Archivos de Pediatria del Uruguay,* 1950, **21,** 81–97.

Rea, J. N. Social and economic influences on the growth of pre-school children in Lagos. *Human Biology,* 1971, **43,** 46–63.

Roberts, O. The physical development and the proportions of the human body. *St. George's Hospital Reports,* 1876, **8,** 1–48.

Robertson, T. B. Studies on the growth of man. IV. The variability of the weight and stature of school children and its relationship to their physical welfare. *American Journal of Physiology,* 1916, **41,** 547–554.

Rona, R. J., Swan, A. V., & Altman, D. G. Social factors and height of primary schoolchildren in England and Scotland. *Journal of Epidemiology and Community Health,* 1978, **32,** 147–154.

Rueda-Williamson, R., Luna-Jaspe, H., Ariza, J., Pardo, F., & Mora, J. O. Estudio seccional de crecimiento, desarrollo y nutrición en 12,138 niños de Bogotá, Colombia. *Pediatria,* 1969, **10,** 335–339.

Rueda-Williamson, R., & Rose, H. E. Growth and nutrition of infants. *Pediatrics,* 1962, **30,** 639–653.

Sabharwal, K. P., Morales, S., & Méndez, J. Body measurements and creatinine excretion among upper and lower socio-economic groups of girls in Guatemala. *Human Biology,* 1966, **38,** 131–140.

Sälzler, A. Übersicht über die Ergebnisse der Messungen von Gewicht und Grösse bei Kindern von 0 bis 3 jahren. *Zeitschrift für Ärztliche Fortbildung,* 1960, **54,** 1228–1235.

Sarram, M., & Saadatnejadi, M. Birth weight in Shiraz (Iran) in relation to maternal socioeconomic status. *Obstetrics and Gynecology,* 1967, **30,** 367–370.

Schiøtz, C. *Physical development of children and young people during the age of 7 to 18–20 years.* Christiania: Jacob Dybwad, 1923.

Schmid-Monnard, K. Ueber den Wert von Körpermassen zur Beurtheilung des Körperzustandes bei Kindern. *Jahrbuch fur Kinderheilkunde,* 1901, **53,** 50–58.

Shakir, A., & Zaini, S. Skeletal maturation of the hand and wrist of young children in Baghdad. *Annals of Human Biology,* 1974, **1,** 189–199.

Sharma, A., Sapra, P., & Mainigi, K. A biometric study of the newborn, gestation period and placental traits. *Indian Journal of Physical Anthropology and Human Genetics,* 1975, **1,** 120–137.

Sikri, S. D. A comparative study of height and weight of government and public school children of Panjabi population. *Indian Journal of Medical Research,* 1972, **60,** 491–500.

Simmons, K., & Todd, T. W. Growth of well children: Analysis of stature and weight. *Growth,* 1938, **2,** 93–134.

Stebbins, T. H. *A nutritional index of new-born infants.* Unpublished Master's thesis, University of Iowa, 1933.

Stinson, S. The effect of high altitude on the growth of children of high socioeconomic status in Bolivia. *American Journal of Physical Anthropology,* 1982, **59,** 61–71.

Swaminathan, M. C. Observation on growth and development of undernourished children of Andhra Pradesh. *Indian Journal of Medical Research,* 1971, **59** (Suppl.), 149–155.

Systems Development Project Staff. Height and weight charts and tables on poverty area children. *Systems Development Project Study Series* 8–9, 1968.

Thomson, F. A. The birth weight of babies in the Federation of Malaya: Effect of race and of economic change. *Journal of Tropical Medicine,* 1962, **8,** 3–9.

Timmer, M. Prosperity and birthweight in Javanese infants. *Tropical and Geographical Medicine,* 1961, **13,** 316–320.

Topp, S. G., Cook, J., Holland, W. W., & Elliott, A. Influence of environmental factors on height and weight of schoolchildren. *British Journal of Preventive and Social Medicine,* 1970, **24,** 154–162.

Tully, A. M. T. The physique of Glasgow school children (1921–22). *Journal of Hygiene,* 1924–25, **23,** 186–197.

Udani, P. M. Physical growth of children in different socio-economic groups in Bombay. *Indian Journal of Child Health,* 1963, **12,** 593–611.

Ulrich, M. Fetal growth patterns in normal mature newborn infants in relation to social status, maternal weight and employment outside the home. II. *Acta Paediatrica Scandinavica Supplement,* 1982, **292,** 18–26.

Underwood, P., Hester, L. L., Laffitte, T., Jr., & Gregg, K. V. The relationship of smoking to the outcome of pregnancy. *American Journal of Obstetrics and Gynecology,* 1965, **91,** 270–276.

van Wering, E. R. *Growth and development of children on Aruba in 1974.* Rotterdam: Bouwcentrum, 1978.

van Wieringen, J. C. *Seculaire groeiverschuiving: Lengte en gewicht surveys 1964–1966 in Nederland in historisch perspectief.* Leiden: Netherlands Instituut voor Praeventieve Geneeskunde TNO, 1972.

Varkki, C., Venkatachalam, P. S., Srikantia, S. G., & Gopalan, C. Study of birth weights of infants in relation to the incidence of nutritional oedema syndrome (kwashiorkor). *Indian Journal of Medical Research,* 1955, **43,** 291–296.

Venkatachalam, P. S. Maternal nutritional status and its effect on the newborn. *Bulletin of the World Health Organization,* 1962, **26,** 193–201.

Vickers, V. S., & Stuart, H. C. Anthropometry in the pediatrician's office: Norms for selected body measurements based on studies of children of North European stock. *Journal of Pediatrics,* 1943, **22,** 155–170.

Vijayaraghavan, K., & Sastry, J. G. The efficacy of arm circumference as a substitute for weight in assessment of protein-calorie malnutrition. *Annals of Human Biology,* 1976, **3,** 229–233.

Wakefield, T., Jr., Disney, G. W., Mason, R. L., & Beauchene, R. E. Relationships among anthropometric indices of growth and creatinine and hydroxyproline excretion in preadolescent Black and White girls. *Growth,* 1980, **44,** 192–204.

Weinberg, W. A., Dietz, S. G., Penick, E. C., & McAlister, W. H. Intelligence reading achievement, physical size, and social class. *Journal of Pediatrics,* 1974, **85,** 482–489.

Weisman, S. A. Contour of the chest in children. III. Environment. *American Journal of Diseases of Children,* 1935, **49,** 52–59.

Wheeler, L. R. A comparative study of the physical status of East Tennessee mountain children. *Human Biology,* 1933, **5,** 706–721.
Wijn, J. F., de, & Haas, J. H., de. *Groeidiagrammen van 1–25 jarigen in Nederland.* Leiden: Nederlands Instituut voor Praeventieve Geneeskunde, 1960.
Wise, F. C., & Meredith, H. V. The physical growth of Alabama white girls attending W.P.A. preschools. *Child Development,* 1942, **13,** 165–174.
Yanev, B. (Ed.). *Physical development and fitness of the Bulgarian people from birth to age twenty-six.* Sofia: Bulgarian Academy of Sciences Press, 1965.
Zellner, M. Über den Einfluss der sozialen Lage auf die Entwicklung der Kleinkinder im Alter von 2–6 jahren. *Klinische Wochenschrift,* 1926, **6,** 1716–1721.

HUMAN SEXUAL DIMORPHISM: ITS COST AND BENEFIT

James L. Mosley and Eileen A. Stan

DEPARTMENT OF PSYCHOLOGY
THE UNIVERSITY OF CALGARY
CALGARY, ALBERTA
CANADA

ADVANCES IN CHILD DEVELOPMENT
AND BEHAVIOR, VOL. 18

ISBN 0-12-009718-4

I. Introduction

The behavioral impact of the biological systems related to human sexual dimorphism is examined in the present article. The past two and one-half decades have witnessed a renewed interest in and a proliferation of research on sex-related differences in behavior (Anastasi, 1958; Maccoby & Jacklin, 1974; Wittig & Peterson, 1979). Much of this research, however, has focused upon the environmental contributors to such differences (Levy, 1978; Sherman, 1978). Little attention has been directed toward the biological mechanisms that serve to differentiate the two sexes and that may indirectly place the male of the species at a disadvantage. The first half of the article includes an examination of the contributions of early protein synthesis, male histoincompatibility, X chromosome inactivation, gonadal organogenesis, masculinization of the hypothalamo–pituitary axis, and a more slowly paced process of physical maturation to outcomes suggestive of a greater survival liability for the male of the species.

The concept of male vulnerability has its genesis in the Darwinian view of natural selection. The contemporary interpretation of Darwin's view is that males are more variable than females and that this variability leads to more male geniuses and more male mental defectives (Sherman, 1978). Such variability leads not only to a greater number of male mental defectives (Jensen, 1971) but also to a higher mortality rate among males (Anastasi, 1958). The research of John Money and his colleagues (see Money & Ehrhardt, 1972) has been instrumental in demonstrating the significance of the biological contributors to psychosexual differentiation while, at the same time, highlighting the greater survival liability of the male (Money, 1963, 1972).

From conception, males are more prone to the occurrence of deviations in the biodevelopmental sequence relative to females. More males are conceived than are females, but by birth this preponderance has been decreased by higher abortion and stillborn rates. During the neonatal and early infancy periods males demonstrate more morbidity and have higher mortality rates relative to females (Singer, Westphal, & Niswander, 1968). Surviving males continue to be disadvantaged in that they grow and mature more slowly than females and they are more susceptible to many diseases. The frequency of males having learning disorders, behavioral disorders, and all levels of mental retardation is greater than the frequency of such occurrences in females.

A cost/benefit approach to human sexual dimorphism is examined in the second half of the article. The cost of human sexual dimorphism can be seen in the preponderance of males exhibiting intellectual, neurological, and behavioral disorders. On the benefit side of the ledger human sexual dimorphism allows for the maximization of the genetic–behavioral potential of the species as evidenced by the greater frequency of males at the positive extremes of behaviors such as intellectual functioning. From the perspective of evolution the increased vulnerability of the male can be viewed as the cost for the greater variability demonstrated by males in many biological and behavioral realms. Such variability provides the species with the ability to adjust to a range of ecological circumstances and thereby assists the species in the essential task of survival.

II. Sex Ratios

Genetic sex is established at the moment of conception. In the human the homogametic state (XX) is considered to be female whereas the heterogametic state (XY) is considered male. The presence of the Y chromosome contains determinants that are essential for the development of maleness. In addition, evidence from single gene mutations has indicated that genes essential for male development are also located on the X chromosome and genes essential to the development of both males and females are located on the autosomes (Wilson, 1978). The genetic determination of maleness is not simply a matter of the presence or absence of the Y chromosome, but rather is dependent upon the interplay of the X and Y chromosomes as well as the autosomes. Such interactions have produced a curious outcome for the male of the species. Human sexual dimorphism has placed the male at a disadvantage relative to the female. One need only compare the primary, secondary, and tertiary sex ratios to ascertain the disadvantage.

Estimates of the primary sex ratio, i.e., the number of males in proportion to the number of females at conception, derived from early abortion data, include 1.60 (Tricomi, Serr, & Solich, 1960), 1.22 (Szontagh, Jakobovits, & Mehes, 1961), and 1.20 (McMillen, 1979). Although some disagreement as to the reliability of the early abortion data exists (Lindley & Mignon, 1979), even the conservative estimate of 1.20 (McMillen, 1979) indicates that more males are conceived. The secondary sex ratio, i.e., the proportion of males to females at birth, in most developed countries is about 1.05 (Larsson, 1973), and Stern (1973) reported a secondary sex ratio of 1.06 for the Caucasian population of the United States of America. More males are conceived relative to females, but these numbers are reduced during gestation. In addition, surviving males continue to be at a disadvantage in that their susceptibility to life-threatening conditions such as disease and stress is greater than that of females, as evidenced by the tertiary sex ratio. Among diseases there are very few that do not affect more men than women (Childs, 1965). Of the 64 specific causes of death listed by the United States Census Bureau, the rate in 57 is higher for men at all ages than for women at comparable ages and of the 7 specific causes for which women have the higher mortality, 5 involve female-specific conditions such as uterine cancer and childbearing. Diabetes and pernicious anemia are the exceptions (Nagle, 1974).

These data indicate that the mechanisms relating to human sexual dimorphism expose the male to a higher probability of deviation from the normal biodevelopmental sequence relative to the female (Money, 1972; Reinisch & Karow, 1977). The genetic mechanisms that contribute to human sexual dimorphism and to the survival liability of the male will be examined.

III. Genetic Contribution to Human Sexual Dimorphism

A. EARLY PROTEIN SYNTHESIS

One of the basic operations of any single cell is to synthesize proteins, which consist of amino acids linked together in a particular sequence. This synthesis involves a transcription of the genetic messages situated on the chromosomal deoxyribonucleic acid (DNA) by messenger ribonucleic acid (mRNA). The mRNA carries the message from the nucleus into the cytoplasm of the cell and via ribosomal ribonucleic acid (rRNA) leaves the message at a ribosome. The message is translated when transfer ribonucleic acid (tRNA) carries the appropriate amino acids to the ribosomal site, where they are linked together in a particular sequence.

In early embryological development the maternal genome controls protein synthesis. Evidence for the posttranscriptional control of early protein synthesis has been found in oviparous species. The operation of masked maternal mRNA has been demonstrated in sea urchin eggs in which artificially activated enucleate fragments have been shown to exhibit increases in the rate of amino acid incorporation comparable to those of nucleate fragments (Denny & Tyler, 1964). Also, eggs fertilized in the presence of a substance that suppresses protein synthesis continue to develop to the blastula stage (Gross & Cousineau, 1964). These findings suggest that (1) the unfertilized egg contains maternal species mRNA that is responsible for determining the course of early embryonic development and (2) that this maternal mRNA is contained in some inactive form not available to the protein-synthesizing system of the unfertilized egg.

In vivaparous species such as the human, the rapid increase in protein synthesis after fertilization is most likely the result of both the initiation of new mRNA synthesis as well as the activation of masked maternal mRNA in the cytoplasm or in the assemblage of active ribosomes. Evidence for this comes from an examination of some of the regulatory mechanisms that may be involved in the process of cell differentiation in mammalian development at the level of transcription. Schultz and Church (1975) demonstrated that most mRNA molecules in mammalian cells contain a sequence of polyadenylic acid [poly(A)] residues that serve as useful markers for studying mRNA in mammalian cells. If

RNA synthesis is required for blastocyst differentiation, this requirement would seem to be fairly nonspecific in that the expression of the male genome is not essential (Schultz & Church, 1975). Many or most of the enzyme activities in preblastocyst embryos are probably derived from the maternal genome (Wolf & Engel, 1972). Lane (1976), in his study of the control of gene expression, demonstrated that any mRNA from cells with a membrane-bounded nucleus can be translated by the oocyte and that any of the oocyte's protein-manufacturing assemblies can be programmed by nuclear mRNA.

The reliance of early protein synthesis on the activity of masked maternal mRNA ties the developing embryo to the genetic constitution of the mother and opens the door to the possibility that the (XY) genome may be exposed to greater risk in the transition from the protein synthesis controlled by the mother and the initiation of new mRNA.

B. MALE HISTOINCOMPATIBILITY

The contact between the human fetus and the mother occurs when the blastocyst becomes firmly attached to the endometrial epithelium of the uterine wall (nidation). The blastocyst, a fluid-filled sphere consisting of an outer cell mass called the trophoblast and a group of centrally located cells known as the inner cell mass or embryoblast, implants itself on approximately the sixth or seventh day after fertilization. At this time the trophoblast invades the endometrial epithelium of the uterine wall. The trophoblast is fetal tissue and has been shown to have antigenic determinants (Loke, 1975). Because the fetus represents a foreign antigenic stimulus via the trophoblast and yet no obvious rejection of the fetus occurs, an immunologically inert physical barrier must exist that gives the trophoblast a privileged immunogenic status with respect to the host. Such a protective barrier notwithstanding, the work of Ohno (1979) and his colleagues has revealed a mechanism that does lead to an immunological response in the female to the male fetus. This response is occasioned by the presence of the H-Y antigen on the plasma membrane of male embryonic cells.

Specifically, antigens are protein molecules that are firmly attached to the surface of nearly all cells. As with other protein molecules, antigens consist of chains of amino acids, but in addition they contain a small amount of carbohydrate and are termed glycoproteins. They are detected and classified by their ability to bind to specific antibodies. Antigens form part of the immunological defense system that protects the body from its own cells when they become infected with bacteria or viruses. Nearly 30 such antigens have been detected in the mouse and each of them can vary in outbred populations (Cunningham, 1977). The nature of histocompatibility antigens has been explored in mice made genetically homogeneous (isogenic) through intensive inbreeding. Such investigations have revealed that the histocompatibility antigens are not only closely associated with the functioning of the immune system but also with embryological development.

In the mouse, fetal and newborn testicular cells (the primordial, Sertoli, and Leydig cells) absorb as much H-Y antibody as some other target cells, yet these cells are totally resistant to the cytotoxic effect of the H-Y antibody. This reflects, in part, the critical role of the H-Y antigen in testicular organogenesis. Notwithstanding the above, however, three well-verified cytotoxic target cell types for the H-Y antibody are found in the mouse (i.e., the epididymal spermatozoa, the male epidermal cells, and preimplantation male embryos).

In the human male fetus testicular organization depends upon the H-Y antigen (Ohno, 1979). As such, male fetuses expose the female via their plasma membranes to the H-Y antigen which, in turn, causes the female to mount an attack on the male fetus via H-Y antibodies. From a natural selection perspective, the immune response is not too effective against so important an antigen. The H-Y antibody is almost always of the immunoglobulin M (IgM) class, being a large γ-globulin. It is rapidly metabolized with the subsequent formation of immunoglobulin G (IgG), which composes 80% of the immune globulins in normal sera. In the human insignificant amounts of immunoglobulins other than IgG reach the fetus transplacentally (Dancis & Schneider, 1975); therefore, the attack is minimal.

Ohno (1979) reported that the cytotoxicity of the H-Y antibody is absolutely male specific. Work with mice indicated that the embryos at the eight-cell stage are extraordinarily sensitive to the cytotoxic effect of the H-Y antibody (Krco & Goldberg, 1976). Karyotyping of the surviving embryos that underwent the H-Y antibody treatment revealed nothing but the (XX) chromosomal constitution, suggesting 100% lysis of male embryos. In the human being, the H-Y antigen, which is specific to the male of the species, predisposes the male fetus to a potentially harmful immunogenic response on the part of the mother and, although the immunogenic response via the H-Y antibody may be minimal, one can argue that the male fetus experiences greater risk in its female uterine environment.

Support for the influence of the H-Y antigen on the increased risk to the male fetus is found in the examination of tumors that originate from the syncytiotrophoblast of the placenta. Trophoblast tumors are unique in that they are the only naturally occurring tumors in the human derived from nonhost tissue. They are analogous to transplanted tumors and therefore focus attention upon the immunological mechanism of the mother. Loke (1975) suggested that, because trophoblast tumors are essentially homologous transplants of fetal tissue in the mother, the possession of very similar antigens between fetus and mother (i.e., between husband and wife) may create a predisposition to the formation of such tumors. In cases of women with choriocarcinoma, an impaired capacity to reject their husband's skin graft, but not those of unrelated donors, suggests that a specific tolerance for their husband's tissues is operational. Such a tolerance has been shown to increase with successive pregnancies and this increase parallels a higher frequency of choriocarcinoma among women experiencing multiple pregnancies.

A finding of importance for the present discussion is that some 80 to 90% of trophoblast tumors are found to be chromatin positive, i.e., have an (XX) constitution. The (XX) constitution of the trophoblast tumor appears to be significantly more compatible with the uterine environment relative to the (XY) constitution. A possible explanation for the significantly low number of (XY) trophoblast tumors may relate to the H-Y antigen. Transplantation studies in isogenic strains of mice have revealed that, although most skin grafts are successful, grafts from a male donor to a female recipient are consistently unsuccessful. The H-Y antigen may account for such male donor–female host rejections (Silvers, Billingham, & Sanford, 1968). An extrapolation to the (XY) genome of the human male fetus would suggest that the presence of the H-Y antigen may, as well, expose the male fetus to a less than optimal uterine environment.

C. X CHROMOSOME INACTIVATION

Although females have twice the number of X chromosomes relative to males, they have approximately the same number of active X genes. This finding has led to the postulation of a dosage compensation mechanism. Such a mechanism was first elucidated by the early work of Liane B. Russell, Mary Lyon, and their colleagues. Russell and Bangham (1961) demonstrated that the autosomal genes translocated to an X chromosome in field mice became inactive if more than one X chromosome was present. The authors concluded that, in the diploid cells of the female, only one X chromosome is active. Littau, Allfrey, Frenster, and Mirsky (1964) provided support for this conclusion by demonstrating that sections of condensed chromatin masses (heterochromatic X chromosome) are inactive in mRNA synthesis in interphase nuclei. Lyon (1963) further demonstrated that the differentiation of the inactive from the active X chromosome is random, so that in 50% of the somatic cells the paternal X is active and in the remaining 50% the maternal X is active. Once differentiation occurs, estimated to be about the sixteenth day of gestation (Whaley, 1974), all the cells derived from the initial cell will have the same X chromosome inactivated. The random inactivation makes the female a mosaic for genes located on the X chromosome. As such, the extent to which the X chromosome is implicated in a range of psychological attributes, female monozygotic twins should show lower degrees of concordance relative to male monozygotic twins. Osborne (1978) obtained this finding on a battery of tests relating to intellectual functioning.

Russell (1963) further demonstrated that only a part and not the whole of the heterochromatic X chromosome is inactive. Russell (1964) noted that the inactivating influence seems to emanate from one point on the heterochromatic X and spread in gradients and that loci on the heterochromatic X are not autonomous as far as random inactivation is concerned. Schmid (1963) demonstrated that in the heterochromatic X, the synthesis of mRNA is not synchronous along its entire length but rather involves initial completion in the area of the centromere, followed by the short arm and the more distal part of the long arm and ending with the proximal part of the long arm. The result of this modification to the Lyon hypothesis is that in the normal female certain segments of the heterochromatic X chromosome are active at some stage in development. Lyon (1974), in a further qualification, noted that, in contrast to somatic cells, both X chromosomes appear to be active in the embryonic germ cells of the ovary.

The study of numerical and morphological sex chromosome anomalies can shed light on the operation of the dosage compensation mechanism in the human and on the contribution of such a mechanism to the phenotypic differences between male and female.

1. Turner's Syndrome

Turner's syndrome is a cytogenetic defect in which one of the pair of sex chromosomes is absent (X0) or its contribution to embryological development is reduced either through the deletion of part of the second X chromosome or through an isochromosome involving the second X chromosome. In the latter cases the phenotype shows a lesser degree of clinical malformation. In the case of the (X0) type of Turner's syndrome the clinical malformations include webbed neck, shieldlike chest, short fourth metacarpals, ovarian dysgenesis with streak gonads and the absence of germinal elements, and extremely short stature. Some 90% of Turner's syndrome females exhibit normal intelligence (Scott & Thomas, 1973). However, a great percentage of these females demonstrate difficulties in the area of spatial abilities (Alexander, Ehrhardt, & Money, 1966; Hier, Atkins, & Perlo, 1980; Money & Alexander, 1966). Generally, their verbal IQ scores tend to be good but they exhibit relatively poor performance IQ scores.

In addition, Turner's syndrome females possess a higher H-Y antigen titer relative to the zero value for normal females and a significantly lower H-Y antigen titer relative to males (Wachtel, Koo, Breg, & Genel, 1980; Wolf, Fraccaro, Mayerová, Hecht, Zuffardi, & Hameister, 1980). The absence of the short arm of one of the X chromosomes is thought to be responsible for this finding. Wolf *et al.* (1980) suggested that a regulator gene that normally represses the H-Y antigen operator–structural gene complex in early embryological development is missing in Turner's syndrome individuals and its absence allows for the synthesis of the low titer of H-Y antigen. The atypical titer of H-Y antigen in Turner's individuals further underscores the importance of two complete X chromosomes for the normal development of the human female in early embryogenesis.

2. Klinefelter's Syndrome

Klinefelter's syndrome is another cytogenetic anomaly, involving, in the male, an additional X chromosome (XXY). The majority of these cases are not detected until puberty because of the absence of consistent phenotypic findings in male infants and preadolescent boys. The clinical findings at puberty consist of very small testes and prostate, absence of sperm because of abnormal structure of the seminiferous tubules in the testes, increased excretion of gonadotropins in the urine, sparse facial and body hair, a female distribution of pubic hair, breast development, and increased stature. The (XXY) karyotype is high among institutionalized mentally retarded males. Money (1975) reported that the pooled data from a number of surveys place the ratio at approximately 1:50. Scott and Thomas (1973) reported that mental retardation occurs in approximately 51% of Klinefelter's males, but Robinson and Robinson (1976) reported subnormal IQs in 25 to 50% of (XXY) males.

According to the Lyon hypothesis, Klinefelter's males should not differ phenotypically from (XY) males if both have only one active X chromosome. However, the clinical picture of Klinefelter's males is far from normal, suggesting that the presence of an extra X chromosome during early embryonic development (Lyon, 1966) moves the normal developmental sequence toward the female end of the sex continuum.

D. SUMMARY

The genetic contribution to human sexual dimorphism lays down a blueprint soon after the zygote is formed and this blueprint has a differential impact on survival of the individual depending upon genetic sex. First, the reliance of early protein synthesis on the activity of masked maternal mRNA ties the developing embryo to the genetic constitution of the mother for the initial 5 to 6 days postfertilization. This reliance raises the possibility that the (XY) constitution of the male embryo may be exposed to greater risk in the transition between the protein synthesis controlled by the (XX) constitution of the mother and the initiation of new mRNA under the control of its (XY) constitution. Second, the H-Y antigen on the plasma membrane of the male embryonic and fetal cells exposes the male to a less than optimal uterine environment beginning at implantation approximately 6 to 7 days postfertilization. Third, the inactivation of one X chromosome in the female makes the female a mosaic for X-linked genes. Prior to inactivation, which occurs at approximately 16 days postfertilization, two active X chromosomes are necessary for the normal development of the female. One too few active X chromosomes (Turner's syndrome) during early embryogenesis influences the regulation of the H-Y antigen operator–structural gene complex.

The interactive nature of these factors provides the biological foundation for the increased survival liability of the male and these mechanisms are inherently tied to the process of human sexual dimorphism.

IV. Hormonal Contribution to Human Sexual Dimorphism

The central nervous system and the endocrine system are adapted for complementary roles in the control of behavior and, not surprisingly, these two regulatory systems influence each other strongly. The nervous system has the advantage of speed, specificity, and transience in its controlling function, but the endocrine system, via hormones, acts very differently. Hormones are not generally secreted quickly nor can they be rapidly removed from the bloodstream. They are able to contact every cell in the body and their speed of movement is limited by that of the blood. But because of these characteristics a given hormone level can be maintained in the bloodstream to provide constant stimulation over days, months, or even years. Hence, in the control of behavior, hormones are important largely in bringing about long-term changes in responsiveness.

Hormones have highly specific target cells and this specificity is related to the presence and density of particular receptors. Some receptors are situated on the outer membranes of the cells and these link to hormones that are too large to diffuse freely in and out of the cell. These large-molecule hormones (peptides) are taken from the blood as it flows by the cells. When the hormone and receptor link up on the cell membrane a message is released intracellularly that triggers a particular piece of cell machinery (Tanner, 1978). The intracellular messenger for most peptides is cyclic adenosine monophosphate (cyclic AMP). Smaller hormones, including the steroids, pass back and forth through the cell membrane. Their presence has an effect only on those cells which contain receptors situated in the cytoplasm where the linkup occurs.

Nowhere is the long-term change aspect of hormonal function more evident than in the development and function of the reproductive system in the human. Sexual differentiation is facilitated through hormones. The steroid hormones, the hypothalamic regulatory peptide hormones, and the pituitary gonadotropins all contribute to sexual differentiation as well as to the sex-related differences in growth and maturation. The complexity of the hormonal interactions also introduces an additional element of risk for the male of the species.

A. PRIMARY SEXUAL DIFFERENTIATION

1. *Gonadal Organogenesis*

Virtually all of the embryonic structures necessary for either sex are laid down morphologically and are present for a time during early embryogenesis. This period is known as the indifferent stage of the reproductive organs and is observed in every individual regardless of genetic sex. The indifferent stage in human gonadal organogenesis begins during the fifth prenatal week and lasts until the end of the seventh prenatal week when the gonad begins to acquire sexual characteristics (Moore, 1974; Wilson, 1978). During the indifferent stage of the reproductive organs primitive germ cells (genocytes) appear interspersed in the substance of the primitive gonad. The genocytes are thought to arise from the yolk sac and hindgut endoderm and they migrate to the genital ridges.

The primitive gonad itself is bisexually organized, containing a central medulla and the cortex that surrounds it. In the male the medulla gradually predominates and in the female the cortex gradually predominates. The differentiation of the gonad does not involve the transformation of one component into the other, but rather the gradual predominance of one component (medulla or cortex) and the regression of the other. The gonadotropic hormones secreted by the anterior pituitary gland control maturation and regulate the action of the gonads. However, the anterior lobe of the pituitary does not appear to be involved in the formation of the gonads themselves (Ebert & Sussex, 1970).

Shortly after the completion of germ cell migration signs of testicular differentiation are seen in the male gonad. Testicular cords are recognizable in the male gonad of human embryos by the forty-ninth day of gestation. As soon as the embryonic gonad develops into a testis, it immediately has to fulfill its role as an endocrine organ. The newly differentiated Sertoli cells of the fetal testis immediately begin to secrete an anti-Müllerian factor to prevent an autonomous differentiation of Müllerian ducts into female genital tracts, fallopian tubes, and uterus. In addition, Leydig cells begin the active synthesis of testosterone from the C_{21} precursors pregnenolone and progesterone (Wilson, 1978) as early as the sixtieth day of gestation, reaching a peak on the ninetieth day, when the Leydig cells compose more than half the volume of the fetal testis. Testosterone is essential for the survival and the differentiation of the Wolffian ducts into epididymis, ductus deferens, seminal vesicles, and ejaculatory ducts, as well as for the masculinization of the urogenital sinus and external genitalia, which include the prostate, scrotum, and penis. In the human the fetal testis synthesizes testosterone prior to differentiation of the neural centers concerned with sexual behavior, i.e., the hypothalamo–pituitary axis.

The familiar embryonic and fetal rule is that something must be added to produce a male. In early embryonic life, testosterone released by the testes has a localized bilateral influence, namely in promoting proliferation of the Wolffian ducts to form the internal male reproductive structures. Anatomically, arrested development as a male is synonymous with development as a female, but the arrested development of a female results in no genitalia at all. In addition, Wilson (1978) noted that many single-gene mutations affect testosterone synthesis or action but, to date, no mutations have been identified that relate to deficient estrogen synthesis or resistance to estrogenic action. The mutations relating to estrogen synthesis or action are probably lethal. Estrogen is essential to life itself, but testosterone, although essential for the survival of the species, is apparently not essential for the survival of the individual. Support for the critical role of estrogen can be found in the lethal nature of the (Y0) genome. One X chromosome is required for the survival of the individual.

2. *Influence of the H-Y Antigen in Gonadal Organogenesis*

A factor of considerable importance in the development of the genital ducts is the H-Y antigen. On the basis of the study of exceptional individuals in the human and other mammalian species, Ohno (1979) concluded that mammalian primary (gonadal) sex is determined by the expression/nonexpression of the H-Y antigen. Through the histochemical visualization of the plasma membranes of Sertoli and presumptive basement cells, Ohno (1979) derived the testes-organizing role of the H-Y antigen. For successful testicular organogenesis, H-Y antigen sites on the plasma membrane of the Sertoli cells couple with their specific receptor sites on the plasma membranes of their immediate neighbors to form the walls of the seminiferous tubules. Although the expression of the H-Y antigen is ubiquitous in the male, that of the specific H-Y antigen receptor appears to be confined to gonadal cells. Female gonadal cells are also endowed with the H-Y antigen receptor, but females do not possess the H-Y antigen. An exception with respect to the H-Y antigen is Turner's syndrome (see Section III,C,1).

B. SECONDARY SEXUAL DIFFERENTIATION

In the human being, male and female embryos grow in the maternal environment dominated by female hormones. This necessitates that the basic embryonic plan is inherently female and so, not only ovarian differentiation, but also female extragonadal development is made independent and autonomous, i.e., not requiring hormonal induction (Money & Ehrhardt, 1968, 1972). Extragonadal masculine development, in contrast, is an androgen-dependent process. The inherent feminine nature of the basic embryonic plan also occasions the earlier differentiation of the male gonad relative to that of the female.

1. *External Genitalia*

Experimental support for the hormonal control of dimorphic differentiation of the external genitalia is found in the infrahuman experiments of Jost (1972), who demonstrated a critical period in fetal life when the presence of the testes is essential if the bipotential anlagen of the external sexual organs are to develop as male instead of female. The critical period is short. In the rabbit, castration on embryonic day 19 was early enough to ensure complete feminization of genital ducts and external genitalia in the genetic male. Castration on day 24 was already too late to interfere with masculine differentiation in favor of resumption of feminine differentiation, with resulting hermaphroditic ambiguity of appearance. Castration did not interfere with female differentiation in the genetic female and castrated female fetuses developed completely female genital ducts and external genitalia. Castrated male fetuses also developed completely as females unless the missing testicular hormones were artificially replaced.

The principle shown in these experiments is that, in the mammalian female, differentiation of the genital ducts and external genitalia is independent of the presence of ovaries, but male differentiation is dependent upon the androgenic substances normally produced by the testes. For masculinization of the external genitalia to occur, the timing and the amount of androgen is critical. This factor further predisposes the (XY) genome to deviations in the biodevelopmental sequence.

2. *Masculinization of the Hypothalamo–Pituitary Axis*

Jost's (1972) studies also demonstrated a critical developmental period for the masculinization of the hypothalamo–pituitary axis. In the rat, which is born extremely immature, the critical period does not begin prenatally. Therefore, the external sex organs of the fetal female can be masculinized by injecting the pregnant mother with androgen so that the clitoris becomes a penis, without disturbing the normal female estrous-cycling mechanism of the hypothalamus. Similarly, the cycling mechanism can be affected without disrupting the mechanism that permits subsequent feminine sexual behavior. The critical period for androgenization of hypothalamic cyclicity peaks from birth until the fifth day and tapers off by the tenth day of age. In animals like the guinea pig, which are more mature than the rat at birth, the critical period begins and ends before birth. During the critical period, a quite brief exposure to androgen is all that is needed. Arai and Gorski (1968), by using an antiandrogen to cancel the effect of androgen, found a 6-hour exposure to androgen to be sufficient to establish acyclic gonadotropin release.

The amount of androgen present during the critical period also affects the degree to which the hypothalamic cycling system will be androgenized. The optimal amount eliminates all estrous cycles throughout adult life. Lesser amounts may reduce the number of cycles that will be experienced, so that cycling begins on time but ceases prematurely.

In the human, the masculinization of the hypothalamo–pituitary axis is likewise an androgen-dependent process. However, not testosterone per se, but the female hormone estradiol converted from testosterone is responsible for the secondary sexual differentiation in the male (Martini, 1978; Ohno, 1979). Both the testis and the ovary utilize the same set of enzymes for their sex steroid hormone synthesis. The microsomal aromatase present in various cell types of both sexes is responsible for the conversion of the androgens into estrogens (Martini, 1978). The majority of the data favors estrogens as the metabolites of testosterone, with the aromatizing pathway as the organizing factor in brain masculinization, i.e., the hypothalamo–pituitary axis (Korenbrot, Paup, & Gorski, 1975; Reddy, Naftolin, & Ryan, 1974). Martini (1978) suggested that circulating estrogens alone are unable to initiate the masculinization process and that local intracerebral aromatization is a necessary initial step.

The influence of sex steroids on the developing brain and subsequent behavior in the human is best demonstrated in clinical syndromes in which the *in utero* levels of androgens have been either excessive or too low during the critical period of hypothalamic differentiation. For the human, this critical period occurs between the fourth and seventh fetal month, according to Dörner (1978). The results of the excess or deficiency of androgens during this critical period in the human parallel the findings of studies of infrahuman mammals subjected to increased doses of androgens or increased doses of antiandrogens. Some animal studies have demonstrated morphological differences between the brains of males and females in response to the steroid hormones. For example, Dörner and Staudt (1968) demonstrated a relationship between the nuclear sizes of the preoptic anterior hypothalamic region and sexual behavior. In female rats, larger nuclear volumes were also found in the ventromedial nucleus of the hypothalamus (Dörner & Staudt, 1969). Apparently, an increase in androgen during the critical period decreases the nuclear size and leads to an increase in male mating behavior.

a. Adrenogenital Syndrome. In the human the adrenogenital syndrome, caused by an autosomal recessive gene, is analogous to the fetal androgenization studies on infrahuman mammals. In this syndrome, production of adrenal androgens in the fetus is excessive because of a defect in the biosynthesis of cortisol. The absence of cortisol causes the pituitary to secrete large amounts of adrenocorticotropic hormone (ACTH) which, in turn, increase the output of the masculinizing steroid by the adrenal glands (Ehrhardt, Evers, & Money, 1968). In males the excess androgen increases muscle growth, causes premature cessation of bone growth, and leads to precocious puberty. In females the excess of fetal androgen masculinizes the external genitalia to varying degrees, in some cases affecting only the clitoris via enlargement and in others also causing fusion of the labia. The internal reproductive organs are differentiated as female. From a behavioral perspective, females suffering from adrenogenital syndrome exhibit (1) high energy levels with a strong interest and participation in outdoor physical activity and a preference for boys over girls in peer contact—tomboyishness (Ehrhardt, 1974; Ehrhardt *et al.*, 1968), (2) a low interest in doll play and infant care plus little concern for clothing, hairdo, or jewelry (Ehrhardt, 1974; Ehrhardt & Meyers-Bahlburg, 1979; Money & Schwartz, 1977), and perhaps (3) high IQ scores as a group (Ehrhardt, Epstein, & Money, 1968; Money & Lewis, 1966; Money, Lewis, Ehrhardt, & Drash, 1967). The question of above-average IQ in fetally androgenized females remains open, given that later studies (Baker &

Ehrhardt, 1974; Reinisch & Karow, 1977) have failed to support the earlier findings.

b. Progestin-Induced Hermaphroditism. Another example of the influence of increased androgens on the human fetus is the syndrome of progestin-induced hermaphroditism, in which exogenous fetal androgenization of the female is induced by progestinic drugs that were, at one time, administered in cases of threatened miscarriage (Ehrhardt & Money, 1967). The progestin induced testosterone-like effects in that some of these pregnancies produced partially virilized female neonates. The external genitalia were masculinized, although not to the same extent as in the adrenogenital syndrome (Ehrhardt & Money, 1967; Reinisch, 1974). Behaviorally, these females also exhibit long-term tomboy behavior, i.e., high energy expenditure in outdoor play, a preference for boys over girls in peer contact, a low interest in doll play and infant care, little rehearsal of the maternal adult role as mother and wife, and they exhibit high IQ as a group (Ehrhardt, 1974; Ehrhardt & Meyer-Bahlburg, 1979; Ehrhardt & Money, 1967).

Although the exposure to excessive levels of fetal androgen is present in both the adrenogenital and the progestin-induced hermaphroditism syndromes and produces similar behavioral outcomes, caution must be exercised in linking the behavioral sequelae directly to the excessive levels of fetal androgen in genetic females. This caution notwithstanding, the findings reviewed here are consistent with those reported in the infrahuman literature (Dörner, 1978; Martini, 1978).

c. Androgen Insensitivity Syndrome. The animal studies that involved antiandrogens or removal of the testes during the critical period of brain differentiation are paralleled by the condition of testicular feminization or androgen insensitivity syndrome. In this condition genetic males are unable to utilize the androgens produced by the fetal testes and develop as morphological females (Money, Ehrhardt, & Masica, 1968). The body responds to the testicular estrogens and the external genitalia are female. The failure of a positive feedback response to estradiol, characteristic of normal women, indicates that the hypothalamo–pituitary axis has been masculinized (Abbott & Hearn, 1979; Van Look, Hunter, Corker, & Baird, 1977). However, the behavior does not differ from that of normal women (Masica, Money, & Ehrhardt, 1971).

C. PHYSICAL GROWTH AND MATURATION

Ounsted and Taylor (1972) have suggested that the Y chromosome permits a fuller expression of the genome in the male by slowing the rate of maturation. Females mature faster than males and this difference is reflected in fetal growth rates; halfway through the fetal period the skeleton of females is some 3 weeks more advanced than that of males (Lowrey, 1978). At birth females are some 4 to 6 weeks ahead of males in terms of maturation. Postnatally, females reach 50% of their adult height 1.75 to 2 years ahead of males and they enter puberty at an earlier age, in some cases 2 years ahead of males. Girls also cease to grow earlier than boys (Tanner, 1978).

1. Prenatal Maturation Rate

The relationship between the rate of maturation and the (XX) and (XY) genomes involves the functions of hormone–receptor complexes. About a dozen hormones are of particular importance in the control of growth. Of focal importance is human growth hormone (hGH), which is synthesized in the pituitary gland. The fetal pituitary has the capacity to synthesize hGH by the end of the first trimester (Lowrey, 1978). However, evidence from anencephalic fetuses and children with a history of growth hormone deficiency suggests that the synthesis of hGH is not essential for physical growth during the fetal period and indeed for some 12 to 18 months postpartum.

Early in gestation the fetal gonads are capable of stimulation by chorionic gonadotropin (hCG), which is produced by the syncytiotrophoblast of the placenta. The fetal pituitary begins synthesis of the gonadotropins luteinizing hormone (LH) and follicle-stimulating hormone (FSH) late in the first trimester and the level of FSH is much higher in the female fetus than in the male fetus. The fetal pituitary production of both LH and FSH increases to maximum at 29 weeks of gestation and thereafter decreases until term. The plasma levels of FSH increase as well, with much higher levels in female fetuses and with a significant fall during the last trimester. This finding suggests that a negative feedback control develops during the last trimester and that the sex-related difference in prenatal gonadotropin secretion may reflect the different inhibitory effects of the steroid output of the fetal testis and ovary, in that placental steroids are high in fetuses of both sexes (Job, 1977). Both FSH and LH are released from the pituitary by hypothalamic luteinizing hormone releasing hormone (LH-RH). The feedback that shuts off LH-RH is triggered by estradiol in the female and testosterone (dihydrotestosterone) in the male. Another ovarian and testicular hormone, inhibin, interacts with the sex steroids and LH-RH in the differential control of LH and FSH secretion and may explain the changes in the ratio of LH and FSH secretion frequently observed in the human (Labrie, Lagace, Beaulieu, Ferland, DeLean, Drouin, Borgeat, Kelly, Cusan, Dupont, Lemay, Antakly, Pelletier, & Barden, 1979). High levels of testosterone in the male fetus and approximately equal estrogens in both sexes may result in a difference in the sensitivity of the negative feedback mechanism that accounts for the differences in the gonadotropins, which, in turn, exert an influence on the differential rate of maturation *in utero* (Lowrey, 1978).

Early postnatal plasma levels of gonadotropins reveal that FSH is significantly higher in female than in male infants and decreases after 1 year of age in girls, but not in boys. Serum levels of LH are similar in boys and girls and do not vary significantly during infancy.

With particular reference to testosterone, the evidence indicates a significant difference in plasma testosterone levels at midpregnancy favoring male fetuses (Abramovich, 1974; Abramovich & Rowe, 1973). In addition, Forest, Cathiard, and Bertrand (1973) reported significantly higher plasma levels of unbound (biologically active) testosterone in male neonates in the first 2 weeks of life. This exposure is short-lived because of an increase in the binding of testosterone. From 10 months to 11 years no significant difference in testosterone concentration was found (Forest *et al.*, 1973).

2. *Postnatal Maturation Rate*

Postnatally, growth and maturation involve the interaction of the sex steroids with hGH. In terms of skeletal growth, hGH does not act directly upon the limb bones but rather upon the liver to stimulate the production of another hormone, somatomedin. Somatomedin acts on the growing cartilage cells located at the ends of limb bones and on the muscle cells, and the receptors for somatomedin in effect control skeletal size.

The sex differences in postnatal growth rate are related to the differences in the proliferation of cartilage cells of the limb bones in that part of the growth plate immediately under the proliferative zone (the epiphysis), which is under the influence of the somatomedin–receptor complex. In general, as bone growth slows down the growth plate gets thinner. In time, the base of the main shaft breaks through the growth plate and eliminates it altogether. At this point, growth in the bone stops and the epiphyses are closed or fused. In the human, the sex hormones bring about the final elimination of the growth plates (see Tanner, 1978).

One of the major influences of both the estrogens and androgens is to accelerate maturation, an index of which is bone age. A normally functioning gonad is essential for the proper development of the child. Children who lack sex hormones demonstrate prepubertal bone age in that the epiphyses remain open but growth is seriously limited because the cartilage cells of the proliferative zone of the growth plate are less responsive to somatomedin. The capacity for these children to grow is reduced considerably. The exact mechanism is not known but may relate to a decrease in the number or affinity of receptors for somatomedin. Also, the presence or absence of some substance may lead to a more active process of receptor repression. Because these children lack sex hormones, a probable mechanism could involve the absence of the androgens and estrogens. For example, females exhibiting Turner's syndrome (X0) are typically extremely short (150 cm or less) and instead of ovaries they possess primitive streak gonads that lack both germ cells and hormone-producing tissue (Mange & Mange, 1980).

Serum hGH concentrations differ between premenopausal females and males with the females demonstrating higher levels (Cryer & Daughaday, 1977). The findings that postmenopausal women have hGH serum levels equaling those of men and that premenopausal females taking estrogen-containing oral contraceptives have secretory rates roughly three times those of premenopausal women not taking these contraceptives suggest that the higher serum levels of hGH in premenopausal females can be attributed to higher estrogen levels. However, a paradox is obvious when one considers that the estrogens inhibit somatomedin production and therefore block the major metabolic action of hGH while at the same time augmenting hGH secretion. The potential resolution of this paradox lies in the finding that hGH exerts negative feedback on its own secretion. The estrogens inhibit somatomedin production and stimulate hGH secretion; therefore, the negative feedback of hGH on its own secretion may well be mediated by somatomedin.

Testosterone, in contrast, although capable of stimulating hGH release does so to a lesser extent and apparently has no effect on somatomedin activity in human serum (Müller, 1979). Therefore, hGH levels in the male are generally somewhat lower. The exception is the male with adrenogenital syndrome who, through excessive androgens, demonstrates premature cessation of bone growth due to early epiphysial closure.

D. SUMMARY

Sexual differentiation is facilitated through steroid hormones, hypothalamic regulatory peptide hormones, and pituitary gonadotropins. The type, concentration, and timing of hormone activity appear to be more critical for male sexual differentiation than for that of the female. Once again, the male is exposed to a greater survival liability by virtue of the hormonal contribution to human sexual dimorphism.

V. Intellectual, Neurological, and Behavioral Disorders: Male Preponderance

The foregoing clearly shows that genetic and hormonal factors influence the ontogenesis of males and females in distinct ways. With respect to biological viability, such influences by and large favor the female and often pose a greater biological risk to the male. As noted earlier, the increased vulnerability of the male can be viewed as the cost for the greater variability demonstrated by the male in many biological and behavioral realms.

A behavioral domain of considerable importance for the human is that of intellectual functioning. Prior to assessing the male preponderance in disorders relating to intellectual functioning it will be helpful to review some of the research that demonstrates that males and females exhibit small but consistent differences in some of the ability areas that comprise the behavioral domain of cognition. These sex-related differences in general cognitive functioning correlate highly with the genetic/hormonal sex-related distinctions outlined earlier in this article.

A. SEX-RELATED DIFFERENCES IN GENERAL INTELLECTUAL FUNCTIONING

In 1968 Donald Broverman and his colleagues concluded that females surpass males on simple overlearned perceptual motor tasks such as color naming, digit symbol, fine manual dexterity, clerical aptitude, discrimination, and some conditioning tasks. Males, in contrast, outperform females on tasks requiring the inhibition of immediate responses to obvious stimulus attributes (mazes, embedded figures, Rod-and-Frame Test). The sex-related differences in cognitive style suggested by Broverman, Klaiber, Kobayashi, and Vogel (1968) were hypothesized to reflect differences in the relationships between adrenergic activating and cholinergic inhibitory neural processes which, in turn, were suggested to be sensitive to androgens and estrogens. On the basis of psychopharmacological studies, Broverman *et al.* proposed that females are more activated or less inhibited than males in their neural and cognitive processes and that the sex difference in the activation–inhibition balance is attributable to the differences in the levels of estrogens and androgens typical of each sex. Furthermore, Broverman *et al.* proposed that variations in the performance of simple perceptual motor and inhibitory restructuring tasks are behavioral representations of the balance between adrenergic activating and cholinergic inhibiting neural processes.

The differential hormonal states among males and females and their potential contribution to the source of the variance observed in spatial abilities were addressed by Petersen (1976), who demonstrated that highly physically androgenized males are more proficient in fluent production tasks than in spatial tasks. The reverse was obtained for less physically androgenized males. However, the more androgenized females were the more proficient on the spatial tasks and the less androgenized females were the more proficient on the fluent production tasks. The degree of sex hormone influence was inferred by Petersen from the degree of secondary sex characteristic development observed in her male and female subjects (i.e., overall body shape, penis or breast size, pubic hair distribution, muscle versus fat distribution).

Petersen's findings suggest that the hormonal influence on behavioral tasks may be curvilinear, in that overandrogenization of males moves them toward proficiency in fluent production tasks, but androgenization in females moves them toward proficiency in spatial tasks. Support for the curvilinear nature of the influence of androgens is provided by males with androgen insensitivity syndrome; they demonstrate superior verbal IQ relative to performance IQ and poor perceptual organization relative to verbal comprehension (Masica *et al.*, 1971). Females with adrenogenital syndrome do not show the expected performance superiority in spatial tasks, but females with progestin-induced hermaphroditism do show marginal performance superiority in spatial tasks (Ehrhardt & Money, 1967; Reinisch, Gandelman, & Spiegel, 1979).

Researchers who infer hormonal status from somatic characteristics have obtained consistent findings with respect to the influence of hormones on cognitive functioning. Androgenized females and normal males tend to demonstrate good spatial abilities. Sex stereotypical females (not androgenized) and under- or overandrogenized males demonstrate better performance on fluent production tasks. However, as Petersen (1979) pointed out, the research on the relationship of hormones to cognitive functioning suffers from methodological problems because of our inability to obtain accurate measures of hormonal activity. Functions such as metabolic clearance rates, production rates, and tissue receptor sensitivity make the assessment of endocrine status extremely difficult. The inference of hormonal status from somatic characteristics must be substantiated by the accurate measurement of hormonal activity.

In the studies conducted by Waber (1976, 1977a), late maturers, determined by observed secondary sex characteristic development, were found to perform better than earlier maturers on spatial ability tasks, and the early maturers excelled on verbal tasks. According to Waber (1977a), the pattern of scores obtained on cognitive tasks varies systematically along a continuum of maturational rate independent of sex. However, because females tend to mature earlier than males, the rate of physical maturation becomes an important determinant of the sex-related difference in spatial ability observed among adults (Waber, 1977a,b). Waber (1977b) proposed a model in which maturational rate influences central nervous system development which, in turn, leads to variation in field dependence and personality characteristics. According to Waber (1977b), endocrinological development influences the organization of higher cortical functions and the variation in such an organization is reflected in both cognitive functioning and personality.

The suggestion that earlier maturation leads to greater symmetry in hemispheric cerebral functioning (Harris, 1978) must be viewed with caution. As

Waber (1976) pointed out, the whole brain acts as an integrated system and sex-related cognitive differences may reflect variation in the mechanisms that integrate the activity of the cerebral hemispheres rather than reflecting variation in the cerebral hemispheres themselves.

1. Spatial Abilities

That males do perform better than females on spatial tasks has been reliably reported by many researchers (e.g., Broverman *et al.*, 1968; Harris, 1978; Maccoby & Jacklin, 1974; McGee, 1979; Vandenberg & Kuse, 1979). From the factor-analytic literature, McGee (1979) identified two distinct spatial abilities viz. spatial visualization and spatial orientation. In addition, McGee cited evidence for a male superiority in the performance of both types of spatial tasks. Harris (1978) examined studies of sex-related differences among a number of different spatial tasks and across different age ranges. Consistent with other reviews (Maccoby & Jacklin, 1974; McGee, 1979; Vandenberg & Kuse, 1979), she reported a developmental trend occurring within such tasks with few reports of performance differences occurring in childhood. The sex-related differences emerged about the time of puberty and continued to adulthood. The tasks in which a male superiority had been reported in childhood were those that involved an orientation ability, i.e., motor tasks requiring a coordination of movements. Harris (1978) also reported findings consistent with the Broverman *et al.* (1968) simple perceptual motor/inhibitory restructuring distinction. For example, males were found to demonstrate superior performance on tasks concerned with geometrical concepts and principles, but negligible sex-related differences were reported for the mechanical parts of mathematics. The mechanical aspects of mathematics, such as numerical addition, would be repetitive, perceptual motor-type tasks, and geometrical skills, as defined by McGee (1979), would involve the extensive mediation of higher cortical processes and thereby would fall into the realm of the inhibitory perceptual restructuring type of task.

The developmental aspect of sex-related differences in cognitive task performance has also been demonstrated by Berlin and Languis (1980). These researchers examined the verbal and spatial abilities of children 5 to 6 years of age and 11 to 12 years of age and, although no sex-related differences were observed in the younger group, differences in performance favoring the males were found in the older group on the Block Design Test. In an investigation of spatial abilities, Richmond (1980) isolated two factors that he identified as the ability to visualize a rigid configuration when it is moved into a different position (S1) and the mental ability to hold onto a configuration against a distraction (C2). Richmond (1980) examined the presence of these factors in a sample of 10-year-old children and found that males and females differed on the S1 factor, with the males demonstrating superior performance. No sex-related differences occurred with the C2 factor. Richmond (1980) suggested that sex-related differences in spatial ability may emerge before the adolescent period, but that such differences are not generalized and remain restricted to specific types of spatial tasks.

Signorella and Jamieson (1978) demonstrated male superiority on a spatial ability task (Card Rotations Test) and also on the Piagetian Water-Level Task among 13- to 14-year-old students. Similarly, Ray, Georgiou, and Ravizza (1979) utilized the Water-Level Task and a spatial ability task (Revised Minnesota Paper Form Board Test) and found the correlation for the scores obtained on the two tasks to be higher for males, suggesting that males have a more integrated spatial processing system than do females. Liben and Golbeck (1980) questioned whether the sex-related differences in spatial ability were due to differences in the level of conceptual maturity acquired by males and females (competence interpretation) or to the manner in which the sexes access the cognitive systems representing space when attacking spatial problems (performance interpretation). Liben and Golbeck tested groups of 8-, 10-, 12-, 14-, and 16-year-old children employing "physical" and "nonphysical" versions of horizontality and verticality tasks. Both males and females performed better on the nonphysical version of the two tasks. The latter finding led Liben and Golbeck to suggest that an inadequate knowledge about such physical phenomena and/or an inability to apply such knowledge may cause the difficulty in performing such tasks. The study also demonstrated that the correlation between the males' verticality and horizontality scores for the physical version was higher than that obtained for the females, but both sexes exhibited virtually identical correlations for the sets of scores obtained from the nonphysical version. According to Liben and Golbeck, these data suggest that females use more variable application procedures or methods of observation when dealing with task-relevant knowledge. Such a conclusion is consistent with results obtained by Allen and Hogeland (1978), who examined problem-solving strategies in relation to spatial tasks (Rod-and-Frame Test and a maze test). From the responses of subjects to a questionnaire that was given following completion of the tasks, Allen and Hogeland concluded that females employed more concrete, nonabstract strategies and used less organized, less efficient methods in solving the problems than did their male counterparts. Allen and Hogeland suggested that the sex-related differences (the male superiority) observed in the performance of the spatial tasks appear to be a reflection of the female's use of ineffective strategies in solving such problems.

Male superiority on spatial tasks has also been reported for atypical populations. For example, Kupke, Lewis, and Rennick (1979) demonstrated that, within a population of adult epileptic individuals characterized by diffuse cerebral dysfunction, males excelled in gross motor performance, visual–spatial abilities, and quantitative skills whereas females exhibited a superiority among tasks requiring psychomotor and verbal abilities. A similar finding has been reported for mild and moderate mentally retarded subjects (Vance, Hankins, Wallbrown, Engin, & McGee, 1978).

2. *Laterality*

The human brain has been suggested to be asymmetrically organized with respect to the function of the cerebral hemispheres. The left hemisphere is most efficient for the processing of verbal and linguistic material; the right hemisphere is most efficient in the processing of perceptual, analytical, and spatial types of stimuli. The concept of hemispheric functional asymmetry is supported by a vast amount of behavioral literature (e.g., Kimura, 1973). Differences in the anatomical structures of the hemispheres, particularly in the auditory regions and in the Sylvian fissure, have also been reported (see Rubens, 1977). Such anatomical differences may underlie hemispheric functional asymmetry (Galaburda, LeMay, Kemper, & Geschwind, 1978).

In addition, evidence indicates the presence of sex-related differences in the anatomical structure of the cerebral hemispheres (Wada, Clark, & Hamm, 1975; Witelson & Pallie, 1973). In infant brains the appearance of an enlarged plenum temporale in the left hemisphere is more prominent in females than in males, suggesting greater physical maturation in the female (Witelson & Pallie, 1973). In adult brains Wada *et al.* (1975) reported that a majority of their cases showed a larger left plenum and that, of these cases, a greater number were female. Of particular interest is the finding that a portion of the right temporal cortex is enlarged more frequently among females than males. The implication is that, as a result, posterior regions are smaller in females and the effectiveness of the right hemisphere as a spatial processor may therefore be less in females. This implication is supported by the behavioral data, which suggest that adult males are more right hemisphere specialized for spatial types of functions and adult females tend to be more bilaterally represented in terms of verbal and spatial functions (see Harris, 1978; McGlone, 1980).

Studies of the performance of children and adults on tasks of lateralization of function suggest a general developmental trend. Studies with children reveal no clear sex-related differences on dichotic listening or tachistoscopic word recognition tasks (Bryden, 1979). The only support for such differences in children is provided by Witelson (1976), who tested males and females between 6 and 13 years of age on the Dichhaptic Stimulation Task. She observed that males demonstrated a greater right hemisphere preference on the spatial task, as indicated by their greater accuracy in performing the task with the left hand relative to the right hand. Affleck and Joyce (1979), also employing Witelson's Dichhaptic Stimulation Task, obtained similar results with a sample of 10-year-old males and females.

For adults, the data indicate that males are more likely than females to show a left hemisphere superiority on verbal tasks and a greater asymmetry for visual–spatial processes (Bryden, 1979). Sasanuma and Kobayashi (1978), employing a task requiring the recognition of the direction of tachistoscopically presented lines exposed in the left and right visual half-fields, observed that adult males demonstrate a trend toward left half-field superiority, and females do not. Levy and Reid (1978) also employed tachistoscopically presented verbal and spatial tasks as measures of cerebral lateralization and concluded that the female subjects were less laterally differentiated than the males.

Studies with clinical populations have also revealed sex-related differences in lateralization. In testing male and female right and left hemisphere-lesioned individuals on measures of language and visual–spatial ability, McGlone and Kertesz (1973) observed a greater spatial impairment among males who had right hemisphere damage than among females similarly affected. The left hemisphere-lesioned females alone showed significant correlations between the verbal and spatial scores. Such findings led McGlone and Kertesz to suggest that the male has a greater degree of right hemisphere specialization for spatial processes and the female utilizes more verbal mediation in spatial tasks. McGlone (1978), in a similar study, obtained further support for this suggestion. Utilizing specific measures from the WAIS verbal and performance IQ scores as indicators of hemispheric function among right and left hemisphere-lesioned males and females, McGlone demonstrated that males with left hemisphere damage had poorer verbal IQ scores relative to their performance IQ scores. The converse was true for males with right hemisphere damage. However, for females the verbal and performance IQ measures were not found to be significantly different regardless of whether the lesion was located in the right or the left hemisphere.

B. CONCLUSION

Descriptions of cognitive differences between the sexes cannot constitute explanations independent of the mechanisms that underlie such differences. Each of the reliably demonstrated sex-related differences (e.g., early female verbal precocity, male superiority in visual–spatial ability, male superiority in analytical skills) suggests the operation of a genetic and/or a hormonal mechanism.

Sherman (1978) argued that the amount of variation in cognitive behavior attributable to sex is not greater than 5% and therefore that the differences are too small to implicate a major biological mechanism. She concluded that such small differences can be attributed to historic and cultural factors that have a basis in biological expectations. For example, Lee and De Vore (1968) and Levy (1978) suggested that males have been the hunters and the leaders of migrations throughout the evolution of the human species and those with good visual–spatial abilities have had the selective advantage. Females, in contrast, have been subjected to selective pressures for the skills involved in child rearing. Such views provide the foundation for the evolutionary explanation of sex-related differences in cognitive functioning.

Among the most salient of the evolutionary factors are sex role prescriptions. Children as young as 2.5 to 3 years of age display stereotypical concepts of sex-appropriate beliefs, traits, and eventual adult roles (Kuhn, Nash, & Brucken, 1978). Also, beginning in the second grade, children perceive verbal and artistic skills as feminine and spatial, mechanical, and athletic skills as masculine (Nash, 1975). Perhaps certain sex-related differences are related to a biological predisposition that is fully or partially realized as a function of attitudes developed over years of socialization.

Most investigators agree that sex-related differences in cognitive functioning are typically small, suggesting a great deal of overlap in the distribution of cognitive abilities across men and women (Anastasi, 1958; Springer & Deutsch, 1981). For example, Hyde (1981), in a reanalysis of the studies reported by Maccoby and Jacklin (1974), determined that the gender differences in verbal ability, quantitative ability, visual–spatial ability, and field articulation accounted for only 1–5% of the population variance. However, when viewed from the biodevelopmental perspective such small but consistent sex-related cognitive differences reflect the operation of biological mechanisms that place the male of the species at greater risk for intellectual, neurological, and behavioral disorders.

C. INTELLECTUAL, NEUROLOGICAL, AND BEHAVIORAL DISORDERS

In nonclinical populations males and females present some fundamental differences in their approach to spatial tasks, in verbal production, and even in the degree to which the cerebral hemispheres are specialized for verbal and nonverbal processing. Although such differences are influenced by environmental factors, the major contributor appears to be the complex of genetic–hormonal interactions that underlies the basic biological differentiation between male and female (Broverman *et al.*, 1968; Waber, 1977b). The suggestion that such genetic–hormonal interactions pose a greater disadvantage for the male is further demonstrated by their preponderance among intellectual, neurological, and behavioral disorders.

1. Mental Retardation

Studies of the prevalence of mental retardation have consistently revealed a higher incidence of retardation among males than among females. Lapouse and Weitzner (1970) reviewed 12 such studies and reported male-to-female ratios ranging from 1.1 to 1.9. Males are also more frequently represented within each of the functional levels of mental retardation (mild, moderate, severe, profound). Abramowicz and Richardson (1975) reviewed 27 community studies of severe mental retardation and their age-specific breakdowns revealed a greater number of males relative to females for all chronological age categories. Lapouse and Weitzner (1970) noted some reported male-to-female ratios of 1.4 for the moderate-to-severe levels and 1.1 for the mild level. Lehrke (1978) reported an excess of males within all levels of retardation from mild to profound and across all ages. For individuals under 21 years, males exceeded females by 48% (mild), 39% (moderate), 44% (severe), and 35% (profound). Among retarded individuals 21 years of age and older, males exceeded females by 10% (mild), 6% (moderate), 34% (severe), and 10% (profound). In total, males were also reported to exceed females by 69% in the borderline range of intelligence. Over all functional levels and across all ages the male population was found to exceed that of the female by 35%.

The 1977 revision of the *Manual on Terminology and Classification in Mental Retardation* (Grossman, 1977) defined mental retardation as "significantly subaverage general intellectual functioning existing concurrently with deficits in adaptive behavior, and manifested during the developmental period" (p. 11). Mental retardation, so defined, refers to a level of behavioral performance without reference to etiology and therefore the term itself does not distinguish between retardation associated with psychosocial influences or with biological deficit. The prevalence of biological etiological factors is known to increase as the functional level of retardation moves from mild to profound and therefore a caution is necessary when sex differences across functional levels are examined. At the mild level of retardation the general survey data may be inflated slightly in favor of males because of biological influences such as the cytogenetic anomalies involving the sex chromosomes (e.g., Klinefelter's syndrome). For the moderate, severe, and profound levels of retardation, biological etiological influences increase considerably and factors such as X-linked genetic disorders account for a high percentage of males who exhibit retardation. In contrast, except for the cytogenetic anomalies involving the sex chromosomes, including the fragile X syndrome (Hagerman, McBogg, & Hagerman, 1983), the male-to-female ratios for autosomal cytogenetic anomalies (e.g., Down's syndrome, Edwards' syndrome, Patau's syndrome) are roughly equal. For example, Gibson (1978) pointed out that the secondary sex ratio for Down's syndrome is similar to that in the general population.

In addition, not only do males outnumber females across the functional levels of mental retardation, but sex-related differences have also been demonstrated within functional levels. For example, Vance *et al.* (1978) analyzed specific cognitive abilities of a sample of mild-to-moderate mentally retarded children from their performance on the WISC-R. They observed that males scored significantly higher than females on the object assembly task and females excelled on the coding task, a finding consistent with the hormonal hypothesis suggested by Broverman *et al.* (1968).

2. Learning Disabilities

Males have also been found in greater numbers among the learning disabled. Unlike the generalized intellectual deficit found in mental retardation, the learning disabled demonstrate near-average, average, or above-average intellectual ability. They do, however, manifest circumscribed impairments in one or a few of the following areas: perception, conceptualization, language, memory, the control of attention, impulse control, and motor control. For hyperactivity Safer and Allen (1976) reported a male-to-female ratio of 4:1, with the prevalence estimated at about 8–9% in elementary school boys and 2–3% in elementary school girls. Profert and Rosenfield (1971) obtained a prevalence rate for stuttering from a population of university students. Of the 115 individuals reported as being present or former stutterers, 74% were male. As well, males are affected by dyslexia much more frequently than are females. Zahálková, Vrzal, and Klobouková (1972) reported that their sample of dyslexics was 86% male. Epidemiological studies concerned with early infantile autism have revealed male-to-female ratios ranging from 3:1 to 4:1. Treffert (1970) reported a ratio of 3:1; Spence, Simmons, Brown, and Wikler (1973) reported an overall male-to-female ratio of 4.7:1 for autism.

Eme (1979) also noted a male preponderance in all disorders that involve a specific delay in development. In a review of learning difficulties, Eme focused on the maturational lag of the male as a contributor to learning disabilities. For Eme, earlier female physical maturation appears to be paralleled by earlier intellectual maturation. For example, Maccoby and Jacklin (1974) reported that between the ages of 2 and 7 years the sex differences that are found in general intellectual abilities usually favor girls.

3. Neurological Disorders

The growth and development of the human brain is susceptible to a number of adverse influences (e.g., genetic, traumatic, infectious), any one or a combination of which can lead to neurological disorders. Generally, the neurological disorders attending such factors do not influence the sexes differentially. However, exceptions to this statement do exist. For example, X-linked recessive disorders involving amino acid metabolism (e.g., Lowe's syndrome), carbohydrate metabolism (e.g., Hunter's syndrome), lipid metabolism (e.g., Fabry's disease), and other metabolic dysfunctions (e.g., Lesch–Nyhan syndrome) lead to impairment in neurological development. The X-linked character of these disorders means that the male expresses the disorder significantly more frequently than the female. Because the male has only one X chromosome (hemizygous) the chance for offsetting genes to modify the expression of genes located on the single X chromosome is nonexistent. Therefore, recessive disorders that have a locus on the X chromosome (X linked) are expressed in the male more frequently than in the female. Heredodegenerative diseases (e.g., Pelizaeus–Merzbacher disease,

Leber's optic atrophy, Charcot–Marie–Tooth peroneal muscular atrophy) and malformations such as agenesis of the corpus callosum and hydrocephalus (aqueductal stenosis) are also more frequently observed in males because of their X-linked character. For a complete listing of X-linked disorders, see McKusick (1978).

In addition, conditions such as cerebral palsy, Sydenham's chorea, hyperthyroidism, fibril convulsions, epilepsy, and early migraine are noted more frequently in boys although these conditions have no genetic predisposition through X linkage (Menkes, 1974). Bradshaw and Lawton (1978) examined a population of 32,709 handicapped children under 15 years of age. Their examination revealed a significantly greater number of males affected with cerebral palsy (56.8%), epilepsy (58.0%), blindness (58.7%), deafness (56.0%), congenital anomalies (57.0%), and, as expected, X-linked conditions such as hemophilia (98.2%), and Duchenne type muscular dystrophy (87.0%). No significant sex differences were reported for meningitis, encephalitis, cystic fibrosis, kidney disease, or bone disease. Females, however, did outnumber males for spina bifida (52.0%). Taylor and Ounsted (1972) reported that females are more prone to severe defects of neural tube closure, relative to males.

Sex differences in the susceptibility to infections have also been reported (Parkman, 1977). The male demonstrates an increased suceptibility to a great variety of infections, including bacterial meningitis (1.8:1) and the septicemias (2:1).

On balance, although males predominate for the overwhelming majority of disease conditions (Childs, 1965), some exceptions exist other than those that are female specific, such as uterine cancer. For example, diseases of the autoimmune group reveal a greater number of affected females (Taylor & Ounsted, 1972).

4. *Behavioral Disorders*

Eme (1979) examined the sex-related differences in the major categories of childhood behavioral disorders. The review revealed a greater male prevalence in adjustment reactions, gender identity disorders, learning disorders, neurotic disorders, and psychotic disorders. This finding was considered to be in marked contrast with adult sex-related differences that, beginning in adolescence, eventuate in a greater female prevalence in neurotic disorders and affective psychotic disorders, a greater male prevalence in personality and gender identity disorders, and no sex-related difference in schizophrenic disorders.

Although no differences in the prevalence rates of schizophrenia according to sex have been reported (Dohrenwend, Dohrenwend, Gottesman, Link, & Neugebauer, 1980), sex differences with respect to the age of symptom onset and first hospitalization have been obtained (Lewine, 1980). Lewine (1980), in a study of 177 schizophrenic patients, established that males are significantly younger than females at onset and at first hospital admission for schizophrenia irrespective of type, except for paranoid schizophrenia, in which no sex-related difference was found. Lewine also confirmed that the reported sex-related differences were independent of both the diagnostic criteria used in the study and any differential tolerance to symptoms that might exist between the two sexes. According to the data reported by Lewine (1980), the typical age of onset and first hospitalization for schizophrenia ranged from 20 to 30 years for males, and the age of onset for females clustered around 30 to 45 years.

The influence of male fetal hormones on schizophrenia in the expectant mother was explored by Taylor (1969), who documented extremely high male fetal mortality in mothers who experienced the onset of prepartum schizophrenia during the first trimester. This finding led Taylor to conclude that the hormonal influence of the male fetus may exacerbate the risk to males in mothers who experience early prepartum schizophrenia. However, if the onset of maternal schizophrenia occurs late in pregnancy, the male fetus may defend itself by the production of functionally high levels of hormones that suppress the disease in the mother. The delivery of the male fetus would then unmask the mother's schizophrenia. The successful treatment of postpartum psychosis by progestins and androgens supports Taylor's view of the protective and masking functions of the male fetal hormones during later pregnancy.

D. Conclusion

The small but consistent sex-related differences in specific areas of cognitive functioning reflect the behavioral influence of the biological mechanisms contributing to human sexual dimorphism. Although the magnitude of such differences suggests a great deal of overlap in the distribution of cognitive abilities across men and women, their consistency, we contend, reflects the differential operation of the genetic–hormonal mechanisms in men and women. Such a difference is directly related to the variability afforded by the (XY) genome. Such variability carries with it a cost, i.e., the preponderance of males exhibiting the disorders noted above.

VI. The Benefit

On the benefit side of the ledger one is compelled to ascribe some advantages to the male (XY) genome. Just as the male represents the greater frequency among abortions, stillbirths, disease, and disorders, so too does he represent the greater frequency among the positive extremes of behaviors such as intellectual functioning (Jensen, 1971; Lehrke, 1972, 1978). The female, in contrast, is less frequently represented at the extremes of the distribution of general intelligence.

The doctrine of greater male variability, however, is not without its opposition. Anastasi (1958) argued that the obtained sex differences in the variability of general intelligence are "extremely small and usually insignificant" (p. 459). Tyler (1965) concluded that "the hypothesis of the greater variability of the male will probably persist as long as no really decisive evidence shows up to disprove it" (p. 251). The reader is referred to Shields (1975) for a chronology of the variability hypothesis polemic.

A. AN X-LINKED MAJOR GENE HYPOTHESIS

Robert Lehrke (1972, 1978) proposed that intellectual functioning is attributable to the X linkage of major genes for intelligence. Lehrke (1972) derived his position from the study of several families that displayed mental retardation with no known physiological correlates. For Lehrke (1978), greater male variability is what would be expected if major genes for intelligence are located on the X chromosome and, indeed, in the retarded (Abramowicz & Richardson, 1975) and gifted (Jensen, 1971) populations males comprise the greater numbers at the extremes of the intelligence continuum.

To support his hypothesis, Lehrke (1978) examined intrafamily comparisons of intelligence test scores. The intrafamily comparison method involves comparing the correlations of IQ scores between family members. The ordering of the correlations by magnitude can reveal the X-linked gene contribution to a characteristic such as intellectual functioning. Because the father passes an X chromosome to his daughters and a Y chromosome to his sons, the expected ordering of the IQ comparisons, if genes located on the X chromosome are influential, would be: (mother–son)=(father–daughter)>(mother–daughter)>(father–son), the latter comparison equaling zero. Lehrke (1978) reported such orderings.

Further support for the X-linked hypothesis is provided by the comparisons of concordance rates between monozygotic female and monozygotic male twins. Female monozygotic twins can be somewhat more unlike than male monozygotic twins because of the random nature of the X chromosome inactivation (Section III,C). To the extent that the X chromosome is implicated in an attribute, female monozygotic twins should show lower concordance than male monozygotic twins. Such a finding was obtained by Osborne (1978) on a battery of tests relating to intellectual functioning.

However, difficulties exist with Lehrke's (1978) hypothesis (Anastasi, 1972; Nance & Engel, 1972; Sherman, 1978). For example, Anastasi (1972) argued that the evidence in support of Lehrke's (1972) hypothesis is too meager to permit an evaluation of the hypothesis. In particular, Lehrke (1972) reported that retarded women married to normal men are twice as likely to have retarded offspring relative to retarded men married to normal women. Anastasi (1972) suggested that because women have more of a role in child rearing, their retardation should have more of a debilitating effect on their offspring than should the retardation of a husband.

B. INTELLIGENCE: A SEX-INFLUENCED TRAIT?

An alternative to the X-linkage hypothesis is to view intelligence as a sex-influenced characteristic. The greater variability of the male with respect to intelligence (Bock & Vandenberg, 1968; Hunt, 1974) could be attributed to a sex-influenced mode of heritability for *some* major intelligence-determining genes. The genes in this case would be located on the autosomes, but in the male they would operate as dominant genes and in the female they would operate as recessive genes. The resultant pattern would be virtually indistinguishable from that of an X-linked recessive characteristic (Mange & Mange, 1980).

Support for the sex-influenced explanation is provided by individuals with (X0) Turner's syndrome. As noted earlier (Section III,C), these females exhibit difficulties in the area of spatial abilities (Alexander *et al.*, 1966; Hier *et al.*, 1980; Money & Alexander, 1966) characteristically unlike (XY) males. However, Turner's individuals do exhibit the male pattern for color blindness, which is an X-linked recessive condition. These findings suggest that intelligence may be not X linked but rather sex influenced. A feature of sex-influenced traits is that the hormones play a significant role in the expressivity of the characteristic (e.g., pattern baldness). In Turner's syndrome (X0), gonadal agenesis is typical and results in a failure to produce gonadal hormones. The absence of hormones may account for the failure of Turner's females to demonstrate the typical male pattern with respect to verbal and performance IQ and would support a sex-influenced interpretation. With respect to spatial ability in particular, Vandenberg and Kuse (1979) reviewed all the available genetic studies of spatial ability, and also failed to find support for X linkage.

The sex-influenced explanation for intellectual functioning encompasses both the genetic and the hormonal components of human sexual dimorphism and, as suggested earlier, an explanation that excludes the hormonal influence (i.e., X linkage) would eliminate a significant link in the gene-to-behavior transaction.

C. INCREASED VARIABILITY AND THE (XY) GENOME

The increase in variability of the genetic–behavioral potential of the species is related to the hemizygous nature of the male (XY) genome. In the male, those genes located on or interacting with genes located on the X chromosome will be fully expressed because of the lack of offsetting alleles. In the female (XX), allelic control from portions of the inactive X chromosome is possible, thus reducing the range of variability in genetic expression. In addition, females are mosaic for genes located on the X chromosome. In approximately 50% of their somatic cells the paternal X is active and in the remainder the maternal X is active. Therefore, the chances for the extreme expression of the genes located on the X chromosome are reduced because particular alleles active in one cell line (maternal or paternal) would be moderated by the active homologous genes in the other cell line.

Consequently, the increase in the variability of genetic–behavioral potential affords the male not only the aforementioned disadvantages but also the advantage of maximizing the genetic potential involved in behaviors such as intellectual functioning.

VII. Conclusion

The human occupies a wide range of available ecologies and the vigor of the species is relative to the ability to adapt to the environment. The development of human intelligence has, by its inventions, allowed the human to modify the environments in which the species lives and to which adaptation is required. The preceding discussion suggests that the biological systems contributing to human sexual dimorphism expose the male to a greater biobehavioral risk, relative to the female. However, human sexual dimorphism also provides the species with a benefit.

The reproductive capacity of a species, and therefore its survival, is determined by the number of propagating females it possesses. A species can ill afford to reduce its number of females, and therefore a mechanism that lowers the genetic risk to females (genetic conservatism) and at the same time provides for the maximum of genetic expression in the species, is advantageous. Human sexual dimorphism is such a mechanism. In this process the X chromosome is passed from female to male to female through successive generations (Ounsted & Taylor, 1972). In the male the X chromosome is subjected to the extraction of maximum genetic expression. In the female, however, both mosaicism and allelic control lead to an attenuation of expression for the genes situated on and interacting with those on the X chromosome. Over generations a balance has been established between the conservation of genetic potential via the female and the expression of genetic potential via the male. By altering the balance of the effect of new variation away from the equality of risk in the two sexes, the human is equipped with a unique mechanism for coping with the challenge of survival, i.e., human sexual dimorphism.

REFERENCES

Abbott, D. H., & Hearn, J. P. The effects of neonatal exposure to testosterone on the development of behavior in female marmoset monkeys. *Ciba Foundation Symposium,* 1979, **62,** 299–316.

Abramovich, D. R. Human sexual differentiation: In utero influences. *Journal of Obstetrics and Gynecology,* 1974, **81,** 448–453.

Abramovich, D. R., & Rowe, P. Foetal plasma testosterone levels at midpregnancy and at term: Relationship to foetal sex. *Journal of Endocrinology,* 1973, **56,** 621–622.

Abramowicz, H. K., & Richardson, S. A. Epidemiology of severe mental retardation in children: Community studies. *American Journal of Mental Deficiency,* 1975, **80,** 18–39.

Affleck, G., & Joyce, P. Sex differences in the association of cerebral hemispheric specialization of spatial function with conservation task performance. *Journal of Genetic Psychology,* 1979, **134,** 271–280.

Alexander, D., Ehrhardt, A. A., & Money, J. Defective figure drawing, geometric and human, in Turner's syndrome. *Journal of Nervous and Mental Disease,* 1966, **142,** 161–167.

Allen, M. J., & Hogeland, R. Spatial problem-solving strategies as functions of sex. *Perceptual and Motor Skills,* 1978, **47,** 348–350.

Anastasi, A. *Differential psychology: Individual and group differences in behavior* (3rd ed.). New York: Macmillan, 1958.

Anastasi, A. Four hypotheses with a dearth of data: Response to Lehrke's "A theory of X-linkage of major intellectual traits." *American Journal of Mental Deficiency,* 1972, **76,** 620–622.

Arai, Y., & Gorski, R. A. Critical exposure time for androgenization of the rat hypothalamus determined by antiandrogen injection. *Proceedings of the Society for Experimental Biology and Medicine,* 1968, **127,** 590–593.

Baker, S. W., & Ehrhardt, A. A. Prenatal androgen, intelligence and cognitive sex differences. In R. C. Friedman, R. N. Richart, & R. L. Vande Wiele (Eds.), *Sex differences in behavior.* New York: Wiley, 1974. Pp. 53–84.

Berlin, D. F., & Languis, M. L. Age and sex differences in measures of brain lateralization. *Perceptual and Motor Skills,* 1980, **50,** 959–967.

Bock, D.R., & Vandenberg, S. G. Components of heritable variation in mental test scores. In S. G. Vandenberg (Ed.), *Progress in human genetics.* Baltimore, Maryland: Johns Hopkins Univ. Press, 1968. Pp. 233–260.

Bradshaw, J., & Lawton, D. Some characteristics of children with severe disabilities. *Journal of Biosocial Sciences,* 1978, **10,** 107–120.

Broverman, D. M., Klaiber, E. L., Kobayashi, Y., & Vogel, W. Roles of activation and inhibition in sex differences in cognitive abilities. *Psychological Review,* 1968, **75,** 23–50.

Bryden, M. P. Evidence for sex-related differences in cerebral organization. In M. A. Wittig & A. C. Petersen (Eds.), *Sex-related differences in cognitive functioning.* New York: Academic Press, 1979. Pp. 121–143.

Childs, B. Genetic origin of some sex differences among human beings. *Pediatrics,* 1965, **35,** 798–812.

Cryer, P. E., & Daughaday, W. H. Growth hormone. In L. Martini & G. M. Besser (Eds.), *Clinical neuroendocrinology.* New York: Academic Press, 1977. Pp. 243–277.

Cunningham, B. A. The structure and function of histocompatibility antigens. *Scientific American,* 1977, **237,** 96–107.

Dancis, J., & Schneider, H. Physiology: Transfer and barrier function. In P. Gruenwald (Ed.), *The placenta and its maternal supply line: Effects of insufficiency in the fetus.* Lancaster: Medical and Technical Publ., 1975. Pp. 98–124.

Denny, P. C., & Tyler, A. Activation of protein biosynthesis in non-nucleate fragments of sea urchin eggs. *Biochemical and Biophysical Research Communications,* 1964, **14,** 245–249.

Dohrenwend, B. S., Dohrenwend, B. P., Gottesman, I. I., Link, B., & Neugebauer, R. Epidemiology and genetics of schizophrenia. *Social Biology,* 1980, **26,** 142–151.

Dörner, G. Hormones, brain development and fundamental processes of life. In G. Dörner & M. Kawakami (Eds.), *Hormones and brain development.* Amsterdam: Elsevier, 1978. Pp. 13–25.

Dörner, G., & Staudt, J. Structural changes in the preoptic anterior hypothalamic area of the male rat, following neonatal castration and androgen substitution. *Neuroendocrinology,* 1968, **3,** 136–140.

Dörner, G., & Staudt, J. Structural changes in the hypothalamic ventromedial nucleus of the male rat following neonatal castration and androgen treatment. *Neuroendocrinology,* 1969, **4,** 278–281.

Ebert, J. D., & Sussex, I. M. *Interacting systems in development* (2nd ed.). New York: Holt, 1970.

Ehrhardt, A. A. Androgens in prenatal development: Behavior changes in nonhuman primates and men. In G. Raspe (Ed.), *Advances in the biosciences: Hormones and embryonic development.* Oxford: Pergamon, 1974. Pp. 153–162.

Ehrhardt, A.A., Epstein, R., & Money, J. Fetal androgens and female gender identity in the early-treated androgenital syndrome. *Johns Hopkins Medical Journal,* 1968, **122,** 160–167.

Ehrhardt, A. A., Evers, K., & Money, J. Influence of androgen and some aspects of sexually dimorphic behavior in women with the late-treated andrenogenital syndrome. *Johns Hopkins Medical Journal,* 1968, **123,** 115–122.

Ehrhardt, A. A., & Meyer-Bahlburg, H. F. L. Psychosexual development: An examination of the role of prenatal hormones. *Ciba Foundation Symposium,* 1979, **62,** 41–57.

Ehrhardt, A. A., & Money, J. Progesterone-induced hermaphroditism: I.Q. and psychosexual identity in a study of ten girls. *Journal of Sexual Research,* 1967, **3,** 83–100.

Eme, R. F. Sex differences in childhood psychopathology: A review. *Psychological Bulletin,* 1979, **86,** 574–595.

Forest, M. G., Cathiard, A. M., & Bertrand, J. A. Total and unbound testosterone levels in the newborn and in normal and hypogonadal children: Use of a sensitive radioimmunoassay for testosterone. *Journal of Clinical Endocrinology and Metabolism,* 1973, **36,** 1132–1142.

Galaburda, A. M., LeMay, M., Kemper, T. L., & Geschwind, N. Right-left asymmetries in the brain. *Science,* 1978, **199,** 852–856.

Gibson, D. *Down's syndrome: The psychology of mongolism.* London and New York: Cambridge Univ. Press, 1978.

Gross, P. R., & Cousineau, G. H. Macromolecule synthesis and the influence of actinomycin on early development. *Experimental Cell Research,* 1964, **33,** 368–395.

Grossman, H. J. (Ed.). *Manual on terminology and classification in mental retardation.* Baltimore, Maryland: Garamond/Pridework, 1977.

Hagerman, R. I., McBogg, P., & Hagerman, P. J. The fragile X syndrome: History, diagnosis, and treatment. *Developmental and Behavioral Pediatrics,* 1983, **4,** 122–130.

Harris, L. J. Sex differences in spatial ability: Possible environmental, genetic, and neurological influences. In M. Kinsbourne (Ed.), *Asymmetrical function of the brain.* London and New York: Cambridge Univ. Press, 1978. Pp. 405–522.

Hier, D. B., Atkins, L., & Perlo, V. P. Learning disorders and sex chromosome aberrations. *Journal of Mental Deficiency Research,* 1980, **34,** 17–26.

Hunt, C. Sex: What's the difference? *New Scientist,* 1974, **16,** 405–407.

Hyde, J. S. How large are cognitive gender differences? A meta-analysis using ω^2 and d. *American Psychologist,* 1981, **36,** 892–901.

Jensen, A. R. The race × sex × ability interaction. In R. Cancro (Ed.), *Intelligence: Genetic and environmental influences.* New York: Grune & Stratton, 1971. Pp. 107–161.

Job, J. C. The neuroendocrine system and puberty. In L. Martini & G. M. Besser (Eds.), *Clinical neuroendocrinology.* New York: Academic Press, 1977. Pp. 487–501.

Jost, A. A new look at the mechanisms controlling sex differentiation in mammals. *Johns Hopkins Medical Journal,* 1972, **130,** 38–53.

Kimura, D. The asymmetry of the human brain. *Scientific American,* 1973, **228,** 70–78.

Korenbrot, C. C., Paup, D. C., & Gorski, R. A. Effects of testosterone propionate or dihydrotestosterone propionate on plasma FSH and LH levels in neonatal rats and on sexual differentiation. *Endocrinology,* 1975, **97,** 709–717.

Krco, C. J., & Goldberg, E. H. H-Y (male) antigen: Detection on eight-cell mouse embryos. *Science,* 1976, **193,** 1134–1135.

Kuhn, D., Nash, S. C., & Brucken, L. Sex role concepts of two- and three-year-olds. *Child Development,* 1978, **49,** 445–451.

Kupke, T., Lewis, R., & Rennick, P. Sex differences in the neuropsychological functioning of epileptics. *Journal of Consulting and Clinical Psychology,* 1979, **47,** 1128–1130.

Labrie, F., Lagace, L., Beaulieu, M., Ferland, L., DeLean, A., Drouin, J., Borgeat, P., Kelly, P. A., Cusan, L., Dupont, A., Lemay, A., Antakly, T., Pelletier, G. H., & Barden, N. Mechanisms of action of hypothalamic and peripheral hormones in the anterior pituitary gland. In C. H. Li (Ed.), *Hormonal proteins and peptides: Hypothalamic proteins* (Vol. 7). New York: Academic Press, 1979. Pp. 205–277.

Lane, C. Rabbit hemoglobin from frog eggs. *Scientific American,* 1976, **23,** 61–71.

Lapouse, R., & Weitzner, M. Epidemiology. In J. Wortis (Ed.), *Mental retardation: An annual review* (Vol. 1). New York: Grune & Stratton, 1970. Pp. 197–223.

Larsson, T. The fate of gene mutations and their impact on human sex ratio. *Acta Psychiatrica Scandinavica,* 1973, **49,** 281–293.

Lee, R. B., & De Vore, I. (Eds.). *Man the hunter.* Chicago, Illinois: Aldine, 1968.

Lehrke, R. G. A theory of X-linkage of major intellectual traits. *American Journal of Mental Deficiency,* 1972, **76,** 611–619.

Lehrke, R. G. Sex linkage: A biological basis for greater male variability in intelligence. In R. T. Osborne, C. E. Noble, & N. Weyl (Eds.), *Human variation: The biopsychology of age, race, and sex.* New York: Academic Press, 1978. Pp. 171–198.

Levy, J. Lateral differences in the human brain in cognition and behavioral control. In P. Buser & A. Rougeul-Buser (Eds.), *Cerebral correlates of conscious experience.* Amsterdam: North-Holland Publ., 1978.

Levy, J., & Reid, M. Variations in cerebral organization as a function of handedness, hand posture in writing, and sex. *Journal of Experimental Psychology: General,* 1978, **107,** 119–144.

Lewine, R. R. Sex differences in age of symptom onset and first hospitalization in schizophrenia. *American Journal of Orthopsychiatry,* 1980, **50,** 316–322.

Liben, L. S., & Golbeck, S. L. Sex differences in performance on Piagetian spatial tasks: Differences in competence or performance? *Child Development,* 1980, **51,** 594–597.

Lindley, M., & Mignon, B. R. Fetal mortality and sex ratio. *Science,* 1979, **206,** 1428.

Littau, V. C., Allfrey, V. G., Frenster, J. H., & Mirsky, A. E. Active and inactive regions of nuclear chromatin as revealed by electron microscope autoradiography. *Proceedings of the National Academy of Sciences,* 1964, **52,** 93–100.

Loke, Y. W. Tumors of the placenta: A breakdown in fetal-maternal relationships. In D. H. Steven (Ed.), *Comparative placentation.* New York: Academic Press, 1975. Pp. 282–293.

Lowrey, G. H. *Growth and development of children* (7th ed.). Chicago, Illinois: Year Book Medical Publ., 1978.

Lyon, M. F. Attempts to test the inactive-X theory of dosage compensation in mammals. *Genetic Research,* 1963, **4,** 93–103.

Lyon, M. F. Sex chromatin and gene action in the X-chromosome of mammals. In K. L. Moore (Ed.), *The sex chromatin.* Philadelphia, Pennsylvania: Saunders, 1966. Pp. 370–386.

Lyon, M. F. Sex chromosome activity in germ cells. In E. M. Coutinho & F. Fuchs (Eds.), *Physiology and genetics of reproduction.* New York: Plenum, 1974. Pp. 63–71.

Maccoby, E. E., & Jacklin, C. N. *The psychology of sex differences.* Stanford, California: Stanford Univ. Press, 1974.

Mange, A. P., & Mange, E. J. *Genetics: Human aspects.* Philadelphia, Pennsylvania: Saunders, 1980.

Martini, L. Role of the metabolism of steroid hormones in the brain in sex differentiation and sexual maturation. In G. Dörner & M. Kawakami (Eds.), *Hormones and brain development.* Amsterdam: Elsevier, 1978. Pp. 3–12.

Masica, D. N., Money, J., & Ehrhardt, A. A. Fetal feminization and female gender identity in the testicular feminizing syndrome of androgen insensitivity. *Archives of Sexual Behavior,* 1971, **3,** 143–149.

McGee, M. G. Human spatial abilities: Psychometric studies and environmental, genetic, hormonal, and neurological influences. *Psychological Bulletin,* 1979, **86,** 889–918.

McGlone, J. Sex differences in functional brain asymmetry. *Cortex,* 1978, **14,** 122–128.

McGlone, J. Sex differences in human brain asymmetry: A critical survey. *The Behavioral and Brain Sciences,* 1980, **3,** 215–263.

McGlone, J., & Kertesz, A. Sex differences in cerebral processing on visuospatial tasks. *Cortex,* 1973, **9,** 313–320.

McKusick, V. A. *Mendelian inheritance in man: Catalogues of autosomal dominant, autosomal recessive and X-linked phenotypes* (5th ed.). Baltimore, Maryland: Johns Hopkins Univ. Press, 1978.

McMillen, M. M. Differential mortality by sex in fetal and neonatal deaths. *Science,* 1979, **204,** 89–91.

Menkes, J. H. *Textbook of child neurology.* Philadelphia, Pennsylvania: Lea & Febiger, 1974.

Money, J. Developmental differentiation of femininity and masculinity compared. In S. M. Faber & R. H. L. Wilson (Eds.), *Man and civilization: The potential of women.* New York: McGraw-Hill, 1963. Pp. 51–65.

Money, J. Determinants of human sexual behavior. In C. J. Sager & H. S. Kaplan (Eds.), *Progress in group and family therapy.* New York: Brunner/Mazel, 1972. Pp. 564–594.

Money, J. Human behavior cytogenetics: Review of psychopathology in three syndromes—47,XXY; 47,XYY; and 45,X0. *Journal of Sex Research,* 1975, **11,** 181–200.

Money, J., & Alexander, D. Turner's syndrome: Further demonstration of the presence of specific cognitional deficiencies. *Journal of Medical Genetics,* 1966, **3,** 47–48.

Money, J., & Ehrhardt, A. A. Prenatal hormone exposure: Possible effects on behaviour in man. In R. P. Michall (Ed.), *Endocrinology and human behaviour.* London and New York: Oxford Univ. Press, 1968. Pp. 32–48.

Money, J., & Ehrhardt, A. A. *Man and woman: Boy and girl.* Baltimore, Maryland: Johns Hopkins Univ. Press, 1972.

Money, J., Ehrhardt, A. A., & Masica, D. N. Fetal feminization induced by androgen insensitivity in the testicular feminization syndrome: Effect on marriage and maternalism. *Johns Hopkins Medical Journal,* 1968, **123,** 105–114.

Money, J., & Lewis, V. I.Q., genetics and accelerated growth: Adrenogenital syndrome. *Bulletin of the Johns Hopkins Hospital,* 1966, **118,** 365–373.

Money, J., Lewis, V., Ehrhardt, A. A., & Drash, P. W. I.Q. impairment and elevation in endocrine and related cytogenetic disorders. In J. Zubin & G. A. Jervis (Eds.), *Psychopathology of mental development.* New York: Grune & Stratton, 1967. Pp. 22–27.

Money, J., & Schwartz, M. Dating, romantic and non-romantic friendship, and sexuality in 17 early-treated adrenogenital families aged 16–25. In P. A. Lee, L. P. Plotnick, A. A. Kowarski, & C. J. Migeon (Eds.), *Congenital adrenal hyperplasia.* Baltimore, Maryland: Univ. Park Press, 1977. Pp. 419–451.

Moore, K. L. *Before we are born: Basic embryology and birth defects.* Philadelphia, Pennsylvania: Saunders, 1974.

Müller, E. E. The control of somatotropin secretion. In C. H. Li (Ed.), *Hormonal proteins and peptides: Hypothalamic proteins* (Vol. 7). New York: Academic Press, 1979. Pp. 123–204.

Nagle, J. J. *Heredity and human affairs*. St. Louis, Missouri: Mosby, 1974.

Nance, W. E., & Engel, E. One X and four hypotheses: Response to Lehrke's "A theory of X-linkage of major intellectual traits." *American Journal of Mental Deficiency*, 1972, **76**, 623–625.

Nash, S. C. The relationships among sex-role stereotyping, sex-role preference, and sex difference in spatial visualization. *Sex Roles*, 1975, **1**, 15–32.

Ohno, S. *Major sex-determining genes*. Berlin and New York: Springer-Verlag, 1979.

Osborne, R. T. Race and sex differences in heritability of mental test performance: A study of negroid and caucasoid twins. In R. T. Osborne, C. E. Noble, & N. Weyl (Eds.), *Human variations: The biopsychology of age, race, and sex*. New York: Academic Press, 1978. Pp. 137–169.

Ounsted, C., & Taylor, D. C. (Eds.). *Gender differences: Their ontogeny and significance*. London: Churchill Livingston, 1972.

Parkman, R. Immunology. In A. J. Schaffer & M. E. Avery (Eds.), *Diseases of the newborn* (4th ed.). Philadelphia, Pennsylvania: Saunders, 1977. Pp. 764–773.

Petersen, A. C. Physical androgeny and cognitive functioning in adolescence. *Developmental Psychology*, 1976, **12**, 524–533.

Petersen, A. C. Hormones and cognitive functioning in normal development. In M. A. Wittig & A. C. Petersen (Eds.), *Sex-related differences in cognitive functioning*. New York: Academic Press, 1979. Pp. 189–274.

Profert, A. R., & Rosenfield, D. B. Prevalence of stuttering. *Journal of Neurology, Neurosurgery, and Psychiatry*, 1971, **41**, 954–956.

Ray, W. J., Georgiou, S., & Ravizza, R. Spatial abilities, sex differences, and lateral eye movements. *Developmental Psychology*, 1979, **15**, 455–457.

Reddy, V. V. R., Naftolin, F., & Ryan, K. J. Conversion of adrenostenedione to estrone by neural tissues from fetal and neonatal rats. *Endocrinology*, 1974, **94**, 117–121.

Reinisch, J. M. Fetal hormones, the brain, and human sex differences: A heuristic, integrative review of the recent literature. *Archives of Sexual Behavior*, 1974, **3**, 51–90.

Reinisch, J. M., Gandelman, R., & Spiegel, F. S. Prenatal influences on cognitive abilities: Data from experimental animals and human genetic and endocrine syndromes. In M. A.Wittig & A. C. Petersen (Eds.), *Sex-related differences in cognitive functioning*. New York: Academic Press, 1979. Pp. 215–239.

Reinisch, J. M., & Karow, W. G. Prenatal exposure to synthetic progestins and estrogens: Effects on human development. *Archives of Sexual Behavior*, 1977, **6**, 257–288.

Richmond, P. G. A limited sex difference in spatial test scores with a preadolescent sample. *Child Development*, 1980, **51**, 601–602.

Robinson, N. M., & Robinson, H. B. *The mentally retarded child: A psychological approach* (2nd ed.). New York: McGraw-Hill, 1976.

Rubens, A. B. Anatomical asymmetries of human cerebral cortex. In T. Harnad, R. W. Doty, L. Goldstein, J. Jaynes, & G. Krauthamer (Eds.), *Lateralization in the system*. New York: Academic Press, 1977. Pp. 503–516.

Russell, L. B. Mammalian X-chromosome action: Inactivation limited in spread and in region of origin. *Science*, 1963, **140**, 976–978.

Russell, L. B. Another look at the single-active-X hypothesis. *Transactions of the New York Academy of Sciences: Series II*, 1964, **26**, 726–736.

Russell, L. B., & Bangham, J. W. Variegated-type position effects in the mouse. *Genetics*, 1961, **46**, 509–525.

Safer, D. J., & Allen, R. P. *Hyperactive children.* Baltimore, Maryland: Univ. Park Press, 1976.

Sasanuma, S., & Kobayashi, Y. Tachistoscopic recognition of line orientation. *Neuropsychologia,* 1978, **16,** 239–242.

Schmid, W. DNA replication patterns of human chromosomes. *Cytogenetics,* 1963, **2,** 175–193.

Schultz, G. A., & Church, R. B. Transcriptional patterns in early mammalian development. In R. Weber (Ed.), *The biochemistry of animal development* (Vol. 3). New York: Academic Press, 1975. Pp. 47–90.

Scott, C. I., & Thomas, G. H. Genetic disorders associated with mental retardation: Clinical aspects. *Pediatric Clinics of North America,* 1973, **20,** 121–140.

Sherman, J. A. *Sex-related cognitive differences.* Springfield, Illinois: Thomas, 1978.

Shields, S. A. Functionalism, Darwinism, and the psychology of women: A study in social myth. *American Psychologist,* 1975, **30,** 739–754.

Signorella, M. L., & Jamieson, W. Sex differences in the correlations among field dependence, spatial ability, sex role orientation, and performance on Piaget's Water-Level Task. *Developmental Psychology,* 1978, **14,** 689–690.

Silvers, W. K., Billingham, R. E., & Sanford, B. H. The H-Y transplantation antigen: A Y-linked or sex-influenced factor. *Nature (London),* 1968, **220,** 401–403.

Singer, J. E., Westphal, M., & Niswander, K. R. Sex differences in the incidence of neonatal abnormalities and abnormal performance in early childhood. *Child Development,* 1968, **39,** 103–111.

Spence, M. A., Simmons, J. Q., Brown, N. A., & Wikler, L. Sex ratios in families of autistic children. *American Journal of Mental Deficiency,* 1973, **77,** 405–407.

Springer, S. P., & Deutsch, G. *Left brain, right brain.* San Francisco, California: Freeman, 1981.

Stern, C. *Principles of human genetics* (3rd ed.). San Francisco, California: Freeman, 1973.

Szontagh, F., Jakobovits, A., & Mehes, K. Primary embryonal sex ratio in normal pregnancies determined by the nuclear chromatin. *Nature (London),* 1961, **192,** 476.

Tanner, J. M. *Foetus into man: Physical growth from conception to maturity.* Cambridge, Massachusetts: Harvard Univ. Press, 1978.

Taylor, D. C., & Ounsted, C. The nature of gender differences explored through ontogenetic analyses of sex ratios in disease. In C. Ounsted & D. C. Taylor (Eds.), *Gender differences: Their ontogeny and significance.* London: Churchill Livingstone, 1972. Pp. 215–240.

Taylor, M. A. Sex ratios of newborns: Associated with prepartum and postpartum schizophrenia. *Science,* 1969, **164,** 723–724.

Treffert, D. A. Epidemiology of infantile autism. *Archives of General Psychiatry,* 1970, **22,** 431–438.

Tricomi, V., Serr, D. M., & Solich, G. The ratio of male to female embryos as determined by the sex chromatin. *American Journal of Obstetrics and Gynecology,* 1960, **79,** 504–509.

Tyler, L. E. *The psychology of human differences* (3rd ed.). New York: Appleton, 1965.

Vance, H., Hankins, N., Wallbrown, F., Engin, A., & McGee, H. Analysis of cognitive abilities for mentally retarded children on the WISC-R. *The Psychological Record,* 1978, **28,** 391–397.

Vandenberg, S. G., & Kuse, A. R. Spatial ability: A critical review of the sex-linked major gene hypothesis. In M. A. Wittig & A. C. Petersen (Eds.), *Sex-related differences in cognitive functioning.* New York: Academic Press, 1979. Pp. 67–95.

Van Look, P. F. A., Hunter, W. M., Corker, C. S., & Baird, D. T. Failure of positive feedback in normal men and subjects with testicular feminization. *Clinical Endocrinology,* 1977, **7,** 353–366.

Waber, D. P. Sex differences in cognition: A function of maturation rate? *Science,* 1976, **192,** 572–574.

Waber, D. P. Sex differences in mental abilities, hemispheric lateralization, and rate of physical growth at adolescence. *Developmental Psychology,* 1977, **13,** 29–38. (a)

Waber, D. P. Biological substrates of field dependence: Implications of the sex difference. *Psychological Bulletin,* 1977, **84,** 1076–1087. (b)

Wachtel, S. S., Koo, G. G., Breg, W. R., & Genel, M. H-Y antigen in X, i(Xg) gonadal dysgenesis: Evidence of X-rated genes in testicular differentiation. *Human Genetics,* 1980, **56,** 183–187.

Wada, J. A., Clark, R., & Hamm, A. Asymmetry of temporal and frontal speech zones in 100 adult and 100 infant brains. *Archives of Neurology,* 1975, **32,** 239–246.

Whaley, L. F. *Understanding inherited disorders.* St. Louis, Missouri: Mosby, 1974.

Wilson, J. D. Sexual differentiation. *Annual Review of Physiology,* 1978, **40,** 279–306.

Witelson, S. F. Sex and the single hemisphere: Specialization of the right hemisphere for spatial processing. *Science,* 1976, **193,** 425–427.

Witelson, S. F., & Pallie, W. Left hemisphere specialization for language in the newborn: Neuroanatomical evidence of asymmetry. *Brain Research,* 1973, **96,** 641–646.

Wittig, M. A., & Petersen, A. C. *Sex-related differences in cognitive functioning.* New York: Academic Press, 1979.

Wolf, U., Fraccaro, M., Mayerová, A., Hecht, T., Zuffardi, O., & Hameister, H. Turner syndrome patients are H-Y positive. *Human Genetics,* 1980, **54,** 315–318.

Wolf, U., & Engel, W. Gene activation during early development of mammals. *Humangenetik,* 1972, **15,** 99–118.

Zahálková, M., Vrzal, V., & Klobouková, E. Genetical investigations in dyslexia. *Journal of Medical Genetics,* 1972, **9,** 48–52.

SYMPOSIUM ON RESEARCH PROGRAMS: RATIONAL ALTERNATIVES TO KUHN'S ANALYSIS OF SCIENTIFIC PROGRESS

INTRODUCTORY REMARKS

Hayne W. Reese, Chairman

Psychologists have long been concerned about the philosophical underpinnings of their science—for example, Kenneth W. Spence published several papers on the philosophy of science underlying the learning theory approach—and developmental psychologists seem to have been especially concerned. Developmental psychology is not only diverse theoretically, but also *simultaneously* diverse in that behavioral and various cognitive approaches to development have coexisted and vied with one another throughout the present century. Thomas Kuhn's analysis of the history of scientific revolutions in terms of competing paradigms seemed closely pertinent and formed the basis for a number of analyses of the theoretical diversity in developmental psychology. Fairly recently, a rational alternative to Kuhn's analysis has been developed by Imre Lakatos and Larry Laudan. The rational alternative, based on the concept of ''research programs'' (Lakatos) or ''research traditions'' (Laudan), is described and contrasted with Kuhn's analysis in this symposium.

In the first paper in this symposium, Overton summarizes historical developments in the philosophy of science, from the positivists to the recent rationalists, and shows parallels in developments in the science of child development. In the second paper, Barker and Gholson use the rationalist perspective to analyze the history of conditioning and cognitive programs as they vied for hegemony earlier in the present century. In the third paper, Beilin uses the rationalist perspective to analyze the historical emergence and interplay of structural cognitivism (in the Piagetian tradition) and functional cognitivism (in the information-processing tradition) in developmental psychology. In the fourth paper Palermo argues that some of Kuhn's detractors have overestimated the irrationality Kuhn attributed to scientists and have overestimated scientists' rationality. The final three papers are commentaries by the other participants on Palermo's remarks and on each other's paper. (The dialogue had to end somewhere, and therefore Palermo and the others were not given an opportunity to respond to the commentaries.)

The first three papers originated as a symposium organized by Barry Gholson and chaired by Hayne W. Reese at the 1982 Southeastern Conference on Human Development. The dialogue continued at the 1983 meeting of the Society for

ADVANCES IN CHILD DEVELOPMENT
AND BEHAVIOR, VOL. 18

ISBN 0-12-009718-4

Research in Child Development, in a symposium organized and chaired by Reese with David S. Palermo as the discussant. The continuation of the dialogue was especially relevant to one of the themes of this meeting, which marked the fiftieth anniversary of the Society, and the symposium was presented as part of an historical program overseen by Alice Smuts as Chair of the Program Committee's Subcommittee on History. The original presentations were edited and revised for the present publication.

WORLD VIEWS AND THEIR INFLUENCE ON PSYCHOLOGICAL THEORY AND RESEARCH: KUHN–LAKATOS–LAUDAN[1]

Willis F. Overton
DEPARTMENT OF PSYCHOLOGY
TEMPLE UNIVERSITY
PHILADELPHIA, PENNSYLVANIA

[1]Portions of earlier versions of this paper were presented at the biannual meetings of the Southeastern Conference on Human Development, Baltimore, Maryland, April, 1982, and at the biannual meetings of the Society for Research in Child Development, Detroit, Michigan, April, 1983. Special acknowledgments are expressed to Kenneth Gergen, Philip Hineline, Richard Lerner, Hayne Reese, and Ralph Rosnow for their critical reading and comments on earlier drafts.

ADVANCES IN CHILD DEVELOPMENT
AND BEHAVIOR, VOL. 18

ISBN 0-12-009718-4

A number of years ago, when my colleague Hayne Reese and I began to explore the relationship between empirical investigations of development and the conceptual foundations that generate these investigations (Overton & Reese, 1973; Reese & Overton, 1970), we were influenced in several ways by the writings of Thomas Kuhn (1962).

Kuhn, more than any other philosopher of science at the time, seemed to present the best articulation of our own belief that very general and abstract conceptual systems exert a categorical influence on the construction of scientific theories and, hence, on empirical investigations that derive from these theories. Following Kuhn and others (e.g., Pepper, 1942), we referred to such general systems as world views or paradigms, and we suggested that any given world view leads to a set of corollaries that acts as an abstract framework defining a research agenda. The world view and corollaries, in turn, generate a set of theories designed to explain or resolve various empirical problems. We referred to such a set of theories as a family of theories, in which the theories exhibit a genetic similarity (the world view and corollaries) but in which each theory deals somewhat differently with the diverse empirical problems it approaches. Members of a family might differ in content and they might differ over specific theoretical issues, but they exhibit a commonality and compatibility of deep structural features.

In addition to Kuhn's position with respect to the relationship between any given abstract conceptual system and empirical investigation, we were also influenced by arguments concerning the relationship between divergent, contradictory conceptual systems. Again, Kuhn's discussion of the issue of "incommensurability" seemed, at the time, to be the best articulation of our own view that incompatible abstract conceptual systems lead to incompatible forms of explanation, families of theories, and ultimately to an incompatibility in the meaning of the empirical phenomena and problems scientists attempt to resolve.

A final important influence of Kuhn's work on our own position involves the understanding of the very nature of scientific activity. Through the 1950s and into the 1960s psychology and other fields were dominated by a philosophy of science that held tightly to an empiricist's epistemology. From this epistemological position, as will be described more fully later, abstract conceptual systems of the type that Reese and I were attempting to examine had no legitimacy in science. Thus, our arguments that such systems perform an essential and necessary function in scientific activity also suffered from a very basic illegitimacy when interpreted within this empiricist framework.

In the late 1950s and early 1960s, however, a radically different version of the nature of scientific activity began to emerge and develop. This was a philosophy of science that admitted a more rationalistic epistemological orientation and maintained that even the seemingly most neutral scientific observations were permeated by abstract conceptual features. Pepper (1942) and Hanson (1958) were early contributors to this reconstruction of the nature of scientific activity, and Kuhn was particularly influential in elaborating and disseminating significant features of it. Because this orientation toward the nature of scientific activity was compatible with our own views, and because this orientation provided our work with a rational scientific legitimacy, Reese and I were naturally influenced by many of its features.

Since the publication of Kuhn's original paper (1962), a good deal of philosophical activity, among those who begin from rationalist epistemological assumptions, has been directed toward elaborating and developing a number of the issues raised by Kuhn. With time, although the basic structure concerning the relationship between conceptual systems and empirical investigation has remained intact, significant elaborations and extensions have also occurred. The best contemporary representations of these elaborations and extensions are defined in Imre Lakatos' theory of "scientific research programs" (Lakatos, 1978a,b) and Larry Laudan's extension of this work into what he refers to as "research traditions" (Laudan, 1977).

In a similar fashion, since the publication of our original papers, Reese and I have developed and modified our positions each in our own way. If the original papers were to be rewritten today several changes would be made. For example, I would move away from various considerations of the nature of truth alluded to in those papers and toward the view presented by Laudan (1977), that a central aim of science is to solve problems, not to seek universal truths about the universe. I would also consider in a more detailed fashion the nature of the incommensurability issue.

However, the most important modification I would make in the original papers is one that I will, in fact, use as a point of focus in the present paper. This is a general reformulation of the early Overton–Reese analysis within the context of philosophy of science issues outlined by Lakatos and Laudan. I believe that the positions articulated by Lakatos and Laudan, with respect to the philosophy of science, strongly support and clarify a number of the key points I have been trying to make with respect to the field of developmental psychology. Specifically, I believe that the early work of Overton and Reese concerning the influence of world views on psychological theory and research is today best interpreted within the context of Lakatos' strategy of scientific research programs, with appropriate modifications being made to incorporate recent advances suggested by Laudan.

In the following pages I will first set the argument by describing some central components of Lakatos' position. Then I will describe and reformulate the early work of Overton and Reese within this context. Finally, I will employ my reformulation to explore some issues related to the role played by mechanistic and organismic research programs in psychological theory and research.

I. Demarcationist Strategies in Science

For both Lakatos and Laudan, the main problem for the philosophy of science is the establishment of normative criteria that demarcate science from nonscience or pseudoscience. Lakatos (1978b) is explicit in rejecting both the view of skeptics (e.g., Feyerabend), who regard scientific theories as just one family of beliefs, equal epistemologically with any other set of beliefs, and elitists (e.g., Toulmin), who claim that no universal criteria are possible and only individual scientists can judge the adequacy of scientific theories. Lakatos and Laudan argue that skepticism and elitism each lead to a view of science as nonrational or irrational and that the rationality of science is preserved only by adopting a demarcationist strategy of attempting to reconstruct universal criteria embedded in past and present scientific activities.[2] Such criteria then serve as standards with which to judge the progress or degeneration of evolving science.

It should be noted that both Lakatos and Laudan included Kuhn among the group of elitists that denys the possibility of universal criteria. However, this view of Kuhn's position appears to be based on a misinterpretation. Although Kuhn's analyses have focused upon the individual differences among scientists that lead to different choices among competing theories he has not denied the existence and discoverability of universal criteria. As he stated, "One must . . . deal with characteristics which vary from one scientist to another without thereby in the least jeopardizing their adherence to the canons that make science scientific. Though such canons do exist and should be discoverable . . . they are not themselves sufficient to determine the decisions of individual scientists" (Kuhn, 1977, pp. 324–325). It is through their analysis of universal criteria—providing the context within which Kuhn's individual factors operate—that the contributions of Lakatos and Laudan may be said to be an elaboration and extension of Kuhn's. The situation in this instance is analogous to some contemporary forms of linguistic theory. For those who take the competence–performance distinction (Chomsky, 1975) seriously, a complete understanding of language requires both an inquiry into universal structures (competence) and individual factors (performance) that affect the expression of competence. So, too, a complete understanding of scientific activity requires the universal criteria described by Lakatos and Laudan and the individual factors described by Kuhn.

Lakatos (1978a) described four rival demarcationist sets of criteria or rival methodologies that have served as universal standards for the acceptance or

[2]The assertion that science is a rational activity is epistemologically neutral. Empiricist models of rationality claim that rationality is a product of observations of nature. Rationalist models claim that rationality is a product of mental activity (reason) and observation.

rejection of theories in science. These included the methodologies of positivism, conventionalism, conventionalism with falsification, and Lakatos' own methodology of "scientific research programs." Laudan's demarcationist methodology, referred to as "research traditions," is an extension and modification of Lakatos' "scientific research programs."

A. POSITIVISM

Two primary universal criteria were set down by positivism as standards of scientific legitimacy. The first was that ultimately, all general propositions in science must be reducible to statements describing hard data, i.e., observations. The second was that general propositions in science must be formulated on the basis of inductive inference and only inductive inference from observables. Thus, positivism claimed that the only propositions admissible into the essential body of science were those that describe observations, or infallible inductive generalizations drawn from observations (Lakatos, 1978a, p. 103). To the extent that deductive inference was accepted, it was employed only to derive from proven empirical generalizations other potentially provable propositions, i.e., propositions that could be reduced to observations.

Ultimately, positivism was widely rejected as a demarcationist position. Most of the friends and all the foes of positivism came to doubt the possibility of reducing general theories to observational propositions and, more importantly, they felt that the laws of science can seldom be adequately described as inductive generalizations (Lakatos, 1978a; Pepper, 1942; Wartofsky, 1968). Although positivism waned in popularity as a general scientific methodology, its ghostly influence continued to be felt in psychology. Guided by this influence, many still distrust any proposed scientific approach that suggests that to some extent theories are determined by more abstract conceptual systems; and many still believe that ultimately, conceptual incompatibilities will be totally resolved on the basis of hard-proven veridical bits of unambiguous data.

B. CONVENTIONALISM

The second demarcationist position or methodology is conventionalism. Conventionalism was built upon positivism and incorporates many of its features, including a heavy reliance on inductive inference (Lakatos, 1978a, p. 106). Conventionalism, however, recognizes that not all scientific propositions can be reduced to observational statements. As a consequence, conventionalism allows for the introduction of propositions, describing nonobservables, including theoretical entities and general theoretical models such as, in psychology, the computer model of information-processing approaches (Lachman, Lachman, & Butterfield, 1979). Although such propositions are held to be irreducible to observational statements, their primary feature is that they operate *only as convenient and conventional ways of ordering and organizing hard data,* i.e., observations. They do not influence the data base itself. Rather, they operate like pigeonholes to classify, arrange, and organize hard data into coherent units. In psychology, the framework of encoding, storage, and retrieval in memory offers a familiar example that is often interpreted from such a conventionalist perspective.

As conventions, theoretical entities or models are lightly held and readily given up when simpler ways are found of organizing hard data. As Lakatos pointed out, "For the conventionalist . . . [theoretical] discoveries are primarily inventions of new and *simpler* pigeonhole systems" (1978a, p. 107). However, the "genuine progress of science . . . takes place [still, as with the positivists] on the ground level of proven facts [i.e., hard data] and changes on the theoretical level are merely instrumental" (p. 106).

Conventionalism results in the creation of two distinct levels of scientific activity. These levels have been termed the context of justification and the context of discovery (Nickles, 1980; Overton, 1976; Reichenbach, 1938). One level (the context of justification) includes observations, experimental manipulations, and inductive generalizations, and this is the level at which genuine progress and explanations take place according to conventionalism. The other level (context of discovery) includes theoretical terms, entities, and models. These propositions may themselves be the products of the scientist's hunches, guesses, creative imagination, or metaphysical presuppositions. The origin of general propositions matters little because, according to conventionalism, this level exerts no real influence on the essential features of science, i.e., those included in the context of justification.

Within either positivistic or conventionalistic interpretations of the nature of scientific activity, the Overton–Reese analysis thus finds no real scientific legitimacy. At best, within conventionalism, the rival world models or world views described by Overton and Reese would be understood as mere convenient devices used to arrange theories and hard data. This, in fact, appears to be the interpretation that Beilin (this volume) gives to the Overton–Reese position and, in turn, Beilin seems to argue that he has found a simpler pigeonhole system, i.e., the "new functionalism." Overton and Reese, however, rejected any conventionalist interpretation. Our thesis has been that world models or world views enter into the essential body of science by providing certain metaphysical and methodological commitments that provide a set of guidelines for the construction of specific theories and the employment of specific methods of procedure. As Laudan emphasized with respect to "research traditions," I would repeat with respect to a world view: "Put simplistically, a . . . [world view] is thus a set of ontological and methodological 'do's' and 'don'ts.' To attempt what is forbidden by the metaphysics and methodology of a . . . [world view] is to put oneself outside the tradition and to repudiate it'' (Laudan, 1977, p. 80).

C. POPPER'S FALSIFICATION CONVENTIONALISM

An important variant of the conventionalist position is Karl Popper's falsification methodology (Popper, 1959). Popper recognized that the acceptance of theories or models based only on comparison of intuitive *simplicity,* as suggested by ''classical'' conventionalism, can be only a matter of subjective taste and hence constitutes a very weak criterion. Popper also recognized that theories or theoretical constructs can be neither verified nor confirmed. As a result, Popper proposed that in order for a theory or theoretical construct to be accepted into the body of science it must be shown to be in principle falsifiable. That is, the scientist, if his or her own theory is to be scientific, must specify results that, if found, would disprove the theory.

This criterion of scientific acceptance, although attaining a good deal of popularity among conventionalists, has also been severely criticized because of the ambiguity over whether falsification of an observational experimental hypothesis can spread to the falsification of the theory that generated the hypothesis. Several arguments against the position that a general theory can be falsified are detailed by both Lakatos and Laudan. One central problem is that when an experiment is conducted, a complex network of theoretical propositions is required to produce the experimental prediction or hypothesis. Falsification of the experimental hypothesis, however, does not unambiguously indicate the location of the error in the network. Another problem is that when the prediction is not supported it is pragmatically difficult to exclude the possibility that the error did not reside in either the inference drawn from the theoretical network or in the manner in which the experimental measures were conducted.

The nonfalsifiability of general theories is central to the understanding of scientific progress as analyzed by Kuhn, Lakatos, and Laudan. Each of these investigators accepted the view that falsified experimental hypotheses do not directly refute a general theory, but rather that they constitute anomalous instances. For Kuhn, anomalies accumulate until they induce a ''crisis'' and the dominant paradigm or general theory is replaced by a new paradigm. However, as noted earlier, Kuhn offers no universal rational criteria for the change from one to another paradigm. For Lakatos and Laudan, scientific progress is judged in terms of the empirical productivity of the general system (i.e., ''scientific research program'' or ''research tradition'') and anomalies are weighed in this context.

Before turning directly to Lakatos' position, I would like to mention a final feature of Popper's demarcationist strategy because of its relevance to the Overton–Reese analysis. Clearly, within the rules proposed by Popper, specific theories may enter the essential body of science but more general propositions, such as metaphysical propositions, may not. For Popper, metaphysical propositions may provide the external stimulus that leads the scientist to falsifiable theories, but the metaphysical propositions themselves are inherently nonfalsifiable, and hence peripheral to science per se. Thus again—as with the classical conventionalist strategy—within a falsification position world views are, at best, convenient heuristic devices but they do not perform the necessary and essential role claimed by Overton and Reese.

D. SCIENTIFIC RESEARCH PROGRAMS AND RESEARCH TRADITIONS

An important point to note is that each of the demarcationist strategies discussed to this point is heavily influenced by an empiricist epistemology. According to this epistemology, ultimately all legitimate scientific knowledge derives directly from fixed observational data free from any theoretical interpretation. The systems of Lakatos and Laudan, however, are much more strongly influenced by a rationalist epistemology.[3] Following Kant, this epistemology asserts that legitimate scientific knowledge is the product of both mental activity (reason) and observation. As mentioned earlier, the contemporary expression of this perspective as it applies to the nature of scientific activity took form in the late 1950s. Gradually it became articulated and elaborated through the analysis of various philosophers of science including Hanson, Hesse, Kuhn, Feyerabend, Pepper, Toulmin, and Wartofsky. The major point of agreement among this group is that although scientific activity is directed toward the solution of empirical problems, the observations that constitute the empirical content are never free from interpretation. As Laudan stated,

> In calling such inquiry situations "empirical" problems, I do not mean to suggest they are directly given by the world as veridical bits of unambiguous data. Both historical examples and recent philosophical analysis have made it clear that the world is always perceived through the "lenses" of some conceptual network or other and that such networks and the languages in which they are embedded may, for all we know, provide an ineliminable "tint" to what we perceive. More to the point *problems* of all sorts (including empirical ones) *arise within a certain context of inquiry* and are partly defined by that context. (1977, p. 15)

[3]Lakatos (1978a) at times referred to himself as a conventionalist. However, his ideas are more appropriately described as epistemologically rationalistic. As Laudan pointed out, Lakatos tried to make Popper's conventionalist "theory of rationality germane, and to fit his own interesting ideas into a Popperian context (where they do not really belong)" (Laudan, 1977, p. 227). Also, Lakatos himself explicitly accepted a Kantian "activist approach to the theory of knowledge" (Lakatos, 1978a, p. 38).

This rationalist orientation toward scientific activity, with its claims that bare, uninterpreted data are not possible and that conceptual systems permeate observations, is obviously compatible with the Overton–Reese analysis. However, a clear expression of the implications of this compatibility required the elaborations and extensions provided by Lakatos and Laudan, as they advanced beyond earlier investigators, particularly Kuhn.

The demarcationist strategy for scientific acceptability provided by Lakatos begins with a unit of analysis that is broader than any observational data base, and broader than any isolated theory or conjunction of theories. Lakatos called this unit a "scientific research program." It can be thought of as being composed of three levels arranged in a hierarchy. From top to bottom, in terms of decreasing levels of generality, these consist of first, a "*hard core*" and second, a "*positive heuristic*." These levels define problems and outline the construction of the third level, called a "*belt of auxiliary hypotheses,*" which are embodied in a family of specific theories.

The hard core itself may consist of various types of propositions, including metaphysical propositions. The potential inclusion of metaphysical propositions is particularly important because, in contrast to positivism and either form of conventionalism, the "hard core" admits into the *essential body of science* propositions that may have no potential falsifiers. Metaphysical propositions, as they may constitute a hard core of a scientific research program, are not, then, simply idle psychological or sociological curiosities, rather they are essential components of scientific activity. They exert a formative influence on lower levels and give meaning to the theoretical concepts of specific theories. For example, Lakatos described how Cartesian metaphysics, i.e., the mechanistic theory of the universe, operated as a hard core of a scientific research program that discouraged work on scientific theories that were inconsistent with it, e.g., Newton's theory of action at a distance, while encouraging work on auxiliary hypotheses that might have saved it from counter evidence (Lakatos, 1978a, p. 48).

In addition to bringing into the essential body of science that which is an external influence in positivism and conventionalism, another characteristic of the hard core is that it is not open to falsification. That is, the hard core is irrefutable. The reason the hard core is irrefutable is open to question. Lakatos claimed it is irrefutable through a "methodological decision of its proponents" (1978a, p. 48). In contrast, Overton and Reese (Overton, 1976; Overton & Reese, 1973) claimed that this characteristic derives from the fact that the categories of the hard core represent the extension of a basic or root metaphor.

The value of the irrefutability of the hard core is that it allows for the development of the "positive heuristic" without unnecessary distraction. The positive heuristic of the research program is influenced by the hard core but it describes the long-term research policy of the program. It is more flexible than the hard core and consists of, to quote Lakatos, "a partially articulated set of suggestions or hints on how to change, and develop the 'refutable variants' of the research programme, how to modify, and sophisticate the 'refutable' protective belt of auxiliary hypotheses" (Lakatos, 1978a, p. 50).

Taken together, the hard core and the positive heuristic of a given program constitute a *conceptual framework* that generates specific theories that within any given program constitute a family of theories. These theories in turn embody the "belt of auxiliary hypotheses," which are sets of observational hypotheses that constitute the falsifiable or refutable component of the scientific research program.

For Lakatos, falsification, i.e., the occurrence of anomalies, constitutes a local and minor criterion of scientific progress. The major criterion of progress of a scientific research program is that it predicts novel or unexpected phenomena with some degree of success. Furthermore, the anticipation of novel events should be guided by a coherent, preplanned positive heuristic rather than via patched-up ad hoc auxiliary hypotheses. Laudan expanded this position by maintaining that science aims "to maximize the scope of solved empirical problems, while minimizing the scope of anomalous and conceptual problems" (1977, p. 66). Thus, scientific progress is measured ultimately by a pragmatic criterion and not by the realist truth criterion of positivism and conventionalism. For Lakatos and for Laudan (1977) the advance of science is best described in terms of problem solving rather than in terms of making observational discoveries (see Nickles, 1980, p. 47).

With respect to the falsification of observational hypotheses, Lakatos claimed that the scientist must note them as they occur "but as long as his research programme sustains its momentum, he may freely put them aside. . . . Only when the driving force of the positive heuristic weakens, may more attention be given to anomalies" (1978a, p. 111). Laudan, in his extension of the general strategy, suggested ways in which anomalies can and should be graded in terms of their cognitive importance (1977, pp. 36–40).

In summary, Lakatos has defined several alternative demarcationist strategies and has put forward his own methodology of scientific research programs as the most adequate normative criteria of science and scientific progress. Lakatos' methodology builds upon but extends several features of Kuhn's analysis, as Laudan's similarly builds upon Lakatos'. I would maintain at this point that my own views with respect to the relationship of deep-seated ontological and methodological commitments to theories and research practices are currently most reasonably interpreted within the framework of research programs or research traditions. I believe that this interpretation both highlights the scientific legitimacy of the early Overton–Reese analysis and supports and clarifies a number of key components of that position.

II. Organismic and Mechanistic Scientific Research Programs

In essence, both Overton and Reese have maintained that two rival programs have continued to exert a strong influence in several scientific domains,[4] including psychology generally and developmental psychology specifically. These rival programs were termed the mechanistic and organismic world views or world models, but for the purposes of clarity, they will now be referred to as scientific research programs.

The thrust of the Overton–Reese analysis has been to articulate the hard core of each research program, to describe the positive heuristic that the hard core generates, and to demonstrate how the hard core and positive heuristic of a program result in a family of theories and testable auxiliary hypotheses. Consistent with both Lakatos and Laudan, we have also maintained that the hard cores of the rival programs are not open to experimental test, i.e., they are irrefutable, the hard cores represent an essential feature of each group's scientific activity, and the hard cores, through their positive heuristic, have an effect on the way the developmental psychologist does his or her research and understands basic terms in the field. The Overton–Reese analysis of the organismic and mechanistic research programs entails both a historical perspective, describing formative philosophical issues that came to represent the hard core ontological commitment of each program, and a parallel perspective describing the categories of each hard core as elaborations of root metaphors (see Table I and Overton, 1976, 1982a; Overton & Reese, 1981).[5]

A. HISTORICAL PERSPECTIVE OF HARD CORES

From an historical perspective, the two issues that have framed the hard cores of these rival programs are the question of the categorical nature of Being or Becoming, and the question of accidental or necessary organization. The issue of

[4]For an analysis of the influence of these programs with respect to classical physics and quantum theory, see Heisenberg (1958), especially Chapter V.

[5]The recognition of the role played by metaphor in the generation and elaboration of the hard core of a research program or tradition facilitates the solution to a problem that existed for both Lakatos and Laudan. Both asserted that "certain elements of a research tradition are sacrosanct, and thus cannot be rejected without repudiation of the tradition itself" (Laudan, 1977, p. 99). Lakatos suggested those elements derive from trial and error but once established they do not change. Laudan insisted that the elements change with time although he offered no solution to how this occurs. Recognition of the metaphorical base of the hard core suggests that the origin of the elements is not a trial and error process and that change is constrained by a systematic elaboration of the metaphor (see Overton, 1976; Pepper, 1942).

TABLE I
Origin and Nature of Scientific Research Programs

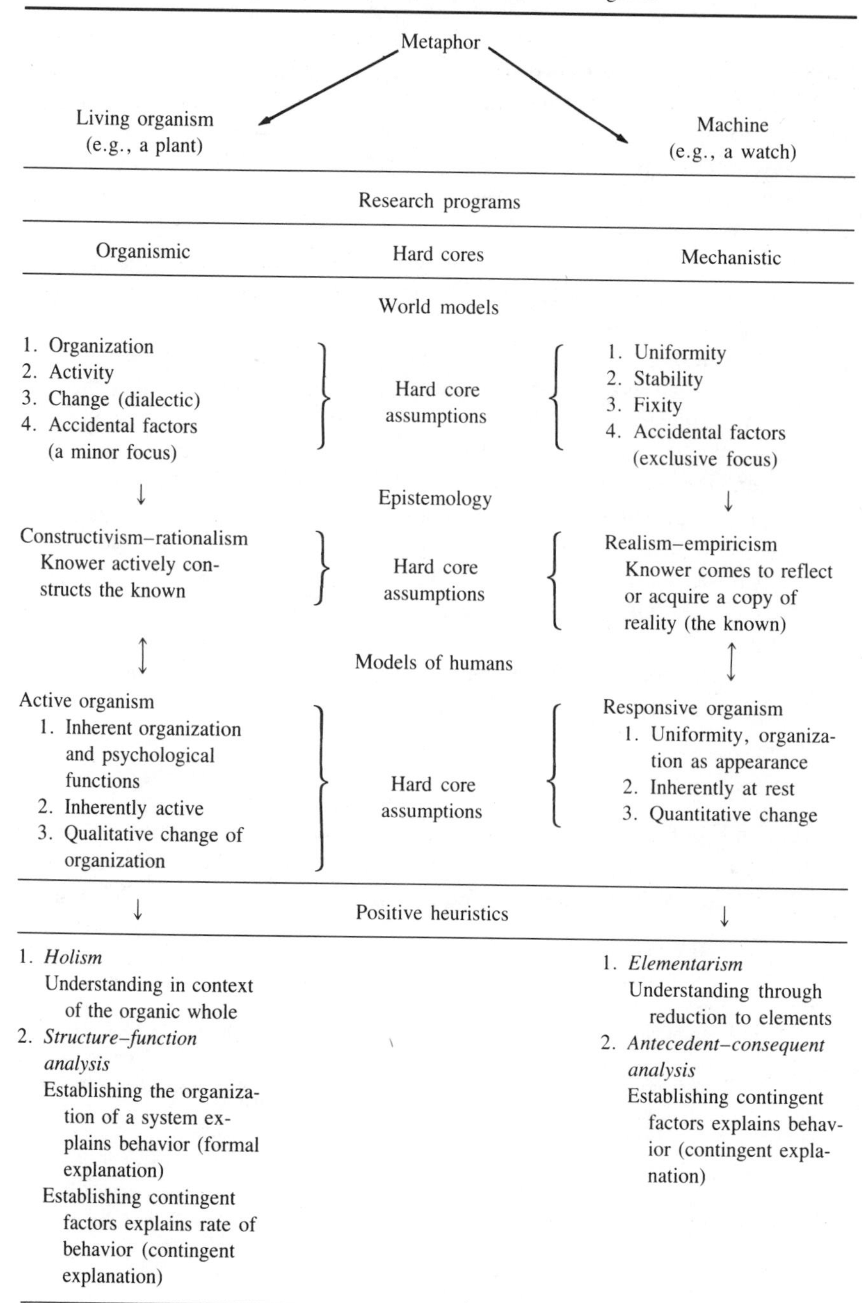

Metaphor		
Living organism (e.g., a plant)		Machine (e.g., a watch)
	Research programs	
Organismic	Hard cores	Mechanistic
	World models	
1. Organization 2. Activity 3. Change (dialectic) 4. Accidental factors (a minor focus)	Hard core assumptions	1. Uniformity 2. Stability 3. Fixity 4. Accidental factors (exclusive focus)
↓	Epistemology	↓
Constructivism–rationalism Knower actively constructs the known	Hard core assumptions	Realism–empiricism Knower comes to reflect or acquire a copy of reality (the known)
↕	Models of humans	↕
Active organism 1. Inherent organization and psychological functions 2. Inherently active 3. Qualitative change of organization	Hard core assumptions	Responsive organism 1. Uniformity, organization as appearance 2. Inherently at rest 3. Quantitative change
↓	Positive heuristics	↓
1. *Holism* Understanding in context of the organic whole 2. *Structure–function analysis* Establishing the organization of a system explains behavior (formal explanation) Establishing contingent factors explains rate of behavior (contingent explanation)		1. *Elementarism* Understanding through reduction to elements 2. *Antecedent–consequent analysis* Establishing contingent factors explains behavior (contingent explanation)

TABLE I (*Continued*)

3. *Necessary change* Establishing the order of organizational change explains development (formal explanation) Contingent factors explain rate of development (contingent explanation)		3. *Accidental change* Establishing the contingent factors explains development (contingent explanation)
4. *Discontinuity–continuity* Emergent systemic properties and levels of organization		4. *Strict continuity* Strict additivity
5. *Reciprocal causality*		5. *Unidirectional causality*
6. *Organized complexity*		6. *Linear causality*
↓	Families of theories	↓
Examples Contemporary structuralist theories: Piaget, Werner, Chomsky, Kohlberg, G. Allport, G. Kelly Humanistic theories: Rychlak Gestalt theories Ego development theories: Erikson, Kegan, Bowlby Bronfenbrenner's ecological perspective		Examples Behavioristic and neobehavioristic theories Operant and classical conditioning theories Observation learning theories Mediational learning theories Information-processing theories: Skinner, Bijou and Baer, Berlyne, Spiker, Bandura, Gewirtz, H. Kendler, Gibson

Being and Becoming entails the question of whether we represent the basic nature of objects and events as ultimately stable and fixed (Being) or as ultimately active and changing (Becoming). The history of the Being position can be traced to the early writings of Thales, Anaximenes, and Democrites, and from there to Locke, Berkeley, and Hume. The history of the Becoming position originates in the writings of Anaximander and Heraclites and leads from there to Leibniz, Vico, Kant, and Hegel (see Overton, 1982a). Representation in terms of the Being position requires that any apparent activity or change be explained by reducing it to stable and fixed elements and then discovering accidental or contingent factors that generated the original complex. Representation in terms of the Becoming position accepts activity and change as necessary. Here the primary task of explanation entails the discovery of the organization, form, or pattern of activity and change.

The distinction between the necessary and the accidental is derived from Aristotle. Activity or change that is accidental is that which is caused by fortuitous or contingent events. Necessary activity and change are free of causal events and are natural to the entity being considered. For example, a plant might be understood as going through a sequence of changes that is as necessary to the essence of the plant as are any other intrinsic features. At the same time, the plant has a history in the sense that accidental events such as favorable or unfavorable nutrients or good or bad weather may occur. The issue of accidental versus necessary organization is similar in the sense that one position claims that it is best to represent objects and events as ultimately uniform and organization as the product of accidental factors whereas the other position claims the best representation is found in considering objects and events as exhibiting necessary organization. The theme of necessary organization was first elaborated by Plato and Aristotle and later developed by rationalist philosophers (e.g., Kant). The theme of uniformity was developed within the historical tradition of philosophical empiricism (e.g., Bacon, Newton, Locke, Hume) (see Overton, 1982a).

The *hard core* of the *organismic* program is expressed in an ontological commitment to a Kantian–Hegelian philosophy of Becoming, wherein activity, change, and organization are understood as natural and necessary features of the cosmos and not simply as the product of contingent accidental factors. Accidental factors can here affect activity, organization, and change, but they cannot explain them. The *organismic positive heuristic* encourages its practitioners to work within a holistic–analytic framework, to consider change and organization as necessary and consequently open to a structure–function analysis, and to represent change as both continuous and discontinuous. The positive heuristic also establishes that both formal and contingent explanations are legitimate and that each serves a different role in providing general explanations (see Overton & Reese, 1981; Rychlak, 1977). Finally, the positive heuristic has led to a family of theories (see Table I) and numerous auxiliary hypotheses such as the set of hypotheses that maintains that the child's conceptual understanding is a necessary reflection of the child's level or stage of structural development.

The *hard core* of the *mechanistic* program is expressed in an ontological commitment to a Lockean–Humean philosophy of Being, wherein stability, fixity, and uniformity are considered basic, and change and organization are understood as the result of contingent or accidental factors only. The *positive heuristic* or research policy that this hard core generates—or what Overton and Reese earlier referred to as corollary model issues—encourages the practitioners of this program to work within a framework of elementaristic or reductionistic analysis, to consider all change and organization as the product of contingent antecedent factors, and to represent all change as strictly additive or continuous in nature. The positive heuristic also establishes that all explanations will be contingent explanations based on efficient or material factors (see Overton & Reese, 1981). Finally, the positive heuristic has, in turn, led to a family of theories (see Table I) and numerous auxiliary hypotheses, such as the set of hypotheses that asserts that the child's conceptual understanding (organization) is a direct product of learning (contingent antecedent factors).

B. ROOT METAPHOR PERSPECTIVE OF HARD CORES

A perspective that is parallel to the historical focuses upon the metaphor that generates the categories of the hard core of the rival programs (see Table I and footnote 5). The basic metaphor for the organismic program is a living organism such as a plant, and the metaphor for the mechanistic program is a simple machine such as a wind-up watch.

If we consider a plant from a relatively naive, common sense perspective it seems to have certain characteristics. For one, the plant has a unique form, structure, or organization that is not characteristic of any of its parts, e.g., its cells, nor a product of the parts simply added together. The organization is a feature of the whole organic unity. Furthermore, the meaning of a part is never complete except in relation to the whole. That is, the parts have no independent existence outside the organization in which they function. A second characteristic is that the plant has an inherent activity in the sense that it draws some things into itself (e.g., carbon dioxide) from the environment, rejects others (e.g., dust), gives back to the environment (e.g., oxygen) and is generally self-regulating or self-maintaining. Finally, the plant changes. This change appears to be as intrinsic to the plant as is its structure. Furthermore, the change is both directional, rather than random, and irreversible. The plant also goes through phases in its directional change and during these phases the structure of the plant changes qualitatively. In addition to these characteristics, the plant may also require nourishment by external factors and it may be subjected to harmful accidental factors acting upon it, but both sets of factors affect rate of activity and rate of change and not the inherent characteristics of the plant.

Given this image of the plant, it is not difficult to see how the basic categories of necessary organization, activity, and change were metaphorically drawn out to form the organismic hard core. Nor is it difficult to see how the focus of explanation is on organizational or formal features and how accidental factors came to be understood as efficient causes that primarily affect rate of activity and rate of change.

If we now consider a simple machine—again from a relatively naive perspective—a contrasting set of characteristics becomes apparent. First, the machine exhibits a uniformity of its parts. The apparent organization that seems to make the thing a watch can be broken down or reduced to these uniform parts. Although the parts operate together, they maintain their identities either in or out of the watch. Thus, the whole is an additive sum of its parts. Second, a machine is inherently at rest. Any activity is ultimately a product of external factors (e.g., winding the watch sets the gears in motion). Finally, a machine does not change. A machine does not go through phases in which its features become transformed. Any apparent changes (the hands on the watch move around the dial) are quantitative in nature and they, like activity, are the product of external factors.

It is easy to see how this machine image leads to the mechanistic hard core with its basic categories of uniformity, stability, and fixity and how accidental factors form the explanatory focus. Beyond generating different research program hard cores of such great scope that they may include virtually any domain of study (i.e., world models), the metaphors also provide guidelines for introducing greater specificity. For example, with respect to a specific focus on the investigation of man, the metaphors provide the categories for both the relationship between man and knowledge (i.e., epistemological models) and for the very nature of man. Thus, given the image that the knower (man), like any other component of the world, is active and possesses an inherent organization, the general organismic categories lead directly to rationalism and the position that the knower actively constructs the known. In contrast, the mechanistic categories of stability and uniformity lead to realism–empiricism and the position that the knower comes to reflect or acquire a copy of reality, and this is the known. Furthermore, a constructivist position concerning knowledge is possible only if one starts from the assumption that man possesses an inherent activity and an inherent organization such that the organization is applied to the world of experience in the creation of knowledge. On the other hand, a realist position is possible only if one basically views man as a kind of neutral mirror (or as Locke's blank slate) that reflects an external reality.

More broadly, when the general categories of the organismic hard core are extended to create a model of man, there results what has been called the *active organism* model (Overton, 1976). This model presents the following representation of man: Man, too, like other components of the universe, exhibits a necessary organization. Properties of this organization include psychological functions, such as representation, perception, and attention. Man, too, is inherently active; man, not the environment, is the source of acts. Finally, psychological growth or development in the sense of necessary, directional, qualitative change of organization and hence change also in the form of psychological functions, i.e., change in the way we represent things, the way we perceive, etc., is a reality, not an appearance.

In contrast, the extension of the mechanistic categories results in a model of man called the *responsive organism* model (Baer, 1976). Here man, like the machine, exhibits a uniformity of structure (Locke's blank slate). Man possesses no necessary organization or inherent psychological functions. If we seem to detect such organization or functions, they are to be treated as appearances that are ultimately understood as the product of external factors. Also, man, like the machine, is understood to be inherently at rest, and activity is the product of external factors. Finally, psychological growth or development, like organization, is to be treated as appearance. Only behaviors change, and these do so in a quantitative manner.

These models, although providing some specificity in terms of the articulation of a limited domain of study, i.e., man, are still quite abstract. They do not constitute psychological theories, nor are they specifically psychological concepts. However, these often implicit categories do form the hard cores of rival programs and they do provide guidelines for the development of the research policies of these programs (i.e., the positive heuristics), the psychological theories of the programs (i.e., families of theories), and specific psychological concepts. In the following section the positive heuristic features of the rival programs will be considered.

C. POSITIVE HEURISTIC COMPONENTS

1. Holism versus Elementarism

The positive heuristic feature of holism derives directly from the organismic categories of considering organization as an active organic unity in which the whole is characterized by systemic properties that do not describe the parts. Holism asserts that parts of an organic unity get their very meaning from these systemic properties. Consider, for example, any of the human biological systems, such as the visual system. It should first be noted that vision is not a property of any of the parts of the system; the retina does not have vision, nor does the optic nerve, nor does the occipital lobe of the brain, etc. Vision is a property of the total, intact, active organization. Furthermore, the parts themselves derive their meaning from the context of this whole system in which they operate. The optic nerve is differentiated from other tissues precisely because it functions as part of the visual system.

In psychology, behavior represents the ultimate parts and, according to this holistic assumption of organicism, specific behaviors derive their meaning and hence can be understood only in the *context* of the system of which they are a part. In essence, holism warns that it is inappropriate to reduce systems, e.g., "thinking," "language," or "perception," to simple behaviors or to assume that the simple behaviors are the sum and substance of the system. This position does not argue that analysis is unimportant. It argues that the best research approach is to analyze in terms of the function or end that the behavior serves in the system. This position leads to the next organismic corollary, structure–function analysis, which will be described shortly.

Before leaving holism it should be mentioned that in addition to influencing the research approach, any theory constructed within the organismic approach will in some way translate this feature and the other heuristic features into its theoretical concepts. The same may be said concerning the mechanistic approach. With respect to holism, an example of this translation is found in Piaget's statement concerning "structures" in his theory. "Wholeness is a defining mark of structures . . . all structuralists . . . are at one in recognizing the contrast between structures and aggregates, the former being wholes, the latter composites formed of elements that are independent of the complexes into which they enter" (1974, p. 6).

The corollary of elementarism derives directly from the mechanistic categories of uniformity and stability wherein apparent organization is understood as an aggregate composed of elements that maintain their identities in or out of the complex. Elementarism asserts that elements or parts constitute the real. As already mentioned, in psychology, behaviors represent the ultimate parts. Elementarism then argues that the best research approach is to reduce any complex phenomenon to these elements. This reduction is the first step in what has been traditionally called mechanical explanation.

2. *Structure–Function Analysis versus Antecedent–Consequence Analysis*

As mentioned above, the best research approach according to the organismic position is to begin from the definable functions of any system or subsystem. Following the specification of function, the investigator seeks to discover (i.e., rationally represent) the organization or structures that serve the function. This approach is familiar in organismically oriented biology. The biologist acts *as if* each organ or structure has a function. He defines the function and inquires into the operation of the structure in serving this function. For psychology, the approach is similar but the structures are psychological and not physical or physiological. Psychological structures refer to the relatively stable organizational properties or patterns of specific behavioral systems. In essence then, having defined the function, the investigator seeks to discover (rationally) the organization. That is, the investigator seeks to establish the formal explanation.

Here we may take Chomsky's (1975) work on language as an example both of the research approach and the theoretical incorporation of this feature. In its general features Chomsky's approach begins with a definition of the function of language as communication and representation. (Note that this excludes some behaviors that on the basis of material identity would be judged as language, e.g., the "language" of the bees and the mimicry of certain birds do not have a representational function.) Given this defining context, Chomsky then examines specific behaviors (written and spoken language acts) and draws inferences in the form of a relatively small number of rules that he believes adequately characterize both the behavior he has examined and all other language behaviors. These rules or structures, he would assert, capture the essential organization of language. Furthermore, the rules describe the psychological organization of the language producer, i.e., man, because man must in some sense (not consciously) possess the rules in order to demonstrate the behavior.

Several features of this approach might be questioned. First, it might be asked whether the approach isn't overly speculative because the rules are actually made up by the investigator. The answer is yes, it is speculative or, as stated earlier, it is a rational construction but the speculation is kept in check by the fact that later empirical tests will be made to determine whether the rules are in fact a good representation of the organization of behavior. Second, there is also a question of whether this approach doesn't demonstrate circular reasoning because the rules are inferred from the behavior and the rules are said to determine the behavior. The answer is that any vicious circularity is avoided if the investigator can show that the rules determine many other behaviors (e.g., other sentences) beyond the few that were used to make the inferences about the rules. In fact, demonstrating this and also demonstrating that the rules would not lead to impossible behaviors (e.g., groups of words that are not acceptable as sentences in a language) is one way of testing whether the rules are a good representation. Third, one might wonder whether the approach isn't descriptive rather than explanatory because the rules describe the behaviors. The answer is that if there were a different rule for each behavior it would be descriptive. Explanatory power in the formal explanatory sense comes from establishing a small set of rules that accounts for a wide range of behaviors.

A final question is whether experimental methods play any role in this approach. It was just pointed out that empirical tests are employed to decide whether the proposed organizations or structure, or rules are good or poor explanatory representations. Usually these tests employ correlational methods to decide whether different sets of behaviors exhibit sufficient coherence to warrant the inference that they are reasonably represented by the proposed organization. However, this still leaves open the question of whether actual experiments are conducted within this approach. An experiment, i.e., the manipulation of an independent variable and the observation of the effect of the manipulation on the dependent variable, is the method for establishing efficient explanations. But inherent organization is not the simple product of efficient factors, it is the formal explanation. Thus, with respect to the momentary organization that we are discussing, the approach does not use experiments to establish the organization.

Experiments *are* used in this approach but their role is that of determining how various situational (efficient) or biological (material) factors influence the way in which the organization is demonstrated in overt behavior (Overton & Newman, 1982). For example, we may know that an individual possesses the necessary structures for language and then we may want to investigate what kind of situational factors will increase the rate at which he or she actually speaks the language. Here, an experiment would be appropriate.

The mechanistic corollary of antecedent–consequent analysis derives from the hard core categories of uniformity and stability and it represents the second and key step in mechanical explanation. Once the phenomenon of interest, e.g., language, has been reduced to its elements, i.e., sounds, the rest of explanation consists primarily of establishing the material and efficient features or antecedents of those behaviors or consequences. This, of course, is done by performing experiments in which the assumed antecedent is the independent variable and the consequence is the dependent variable. Explanation is complete when the regularity between antecedent and consequent is reliable to the point that we inductively understand it to be scientific law.

3. *Necessary versus Accidental Change*

The foregoing positive heuristic features do not in themselves address the problem of change, which is the primary focus of developmental psychology. Rather, they establish the necessary features of general approaches to psychology and provide the basis for considerations of development. A number of theories have, in fact, been constructed on the basis of only these two sets of corollaries and these exhibit little interest in issues of development per se. Chomsky's work is an example of an organismic theory that ignores the issue of change and various contemporary cognitive information-processing approaches (see Lachman *et al.*, 1979) typify nondevelopmental mechanistic approaches.

As already discussed, the organismic model asserts that change and, hence, development are necessary, intrinsic, directional rather than random, and irreversible. What this means as a research approach is that the investigator must define the end or function of change, hence establishing the direction, and then discover (rationally) the organization or rules according to which the change occurs. Notice that the approach here is identical to that taken with respect to a structure–function analysis. But here the focus is upon the organization of change rather than upon momentary organization. Here also the momentary structure–function organizations are the part systems that change in accordance with the rules of the overall organization of change. Piaget's equilibration process, Werner's orthogenetic principle, and Erikson's epigenetic ground plan are all examples of such developmental rules. For Piaget, there is a necessary sequence of structures that proceeds from biological structures to sensorimotor structures to concrete operational structures to formal operational structures, all in accordance with the rules described by the equilibration process, always moving toward the end of intellectual maturity.

One may again question the speculative nature of having the investigator involved in yet more rational construction of rules. But here, as with the momentary structure–function analysis, the speculation is later empirically assessed by conducting investigations to determine whether the rule of change is a good representation of the changes of the structures of behavior. Both *cross-sectional* and *longitudinal* investigations can be directed toward examining whether the sequence is as universal as, e.g., Piaget claims, and correlational techniques can be employed to assess the changes in behavioral coherence across the sequence.

Experiments can also be conducted within the context of the rationally constructed rule of necessary change. For example, one might do an experiment to determine whether a group of children exposed to a poor educational environment is slowed down in the rate in which changes of organization are shown. Or training studies might select variables under the hypothesis that certain factors will speed up the rate of change. But it is most important to be aware that the *variables* chosen (efficient or material factors) for these or any other *experiments can never be used to explain the change itself* (Overton & Newman, 1982). They explain rate of change, the rule explains the development, and the rule cannot be directly tested by experimentation.

The mechanistic model asserts that fixity is basic and as a consequence change is produced by extrinsic accidental factors. Thus, the mechanistic group would claim that rules of change, like momentary organization, can be reduced to specific behaviors and full explanation is found by observing the antecedent causes that produce behavioral change. Thus, from this perspective, cross-sectional and longitudinal research is purely descriptive whereas the experiment provides the full explanation of change. To find that education has an effect on behavior or that training has an effect explains development from the mechanistic perspective.

4. Discontinuity–Continuity versus Strict Continuity

The final positive heuristic features to be considered here (see Overton & Reese, 1973, for others) involve the issue of whether change entails qualitative as well as quantitative features. As a model issue the debate is over whether, with change, later types of organization exhibit novel features that cannot be reduced to earlier organization and ultimately to behavior per se (discontinuity), or whether they are reducible (continuity). As a model issue it is completely irrelevant whether observed behavioral change is gradual or abrupt, small or large (Overton & Reese, 1981; Reese & Overton, 1970).

As already discussed, from the organismic model and its holistic corollary, any momentary organic system has systemic properties that are characteristic of organization as a whole, and not of any of the individual parts. From a psychological point of view, functions such as representation, symbolization, thinking, and language are all examples of systemic properties of active behavioral systems, just as in our earlier example the function vision was a systemic property of a particular biological system. Furthermore, as just described with respect to organismic change and earlier with respect to Hegel's contribution to this view, less advanced momentary structure–function relationships become transformed and integrated with later ones and, thus, as each new organization progresses further novel systemic properties emerge. The effect of this is that the later levels of organization cannot be *completely* analyzed into or reduced to earlier levels or ultimately to simple behavior. Language, for example, is a system of signs and symbols. Certainly early speech sounds may be significant precursors to later language, but from the organismic perspective, language can never be completely analyzed into these simple elements. Similarly, as discussed earlier, Piaget's later levels of organization, i.e., structures, cannot be completely reduced to the behaviors of infancy any more than a single level can be completely reduced to contemporary specific behaviors. The impossibility of complete reduction across the progressive levels of organization is called *discontinuity*.

Discontinuity entails qualitative change, i.e., the novel systemic properties, but this does not mean that it denies that any quantitative change is possible. Recall that earlier it was stated that from an organismic position analysis of the parts of any system is appropriate as long as it occurs in the context of the whole. Similarly, analysis of the behaviors and systems that are precursors to later levels of organization is appropriate as long as it is explicitly recognized that they are precursors to and not the ultimate elements of the later organization. Thus, for example, from this perspective it is appropriate to analyze the quantitative nature of the movement from early speech sounds to mature language, while recognizing that early speech sounds are precursors to language rather than elements because they do not serve the representational function of language. The organismic position, therefore, maintains that development involves both discontinuity and continuity.

As with other corollaries, discontinuity between levels of organization is translated into any theory constructed within an organismic framework. The specific theoretical concept that is used to demonstrate a model commitment to discontinuous levels of organization is "stage." Stage, then, in any organismic theory refers to a level of organization that exhibits novel or emergent systemic properties that are not completely reducible to specific behaviors. Because "stage" reflects model assumptions it is not in itself open to empirical tests of truth or falsity. If one is working within an organismic framework it is simply meaningless to ask the question, are there really stages of development? This, in fact, is a mechanistic question because it implies stages are things to be observed rather than formal explanatory constructs. However, although "stage" is not open to empirical testing, the specific representation of a stage (i.e., the particular structural description) that is provided by the theorist can be empirically assessed. That is, the organismically oriented investigator cannot ask, are there really stages, but he or she can ask, are the specific stages such as those that Piaget, Werner, or Erikson describe good representations? The specific procedures for this assessment were presented earlier under the structure–function and necessary change corollaries.

The mechanistic corollary of strict continuity derives from the position described earlier of reductionism and accidental change. Simply stated, the mechanistic position is that all change is to be understood as completely additive. Later, apparent organization is completely reducible to earlier behavior. On occasion the mechanistic group will use the concept "stage" but here, as in other cases, I will present shortly that the term has a different meaning than the one deriving from the organismic framework. For the mechanistic group, "stage" is at best a descriptive device used to give a summary statement about a group of behaviors. Like organization, "stage" is not necessary to explanation, and ultimately "stage" will be eliminated when the organization is fully reduced to behaviors and the effective antecedent causes of the behaviors have been discovered.

In summary to this point, the primary contribution of the Overton–Reese analysis has been to articulate what was earlier implicit. The goal of such an analysis is to demonstrate the continuing influence of these often implicit ontological and methodological commitments on day-to-day research strategies. In doing this, we expected that recognition of the hard cores and positive heuristics of rival programs will provide more coherent and explicitly defined research policies. In addition, by making the implicit explicit, an analysis of this type provides a more well-defined basis for the critical appraisal of the adequacy and progress of rival programs as they go about their task of solving both empirical and conceptual problems.

D. THE MEANING OF BASIC TERMS

A related consequence of the type of analysis conducted by Overton and Reese concerns the clarification of the nature of the meaning of basic terms as they are used in psychology generally, or developmental psychology specifically. Both positivist and conventionalist methodologies assume that there is a neutral observational language independent of any deep-level ontological and methodological commitments. Basic terms are defined either through operational definitions or, in the case of conventionalism, they are often left relatively undefined and simply operate as pigeonholes used to order experimental findings. The difficulties with the positivist's position have been well documented; the difficulty with the conventionalist's position is that in avoiding the issue of meaning it leads to a worst-case scenario of vagueness, ambiguity, and degenerate eclecticism.

Consider, for example, Beilin's analysis (this volume) of early, middle, and new "functionalism." The primary basic term employed in this historical analysis is "function." However, the meaning of this term is left undefined. New functionalists consist of a group "dominated ideologically by information processors at one pole, and by Vygotskyans at the other" (Beilin, this volume, p. 254). Piaget's theory is included. Middle functionalists included Woodworth and non-Hullian learning theories. " 'Early' and 'middle era' functionalists made much of their rejection of mentalistic language . . . although they never went as far as Watson or Skinner in their positivism" (this volume, p. 254). Beilin, taking a conventionalist perspective, appears to group everyone—excepting avowed positivists—who employs the term "function" under the rubric "functionalists." The effect of this procedure is to blur significant distinctions in the way the basic term is applied and, thus, to ignore significant distinctions in basic research strategies.

From the perspective of a research program analysis as described by Overton and Reese, the meaning of basic terms is generated to a significant extent by the hard core and positive heuristic of a program. The deep-level hard core and positive heuristic of a program form, as Lakatos and Laudan have pointed out, the conceptual foundation of the program and this foundation generates meanings for the surface-level terms in a field. The point of overwhelming importance here is that in different research programs the same surface-level term may have different meanings and hence different implications for methods and procedures employed to investigate problems (Overton, 1982a). [An example from physics is that basic terms such as "time," "length," and "velocity" all change in meaning depending on whether they are interpreted within a classical Newtonian model or a relativity model (Feyerabend, 1971).]

In the earlier section (II,A) on the nature of the mechanistic and organismic research programs, I briefly alluded to the fact that the very meaning of the term "concept" changes depending upon whether it is generated by one or the other program. Here, I will try to demonstrate the point by considering two basic terms that have been widely used in psychology and that play important roles in Beilin's analysis. These are the terms "structure" and "function."

For both Wundt and Titchener, "structure" was a basic term in their "structuralist" school of psychology. However—at least in the sphere of experimental psychology—both Wundt and Titchener were committed to working within a mechanistic research program and, as earlier noted, such a commitment entails a further commitment to an elementaristic analysis. As a consequence, "structure" was defined within this system as the elements of consciousness, and a research strategy was employed in an attempt to reduce the complexity of thought to these elements. "Structure" is also a basic term for Piaget and Chomsky. But here, "structure" is defined as the abstract organization or form of knowledge and language. This definition reflects an organismic research program commitment to the assumption of necessary organization, and research strategies, quite incompatible with those of Wundt and Titchener's, have been developed to explore the nature of such structures. Without the benefit of a deep-level research program analysis one might easily but improperly conclude that the research approaches of Wundt, Titchener, Piaget, and Chomsky were for all significant purposes identical because each sought to identify "structures."

The situation is similar, if more complex, with respect to the term "function." One meaning of "function" is the natural, proper, or characteristic action of anything, such as an organ of the body (Random House Dictionary of the English Language, 1967). Within the confines of this definition, a reciprocal relationship exists between the thing, e.g., the organ, and its function. Given the organ stomach we can ask about its function, or given the function of digestion we can explore the organ. The relationship here is one of structure and function, and except for purposes of abstraction one cannot be analyzed without reference to the other.

This meaning of "function" is exactly that which is generated by the organismic program, with its hard core commitment to an interrelationship between necessary organization (structure) and activity (function) and with its consequent research policy of requiring that the exploration of structures proceed within the context of their specified functions, i.e., a structure–function analysis (see Table I). This meaning generated by the organismic research program is, in turn, exactly that employed by both Piaget and Chomsky as the one considers the function of intelligence and explores the structures that serve it and the other considers the function of language and explores the structures that serve it. The fact that at one time or another the functional or structural side of the equation is relatively more elaborated does not necessarily lead to difficulty in determining whether Piaget's system is primarily functionalist or structuralist (Beilin, this volume, p. 254). To suggest otherwise misses the point of the program-generated deep-level meaning of these basic terms. Similarly, to ignore Chomsky's consideration of function is to ignore what Papert called "Chomsky's 'organicist' tendency to see mental functions as . . . organized into organs of the mind" (Papert, 1980, p. 92).

A second meaning of "function" drops the characteristic feature of the activity as well as the object and focuses simply on the verb form, to act (Random House Dictionary of the English Language, 1967). If "function" is taken to mean a commitment to activity in general, then one need have no concern with organization or structure. Clearly here, such a meaning would not be generated by an organismic research program. Furthermore, because the commitment to activity is left vague, an ambiguity arises: Is the activity involved to be understood as origin or as outcome?

This vague definition of function best describes the meaning it held for Beilin's (this volume) "middle functionalism" group, including Harvey Carr and Robert S. Woodworth. However, in the views of these investigators, the meaning of the term acquired additional connotations from the mechanistic research program. For both Carr and Woodworth the activity or function was the product of other forces. That is, deriving from the mechanistic program, the organism was considered inherently stable and activity or function was the product of antecedent stimuli or drives. In fact, in his original statement of the drive concept, Woodworth (1918) was explicit in making this commitment: "The drive is the power applied to making the mechanism go. . . . The mechanism without the power is inactive, dead, lacking in disposable energy" (p. 37). Rychlak (1977) provided a more elaborate historical analysis of the manner in which this brand of functionalism, as well as later mediational theorists, continued to demonstrate mechanistic hard core commitments to a Lockean–Humean set of philosophical assumptions. The fact of significance here, however, is that again the meaning of the basic term is generated by the research program. Ignoring this deep-level analysis of meaning and grouping according to the surface-level labels has the effect of tearing apart the integrative coherence of any general research program, and leads to conceptual and methodological confusion.

A third meaning of "function" refers to a factor related to or dependent on other factors. This meaning has been applied by those favoring an operant or experimental analysis of behavior approach (e.g., Bijou & Baer, 1963; Gewirtz, 1969; Skinner, 1974) as a method of analyzing antecedent–consequent relationships without recourse to causal statements. Thus, proposals from this group for a functional analysis of behavior reflect a mechanistic research program commitment to an analysis of antecedents and consequences.

III. World Views and Scientific Research Programs

In the foregoing general discussion I have attempted to highlight the fact that the philosophical progression from Kuhn to Lakatos and Laudan establishes a rational context for an elaboration of the early Overton–Reese analysis of the role of world views as they impact on scientific activity in psychology. As both Lakatos and Laudan argued, world views can and do form a necessary and rational dimension to scientific research programs and traditions. From this perspective, they are not, as Beilin and other conventionalists would maintain, merely an added "psychological and sociological dimension" (Beilin, this volume, p. 256).

A. World Views in Science

Several other issues concerning the role of world views as they enter scientific research programs and traditions require clarification, particularly as they relate to my understanding of the impact of world views on psychology. A first issue concerns the question of whether the organismic and mechanistic world views provide the only possible basis for research programs in psychology. The answer here is simply no. Both Overton and Reese have maintained that these world views appear to have had the greatest impact on psychology, but it was never asserted that these are the only possible sources of research programs. However, the burden of proof in establishing alternative research programs lies with their proponents. To simply assert that it appears that some part of some investigator's work is more formistic or contexualistic than mechanistic or organismic does not satisfy the demands of this task. The task necessarily requires the explicit articulation of a coherent set of assumptions forming a hard core; the demonstration that the hard core influences the formulation of an explicit research policy or positive heuristic; evidence that the hard core and positive heuristic influence the formulation of a family of theories; and an analysis of the ways in which the hard core and positive heuristic have a determining effect on the meaning of key terms in a field and on day-to-day research strategies.

A closely related issue involves the question of whether any of the *currently available* world views, aside from organicism and mechanism, can, in fact, form the basis for a *scientifically* viable research program. This is a complex and arguable issue, but for myself and not speaking for Reese, I would again submit that the answer is no. Consider first the very nature of science. Although significant disagreements have occurred and do exist about the specific nature of scientific activity, agreement has been uniform that a central aim of science is to establish an "organized or systematic body of knowledge" (Wartofsky, 1968, p. 23). That is, science aims at introducing order and organization into the vagueness and ambiguity of common sense perceptions and understandings. Any viable approach to science must therefore provide some means of *integration* of disparate and seemingly divergent data sources. For positivists and conventionalists the means of integration consist of careful observation, inductions, and ever simpler pigeonhole systems. From a rationalist perspective, in contrast, the primary vehicle for integration resides in the deep-level assumptions of the research program or research tradition's hard core and positive heuristic.

Any scientifically viable research program, then, must include the means for achieving integration as a part of its basic assumptions. To the extent that a research program is based upon or incorporates the assumptions of a world view into its hard core, *the world view must be integrative in nature*. But here is exactly where the problem arises. For of the currently available world views, only organicism and mechanism are integrative; others, in fact, reject the idea of integration.

If we take as the class of currently available world views those that have been relatively well defined and articulated, then this class is composed of formism, contextualism, mechanism, and organicism (Pepper, 1942). But as Pepper pointed out, only mechanism and organicism are integrative in nature; formism and contextualism are dispersive. "That is to say, the categories of formism and contextualism are such that . . . facts are taken one by one from whatever source they come and are so left. The universe has for these theories the general effect of facts rather loosely scattered about. . . . The cosmos for these theories is not in the end highly systematic'' (Pepper, 1942, pp. 142–143). And specifically with reference to contextualism, ''disorder is a categorical feature of contextualism'' (p. 234). Thus, for whatever else their value, formism and contextualism as world views cannot form the basis for scientifically viable research programs—unless science were to abandon its attempt to establish an organized and systematic body of knowledge, which is unlikely. Therefore, although mechanism and organism do not form the only possible basis for scientific research programs, they do seem from my point of view to be the only *currently available* world views to serve this purpose.

B. CONTEXTUALISM AND DIALECTICS

Because the proposal has been made (e.g., Lerner, 1982; Moshman, 1982; Reese, 1976; Riegel, 1976, 1979; Sigel, 1981) that, for purposes of understanding development, contextualism may be a viable alternative to organicism, a few additional points should be made about this option. Two underlying assumptions appear to be implicated in making such a suggestion. The first assumption is that change must be understood as a dialectic process and such an understanding requires contextualism. Although I have agreed, and indeed have argued that development is a dialectic process (e.g., see Overton & Reese, 1981, pp. 108–109), the plain and simple fact of the matter is that the dialectic is a category of organicism. As Pepper specifically stated, ''The early organicists, notably Hegel, thought that there was one and only one course of progress from maximum fragmentariness to ultimate integration. . . . Thesis-antithesis-synthesis is the ever recurring form'' (Pepper, 1942, p. 293). Furthermore, as Pepper also clearly stated, although later organicists rejected the rigid picture of a single path of development, they maintained the central category of the dialectic (pp. 294–295). Therefore, any assumption that dialectic change requires contextualism is mistaken.

The second assumption underlying the use of a contextualist world view, with respect to the understanding of development, begins with the recognition that change is a category of contextualism. This recognition then seems to lead to the assumption that change is not a category of organicism. However, the assumption that change is not a category of organicism is based on a subtle misinterpretation of organicism. Organicism, as a world view, is composed of two sets of categories. The first of these consists of the progressive categories in which events proceed from fragments through a dialectic process *toward* an ultimate organic whole. Quite clearly, this set of progressive categories constitutes the change or developmental feature of the system. In contrast, the second set of categories describes the ideal absolute state that would occur if all contradictions were actually resolved and the dialectic ceased. Here, indeed, change or development would cease. In modern interpretations, the ideal or the absolute is an end toward which events progress, it is not an end achieved. Only if an interpretation is made that the absolute is an end achieved, can organicism be viewed as a nonchange or nondevelopmental position.

Beyond these two flawed reasons for proposing contextualism as an alternative to organicism, a certain ambiguity exists with respect to contextualism that seems to heighten its appeal to many. That is, as discussed by Pepper, contextualism consistently shows a tendency to lose its identity and to become a part of mechanism or of organicism. On the one hand, when contextualism combines with mechanism the concept "context" simply functions as yet another antecedent variable in the sense of asking the question, "How did the situation or context affect the behavior"? Thus, by adopting the facade of contextualism, mechanism gains the appearance of greater scope while maintaining the reality of virtually no basic change in assumptions.

On the other hand, as Pepper stated, "contextualism and organicism are so nearly allied that they may almost be called the same theory, the one with a dispersive, the other with an integrative plan" (p. 147). When contextualism combines with organicism, the integrative plan takes precedence and the category "context," as well as other contexualist categories, serve to specify and articulate the nature of the organic whole or holism. Here, "context" is not one antecedent event among others; "context" is the organic functioning whole that gives meaning to its parts and that can never be analyzed into simply the sum of its parts. From this interpretative framework I have myself had occasion to discuss contextualist assumptions (see Overton & Reese, 1981).

It should be emphatically stressed that taking advantage of contextualism's identity problems by both mechanists and organicists does not in any sense lead to a synthesis of the three positions. In fact, taking advantage of contextualism's identity problems has a strong tendency to lead to conceptual confusion because doing this usually leaves unclear whether an author is making an argument from a mechanistic–contextualistic viewpoint or from an organismic–contextualistic position. If, as Laudan argued, one of the major aims of science is to resolve conceptual problems as well as empirical problems, this value would be enhanced if investigators would drop the surface-level concept "contextualism"—given that, as argued earlier, such a position as a world view cannot serve as the basis for a scientific research program—and explicitly acknowledge when they mean mechanistic–contextualistic and when they mean organismic– contextualistic.

C. RESEARCH PROGRAMS AND FAMILIES OF THEORIES

The next general issue involves a problem of the relationship of the ontological and methodological commitments of a scientific research program and the family of theories entailed by the program. More specifically, the question concerns the extent and manner in which theories can disagree among themselves and still constitute a family of theories. A part of the answer to this question was already given in an earlier quote from Laudan: "to attempt what is forbidden by the metaphysics and methodology of a research tradition [research program] is to put oneself outside that tradition and to repudiate it" (1977, p. 80). That is, to the extent that theories are formulated in a manner that is consistent with or, at a minimum, does not violate the strictures of the hard core and positive heuristic of a research program, they constitute a family of theories regardless of other mutual inconsistencies (Laudan, 1977, p. 81).

Because Overton and Reese have maintained that Piaget's and Chomsky's theories are two members of the organismic family and Beilin (this volume) argued that each implicates a different research program, these theories will be used as illustrative. First, both Piaget and Chomsky explicitly accept and incorporate the organismic hard core assumptions of the integrated relationship of necessary organization and activity. As Piattelli-Palmarini pointed out with respect to the debate between Piaget and Chomsky, both accept the assumptions that: "(1) nothing is knowable unless cognitive organization of some kind is there from the start; and (2) nothing is knowable unless the subject acts in one way or another on the surrounding world" (1980, p. 54). Furthermore, each theory also incorporates the organismic positive heuristic features of holism and structure–function analysis and places primary emphasis on formal explanation.

Here then, one has every reason to assert and none to deny that Piaget and Chomsky's theories constitute two members of the organismic family of theories. The primary conflict between Piaget and Chomsky concerns the specific nature and extent of the initial organization or fixed nucleus and not the hard core assumption of organization itself. Although Piaget's constructivist position and Chomsky's innateness position constitute a significant theoretical debate (Piatelli-Palmarini, 1980) with respect to the nature and extent of the organization, they do not implicate different scientific research programs. In fact, by the end of the debate, several potential compromises, each of which was compatible with an organismic research program, were offered and developed by participants in the debate (e.g., Cellerier, 1980; Changeux, 1980).

Another feature of the relationship between Piaget and Chomsky's theories as they implicate the organismic research tradition concerns necessary change. The hard core and positive heuristic components of this feature are strongly emphasized within Piaget's theory but they are relatively undefined within Chomsky's. In considering this feature of necessary change, note first that Chomsky did not reject it. That is, Chomsky did not violate the strictures of the organismic program and put himself outside this tradition by, for example, asserting that all change is ultimately a product of direct experience (mechanistic commitment). Rather, this feature is simply not extensively articulated in the theory.

One might deal with Chomsky's failure to articulate necessary change in his theory by simply noting that Chomsky is not very interested in development. Or it might be said that Chomsky's theory, like Gestalt theory, or George Kelly's personality theory, represents a kind of truncated organicism. However, although such statements are not incorrect, they miss an important component of the nature of scientific research programs, i.e., the manner in which empirical problems serve to initiate an elaboration of a program's positive heuristic.

Scientific research programs function to solve empirical problems. But empirical problems are not all of one sort; they vary in both their nature and generality. Thus, when an investigator confronts a particular empirical domain, the features of the positive heuristic of a program will be differentially elaborated depending upon the kinds of empirical problems being addressed. The elaboration of the positive heuristic depends to a large extent upon the problems or puzzles the investigator is confronted with *at any particular time* with respect to his or her field of investigation (Overton, 1982b).

From this perspective one can see how Piaget, in focusing on the intellectual domain and being faced with seemingly major transformations that occur in this domain between infancy and adulthood, was led to elaborate the necessary change feature of the organismic positive heuristic as well as the holism and structure–function features. Chomsky, however, in focusing on the domain of language, was faced with the relatively early sudden expression of universal components of syntax. As a consequence, the empirical problems that this issue posed required an elaboration of the holistic and structure–function features, but not the necessary change feature of the organismic program's positive heuristic. This difference in the elaboration of the positive heuristic does not, however, mean that Piaget and Chomsky pursue rival research programs. Different puzzles or problems facing different investigators will lead to the differential elaboration of the various features of the positive heuristic within any family of theories.

D. INCOMMENSURABILITY

A final general issue is that of incommensurability. In the original Reese and Overton (1970) paper we accepted Pepper and Kuhn's position on this issue and maintained that "different world hypotheses cannot be compared evaluatively with one another, because of the basic lack of communication. . . . Only internal evaluation is possible" (p. 122). At this point I would reject this radical form of the incommensurability thesis and agree with a thesis that is more compatible with the arguments by Lakatos and Laudan. The primary problem with Pepper and Kuhn's position is that, if accepted without qualification, then no rational standard of scientific progress is possible. That is, if *only* internal evaluation is possible, scientific acceptability and scientific progress can be defined only in terms of psychological and sociological criteria (Lakatos, 1978b, elitism criteria). In this context "rival" research programs or traditions are not even rivals and the choice of one or another program is determined by psychological and sociological factors that influence one or another group of investigators.

Laudan proposed that the scientific progressiveness (or regressiveness) of a specific research program or tradition be characterized in terms of whether, in time, it has expanded its domain of explained problems, and has minimized the number and importance of its conceptual problems and anomalies. This rational criterion then allows for a progressiveness ranking among rival research programs or traditions at any given time. Thus, it is possible "to be able to compare the progressiveness of different research traditions [programs], *even if those research traditions are utterly incommensurable in terms of the substantive claims they make about the world!*" (Laudan, 1977, p. 146).

The revised form of the incommensurability thesis is consistent with the evolution of my own understanding of rational standards of scientific acceptability and scientific progress and the nature of rival scientific programs. However, it still leaves the important issue of "incommensurability" unresolved. Incommensurability involves both issues of standards of evaluation and issues of the lack of communication between rival world views and their constituent research programs and theories (Kuhn, 1970, pp. 148–150). The problem originally arose from the rationalist rejection of the idea of the existence of a neutral observational language and the acceptance of the position that every theory has its own observational language. Thus, to the extent that a research program or tradition "is a set of general assumptions about the entities and processes in a domain of study" (Laudan, 1977, p. 81) and to the extent that these assumptions influence the definition of basic terms, rival programs do exhibit incommensurability.

However, the incommensurability argument has both a strong and weak form. The strong form is that virtually all features of the observational language are determined at all times by each research program. If this were the case, communication would indeed be impossible. The weaker argument, although accepting that no pure observations are possible, begins from a position that a wide variation exists in the extent to which a specific observation is dependent on any given program at any given time. For example, the observation "that is a human being" usually entails little specific dependence on any given psychological theory (note, however, that this is not the case in paleoanthropology). In contrast, the observation "that is a concept" or "that is a psychological structure" entails maximum dependence on psychological theories. From this perspective, when two programs are at a point of incommensurability (e.g., "What is a concept, a symbol, a representation, a structure?") the proponents can withdraw, not to a pure observational language but to an observational language whose theoretical assumptions are not immediately at issue (Barbour, 1974).

The weaker incommensurability argument best characterizes my own contemporary position. That is, at any given time an incommensurability may, in fact, exist between the organismic and mechanistic research programs with respect to the meaning of "development," "structure," "function," "representation," "intelligence," "language," "symbol," "concept," "attachment," etc. This component of incommensurability is eliminated by appealing to a *currently* more neutral language. Thus, for example, using this technique facilitated recognition that the mechanistic program led Wundt and Titchener to understand structure as "elements of consciousness" and that the organismic program led Piaget and Chomsky to understand structure as "abstract forms of knowing." Here, communication has been restored and incommensurability eliminated. However, and this is a point of central importance, the elimination of incommensurability in turn makes salient the incompatible and competitive nature of the rival research programs (see Lakatos, 1978a, p. 91).

IV. An Organismic–Mechanistic Compromise?

In this paper I have tried to demonstrate ways in which my own understanding concerning the functioning of rival scientific research programs in psychology has evolved along lines that are consistent with the philosophical evolution from Kuhn to Lakatos and Laudan. In closing, I would like to address very briefly a question that is often asked with respect to the rival mechanistic and organismic programs: Is a compromise possible? For myself, I tend to mistrust attempts at such compromise. The reason is that virtually all potential compromises destroy the core integrity of one or the other of the programs and, as Laudan pointed out, "it is precisely that integrity which stimulates, defines, and delimits what can count as a solution to many of the most important scientific problems" (1977, p. 80).

Having made this disclaimer, I will briefly sketch my own version of a "compromise." In essence, it is a "compromise" that leaves the organismic program intact and destroys the integrity of the mechanistic program. As a starting point for this compromise, consider the fact that in the past investigators have tended to approach the explanation of behavior and development from two extremes of a bipolar dimension. One group—organismic in nature—being impressed with the constancy and universality of behavior and development, has offered formal explanations in terms of universal structures (both synchronic and diachronic) and has treated contingent explanation as relatively unimportant. The second group—mechanistic in nature—being impressed with the variability and individuality of behavior and development, has proposed that universal structures are, at best, temporary heuristics and that ultimately all phenomena will be explained by contingent explanation. The proposed compromise is one that requires that the organismic group maintain its focus on formal explanation but increase its emphasis on contingent explanation (easily done because the organismic program admits both types). It also requires that the mechanistic group abandon its hard core and its positive heuristic features of elementarism and strict continuity. The compromise leaves the mechanistic group to focus its techniques and research strategies on contingent explanation but always in the context of organismic structures and stages of structures, i.e., contingent factors explain rate of behavior and rate of change (see Table I) (see also Moshman, 1982) and deviations from the normal course of development (Overton, 1982a; Overton & Newman, 1982; Overton & Reese, 1981).

I have elaborated this compromise in other contexts where I have referred to it as a competence–activation–utilization approach or a competence– moderator–performance approach (Overton, 1982b; Overton & Newman, 1982). In essence it elevates formal and contingent explanation to a more equal partnership in which each plays a distinct and mutually supportive role in the general explanatory effort. Formal explanation operating within the hard core and positive heuristic of the organismic program yields the abstract idealized models of competence and the development of competence. It provides the laws of the universal, the regular, the normal, the necessary. Contingent explanation focuses on moderators and provides answers to questions of how competence and the development of competence is accelerated, retarded, or deflected from its normal course; how the activation or utilization of competence is facilitated or hindered by specific psychological processes and situational factors.

With the "compromise," theories such as Piaget's, Werner's, or Chomsky's could be wed to truncated forms of theories such as Skinner's or Bandura's, i.e., truncated in the sense that they are shorn of mechanistic hard core assumptions and elementaristic and strict continuity features. Here, for example, contingencies of reinforcement might well account for why one group of formal operational adolescent children (competence) utilizes this knowledge in situations whereas another group does not. Or, given that the nature of imitation is limited by cognitive level, Bandura's emphasis on the status of the model could account for differential amounts of imitation within any level. Similarly, given that a theory like Piaget's equilibration model (a diachronic competence) would account for the normal course of development, various deprivation or enrichment theories could explain the retardation or acceleration of this normal course. It is, of course, questionable whether this general proposal is in fact a compromise or simply a further elaboration of the organismic positive heuristic. However, when viewed as an elaboration it offers the added advantage, noted by Laudan (1977, p. 94), of suggesting ways in which modified theories can be taken over by an alternative research program or research tradition.

V. Conclusions

In summary, then, my own views with respect to the early Overton–Reese analysis have evolved in ways that are consistent with the philosophical evolution from Kuhn to Lakatos and Laudan. This evolution has served to highlight, extend, and modify a number of points. Today the mechanistic and organismic positions are best interpreted as scientific research programs or traditions including hard cores, positive heuristics, and families of theories. These programs bring metaphysical and methodological commitments into the essential body of science and in so doing they exert a determining influence on theories, basic terms, and research strategies. Of the currently available world views, only mechanism and organicism seem adequate to form constituent parts of scientific research programs. The Lakatos and Laudan analyses provide a more adequate interpretation for the rival relationship between the mechanistic and organismic programs. These analyses also provide a more adequate rational explanation for comparing these programs in the context of scientific progress. Compromises between the two programs must be suspect because, in fact, they tend to destroy the integrity of one or the other program.

REFERENCES

Baer, D. The organism as host. *Human Development,* 1976, **19,** 87–98.

Barbour, I. G. *Myths, models and paradigms.* New York: Harper, 1974.

Bijou, S. W., & Baer, D. M. A systematic and empirical theory. In *Child development* (Vol. 1). New York: Appleton, 1963.

Cellerier, G. Cognitive strategies in problem solving. In M. Piatelli-Palmarini (Ed.), *Language and learning: The debate between Jean Piaget and Noam Chomsky.* Cambridge, Massachusetts: Harvard Univ. Press, 1980.

Changeux, J. Genetic determinism and epigenesis of the neuronal network: Is there a biological compromise between Chomsky and Piaget? In M. Piatelli-Palmarini (Ed.), *Language and learning: The debate between Jean Piaget and Noam Chomsky.* Cambridge, Massachusetts: Harvard Univ. Press, 1980.

Chomsky, N. *Reflection on language.* New York: Pantheon, 1975.

Feyerabend, P. K. Problems of empiricism, part 2. In R. Colodny (Ed.), *The nature and function of scientific theory.* Pittsburgh, Pennsylvania: Univ. of Pittsburgh Press, 1971.

Gewirtz, J. Levels of conceptual analysis in environment-infant interaction research. *Merrill-Palmer Quarterly,* 1969, **15,** 7–47.

Hanson, N. R. *Patterns of discovery.* London and New York: Cambridge Univ. Press, 1958.

Heisenberg, W. *Physics and philosophy: The revolution in modern science.* New York: Harper, 1958.

Kuhn, T. S. *The structure of scientific revolutions.* Chicago, Illinois: Univ. of Chicago Press, 1962.

Kuhn, T. S. *The structure of scientific revolutions* (2nd ed., enlarged). Chicago, Illinois: Univ. of Chicago Press, 1970.

Kuhn, T. S. *The essential tension.* Chicago, Illinois: Univ. of Chicago Press, 1977.

Lachman, R., Lachman, J. L., & Butterfield, E. C. *Cognitive psychology and information processing.* Hillsdale, New Jersey: Erlbaum, 1979.

Lakatos, I. *The methodology of scientific research programmes: Philosophical papers* (Vol. 1). London and New York: Cambridge Univ. Press, 1978. (a)

Lakatos, I. *Mathematics, science and epistemology: Philosophical papers* (Vol. 2). London and New York: Cambridge Univ. Press, 1978. (b)

Laudan, L. *Progress and its problems: Towards a theory of scientific growth.* Berkeley, California: Univ. of California Press, 1977.

Lerner, R. M. *Individual and context in developmental psychology: Conceptual and theoretical issues.* Papers presented at a conference on individual development and social change, Max-Planck-Institut fur Bieldungsforschung, Berlin, 1982.

Moshman, D. Exogenous, endogenous and dialectical constructivism. *Developmental Review,* 1982, **2,** 371–384.

Nickles, T. Introductory essay: Scientific discovery and the future of philosophy of science. In T. Nickles (Ed.), *Scientific discovery, logic and rationality.* Boston, Massachusetts: Reidel, 1980.

Overton, W. The active organism in structuralism. *Human Development,* 1976, **19,** 71–86.

Overton, W. F. *Historical and contemporary perspectives of development.* Unpublished manuscript, 1982. (a)

Overton, W. F. *Scientific methodologies and the competence-moderator-performance issue.* Invited address presented at the annual symposium of the Jean Piaget Society, Philadelphia, 1982. (b)

Overton, W. F., & Newman, J. Cognitive development: A competence-activation/utilization approach. In T. Field, A. Houston, H. Quay, L. Troll, & G. Finley (Eds.), *Review of human development.* New York: Wiley, 1982.

Overton, W. F., & Reese, H. W. Models of development: Methodological implications. In J. R. Nesselroade & H. W. Reese (Eds.), *Life-span developmental psychology: Methodological issues.* New York: Academic Press, 1973.

Overton, W., & Reese, H. Conceptual prerequisites for an understanding of stability-change and continuity-discontinuity. *International Journal of Behavioral Development,* 1981, **4,** 99–123.

Papert, S. The role of artificial intelligence in psychology. In M. Piatelli-Palmarini (Ed.), *Language and learning: The debate between Jean Piaget and Noam Chomsky.* Cambridge, Massachusetts: Harvard Univ. Press, 1980.

Pepper, S. *World hypotheses.* Berkeley, California: Univ. of California Press, 1942.

Piaget, J. *Structuralism.* New York: Basic Books, 1974.

Piatelli-Palmarini, M. (Ed.). *Language and learning: The debate between Jean Piaget and Noam Chomsky.* Cambridge, Massachusetts: Harvard Univ. Press, 1980.

Popper, K. R. *The logic of scientific discovery.* London: Hutchinson, 1959.

Reese, H. W. Memory development in childhood: Life-span perspectives. In H. W. Reese (Ed.), *Advances in child development and behavior* (Vol. 11). New York: Academic Press, 1976.

Reese, H. W., & Overton, W. R. Models of development and theories of development. In L. R. Goulet & P. B. Baltes (Eds.), *Life-span developmental psychology: Research and theory.* New York: Academic Press, 1970.

Reichenbach, H. *Experience and prediction.* Chicago, Illinois: Univ. of Chicago Press, 1938.

Riegel, K. F. The dialectics of human development. *American Psychologist,* 1976, **31,** 689–700.

Riegel, K. F. *Psychology mon amour.* Boston, Massachusetts: Houghton-Mifflin, 1979.

Rychlak, J. *The psychology of rigorous humanism.* New York: Wiley, 1977.

Sigel, I. E. Child development research in learning and cognition in the 1980s: Continuities and discontinuities from the 1970s. *Merrill-Palmer Quarterly,* 1981, **27,** 347–371.

Skinner, B. F. *About behaviorism.* New York: Knopf, 1974.

Wartofsky, M. *Conceptual foundations of scientific thought.* New York: Macmillan, 1968.

Woodworth, R. S. *Dynamic psychology.* New York: Columbia Univ. Press, 1918.

THE HISTORY OF THE PSYCHOLOGY OF LEARNING AS A RATIONAL PROCESS: LAKATOS VERSUS KUHN[1]

Peter Barker
DEPARTMENT OF PHILOSOPHY
MEMPHIS STATE UNIVERSITY
MEMPHIS, TENNESSEE

Barry Gholson
DEPARTMENT OF PSYCHOLOGY
MEMPHIS STATE UNIVERSITY
MEMPHIS, TENNESSEE

I. Introduction

In this paper we present an alternative account to the view of science, and particularly of psychology, that was introduced by Pepper (1942) and developed in the last two decades under the influence of Thomas Kuhn (1962). Psychologists may be most familiar with this view as presented by Reese and Overton

[1]Barker acknowledges the support of a Faculty Development Leave from Memphis State University. Earlier versions of this paper were presented at the meeting of the Southern Society for Philosophy and Psychology, 1981, and at the seventh biennial Southeastern Conference on Human Development, 1982.

ADVANCES IN CHILD DEVELOPMENT
AND BEHAVIOR, VOL. 18

ISBN 0-12-009718-4

(1970). Our aim is to present an alternative to the Kuhnian viewpoint by drawing on the work of Imre Lakatos (1970, 1978).

One feature of Kuhnian orthodoxy is that it leads to quite specific expectations about the developmental pattern of a scientific discipline. A second feature of the position is the claim that no basis exists for choice among the largest units identifiable in the development of a discipline (Pepper's "world hypotheses," Kuhn's "paradigms"). Lakatos' model of the history of science leads to different expectations about the historical pattern of a discipline's development and it provides a mechanism for choice among large-scale units. We will suggest that the sort of competition among large-scale units described by Lakatos can readily be identified in the history of the psychology of learning and show that the pattern of historical development in the last 50 years conforms to Lakatos' model and not to Kuhn's.

The paper is divided into two parts. In the first an outline of Lakatos' ideas on methodology is presented against the background of the Kuhnian position. In the second part a sketch of the recent history of the psychology of learning is presented, using Lakatos' concepts.

II. Lakatos' Analysis versus Kuhn's

Recent work in psychology has shown a remarkable sympathy for relativism; the view that some scientific theories are so radically different from one another that no entirely rational grounds can be offered for accepting or rejecting one theory in preference to a rival. In an influential paper, Reese and Overton (1970) concluded that:

> [P]retheoretical models have a pervasive effect upon theory construction. Theories built upon radically different models are logically independent and cannot be assimilated to each other. They reflect representations of different ways of looking at the world and as such are incompatible in their implications. Different world views involve different understanding of what is *knowledge* and hence the meaning of *truth*. There, synthesis is, at best, confusing. (p. 144)

Reese and Overton drew on two main sources: Pepper (1942), who introduced the term "world hypotheses" for such different ways of looking at the world, and Kuhn (1962), who later placed similar ideas before a wider audience.

Kuhn's book, *The structure of scientific revolutions* (1962, 1970), introduced a new technical meaning for the word "paradigm," which passed into the vocabulary of working scientists. Although addressed to philosophers of science, by appealing to a broad audience in the social sciences the book became the most influential work on general methodology since the high tide of logical positivism. Psychologists, sociologists, and economists adopted Kuhn's ideas, sometimes to defend the legitimacy of their own (for an extensive bibliography see Gutting, 1980).

According to Kuhn (1962), the history of science is to be understood as a series of eras of stability and consensus, punctuated by brief interludes of chaos. During these interludes all fundamental beliefs are jettisoned and replaced. A paradigm was taken to be the set of fundamental commitments to an ontology, an epistemology, and a methodology which, gaining universal acceptance for a certain period, stabilized a given science and provided the foundation for effective research. The commitments constituting the paradigm were taken to be so fundamental that they were immune from empirical testing. Experimental failures might lead to the abandonment of theories, but the paradigm itself was to remain untouched and to direct the construction of successor theories. The paradigm provided a way of making sense of the world; without it nothing existed to construct theories about. The occasional replacement of one paradigm by another was therefore a cataclysmic event: A world was destroyed with the old paradigm and a new world was created with its successor. This process was supposed to represent the most spectacular sort of scientific change, known as a scientific revolution. The simplest model of science that could be constructed from Kuhn's account portrayed history as a linear, nonrepeating sequence of paradigms punctuated by scientific revolutions (Barker, 1980).

Two consequences of Kuhn's account were apparent to philosophers, if not to scientists. First, Kuhn had removed empirical evidence (the results of experiment) from the central place it had occupied in all previous accounts of science. Kuhn specifically denied that empirical evidence is a decisive factor in the most dramatic sort of scientific change, such as the scientific revolutions exemplified by the transitions from the world of Aristotle to the world of Newton and from the world of Newton to the world of Einstein. Second, no claim of objective superiority of one paradigm over any other was defensible. Kuhn suggested that all rules for appraising scientific procedures as good or bad are supplied by paradigms, with different rules being supplied by different paradigms. Any judgment based on such rules would favor the paradigm from which the rules were selected. Because no rules exist apart from paradigms, no neutral standpoint exists from which to judge among rivals. Kuhn concluded that paradigms are *incommensurable* (i.e., they lack a common basis for comparison) and hence that scientific revolutions are not entirely rule governed. This conclusion was taken as an abdication of the claim that scientific change is rational by those who equated rationality with rules (Scheffler, 1967; Suppe, 1977). The account of consensus formation Kuhn offered in its place was dismissed by some as an appeal to "mob psychology" (e.g., Lakatos, 1970). During the 1970s several new models of the history of science were proposed in a conscious attempt to improve upon Kuhn's and remedy the alleged defects of incommensurability and irrationalism (Lakatos, 1970, 1978; Laudan, 1977; Stegmuller, 1976). In order to show how conclusions like those reached by Reese and Overton may be avoided, we will contrast Kuhnian ideas with those of Lakatos.

Lakatos (1970) accepted Kuhn's notion that some aspects of science are relatively immune from empirical refutation, but he was particularly concerned to avoid the incommensurability problem posed by Kuhn. Lakatos replaced Kuhn's *paradigms* with a large-scale entity called a *research program,* conceived as a succession of theories. Unlike Kuhn, Lakatos expressly specified that several research programs may exist during the same period in a discipline's history and he provided a framework for choosing among them. The framework he proposed is not an a priori superstructure like the positivists' theories of confirmation but a naturalistic methodology based on the consideration of actual scientific practice in case studies similar to those offered by Kuhn.

Lakatos' basic idea was that a good theory does more for you than you expected. His research programs are sequences of theories, linked by a common *hard core* of shared commitments. Each theory in the sequence is conceived as a new and usually more detailed articulation of these commitments. The first theory of a given research program may be quite primitive, so primitive that no one would seriously entertain it as a description of the world. For this reason some people may be happier using the word "model," with its connotation of recognized artificiality, in preference to "theory," which has come to mean "candidate representation of reality." What is important about the "first theory" in Lakatos' conception of a research program is its ability to stimulate the development of more complex and adequate theories. Lakatos took this capacity for development to be an objective feature of the theory or, more precisely, of the research program of which the theory is a start. Lakatos called this feature the *heuristic* of the program.

These features of Lakatos' methodology capture several features of scientific practice. When faced with a model or theory that is known to be inadequate, scientists are normally quite capable of reaching agreement on which features of the theory or model are indispensable (hard core) and which are modifiable. The dispensable features of the theory form a "protective belt" sheltering the hard core from experimental refutation. The core is protected by constructing a new theory, or model, that retains the same core commitments but changes some dispensable features of the theory, such as simplifying assumptions.

Although the statements in any theory may be separated into dispensable and indispensable elements, not all theories lend themselves equally to such division. Similarly, not all theories indicate the direction in which to seek their successors with equal clarity, nor do they lead to equally attractive successors. Thus, research programs may be said to have strong or weak heuristics.

The normal motivation for replacing a theory within a research program is an experimental failure (Lakatos, 1970). To be an acceptable replacement a new theory must both accommodate the success of its predecessor and explain the experimental data that brought its predecessor into question. But according to Lakatos a really good theory does even more; it also leads to completely new predictions that are verified when checked experimentally. A research program comprising theories that succeed one another in this fashion is said to be *progressive*.

Lakatos repeatedly emphasized that the generation of new predictions is what makes a research program attractive; thus, an important issue is to clarify what constitutes a new prediction. Lakatos' original idea was clearly that the prediction should be about something quite unknown before the introduction of the new theory, for example, a domain of phenomena untouched by predecessor theories. But his student Zahar (1976) pointed out that many theories are valued for their ability to explain effects well known before the theory appeared. Zahar (1976), therefore, widened the scope of "new predictions" to include any effect the theory was not specifically designed to explain.

Lakatos also distinguished empirical progress from theoretical progress. The replacement of one theory by another is *theoretically progressive* if it leads to new predictions. It is *empirically progressive* if some of these predictions are verified experimentally. In both cases we are talking about sequences of theories, so the terms may be applied to the research programs comprising the theories as well as to the theories themselves. A progressive program need not be simultaneously progressive at both levels. Lakatos suggested that consistent theoretical progress with only occasional empirical verifications is enough to keep a research program alive. The relative independence of the theoretical and empirical sides of progress explains why the theoretical side of the program is, in the short term, immune from empirical failure. Theoreticians may, with clear conscience, wait for empirical confirmation that is a long time coming. They may also disregard apparent counterevidence in the expectation that later work will convert it into empirical support, provided that the program is theoretically progressive and shows *some* empirical progress. The basic idea, then, is that a good theory always does more for you than you anticipated. A research program consisting of such theories will continually expand the boundaries of knowledge.

If a program is not progressing, then it is *degenerating*. In practice this may mean that the program has temporarily ceased to yield new predictions. But if empirical anomalies can only be met by ad hoc maneuvers rather than by introducing successful new theories, or if new theories raise more problems than they solve, then the heuristic of the program may be exhausted and the time may have come to look for a new core.

The appraisal of a program as progressive or degenerating is not absolute. The judgment is made at one moment in history, based on the recent performance of the program. Given sufficient time, negative appraisals may become positive and vice versa. A single program may be progressing in one epoch and degenerating in a second, but return to progressiveness in a third (Lakatos, 1970). Consequently, choices among programs are not final. If one program is degenerating at a time when another is clearly progressive, then the choice between them is clear. In most cases, however, one program's higher rate of progress is what makes it more attractive than a rival, although the rival is still progressing. Variations in the progressiveness of a program over time permit the weaker program to overtake its rival by undergoing a new spurt of theoretical and empirical progress. All the weaker program needs is a new theory that accommodates the experimental failures of the last theory in the program progressively, that is, by both explaining the previous failures and producing successful new predictions.

The episodes Kuhn describes as scientific revolutions, Lakatos treats as the defeat of one research program by another. The most important historical cases, in which a major scientific system was abandoned in favor of an incompatible rival, fit the model quite well, but the revisability of judgments that a program is progressive or degenerating makes final appraisals of contemporary science difficult. Nevertheless, Lakatos' model shows one clear way to make long-term choices between rival research programs. The grouping of similar theories under a hard core with a linking heuristic is a valuable idea, and the key notion that progress consists of making new, successful predictions offers a useful short-term measure of theory comparison.

III. Applications to Physics

Lakatos disagrees with the Kuhnian view of history. Lakatos' analysis shows that the simultaneous existence of several research programs is the most common historical occurrence, that these rival programs contribute elements to each other's development, and that superseded programs may be revived. Although Kuhn (1970) denied that a given discipline must embody only a single paradigm at any given time, many people drew that conclusion from his account (Shaffner, 1972; Watkins, 1970). One is tempted to read the history of physics as a linear progression beginning with the Aristotelian–Ptolemaic paradigm, which was superseded by the Copernican–Newtonian paradigm, which was superseded in turn by the Einsteinian paradigm. From a Kuhnian view we cannot claim that any of these historical replacements represent progress, or that the later paradigms are better than the earlier ones.[2] From Lakatos' viewpoint the situation is very different.

[2]Although Kuhn says that resolving an anomaly that led an old paradigm to crisis is often the most effective argument in favor of a new paradigm (1970, p. 153) and a new paradigm may be preferred on grounds of increased precision and the prediction of new effects (1970, p. 154), he also says that "these arguments are neither individually nor collectively compelling" (1970, p. 155).

We will briefly review the Copernican and Einsteinian revolutions to illustrate Lakatos' techniques. The first point to emphasize is that both revolutions involved competition between more than two research programs. In the case of the Copernican revolution two major programs appeared as candidates to replace the Aristotelian–Ptolemaic system: one due to Descartes and a second due to Newton. The hard core of the Cartesian program was action by contact. The Cartesians explicitly denied the action-at-a-distance concept of Newtonian gravitation. Both programs were theoretically progressive with respect to their Aristotelian predecessor. Both claimed to be able to account for the motions of comets and the tides, new predictions not made by the Aristotelians, and each made new predictions not made by its rival. The Cartesians, for example, claimed to be able to explain why the moon always kept the same face toward the earth, and why all the planets moved around the sun in the same direction. The Newtonians could predict that the planets would exert forces on one another (Aiton, 1972).

Lakatos used Newton's work as his main example of progress within a research program. Taking as hard core the laws of motion and universal gravitation, Newton in his early theories or models began by treating the planets as point particles. Later, in more realistic theories, planets were treated as symmetrical extended bodies, then as possibly asymmetrical extended bodies. At the same time the description of the motions of the planets became progressively more sophisticated. Early theories, in which planets were said to move in circles around a geometric center, were replaced by more sophisticated versions in which both the planets and the sun were said to move in elliptical orbits around their common center of mass. Laplace's demonstration of a technique for accommodating the influence of the planets on each other may be seen as the next logical step in this program. Lakatos pointed out that each of these changes led to new predictions (theoretical progress) and that these predictions proved correct (empirical progress) often enough to make the program highly attractive to scientists.

As noted above, the programs of both Newton and Descartes were progressive in comparison to the Aristotelian program; but Newton's program gained universal acceptance by outperforming Descartes'. After the death of its founder the Newtonian program continued to yield new and more accurate tables for planetary motion, the motion of the moon, and the motions of the tides. The Cartesian program did not continue to yield successful predictions of novelties and was quickly reduced to attempting to explain, after the fact, the latest successes of the Newtonians. Within a century of the publication of Newton's work, the Newtonian program was obviously making much more progress than the Cartesian program and Cartesian physicists began changing sides. The conversion was particularly complete in this case and led to a period of universal acceptance of Newtonian physics (Aiton, 1972).

The complete victory of the Newtonian program over its rivals is, however, the exception rather than the rule in the history of science. Excessive emphasis on this case may have led to the myth (denied by Kuhn) that only one paradigm exists at a given time and that all scientists subscribe to it. Even the Newtonian system enjoyed only a very brief period of universal acceptance. By the last quarter of the nineteenth century the Newtonian program had ceased to yield new discoveries and was being challenged by at least two rivals. The first rival program, led by Lorentz, took the laws of electromagnetism to be the basic principles of physics and claimed the prediction and detection of radio waves as impressive theoretical and empirical progress. The second program, led by Mach and Kirchoff, advocated a physics that made no recourse to unobservable entities. In the first two decades of the twentieth century, two even newer rivals to Newton's program emerged, Einstein's relativity theories and the quantum theories. All three previous programs were eventually supplanted by the two newcomers.

Some of these changes can be argued to have involved the replacement of a degenerating program by a progressive one, but in at least one important case this was not true. Both Lorentz's electromagnetic program and Einstein's relativity program were progressive and could claim new theoretical and empirical findings. Einstein's program ultimately won because it was *more* progressive. As Zahar (1976) has argued at length, it *outperformed* a strong rival from which it also appropriated certain important elements (the Lorentz Transformations, which still indicate their origin in their name). This is a further critical point against the Kuhnian view, in which the transition from one paradigm to the next is not supposed to be achieved by articulating with, or extending, the old paradigm. Although the problems solved by competing paradigms may overlap to some extent during the transition period, according to Kuhn a change of paradigm revises the field's elementary generalizations and replaces old theories with new ones that are logically incompatible. But in the case of the relativity program (at least), important elements were appropriated from Lorentz's rival electromagnetic program.

The present state of physics illustrates another important feature of Lakatos' account—the revival of a research program after a period of degeneration or stagnation. After its initial successes, Einstein's program entered a period of stagnation lasting from the 1930s to the 1960s. The last major piece of theoretical and empirical progress was the explanation of the Hubble recession law by the expanding universe model, although some theoretical progress continued, for example, the early work on gravitational collapse and Einstein's demonstration that the equations of motion in general relativity theory are derivable from the general field equations. During the same time period, however, the quantum mechanical program had progressed from Bohr's quantized solar atom, through the wave and matrix mechanics theories of the 1920s, to Dirac's relativistically consistent theory, with successful new predictions at each turn. This progress continued during the period of the relativity program's stagnation with the elucidation of the structure of the atomic nucleus and the development of quantum electrodynamics. It continues today with the quark model. However, in the early 1960s the relativity program became progressive again. A host of astronomical discoveries, such as quasars and pulsars, stimulated new theoretical progress leading to the modern theory of stellar evolution and the now conventional "hot big bang" cosmology. At present both programs are viable.

The present and past of physics are decisively at odds with the Kuhnian model of history. The Kuhnian model suggests one paradigm dominates each period of stability,[3] denies that a paradigm can contribute to the foundations of its successor (except through translation, which is always partial), and makes no allowance for the reappearance of a superseded paradigm. As the preceding sketch shows, each period in the history of physics has been marked by a number of competing viewpoints, each of sufficient generality to count as a paradigm. These competing viewpoints are not watertight compartments, as shown by the Lorentz Transformations, which became a central feature of Einstein's relativity program, although they developed as part of the rival electromagnetic program. The temporary degeneration and later revival of a research program is also illustrated by the fortunes of relativity theory during the last half century. Similar events, including this pattern of stagnation and revival, will be described in the psychology of learning in the second half of this paper. The last, and perhaps most important point to make is that decisions among rival programs were based on rational considerations involving experimental evidence. This mode of competition is completely consistent with Lakatos' model.

IV. Applications to Psychology

Historically, two conflicting approaches have, at different times, achieved wide enough acceptance among researchers and theorists concerned with learning and related processes (Reese & Overton, 1970) to justify their classification as "world hypotheses" (Pepper, 1942), "paradigms" (Kuhn, 1962), or "research programs" (Lakatos, 1970). For reasons already outlined, in this paper we approach the subject through Lakatos' concept of a research program. One group of theories may be represented as a research program based on a mechanistic cosmology (Pepper, 1942). These are variously referred to as "associationist," "behaviorist," "Pavlovian," or "conditioning" theories. We will adopt the last of these terms to label the corresponding research program. The core commitments of the program include the assumptions that learning is to be

[3]"Revolutions close with a total victory for one of the two opposing camps" (Kuhn, 1970, p. 166).

accounted for in terms of the conditioning and extinction of specific stimulus–response associations and that the organism is reactive, that is, change can be caused only by the application of external force.

The competing research program is said to be based on an organismic cosmology (Pepper, 1942). The core commitments of this program include the notions that learning is achieved through testing rules or "hypotheses," which are evaluated in terms of environmental feedback, and that the organism is said to be an active information seeker. Change is induced by internal transformations. Theories in this program include approaches as diverse as nineteenth century structuralism, gestalt theory, Piaget's theory, and some modern versions of information-processing theory. They are referred to collectively as "cognitive" theories and we will adopt that label for the corresponding research program.

Philosophers have explored implications of the two viewpoints for centuries and, as already indicated, theories of learning reflecting each were current by the late nineteenth century. In this essay, however, we will consider only developments during the past half century. We do this in order to reduce the scope of the paper to a manageable size, and because the conditioning program and the cognitive program were in clear confrontation by the 1930s.

As is well known, John B. Watson (1914, 1919) introduced the term "behaviorism" during the second decade of this century. His work and that of others (e.g., Pavlov, 1927) were well established by the early 1930s and the conditioning program had attracted many advocates. The cognitive program was also well established within the psychology of learning in the early 1930s, in the form of two highly visible representatives: gestalt theory (Koffka, 1935; Köhler, 1925, 1929, 1930; Lewin, 1935) and hypothesis theory (Krechevsky, 1932a,b, 1933a,b, 1937; Lashley, 1929; Tolman, 1932).

When the battle between the research program based on a hard core of conditioning theory assumptions and the program embodying cognitive assumptions was joined during the 1930s, the conditioning program clearly became progressive in Lakatos' technical sense. The progress of the conditioning program relative to its rival may be illustrated by two central examples: In each case the conditioning program both resolved an experimental problem and made a new prediction that was confirmed; that is, it made both theoretical and empirical progress. First, consider the clash with hypothesis theory, modern versions of which had their origins in the work of Lashley (1929). In discussing the behavior of rats during the learning of a brightness discrimination, Lashley offered two observations: First, "attempted solutions," such as position preference, position alternation, or reactions to other cues irrelevant to solution, frequently preceded acquisition of the "correct solution"; and, second, as long as the animal exhibited these attempted solutions, training had no effect on the final acquisition of the correct association.

Although Lashley had little more to say on the issue, his comments influenced a graduate student named Krechevsky who was working with Tolman at the time

(Tolman, 1932). There followed a series of research reports in which Krechevsky investigated systematic response patterns exhibited by rats prior to solution in various learning tasks (Krechevsky, 1932a,b, 1937). He labeled these response patterns "hypotheses" and discussed them in the language of the cognitive program.

Spence and others working in the conditioning program were quick to respond to the challenge presented by the cognitive program. In a series of influential papers, Spence (1936, 1937, 1940) argued, convincingly, that any response patterns observed prior to solution were an uninteresting by-product of the animal's earlier conditioning history. Because reinforcement and extinction processes were presumed to account for *all* behavior (this was a core commitment of the conditioning program and therefore was unmodifiable), systematic response patterns themselves were of no intrinsic interest. In one paper, for example, Spence (1936) provided a reasonably precise mathematical theory which showed not only that conditioning theory could account for systematic response patterns (hypotheses), but also that it could predict both which specific patterns would occur (e.g., position preference, position alternation) and when they would occur during the course of learning. Krechevsky's theory led to no such predictions. Spence's work may be seen as a classic example of a research program overcoming an empirical anomaly in a content-increasing fashion, and hence exhibiting both theoretical and empirical progress according to Lakatos' definition.

Spence's defense of the conditioning program was so successful that in the ensuing dialogue the emphasis shifted to Lashley's second claim, that training produced no effect on final learning as long as the presolution response patterns persisted. Out of this the continuity–discontinuity controversy was born and the analysis of response patterns—the original concern of both Lashley and Krechevsky—ceased to be studied. By the early 1940s the rivalry between the research programs was temporarily resolved in favor of the conditioning program. Although an occasional new experiment was reported (e.g., Postman & Bruner, 1948, 1952), the cognitive research program represented by hypothesis theory was effectively eclipsed for the ensuing decade and a half, that is, it went into a period of degeneration.

At about the same time, a second representative of the cognitive program, the gestalt theory of learning, came into conflict with the conditioning program in the context of what is called "transposition" learning (Klüver, 1933; Köhler, 1918; Spence, 1937). To understand this controversy, consider a simple problem in which two circles are presented side by side on each of a series of trials. One circle is 10 cm in diameter and the other is 15 cm, with the positions varied randomly from one trial to the next. The task for the animal is to learn to choose the 15-cm circle, that is, reinforcement or reward (e.g., a food pellet) follows the correct choices, but nothing follows choices of the 10-cm circle.

After some learning criterion is met, for example, 12 consecutive correct responses, the experimental arrangement is altered. The 10-cm circle is eliminated and the 15-cm circle is now paired with a 20-cm circle. If allowed a free choice, animals almost always choose the 20-cm circle in the transfer (transposition) task. A core commitment of the conditioning program is that the stimulus–response bond is established between a specific stimulus (here, the 15-cm circle) and response. What the animals appeared to learn, however, was a relational response, that is, "choose the larger circle." Gestalt theorists, therefore, presented transposition data as a critical refutation of a core commitment of the conditioning program (e.g., Klüver, 1933). The experimental anomaly remained an embarrassment to conditioning theory until about 1937.

Immediately after his successful defense of the cognitive program against hypothesis theory, Spence (1937) showed that conditioning theory could account for transposition findings of the type just described. He did this by expanding two of the conditioning program's basic mechanisms to include the notion of generalization. He proposed that the strength of the stimulus–response bond, called "habit strength," which increases as a function of the number of reinforced trials, generalizes to similar stimuli. The less similar the stimuli the less habit strength generalizes. Similarly, inhibition, which is the tendency to avoid a stimulus, increases as a function of the number of nonreinforced trials. The generalization of inhibition is also directly related to stimulus similarity. That is, the more similar a given stimulus is to the nonreinforced stimulus, the more inhibition will generalize to it.

Using the mechanisms of habit, inhibition, and generalization, Spence (1937) demonstrated that conditioning theory predicted the transposition finding that gestalt theorists had presented as a crucial refutation of the core of conditioning theory. In addition, Spence showed that conditioning theory made a new prediction concerning transposition, which gestalt theory did not make. In the problem described above the 15-cm circle, choice of which was reinforced in the first task, was paired with the 20-cm circle in the transposition task. This pairing is called a "near" test, because the originally rewarded stimulus is included and proportionality is maintained. In a "far" test the proportions remain the same but the absolute sizes change more drastically. Circles of 20 and 25 cm or 25 and 30 cm, for example, are paired in the transfer task.

Gestalt theorists (e.g., Klüver, 1933) predicted that animals would respond relationally in both near and far tests, that is, they would choose the larger circle in both. Conditioning theory, however, predicted that the larger circle would be chosen consistently only in the near test. Empirical findings supported conditioning theory and once again Spence had defended the conditioning program by accommodating an anomaly in a way that was both theoretically and empirically progressive.[4] Gestalt approaches to learning, like hypothesis theory, entered a

[4]Although it was not apparent at the time, later analyses revealed that Spence's predictions were only broadly supported (see Reese, 1968, pp. 273–308).

long period of stagnation. Skinner's classic (1938) was soon published, as was Hull's (1943). The influence of the conditioning program reached its zenith in the mid-1940s and little was heard from the cognitive program until about 1960.

One contribution to the revival of the cognitive program began with Harlow's (1950) demonstration of learning set in monkeys. He presented each animal with a long series of short problems, each with different stimulus objects but all involving a common type of solution. A pair of stimulus objects was presented in each trial, with the left–right position of the correct object varied at random. A learning set was said to be acquired when the solution to each new problem was immediate, that is, when the monkey needed feedback from only the first-trial response to obtain solution. The research provided measures of learning within each individual problem and a measure of the cumulative improvement in performance across a series of problems.

Once the learning set was established, monkeys showed essentially perfect performance on each consecutive problem, although the solutions differed. Thus, Harlow's findings were a challenge to the conditioning program (cf. Reese, 1964; Restle, 1958). Harlow observed, as had Lashley and Krechevsky, that several types of systematic response sequences (e.g., position alternation, stimulus perseveration) dominated the animals' behavior prior to the achievement of learning set. These response sequences, which he labeled "error factors," masked the learning process. Harlow concluded, therefore, that he should chart the time course of each error factor during acquisition.

Initially, Harlow (1950) identified four error factors. Each one occurred in some of his monkeys, and different error factors seemed to dominate behavior in successive phases of the acquisition process. In the next few years, Harlow, his students, and other primate researchers performed error factor analyses on data derived from various kinds of learning set problems. Consequently, the number of published accounts increased very quickly, as did the list of error factors. By the mid-1950s the domain had become somewhat chaotic; each article seemed to specify a different set of error factors and those that were identified never seemed to be related to one another. We see here an example of the degeneration of a research program when its heuristic has played out. The later work only expanded the number of error factors. It failed to relate error factors to each other, failed to resolve the problems posed for the conditioning program by Harlow's earlier work, and no theoretical progress was forthcoming. In an important sense, "error factor theory" was really the demonstration of an empirical phenomenon in search of a theoretical explanation (cf. Reese, 1964; Restle, 1958).

The various problems were resolved when Levine (1959, 1963), a graduate student working with Harlow, systematized error factor analysis, beginning in 1959. He defined error factors in a way that permitted a standard mode of measurement, and he provided a quantitative theory from which the measurement was derived. Levine enlarged the class of systematic response patterns to be considered and redefined the means by which each was identified. His enlarged system also included a response pattern that corresponded to the acquisition of learning set. Correct responding, then, was treated simply as another response pattern. As the label ''error factor'' was no longer appropriate for the class of all response patterns, Levine adopted Krechevsky's (1932a,b) term ''hypothesis'' from the cognitive program.

During the decade of the 1950s another set of events, at first at odds with the cognitive program, but important to its revival in the 1960s, took place within the mainstream of the conditioning program. The movement involved a group of conditioning theorists (e.g., Bush & Mosteller, 1955; Estes & Burke, 1953; Restle, 1955) that elaborated stimulus-sampling theory, which is based on Guthrie's (1935, 1942) contiguity theory, into what became commonly known as ''mathematical learning theory.'' The theory makes reference only to observable (or potentially observable) events: a set of stimuli, a set of responses, and a set of stimulus–response connections. The total set of connections defines a state of conditioning.

To illustrate the general approach, consider a two-choice task involving a circle and a square. One of the forms is designated as correct and responses to it are always followed by a reinforcer. Responses to the other form are never reinforced. At the start of each trial the subject takes a random sample of the stimulus cues available from the environment. Three features of the random sample are important. First, any stimulus element is conditioned to, at most, one response. Second, the probability of a given response is a function of the number of cues in the sample that are conditioned to it; the probability of choosing the square, for example, is a function of the proportion of cues in the sample that are conditioned to that response. Also, all the conditioning produced by the reinforcement applies only to the cues sampled in that trial, that is, the conditioning state of unsampled cues does not change. In the next trial the sample is returned to the universe of cues and a new random sample is taken, and so on. The central idea is that all the cues corresponding to the correct form will eventually be conditioned. Similarly, all the cues that correspond to the unreinforced form will eventually be extinguished. Thus, the probability of a correct response will increase incrementally with the number of trials.

Quantitative predictions derived from this simple but elegant formulation were applied successfully to numerous tasks and subject populations, ranging from simple conditioning in rats to complex concept identification in college students. In Lakatos' terms, the theory made rapid theoretical and empirical progress. Consecutive statements of mathematical learning theory broadened its scope and remedied the deficiencies of earlier versions almost, it seemed, before they were recognized as defects (Bourne & Restle, 1959; Restle, 1955). Because consecutive theoretical formulations were mathematically cast, rigorous, and clear in their implications, they set a demanding standard for competitors.

At about the same time, however, Rock (1957) published a challenge to one of the conditioning program's strongly held commitments: the assumption that learning is incremental. Rock compared two groups of college students in a paired associate task. One group went through a standard list of paired associates on successive study and test trials until the correct response was given to each stimulus item. The other group began with the same list but each time an incorrect response was given that particular item was removed from the list and replaced with a new pair. The latter group, then, had to learn a few new items on successive presentations of the list. If each pair was learned by a gradual, or incremental, conditioning process, then the group that received the same list throughout should learn faster than the group for which pairs were substituted following errors. Rock, however, found no differences between the groups. On this basis he argued that prior to the acquisition of a given stimulus–response relation, the strength of the bond between them was zero. Rock concluded that learning is an all-or-none process.

If learning is not an incremental process, then a core commitment of the conditioning program was suspect, no matter how elegantly the theories were formulated. Consequently, Rock's findings were critically examined by many active researchers, and although this sketch greatly oversimplifies the ensuing history, the next events of importance to the revival of the cognitive program were produced by researchers in the conditioning program. Estes (1960), a leading figure in the mathematical learning movement, is an example of someone who took the issue seriously. Rock's results, with some of his own, led Estes to conclude that learning is indeed an all-or-none process. He announced this view, provided supporting data, and rejected an incremental position in 1960.

The final episode we will mention in the revival of the cognitive program was a restatement of stimulus-sampling theory (Restle, 1962). According to this latter view, conditioned cues are sampled from the environment and determine the subject's response. Thus, in retrospect, a reasonable restatement places the response-determining cues in some repertoire inside the subject to be selected and tested until one cue that results in solution is located. Restle, another leading mathematical learning theorist, announced this innovation in 1962. Restle (1962, p. 362) remarked that his model was similar in intent to Krechevsky's and because "conditioned cues" no longer seemed an appropriate label for the class of all response determinants, Restle (1962, 1965), like Levine, substituted Krechevsky's term "hypothesis."

Thus, spokesmen for two different approaches, Levine for error factors and Restle for mathematical learning, had in rapid succession converged on a theoretical statement in which the term "hypothesis," from the old cognitive research program, was again used to identify a core commitment. Although the term was pressed into service in contexts not considered by workers in the cognitive program before its degeneration in the 1930s, the core commitments adopted by people such as Levine and Restle in the 1960s were those of the cognitive program and not of the conditioning program. During the 1960s the cognitive program flourished in the mainstream of the psychology of learning. After its abrupt reemergence in the early part of the decade, theoretical and empirical progress was so rapid that by 1969 it was fairly characterized as "the leading theory of discrimination learning by the adult human" (Levine, 1969, p. 101).[5] Of course, theories within the conditioning program continued to have adherents, and thus the program may enter a new progressive phase in the future. But theories based on the cognitive program's core assumptions have progressed rapidly and during the past decade have produced important theoretical and empirical advances in domains as diverse as clinical, neurological, and developmental psychology.

V. Conclusions

In conclusion, let us recapitulate our main contentions. We are suggesting that the history of the competition between the cognitive program and the conditioning program conforms to Lakatos' description of science rather than to Kuhn's. Three points in particular support this conclusion: (1) the existence of more than one large-scale position throughout most of the half century in question; (2) the experimental commensurability of the programs as indicated by the contributions made by theorists in the conditioning program to the revival of the cognitive program; and (3) the 20-year pattern of decline of the cognitive program followed by its abrupt and progressive revival. We described how Spence, from 1936 onward, made a brilliant defense of the conditioning program against threats from the cognitive program as represented by Krechevsky's hypothesis theory and gestalt theory. In each case Spence's work was both theoretically and empirically *progressive* in Lakatos' technical sense, as was the work of countless others who shared the core commitments of conditioning theory during the ensuing decades. In Lakatos' terms it was, therefore, to be expected that the conditioning program would dominate the field from the 1940s onward, while the cognitive program degenerated.

The revival of the cognitive program and the conversion of many well-known theorists from the core commitments of the conditioning program to those of the cognitive program were affected, of course, by many developments within both psychology and related disciplines (e.g., linguistics, computer science). A description of all these events was far beyond the scope of this paper. Our aim, instead, was to identify the major currents affecting the mainstream of the psy-

[5]Levine was, of course, an important contributor to the revival of the cognitive program.

chology of learning and to demonstrate that Lakatos' analysis provides a more veridical description of the mainstream's course than does Kuhn's.

REFERENCES

Aiton, E. J. *The vortex theory of planetary motions*. London: Macdonald, 1972.

Barker, P. Can scientific history repeat? *Philosophy of Science Association*, 1980, **1,** 20–28.

Bourne, L. E., & Restle, F. Mathematical theory of concept identification. *Psychological Review*, 1959, **66,** 278–296.

Bush, R. R., & Mosteller, F. *Stochastic models for learning*. New York: Wiley, 1955.

Estes, W. K. Learning theory and the new "mental chemistry." *Psychological Review*, 1960, **67,** 207–223.

Estes, W. K., & Burke, C. J. A theory of stimulus variability in learning. *Psychological Review*, 1953, **60,** 276–286.

Guthrie, E. R. *The psychology of learning*. New York: Harper, 1935.

Guthrie, E. R. A theory of learning in terms of stimulus, response and association. In *The psychology of learning*. National Social Studies Education, 41st Yearbook, Part II, 1942.

Gutting, G. (Ed.). *Paradigms and revolutions*. Notre Dame, Indiana: Univ. of Notre Dame Press, 1980.

Harlow, H. F. Analysis of discrimination learning by monkeys. *Journal of Experimental Psychology*, 1950, **40,** 26–39.

Hull, C. L. *Principles of learning*. New York: Appleton, 1943.

Klüver, H. *Behavior mechanisms in monkeys*. Chicago, Illinois: Univ. of Chicago Press, 1933.

Koffka, K. *Principles of gestalt psychology*. New York: Harcourt, 1935.

Köhler, W. *The mentality of apes*. New York: Harcourt, 1925.

Köhler, W. *Gestalt psychology*. New York: Liveright, 1929.

Köhler, W. Some tasks of gestalt psychology. In *Psychologies of 1930*. Worchester, Massachusetts: Clark Univ. Press, 1930.

Krechevsky, I. "Hypotheses" in rats. *Psychological Review*, 1932, **39,** 516–532. (a)

Krechevsky, I. "Hypotheses" versus "chance" in the pre-solution period in sensory discrimination learning. *University of California Publications in Psychology*, 1932, **6,** 27–44. (b)

Krechevsky, I. The docile nature of "hypotheses." *Journal of Comparative Psychology*, 1933, **15,** 429–443. (a)

Krechevsky, I. Hereditary nature of "hypotheses." *Journal of Comparative Psychology*, 1933, **16,** 99–116. (b)

Krechevsky, I. A note concerning "the nature of discrimination learning in animals." *Psychological Review*, 1937, **44,** 97–104.

Kuhn, T. S. *The structure of scientific revolutions*. Chicago, Illinois: Univ. of Chicago Press, 1962.

Kuhn, T. S. *The structure of scientific revolutions* (2nd ed., enlarged). Chicago, Illinois: Univ. of Chicago Press, 1970.

Lakatos, I. Falsification and the methodology of scientific research programs. In I. Lakatos & A. Musgrave (Eds.), *Criticism and the growth of knowledge*. London and New York: Cambridge Univ. Press, 1970.

Lakatos, I. *The methodology of scientific research programs*. London and New York: Cambridge Univ. Press, 1978.

Lakatos, I., & Musgrave, A. (Eds.). *Criticism and the growth of knowledge*. London and New York: Cambridge Univ. Press, 1970.

Lashley, K. S. *Brain mechanisms and intelligence*. Chicago, Illinois: Univ. of Chicago Press, 1929.

Laudan, L. *Progress and its problems*. Berkeley, California: Univ. of California Press, 1977.

Levine, M. A model of hypothesis behavior in discrimination learning set. *Psychological Review*, 1959, **66,** 353–366.

Levine, M. Mediation processes in humans at the outset of discrimination learning. *Psychological Review*, 1963, **70,** 254–276.

Levine, M. Neo-noncontinuity theory. In G. H. Bower & J. T. Spence (Eds.), *The psychology of learning and motivation* (Vol. 3). New York: Academic Press, 1969.

Lewin, K. *A dynamic theory of personality*. New York: McGraw-Hill, 1935.

Pavlov, I. P. *Conditioned reflexes*. London and New York: Oxford Univ. Press, 1927.

Pepper, S. *World hypotheses*. Berkeley, California: Univ. of California Press, 1942.

Postman, L., & Bruner, J. S. Perception under stress. *Psychological Review*, 1948, **55,** 314–323.

Postman, L., & Bruner, J. S. Hypothesis and the principle of closure: The effect of frequency and recency. *Journal of Psychology*, 1952, **33,** 113–125.

Reese, H. W. Discrimination learning set in Rhesus monkeys. *Psychological Bulletin*, 1964, **61,** 321–340.

Reese, H. W. *The perception of stimulus relations: Discrimination learning and transposition*. New York: Academic Press, 1968.

Reese, H. W., & Overton, W. F. Models of development and theories of development. In L. R. Goulet & P. B. Baltes (Eds.), *Life-span developmental psychology*. New York: Academic Press, 1970.

Restle, F. A theory of discrimination learning. *Psychological Review*, 1955, **62,** 11–19.

Restle, F. Toward a quantitative description of learning set data. *Psychological Review*, 1958, **65,** 77–91.

Restle, F. The selection of strategies in cue learning. *Psychological Review*, 1962, **69,** 329–343.

Restle, F. Significance of all-or-none learning. *Psychological Review*, 1965, **64,** 313–325.

Rock, I. The role of repetition in associative learning. *American Journal of Psychology*, 1957, **70,** 186–193.

Schaffner, K. *Nineteenth century aether theories*. Oxford: Pergamon, 1972.

Scheffler, I. *Science and subjectivity*. Indianapolis, Indiana: Bobbs, Merrill, 1967.

Skinner, B. F. *The behavior of organisms: An experimental analysis*. New York: Appleton, 1938.

Spence, K. W. The nature of discrimination learning in animals. *Psychological Review*, 1936, **43,** 427–449.

Spence, K. W. The differential response in animals to stimuli varying within a single dimension. *Psychological Review*, 1937, **47,** 271–288.

Spence, K. W. Continuous versus noncontinuous interpretations of discrimination learning. *Psychological Review*, 1940, **47,** 271–288.

Stegmuller, W. *The structure and dynamics of theories*. Berlin and New York: Springer-Verlag, 1976.

Suppe, F. *The structure of scientific theories* (2nd ed.). Urbana, Illinois: Univ. of Illinois Press, 1977.

Tolman, E. C. *Purposive behavior in animals and men*. New York: Appleton, 1932.

Watkins, J. W. N. Against normal science. In I. Lakatos & A. Musgrave (Eds.), *Criticism and the growth of knowledge*. London and New York: Cambridge Univ. Press, 1970.

Watson, J. B. *Behavior. An introduction to comparative psychology*. New York: Holt, 1914.

Watson, J. B. *Psychology from the standpoint of a behaviorist*. Philadelphia, Pennsylvania: Lippincott, 1919.

Zahar, E. Why did Einstein's programme supersede Lorentz's? In C. Howson (Ed.), *Method and appraisal in the physical sciences*. London and New York: Cambridge Univ. Press, 1976.

FUNCTIONALIST AND STRUCTURALIST RESEARCH PROGRAMS IN DEVELOPMENTAL PSYCHOLOGY: INCOMMENSURABILITY OR SYNTHESIS?[1]

Harry Beilin
DEVELOPMENTAL PSYCHOLOGY PROGRAM
CITY UNIVERSITY OF NEW YORK
GRADUATE SCHOOL AND UNIVERSITY CENTER
NEW YORK, NEW YORK

I. Introduction

Understanding scientific progress is presently complicated by the fact that the usual model for such understanding, the philosophy of science, has itself been the subject of radical change. Philosophic orientations within our science nevertheless have an important influence on how we think about and conduct our research. An example from the *Journal of Experimental Child Psychology* illustrates this point. In 1972, the *Journal* published a paper by authors from a midwestern university on a test of some predictions derived from Hull–Spence

[1]A shorter version of this paper was presented at the symposium, "Research programs: A rational alternative to Kuhn's analysis of the history of scientific revolutions." Southeastern Conference on Human Development, Baltimore, Maryland: April, 1982.

ADVANCES IN CHILD DEVELOPMENT
AND BEHAVIOR, VOL. 18

ISBN 0-12-009718-4

discrimination learning theory. The authors were among the principal inheritors of the behaviorist tradition, which had an intimate ideological association with logical positivism and empiricism. It would be fair to say that by 1972 behaviorism had seen better days, and logical empiricism was under vigorous attack. In the process of reviewing the aforementioned paper, a former adherent to the same orientation made the point that the reported data could be analyzed and interpreted just as well in accord with another model. He argued that the authors had an obligation to test alternative interpretations of the findings (Bogartz, 1972). The authors rejected the suggestion, arguing in turn that the investigator had the prerogative to pursue his or her own theoretical direction. In reply to a critical note by the reviewer, which was published with the original paper, the authors rejected "any implication that the direct comparison of two or more theories is a prerequisite to theoretically significant contributions" (Spiker, Croll, & Miller, 1972, p. 586) and went on to defend "successful" theories of large scope from being compared to ad hoc theories of lesser or more limited scope, although the latter could apply equally well to the data.[2] Neither the authors nor the critic cited philosophers of science to buttress their arguments, but they were playing out in a side ring the drama being enacted in the main ring between the logical positivists and their critics, such as Toulmin, Kuhn, Feyerabend, Hanson, Lakatos, and others. (For an excellent description and commentary—on which the synopsis given here is based—see Suppe, 1977.)

This event is now more than 10 years past; much has transpired in the interim, both in the philosophy of science and in developmental theory. I will review some of these events to show that "revolutions" in developmental psychology are still occurring, although theory in the philosophy of science to account for them is not exactly in a stable state itself. I will also suggest that the application of a Kuhnian model (in the earlier views of Overton & Reese, 1973) is no longer helpful to an understanding of the current state of developmental theory.

II. The Demise of Logical Positivism

Logical positivism, and its later form, logical empiricism, fell into disfavor despite its hold on the loyalties of two generations of philosophers of science and scientists themselves, because of its inability to defend its most important assumptions from logical and historical attack. One of the original aims of the unity-of-science movement, associated with the Vienna Circle and logical

[2]The critical note and the authors' reply were written at the suggestion of the editor in the interests of exposing the kind of philosophy of science debate already evident in the field, although few appear to have seen it in those terms at the time.

positivism, was to unify the sciences through the development of formal languages (symbolic logic and mathematics) that would aid in the axiomatization of each of the sciences. What became clear, at least to the critics from both within and without logical positivism, was that even when achieving axiomatization was possible in the most advanced of the physical sciences, achieving it was not necessarily fruitful. Axiomatization itself could take place only if a distinction could be maintained between theoretical and observation languages, which in turn relied on the Kantian distinction between analytic and synthetic knowledge.

Although some scientific statements are clearly analytic (i.e., logically derivable) and others clearly synthetic (i.e., validated by observation alone), many scientific statements are neither synthetic nor analytic but have the properties of both. Many ostensibly clear-cut examples of observation and theoretical terms are in fact incapable of being precisely categorized (e.g., "temperature" as a theoretical term). In addition to the difficulties with the distinction between observation and theoretical terms, difficulties are found in relating theory to observation in the test of scientific theories. The test of a theory with observation data, according to logical empiricism, is achieved through correspondence rules, or operational definitions. The interpretation of correspondence rules rests on the distinction between observation and theoretical terms, which was shown at best to be imprecise, and therefore the correspondence rule model has been judged to be equally untenable.

One of the strongest tenets of logical positivism also under attack was Hempel's "covering law of explanation," according to which prediction and explanation are essentially the same operation, the critical distinction being that one comes before the other. The realization that, among other things, one could have explanation without prediction, as in evolutionary theory, and prediction without explanation, as in astronomy, undercut at least some of the force of the covering law model. That model, which holds that causal explanation of the relationship between two events requires that some lawful relationship be applicable to "cover" them, was not completely rejected but has certainly had its scope of application substantially narrowed in the general rejection of logical empiricism. Another aspect of logical positivism under serious attack was the claim that scientific progress occurred when theories explained new facts, or when confirmed theories were included in or reduced to more inclusive theories.

In summary, the attack on logical positivism and logical empiricism was directed at the distinction between theoretical and observation languages and the entailed analytic/synthetic distinction, the goal of formalization and axiomatization of theories, the basis of explanation and prediction defined in terms of the covering law model, and the characterization of theories in respect to their structural characteristics (statically) delineated at particular stages of their development.

A. *WELTANSCHAUUNG* THEORIES

The contested issues are seen even more clearly in the alternative models proposed. These issues were principally embodied in the views of Kuhn and Feyerabend, although their position in many respects developed from ideas expressed by Popper, Toulmin, and Hanson. These critics collectively accepted the distinction made by logical positivists between the *logic of discovery* and the *logic of justification,* but differed from the logical positivists in not rejecting the logic of discovery as a legitimate aspect of an understanding of scientific theory and scientific progress. In particular, they accepted the possibility that psychological and sociological facts could provide insights into the nature of scientific knowledge, which in the logical positivist model was confined to logical and rational analysis of the structure of theories and their relation to the data of experience. Thus, contrary to the positivist view that theories are tested and either confirmed or disconfirmed, leading to their acceptance or rejection, the *Weltanschauung* or "world view" position is that theories can only be falsified (in the Popper sense) and are replaced not on logical grounds but because the conceptual framework or world view of which the theory is a part has lost credibility. Such a *world view, conceptual framework, paradigm,* or *disciplinary matrix* (as Kuhn later characterized paradigms) determines which questions are worth asking and what answers are acceptable, and is tied to one's language, which shapes the way we look at the world. Conceptual frameworks are shared by a scientific community and tend to dominate a science at particular periods. They are also essentially incommensurable in Kuhn's view with other disciplinary matrices. They change only during revolutionary periods because the problems within a paradigm or matrix cumulate to the point at which the members of the scientific community begin to see more defects than assets and search for new ways of dealing with the same issues. Ordinary scientific activity is dominated by "normal science," which is problem-solving science. Defects exposed during periods of normal science do not lead to rejection of a theory, even if they disconfirm it. In this view, despite the possession of common vocabularies and concepts, different paradigms or world views are resisted by their antagonists inasmuch as others view data and even logic within their own standards and values and apply different meanings to commonly used terms and concepts. Logical argument, then, cannot show the superiority of one view over another. Not even a neutral observation language exists, inasmuch as observation is interpreted in the context of the disciplinary matrix, i.e., "all observations are theory-laden."

When scientific revolutions occur, the cumulations of knowledge characteristic of normal science give way to the doubts also cumulated in that period. The revolution is the consequence of a "gestalt switch," when what is "in" suddenly is "out," and alternatives proliferate until one view emerges as the victor and a new community organizes around it. The incommensurability of world views is particularly emphasized in Overton and Reese's (1973) model for developmental theory.

Although the so-called *Weltanschauung* or world view position had great appeal for a time, particularly as the logical empiricist position was receding in favor, it came under considerable criticism itself, with the consequence that its own influence, at least among philosophers of science, has considerably diminished, if not extinguished. The main thrust of the criticism against it is directed at the world view model's subjectivist assumptions and incommensurability thesis, which bars discourse between world views and makes objective and rational tests of the empirical claims of theories impossible. Kuhn responded to these criticisms, but in doing so made his theory appear more like the logical empiricist position he rejected. Feyerabend's refusal even to acknowledge criticism has effectively led others to seek more rational interpretations of the nature of scientific activity (Suppe, 1977).

B. RATIONALIST THEORY: LAKATOS

The direction that the contemporary philosophy of science has taken, then, is one that seeks a more rational basis for the growth of knowledge. In Lakatos' view, science concerns itself with key ideas that are elaborated upon and developed in a sequence of related theories he termed a "research program." Research programs are persisted in despite experimental evidence that appears to falsify them, and despite the ability of competing theories to explain the data equally well. Built into research programs are positive and negative heuristics. Negative heuristics reflect defensive tactics that do not advance the program; positive heuristics entail a response to criticism that moves the theory forward. Negative heuristics isolate a hard core in the program and build a protective wall that prohibits modification or rejection of that hard core.[3] For Lakatos, the history of science is one of competing research programs and not of normal science monopolized by a dominant paradigm or disciplinary matrix. Theoretical pluralism is and should be the rule, to permit the relative merits of research programs to be compared and assessed. Progress occurs in a "problem shift" when a new theory emerges that is able to predict new and novel facts over that of its predecessor, in addition to the empirical content covered by the predecessor. A program is degenerating when it experiences consistent falsification without the generation of new facts or theory.

In summary, a rational way of doing science is to have a research program

[3]Overton (1984) appears to substitute Lakatos' description of hard core theory assumptions for Kuhn's incommensurability thesis to make it appear that world views (now research programs) are incapable of being tested against one another. I believe this is contrary to Lakatos' intention to provide a rational basis for evaluating the worth of competing theories.

with progressive "problem shifts" in the attempt to falsify competing theories and, as necessary, to modify one's theories by the addition of new hypotheses or through semantic reinterpretations of the theory under the guidance of a positive heuristic. A program should be stopped or rejected when it is degenerating, although even then it can be continued if it is theoretically progressive and only intermittently empirically so. Lakatos emphasized the impossibility of inductively confirming theory. Also, because all hard cores of research programs are likely to be false, no amount of testing can establish the validity of a theory. At the same time, inasmuch as one must perforce suppose one's own theory to be true, science ought to encourage the proliferation of competing theories.

Lakatos has himself been criticized (Suppe, 1977) for having little to say as to how rationality operates in theories, except to suggest one avenue of approaching it, and for exaggerating the importance of being theoretically and empirically progressive in deciding whether pursuit of a particular research program will be fruitful. Thus, too much emphasis is said to be placed on theory changes through thought experiments, in that theoretical development is little influenced by experimental results. More recent suggestions by Toulman, Shapere, and others place greater emphasis on patterns of rationality in the process of scientific discovery, leaving the field, in summary, in the position of having a number of helpful notions about scientific progress and an uncertain set of criteria, if any at all, for knowing when theories are true or worth pursuing. With the foregoing as a framework, I wish to consider the "revolutionary" events that have been taking place in developmental psychology, and to anticipate what may yet occur.

III. Research Programs and Revolutions in Developmental Psychology

Two significant revolutions in developmental psychology occurred in the past 30 years. This assertion implies acceptance of the idea that revolutions take place in science and that a particular theoretical program tends to dominate between revolutions. This position is not incompatible with the Lakatosian view that competition among alternative theories or between research programs is, in fact, the norm. Thus, a particular research program can dominate a field at the same time intense competition occurs among alternative views. Such, I believe, is evident in the history of developmental psychology.

A. THE COGNITIVE REVOLUTION

The first of the recent revolutions occurred in the 1950s and 1960s in the transition from behaviorism to cognitivism; the second is the transition still underway from structural cognitivism to what I have called the new functionalism (Beilin, 1981, 1984). The cognitive revolution of the 1950s and 1960s was fueled by a number of sources. First, despite the general dominance of behaviorism in the period from the 1920s to the 1950s, continual confrontation occurred between gestalt theory and behaviorist theories. This state of affairs alone is enough to discredit the view that it was a period of "normal science" in the Kuhnian sense, although certainly a fair amount of "normal science" activity can be seen in the many studies of discrimination learning, conditioning, etc. One aspect of the confrontation between gestalt and behaviorist theories that probably prolonged the debate between them was that gestalt theory took the nature of perceptual organization as its principal model, and behaviorists' concerns were more with learning. Gestaltists began to make serious inroads on the dominant behaviorist position when they undertook experiments in learning and problem solving, such as the latent learning and transposition experiments, the results of which began to embarrass behaviorist theories. Behaviorism did not yield easily, and in true Lakatosian fashion, Spencian elaborations of Hullian theory showed how it was possible to progress the theory through simple modifications and extensions; in turn, some of the consequent transposition studies embarrassed gestalt theory. One element that helped undermine behaviorism, and the positivist–empiricist base upon which it rested, was the increasing use of human subjects, to which the study of children added a significant dimension. The studies of Margaret Kuenne and the Kendlers, who came out of the Iowa Hull–Spence tradition, did much to undermine that tradition, with the idea that developmental change could be discontinuous and involve the emergence of mediating concepts at about 5 to 6 years of age. I believe that the role played by investigators like the Kendlers is typical of what occurs in a research program when those within a tradition itself undertake research, which despite being seen as an important advance, is instrumental in undermining confidence in the older tradition. The Kendlers and other mediationists are usually characterized as neobehaviorists, but I see them as the forerunners of what has emerged as the *new functionalism*.

Three sources underlay the research program we now refer to as cognitivism in developmental psychology: The neobehaviorists who discovered that children are more interesting subjects than rats and pigeons, and, more importantly, appear to employ processes barred to these other species; the Wernerians, who transformed gestalt theory by attempting to make an ahistorical theory historical; and experimentally oriented developmentalists, who discovered that Piaget and his colleagues had spent the war years building an imposing cognitive architecture on a theory that had already been around for at least 20 years. At that, Piaget's theory of the 1930s and 1940s was in constant contention with behaviorist theories of concept development, moral development, language development, and other aspects of development to which behavior theory was being applied. These three sources, together with the quasi-experiments that resulted from the blend of neobehaviorist and Freudian theory current in the 1950s, came together to forge the basis of a cognitive revolution in developmental psychology, which in turn affected psychology as a whole.

The cognitive era, ushered in by the cognitive revolution, if it can be said to have a program, is in actuality a number of competing theories, each with a different loading of cognitive components. We discern two types of cognitive theories. Type I theories are those concerned with cognitive *processes* as they relate to behavior. Verbal mediationist theories are of this type, as are hypothesis-testing theories that appeared in neobehaviorism. Type II theories are more properly cognitive *theories* in offering cognitive explanations that are structuralist or organismic in nature; Piaget's theory, Werner's theory, and psychoanalytic theories are examples. Neobehaviorist theories are identified by some with a mechanistic world view, the other theories with an organismic world view, but the division between mechanistic and organismic, which Overton (1983) made much of, although it simplifies and organizes our perceptions, does not necessarily clarify them. Such is evident in respect to understanding the considerable influence on psychology's cognitive revolution in Chomsky's theory, initiated by his review of Skinner's *Verbal behavior*. Overestimating the effect on changing attitudes toward behaviorism, occasioned by Chomsky's attack on the fundamental tenets of behaviorism and positivism, is difficult. Chomsky's review did much to swell the ranks of adherents to structuralist theories and also to generative transformational studies of language that became the rage for the next 20 years. The decline in influence of mediationist and Wernerian theory in the 1960s and 1970s left Piagetian and Chomskyan structuralist theories in a dominant position in developmental psychology but, again, not without constant criticism from within and without. Despite their common structuralism, Chomsky and Piaget were themselves constant adversaries over cognitivism, nativism, and language acquisition (Piattelli-Palmarini, 1980). Both their commonalities and differences make the mechanistic–organismic distinction outdated, for although Piaget's theory is easy to characterize as organismic, Chomsky's is not.[4] At the same time, Chomsky's theory is hardly mechanistic, and however it is viewed it does not fall under the mantle that would cover Hull, Skinner, and the current functionalists.

The last developments that undermined behaviorism arose from within behaviorism itself, or more strictly from what I refer to as middle functionalism (Beilin, 1983). Middle functionalism was the movement that survived the attack of (Watsonian) behaviorism and is best represented by Woodworth and the non-

[4]In Pepper's (1970) classification, which Overton and Reese adopted in part, Chomsky's theory would more appropriately be considered as formalist. Neither this nor the contextualist category of Pepper were included among Overton's delineation of world views in developmental psychology. The latter category would include most of current Soviet developmentalists and cross-cultural researchers.

Hullian learning theorists of the 1930s, 1940s, and 1950s. The events I am referring to were those that gave rise to mathematical psychology (with mathematical models of learning), soon joined by information theory, which was influenced by communications theory and particularly the works of Shannon, and information-processing theory, which was modeled on a combination of cybernetic theory and the (principally software) functions of the computer. The last group, the information-processing theorists, are the ones who, to a greater or lesser extent, define the nature of the contemporary era in experimental psychology and whose theories form the core of what I characterize as the new functionalism.

B. DEVELOPMENTAL PSYCHOLOGY: STRUCTURALISM

This functionalist program succeeded in undermining confidence in structuralist theories and has superseded them as the dominant program in developmental psychology. The transition from structural cognitivism to the new functionalism thus defines the second of the revolutions in developmental psychology of the past 30 years. What is significant in that transition is the way in which research programs confront one another and how they undergo change as a function of the confrontation.

First, one may ask why confidence in Piaget's program eroded, despite its many successes, and despite the fact that for many domains in development to which the theory has been applied no adequate substitute is evident. Piaget's program was undermined on both theoretical and empirical grounds. Empirically, considerable damage was done by the many successful training studies in conservation, which for years had been used as a test case for the validation of the theory. Piaget had at first argued that training should not be effective, and if such training were effective it should occur as a function of an equilibration-based process. This assertion was soon shown to be questionable (Beilin, 1971). Second were the studies that showed inconsistent, stagelike behavior where early Piagetian theory argued mainly for consistency. When later Piagetian theory introduced and emphasized horizontal and oblique decalage and provided a logical account of how one could have both consistency (i.e., stage structure) and inconsistency (i.e., decalage), this argument was largely ignored and the principal theoretical attack was directed at the stage concept. In addition, claims concerning particular stage properties were attacked on the basis of evidence inconsistent with the logical claims of the theory. Other analyses attempted to show that Piaget's theory was incorrect in claiming formal logical competence in adolescence, as in combinatorial thinking, and, paradoxically, for claiming too much logical competence in adolescence by showing the extent to which adolescent and adult thoughts are nonlogical. Arguments to save the theory by emphasizing the distinction between competence and performance models, with

Piaget's theory as an example of the former, increasingly fell on deaf ears. In addition, Piaget's genetic epistemology models adapted from mathematics and logic have been criticized for their deviation from mathematical models themselves and for the very use of those models in a logicist fashion. Despite Piaget's constant refinement and even substitution of more for ostensibly less adequate logical and mathematical models, critics have generally ignored the changes or have failed to see that Piaget's system is really a research program in the Lakatosian sense, with changes made in the theory almost every year either through expansion to new domains of knowledge, or through major revisions in basic assumptions of the theory, as is evident in the recent introduction of correspondences and morphisms into the theory. Many other aspects of the program were under critical attack, but what they collectively showed was a hard core to the theory that could not change and which became more difficult to defend—in fact, no effort was made to defend it, although some of the hard core elements of the theory, such as the equilibration model and the nature of stages, have been modified. Other aspects of the program underwent constant modification—first elaboration and then substitution as with the logicomathematical models. Perhaps the most interesting attempt at program change was the emphasis in Geneva on the functional aspects of the theory. The functional component was an original element in the theory but in recent years it has become an increasing focus of Genevan research, just as general interest in functionalism has grown outside the Genevan group. Thus, one finds in the updated version of Piaget's program an almost primary emphasis on its functional aspects. This emphasis is evident in the recent work of Inhelder (1978; Inhelder, Sinclair, & Bovet, 1974), Karmiloff-Smith (1979), and Mounod (1981), among others. In essence, the functionalist elements in the theory have been expanded upon, at the same time preserving to the maximum extent possible a structuralist framework. Increasingly, however, that framework is reduced so that some of the cited work is difficult to identify as primarily functionalist or structuralist, a state of affairs that holds particularly for such self-styled neo-Piagetians as Pascual-Leone (1978) and Case (1974).

C. THE NEW FUNCTIONALISM

The functionalist alternative itself is not a monolithic metatheoretical orientation. Although the new functionalists are dominated ideologically by the information processors at one pole and by Vygotskyans at the other, with a shared set of assumptions that make them look like a single paradigm, their differences are considerable. "Early" and "middle era" functionalists made much of their rejection of mentalistic language and concepts, arguing for concepts closely related to observation, and although they never went as far as Watson and others in their positivism, they nevertheless considered anathema the kind of organizational constructs and systems that were characteristically a part of structuralist theorizing typical of Type II cognitive theories. If one looks at the history of information-processing models, however, what one sees is an increasing accomodation to structuralist theorizing in important ways. Worth noting is the core conception of humans as symbol processors and the willingness to investigate previously proscribed mentalistic constructs, such as imagery. What is of especial import is that recent models for the organization of memory, particularly in respect to declarative knowledge, embody many structuralist elements. Anderson's ACT model (Anderson, 1976) is an example with its abstract systems of representation that have structure-like properties and forms that subsume linguistic and visual processing. If this trend continues, and I believe a number of similar instances of change could be cited, functionalist theories will become increasingly indistinguishable from structural theories in critical respects.

If structural theories like Piaget's became increasingly functional and functionalist theories became increasingly structural, what is to be said for the incommensurability theses of Kuhn and Feyerabend, and of Overton and Reese in the developmental context?

For one, I believe the evidence contradicts the incommensurability thesis. Although the claim can be made and justified that fundamental theoretical differences remain at the core of structuralist and functionalist theories, these differences nevertheless do not parallel the organismic–deterministic world view distinction that Overton (1984) proposed to a degree that makes that distinction useful for us today. Second, structural and functional analyses are not so theory laden as to preclude their application in either orientation. As a consequence, one can expect to see the increasing application of both structural and functional analyses within the same framework in the future. Does this mean that the theories of the future will be a synthesis of both traditions? If thought of in the sense of a Hegelian dialectical synthesis that derives from a confrontation of theses and antitheses, then I believe the recent evidence, at least in psychological theory, suggests they will not. Instead, we should see an adaptation of the essential strengths of competing metatheories as they are incorporated into existing programs to the point at which the distinctions between them became increasingly blurred.

What, then, should be encouraged, as opposed to expected, in respect to developmental theory? I, for one, look to continual confrontation between different research programs and theories on the assumption that, on rational grounds, it is clear when a theory is able to establish its claims, and a promissory note that is never paid is distinguishable from one that is. At the same time, I believe that nonrational elements enter into beliefs about research programs that affect the persistence of theories and the search for alternatives. The fact that Chomskyan generative transformational theory is no longer the mode in psychology is not because a better syntactic theory is available. Nor is the fact that Piagetian theory is not the focus of attention it was 10 years ago a function of the availability of better theories. Some of the irrational reasons for change bear on the search for novelty, on the frustration over intractible problems, on the politics of publication and grantsmanship, and a myriad of other causes, in addition to some very rational ones.

In summary, although the world view idea has added a necessary psychological and sociological dimension to an understanding of scientific theory building, it oversimplifies and fails to capture some of the critical dynamics of change that characterize recent developments in developmental psychology.

REFERENCES

Anderson, J. R. *Language, memory and thought.* Hillsdale, New Jersey: Erlbaum, 1976.

Beilin, H. The training and acquisition of logical operations. In M. F. Rosskopf, L. P. Steffe, & S. Taback (Eds.), *Piagetian cognitive-development: Research and mathematical education.* Washington, D.C.: National Council of Teachers of Mathematics, 1971.

Beilin, H. *Piaget and the new functionalism.* Invited address presented at the annual symposium of the Jean Piaget Society, Philadelphia, June, 1981.

Beilin, H. The new functionalism and the Piagetian program. In E. K. Scholnick (Ed.), *New trends in conceptual representation.* Hillsdale, New Jersey: Erlbaum, 1983.

Bogartz, R. S. Three-cue selection models applied to multidimensional stimulus classification: Alternatives to the Spiker, Croll and Miller analysis. *Journal of Experimental Child Psychology,* 1972, **13,** 573–584.

Case, R. Structures and strictures: Some functional limitations on the course of cognitive growth. *Cognitive Psychology,* 1974, **6,** 544–573.

Inhelder, B. New currents in genetic epistemology and developmental psychology. In J. S. Bruner & A. Garton (Eds.), *Human growth and development.* London and New York: Oxford Univ. Press, 1978.

Inhelder, B., Sinclair, H., & Bovet, M. *Learning and the development of cognition.* Cambridge, Massachusetts: Harvard Univ. Press, 1974.

Karmiloff-Smith, A. *A functional approach to child language: A study of determiners and reference.* London and New York: Cambridge Univ. Press, 1979.

Mounod, P. Cognitive development: Construction of new structures or construction of internal organizations. In I. E. Sigel, D. M. Brodzinsky, & R. M. Golinkoff (Eds.), *New directions in Piagetian theory and practice.* Hillsdale, New Jersey: Erlbaum, 1981.

Overton, W. F. Historical and contemporary perspectives of development. In I. E. Sigel & D. M. Brodzinsky (Eds.), *Developmental psychology.* New York: Holt, 1984.

Overton, W. F., & Reese, H. W. Models of development: Methodological implications. In J. R. Nesselroad & H. W. Reese (Eds.), *Life-span developmental psychology: Methodological issues.* New York: Academic Press, 1973.

Pascual-Leone, T., Goodman, D., Ammon, P., & Subelman, I. Piagetian theory and neo-Piagetian analysis on psychological guides to education. In J. M. Gallagher & J. A. Easley, Jr. (Eds.), *Knowledge and development.* (Vol. 2). New York: Plenum, 1978.

Pepper, S. C. *World hypotheses: A study in evidence.* Berkeley, California: Univ. of California Press, 1970.

Piattelli-Palmarini, M. (Ed.). *Language and learning: The debate between Jean Piaget and Noam Chomsky*. Cambridge, Massachusetts: Harvard Univ. Press, 1980.

Spiker, C. C., Croll, W. L., & Miller, A. A. On the comparison of psychological theories: A reply to Professor Bogartz. *Journal of Experimental Child Psychology,* 1972, **13,** 585–592.

Suppe, F. (Ed.). *The structure of scientific theories* (2nd ed.). Urbana, Illinois: Univ. of Illinois Press, 1977.

IN DEFENSE OF KUHN: A DISCUSSION OF HIS DETRACTORS

David S. Palermo
DEPARTMENT OF PSYCHOLOGY
THE PENNSYLVANIA STATE UNIVERSITY
UNIVERSITY PARK, PENNSYLVANIA

In reviewing the papers of this symposium, some of Lakatos' work, Kuhn's writings, and some more recent work in the philosophy of science, I am somewhat surprised at (1) the easy dismissal of Kuhn's proposals in favor of the work of Lakatos (1970), Hanson (1958), and Laudan (1977), (2) the focus upon rationality as the sole basis of scientific decision making by individual scientists, and (3) the failure to recognize that science is a social enterprise in which individuals seeking to achieve their own goals yield a social matrix of interactions that direct the flow of science in not necessarily irrational, but certainly unpredictable ways. As an aside, I would add that I found it particularly surprising that psychologists who advocate a stage theory of psychological development in which one stage emerges in a discontinuous manner from another, creating new and incommensurable meanings for the child, would argue so strongly, when they put on their philosopher of science hats, that such a conception of scientific development should be rejected because it smacks of irrationality.

Before examining the issues concerning the different views of science, I should point out an important problem with which we are all faced in this process of analyzing science. We should recognize in analyzing any theory of the development of science that the history we are discussing comes from texts. Texts are reconstructions after the fact of the historical events. Those reconstructions are based upon some theory nested within the world view the author of the written record holds with respect to the history. The history is, in turn, read by a person holding his or her own theory within a world view that may or may not be the

ADVANCES IN CHILD DEVELOPMENT
AND BEHAVIOR, VOL. 18

ISBN 0-12-009718-4

same as that of the author. Thus, given the ambiguity of the record, the available data may be given different emphases and meanings in light of the paradigmatic view brought to it. In short, our own paradigmatic view of the history of science influences our reconstruction of that science and the processes we are trying to explain (Weimer, 1974a,b).

Let's look at what Lakatos has to say very briefly and then reexamine Kuhn's original thesis for comparison purposes. From my perspective it will become clear that Lakatos has done little more than reword, with some clarification and added precision, what Kuhn had already proposed but, more important in some ways, Lakatos has shorn the Kuhnian proposal of its organismic (read human) characteristics in favor of a mechanistic rationality.

Lakatos argues that any scientific discipline is characterized by its research programs. Any discipline may have more than one research program at any point in time. Each research program has its hard core that consists of unchallengeable basic assumptions upon which any theory conceived within the framework of the research program is based. There is, in Lakatos' terms, a negative heuristic that is a rationally established decision to protect those basic assumptions. Only under conditions in which the theories generated by the research program are not corroborated by the empirical will a logically and empirically based decision to challenge or refute the hard core be made (Lakatos, 1970, p. 134).

In addition to the negative heuristic associated with the irrefutable hard core, there is a positive heuristic that ''consists of a partially articulated set of suggestions or hints on how to change, develop the 'refutable variants' of the research-programme, how to modify, sophisticate, the 'refutable' protective belt'' (Lakatos, 1970, p. 135). The protective belt is that portion of the research program that is defined as changeable or refutable and that allows for progressive theoretical problem shift. Within this framework, ''The positive heuristic . . . saves the scientist from becoming confused by the ocean of anomalies. The positive heuristic sets out a programme which lists a chain of ever more complicated *models* simulating reality: The scientist . . . ignores the *actual* counterexamples, the available 'data' '' (p. 135). In Lakatos' view, the theorist within a research program foresees the problems with the initial theory and which aspects of the theory will need to be revised because initial conditions are known to be wrong and bound to be replaced by means known more or less to the scientist. Thus, refutations may be ignored and verifications rather than refutations are the main contact with reality although verification, of course, does not verify a program, only its heuristic power. Thus, theoretical science is relatively autonomous from anomalies that ''are listed but shoved aside in the hope that they will turn, in due course, into corroborations of the programme'' (p. 137).

Lakatos then goes on to prescribe, as opposed to describe, that

> One must never allow a research programme to become a *Weltanschauung*. . . . The history of science has been and should be a history of competing research programmes (or, if you wish,

> 'paradigms'), but it has not been and must not become a succession of periods of normal science: The sooner competition starts, the better for progress. 'Theoretical pluralism' is better than 'theoretical monism': On this point Popper and Feyerabend are right and Kuhn is wrong. (Lakatos, 1970, p. 155)

I cannot refrain from noting here that what scientists should do and what they actually do may be two quite separate matters. I should also note that Kuhn did not deny the existence of theoretical pluralism within the framework of a paradigm—theoretical differences within the paradigmatic fold were clearly articulated by Kuhn—nor did he argue that more than one paradigm could not exist within a scientific community at one time. He specifically noted the possibility of paradigm plurality and discussed at length theoretical differences leading to arguments within a paradigmatic framework. Kuhn's distinction between paradigm and theory is important and more clearly articulated than Lakatos' distinction between hard core and protective belt.

How, then, are research programs eliminated on Lakatos' account? They cannot be eliminated, to use Lakatos' own words, by "some old fashioned 'refutation,' or a Kuhnian 'crisis'. . . . *Can there be any objective* (as opposed to socio-psychological) *reason to reject a programme, that is, to eliminate its hard core and its programme for constructing protective belts?*" (p. 155). His answer is "that such an objective reason is provided by a rival research programme which explains the previous success of its rival and supercedes it by a further display of *heuristic power*" (p. 155). In short, the new research program must explain progressively in contrast to the degenerate explanations of the defeated research program. "But scientists, of course, do not always judge heuristic situations correctly" (p. 173) and "rationality works much slower than most people think, and, even then, fallibly" (p. 174). Here Lakatos slips from his strict rationality to a veiled recognition that science is conducted by humans who are themselves fallible at least with respect to rationality. The questions left open by Lakatos, and directly faced by Kuhn, are why the so-called rational scientist is unable to recognize the heuristic power of an alternative research program and why rationality takes such a long time. The answers, so succinctly presented by Kuhn, are that scientists cannot see the alternatives because of their paradigmatic (not theoretical) glasses and rationality takes a long time because it occurs an individual at a time and it is only seen to work from an historical perspective, when the sociological mass that has gained the rational insight is large enough to be recognized. Because Lakatos fails to understand these psychological and sociological phenomena about which Kuhn was so clear, he is able to offer a second prescription for scientists,

> *that we must not discard a budding, research programme simply because it has failed to overtake a powerful rival. We should not abandon it if, supposing its rival were not there, it would constitute a progressive problem shift. And we should certainly regard a newly interpreted fact as a new fact. . . . As long as a budding research programme can be rationally*

> *reconstructed as a progressive problem shift, it should be sheltered for a while from a powerful established rival.* (p. 157)

This prescription, as the prior one, could be implemented by robots programmed to rational rules alone but scientists turn out to be humans who are social–psychological beings, with all their nonrational as well as rational characteristics. Anyone with any knowledge of psychological research on rational behavior recognizes this.

Although Kuhn has been criticized, and rightly so, for his lack of precision in the use of the terms paradigm and incommensurability, there is no reason to throw the baby out with the bath and to reject the basic insights these terms have stimulated as well as the ideas related to factual relativity and social– psychological phenomena that influence the scientific enterprise. It was, after all, the intuitive appeal of these ideas as representing the knowledge by acquaintance that scientists who have been through a scientific revolution recognize. It was, at least in part, because Kuhn captured this knowledge that he gained such widespread attention. In contrast, the efforts of Lakatos force scientists into a rational mold, a mold unfamiliar to the practitioners of science. It is this difference that clearly separates his analysis of knowledge about how science works from that of Kuhn.

Let me try to clarify some aspects of Kuhn's position prior to discussing some specifics of the papers presented here. While Kuhn (1962) emphasized the incommensurability of pre- and postrevolutionary communication among scientists, he did not say they lack any point of contact as Lakatos and others have suggested. What he did say is that "proponents of competing paradigms must fail to make complete contact" (p. 148). They are "always at least slightly at cross purposes" (p. 148) and "Communication across the revolutionary divide is inevitably partial" (p. 149). The reason this problem exists, as Kuhn notes, is that "Since new paradigms are born from old ones, they ordinarily incorporate much of the vocabulary and apparatus, both conceptual and manipulative that the traditional paradigm had previously employed. But they seldom employ these borrowed elements in quite the traditional way" (p. 149). One need go no further than the concept of intelligence as defined in the surface structure terms of what an intelligence test measures to the use of intelligence within the deep-structure analysis of Piaget, to understand what Kuhn means here.

Consider now what Kuhn wrote about how a new paradigm achieves success. He notes first that "The single most prevalent claim advanced by proponents of a new paradigm is that they can solve the problems that have led the old one to crisis. . . . This is often the most effective one possible" (p. 153). Second, "Claims of this sort are particularly likely to succeed if the new paradigm displays a quantitative precision strikingly better than its older competitor" (pp. 153–154). Third, the new paradigm may permit "The prediction of phenomena that had been entirely unsuspected while the old one prevailed'' (p. 154). As Kuhn notes, and I quote again, ''To scientists those arguments are ordinarily the most significant and persuasive'' (p. 155). Thus, the rational arguments are significant and persuasive in Kuhn's words. But then he adds the human, or psychological, element by adding that these arguments ''are neither individually or collectively compelling'' (p. 155). Other considerations are required and here he lists, first, the requirement that the new paradigm needs also to ''appeal to the individual's sense of the appropriate or the aesthetic'' (p. 155). He notes here, however, that

> The early versions of most new paradigms are crude. By the time their full aesthetic appeal can be developed, most of the community has been persuaded by other means. Nevertheless, the importance of aesthetic considerations can sometimes be decisive. Though they often attract only a few scientists to a new theory, it is upon those few that its ultimate triumph may depend. If they had not quickly taken it up for highly individual reasons, the new candidate for paradigm might never have been sufficiently developed to attract the allegiance of the scientific community as a whole. (p. 156)

The second factor Kuhn notes is one of faith. The decision to adopt a new paradigm by an individual scientist is based not on past achievement but on future promise. ''He must, that is, have faith that the new paradigm will succeed with the many large problems that confront it, knowing only that the older paradigm has failed with a few. A decision of that kind can only be made on faith'' (p. 158). He then adds that ''This is not to suggest that new paradigms triumph ultimately through some mystical aesthetic'' (p. 158). In short, scientists, like any other group to be persuaded, turn to a new conceptualization of their science as individuals. Some find rational arguments convincing, others are convinced by data from what seem to be crucial experiments, others by mathematical precision, others by the promise of future solutions, and still others by the aesthetic characteristics of the new ideas. I suspect there are still more reasons but that would require a psychology of the scientist, a sociology of the scientific community, and an understanding of rhetoric; I must turn to other matters.

My reason for taking the time to compare Lakatos and Kuhn here was to try to show that Lakatos has accepted Kuhn's notions of paradigm but relabeled them as a research program. He has argued that more than one research program may exist in a scientific discipline at one time, as Kuhn explicated in his first presentation. He accepts Kuhn's notion of normal science but argues for theoretical and occasional empirical progression to sustain normal science within a research program, a position perhaps better articulated by Lakatos but hardly something with which Kuhn would argue. He disparages the need for the concept of crisis but substitutes program degeneration, which seems little different in meaning or operation and has the same effect of leading to the dominance of an alternative research program. Kuhn was explicit in stating that a crisis is not the only precipitator of a paradigm shift because the insight created by a single crucial experiment for a single scientist could lead to a new paradigm for that scientist. Both agree that the shift from one paradigm or program would take time. Both agree that changing paradigms leads to changes in world view, i.e., the relative nature of facts. Kuhn, however, is more explicit here and Lakatos would reject revolution as a descriptive term for the shift. And finally, both agree that the scientists working within a paradigm, and the theories they spawn, can and do ignore anomalous research findings, i.e., most data are not crucial to the practice of a particular scientific viewpoint. On the other hand, Lakatos strips Kuhn's contribution of the psychological and sociological variables affecting the scientist and the scientific community. He ignores the abstract structure, or tacit knowledge, underlying the behavior of the people interacting in the scientific enterprise. Instead, Lakatos offers prescriptions for the rational conduct of science as if it were conducted in a mechanistic, albeit sometimes inefficient, manner. From my perspective the mechanistic prescription of Lakatos, although presented with greater precision of word, does not ring true to the principles that seem to underlie the behavior of scientists so aptly captured in Kuhn's analysis.

With this background in mind, let me turn to the papers at hand. Turning first to Overton's paper, it seems to me that he is correct in emphasizing that science, or more appropriately its practitioners, is guided by very general abstract conceptual systems from which various particularistic theoretical views are derived and which, in turn, suggest empirical tests bearing on those theories. Furthermore, he is correct in recognizing the importance of those abstract conceptual systems and theoretical views in determining how the particulars in the empirical realm are given meaning, i.e., the idea of factual relativism—although he seems to waffle on the latter at times. He is also correct in dismissing positivistic philosophies of science, a point on which almost all philosophers of science are currently agreed. More important, he is correct that, although philosophers of science recognize the shortcomings of the positivist philosophy, that philosophy is still a strong, and often covertly adhered to, underlying position of many, if not most, psychologists. Among psychologists, the data are crucial; the theory and conceptual presuppositions underlying the theory, and thus the interpretations of the data, are often ignored and seldom specifically confronted. One need read no further than the restatements of the results that pass as discussion sections of our research reports to understand this fact. Overton's arguments with respect to the weaknesses of falsification procedures advanced by Popper (1963) are sound as well, although it should be noted that Popper himself advanced at least three versions of his position (cf. Weimer, 1979) in an effort to meet some of the weaknesses Overton notes.

But it is at this point in his presentation that I must begin to take issue. As Overton puts it, research findings that run counter to a currently held theory can be considered anomalous rather than as falsifications but, from a Kuhnian perspective, the accumulation of some anomalies eventually leads a scientist, or a subset of scientists, to abandon the paradigm in favor of an alternative paradigm. I have altered Overton's description in two important ways. First, I have noted that it is the paradigm that is abandoned and not a theory—changing theories within a paradigm is not revolutionary. Second, it is scientists, one or more, who abandon the paradigm as a function of their evaluation of the anomalous findings. The latter is important because it involves a rational component in the decision by the people involved regarding the evaluation of the relationship between what the old paradigm promised and what it has produced, both theoretically and empirically.

What Overton wishes to substitute, appealing to Lakatos and Laudan, is a system in which scientific progress is measured in terms of the empirical productivity of the research program (to be true to Lakatos, he should have added the more important element of theoretical progress) and anomalies are weighted in the context of that productivity. If this is not mere relabeling of Kuhnian concepts, then some rational metric for empirical and theoretical progress as well as anomaly weighting is required and none is even hinted at by either Lakatos or Overton. We are left with a human decision-making machine and, alas, it is not entirely rational and certainly not a machine unless we are presupposing a mechanistic paradigm for our philosophy of science. The basic problem, and Lakatos makes the point himself, is that "we cannot articulate and include *all* 'background knowledge' (or 'background ignorance'?) into our critical deductive model" (Lakatos, 1970, p. 131). Unfortunately, much of that knowledge is tacit, which makes the task much more difficult than suggested. In order to make rational decisions we must have all the relevant background knowledge in mind to make those decisions. If we had all that knowledge we would have a complete theory, which is, of course, what the search is all about. Thus, decisions about empirical results, theories, and paradigms cannot, by definition, be totally rational and we find the appeal of Kuhn's analysis (in terms of the sociopsychological factors that affect such decision making in the face of incomplete knowledge) most appealing. One must understand the belief system of the scientist as it interacts with the objectivity of his or her empirical claims to understand the process of science. Weimer (1979) has referred to this combination as the warrantability of knowledge claims. We need an adequate psychology of inference and a sociology of research communities in order to articulate an adequate theory of science and its history. Kuhn comes closest to understanding that and Weimer has made the issues involved explicit.

Overton, in this paper and in the others he has published with his collaborator Reese (e.g., Overton & Reese, 1973), has done a valuable service in analyzing the mechanistic and organismic paradigms and their associated sets of theories. I find it disturbing to find Overton, at least, casting aside his well-demonstrated psychological knowledge and talents when he enters the area of philosophy of science, which is, in my opinion, an effort after explanation of the cognitive processes of the scientist.

Valuable as Overton's contributions may be, there are serious questions that may be asked about the analyses of the hard core and positive heuristics, as he now wishes to call the characteristics of the two paradigms he discusses. Because Overton is presuming to make the implicit explicit, one may raise the question of how his insights came about. How do we know, for example, that the characteristics listed as composing the implicit structure of the mechanistic paradigm are more appropriate than, say, a list I created over 10 years ago (Palermo, 1971) when I first became interested in such analyses? The question is one of the validity of the analyses, regardless of the analyzer. In some sense, it seems to me that we need a theory of the abstract underlying cognitive structures of scientists as individuals and as groups before such lists can be viewed as more than intuitive reflections on the nature of scientists and paradigms. We need such a theory no less than a developmental theory of the human. Thus far, we have progressed no further than to argue over the outline of what such a theory might look like. If Overton's analysis of the abstract structure of mechanistic and organismic research programs is correct then, of course, the rest of his arguments in this and previous papers follow but otherwise we are no more clear on the issues than before. I would suggest that he is not all wrong, but I would be much more confident with an explicit framework within which to evaluate his contentions, especially with respect to the less clear cases.

I could stop here but there are one or two other points in Overton's paper on which I feel compelled to comment. The first has to do with incommensurability. As I noted earlier, Kuhn did not take the extreme position attributed to him but he did not waffle as Overton seems to do in his presentation. At one point Overton takes a Kuhnian position in stating that "The point of overwhelming importance here is that in different research programs the same surface-level term may have different meanings and hence different implications for methods and procedures employed to investigate empirical problems" (Overton, this volume, p. 214). He then criticizes Beilin's discussion of structure and function based upon the incommensurable meanings of these terms for scientists from different research programs. Later, Overton tries to invoke a neutral language, already admitted to be outside the pale for any scientist viewed from Lakatos' or Laudan's point of view. Whereas a version of the weaker incommensurability argument has already been given by Kuhn, Overton's version will not work. A concept, to use Overton's example, in one view is a concept in that view regardless of the language used because the language presupposes the world view. The term "human being" may be used with the same meaning by people holding both views because both can agree on the referent but, beyond that, they disagree incommensurably with respect to the nature of the functioning of that human being with respect to concepts, for example. It is only where the deep structure of the two world views overlap that communication can occur unambiguously.

A second point relates to the characterization of Wundt. I would suggest that Blumenthal's presentation of Wundt (Blumenthal, 1970) bears little relation to that of Overton. If Blumenthal is correct, that Wundt's paradigmatic view is much closer to that of Chomsky than Overton portrays, we are in need of a better metric for validating the hard core character of research programs.

Finally, I am disturbed by Overton's characterization of scientific research programs as having the function of solving empirical problems. That seems to me analogous to arguing that psychology is the study of behavior. In some sense we are less interested in the empirical problems than the underlying rules or principles which relate to the empirical but do not necessarily solve the empirical. Perhaps an example can make the point more clearly. We are more interested in the abstract law of gravity than we are in solving the empirical problem of the path of a leaf falling from a tree.

Turning now to Beilin's presentation, I must agree with Overton that Beilin never tells us what he means by function or functionalism. It appears that the listener is already supposed to have a full grasp of the meaning and yet Beilin seems to use the term in rather diverse ways in his paper without making clear where he stands. This confusion is exacerbated by Beilin's lumping together theorists who have diverse paradigmatic or hard core presuppositions.

The matter becomes clearer, however, if we read Beilin's earlier papers (e.g., Beilin, 1983), in which he traces the history of functionalism from James and Dewey through Watson and Woodworth, and he might have added Thorndike, to those he characterizes as functionalists today.The latter include those who have taken some form of computer modeling as their methodological approach, those who are loath to free themselves from a learning theory model, those who work within the Piagetian framework, those who work within a general Chomskyan framework, and others not always easy to classify. If it is the case, as Beilin maintains, that all of these people are functionalists, then it becomes clear that functionalism, at least by Beilin's definition, is not a cohesive scientific approach in the sense of Popper, Kuhn, Lakatos, or anyone else who has attempted to analyze the scientific endeavor. Functionalism crosses the lines of paradigms or research programs. Functionalists, as a group, do not have a common set of commitments. As Beilin describes them, they are tolerant but critical with respect to vocabulary and method and relativistic with respect to the origin of psychological activities; they prefer continuity in function, experimentation in method, and associationistic and environmental accounts of psychological phenomena. Although these are their biases, these are not their commitments, as Beilin points out.

These characteristics, however, describe the group of scientists with functional interests. The individuals in the group, however, do have commitments.

Some of them are committed to some variant of the mechanistic research program or paradigm whereas others are committed to some variant of the organismic research program or paradigm. What separates them is that some make an underlying assumption that one can deal in an explanatory manner with psychological phenomena by considering only surface structure analyses whereas the others assume that one needs to postulate an abstract or deep-level system that allows explanation of surface structure exemplars of psychological phenomena. In short, one group assumes that structure is needed to account for function whereas the other rejects this requirement.

Once this becomes clear, we can see that the questions regarding function that Beilin puzzles over can be clarified. Some researchers are asking how the structure functions. They are the structuralists who have gone beyond the question of what the structure is and how it develops to questions of how, given a particular structure, that structure leads to particular psychological phenomena—behaviors, if you wish. The nonstructuralists, or mechanists in Overton's terms, are short-circuiting the procedure on the assumption that one can account for behavior without bothering with the need to postulate an underlying structure. In responding to Overton's blurring of the distinction between structure and process or function, Beilin has created another confusion, which does not seem to me to help clarify what is happening in the scientific endeavor. I think he was led to this by his own presupposition that structuralism is a prerequisite to a successful functionalism but that leaves him in a position of not knowing what to do with those he classifies as functionalists but who do not share his presupposition. I share his presuppositional position and I think his earlier analysis makes clear who falls in each functionalist camp, so I will not try to elaborate on his analysis here. I cannot refrain, however, from pointing out that the ease with which one can separate the two groups is made more difficult by the adoption of structuralist terminology by the mechanist camp. The information processors, for example, who take the computer as their simulation model are clearly mechanists. Their model is a machine! Such a model cannot succeed in principle, as Kleindorfer and Martin (1983) have pointed out. The Kleindorfer and Martin argument focuses upon values and principles, as opposed to rules, which are so important to human functioning but which cannot be incorporated into the computer model. Beilin, however, sorts the groups and individuals out rather nicely and I recommend that you read his earlier papers for clarification.

Gholson and Barker, like both Overton and Beilin, seem to accept Kuhn at times and to reject him at other times and it is not always clear what they are accepting and what they are rejecting, or why. They point out, for example, that the rationalist philosophers found Kuhn's account irrational and, in focusing upon that, failed to note the consensus formation account Kuhn proposed. But Gholson and Barker do nothing with this observation. Second, they correctly note Kuhn's emphasis on the relativity of fact (or scientific truth, as they call it), leaving the impression that they do not hold that position but they do nothing with that either.

Gholson and Barker argued that "Kuhn denied that the replacement of one paradigm by another constituted progress" (this volume). Kuhn, however, devoted a whole chapter to this issue. A single quote makes his position clear, "though new paradigms seldom or never possess all the capabilities of their predecessors, they usually preserve a great deal of the most concrete parts of past achievement and they always permit additional concrete problem-solutions besides" (p. 169).

Gholson and Barker's account of the demise of the gestalt paradigm in this country, due to the genius of Spence, is well taken. They should take care, however, to not include Tolman in their discussion of this issue without a thorough examination of his position. It seems to me that although Tolman was a controversial figure in the learning theory era he accepted the behavioristic paradigm and worked within it. Although he was clearly unhappy with portions of the assumptions he tacitly assumed, he did not bolt the paradigm. If he had done so, he would likely have received little attention and would have had as little influence on the development of learning theory as Kurt Lewin, for example, had on developmental psychology. Lewin, of course, did not accept the behavioristic paradigm. Incidentally, if one is tempted to take seriously the rational position with respect to the manner in which science is conducted, they should read some of Spence's papers, in which he made footnote references to Lewin, who occupied an office four floors above Spence's at the University of Iowa. Finally, I would add that Harlow also remained within the fold.

I would also note that Piaget generated a great deal of research and theory in Geneva and was almost totally ignored by those in this country who had accepted a different paradigm. In fact, some efforts to test Piaget's theory by developmental psychologists in this country were total disasters in the sense that Piaget cannot be understood from a behaviorist viewpoint. The research of the 1930s and 1940s clearly demonstrates this.

Finally, I would suggest that a great deal more documentation would be required before I would be convinced that the mathematical learning theorists had abandoned the behavioristic paradigm despite their one-trial learning theories, the use of the term "hypothesis," and the questions about the need for reinforcement. [Spence, in his Silliman lectures (1956), noted the various uses of the latter term within this paradigm.] The problem with Gholson and Barker's analyses of psychology, I emphasize again, and which was made clear by Overton and Reese, is that mechanistic theories assume surface structure analyses even with mediation, flow diagrams, stimulus sampling, and hypotheses, whereas cognitive psychologists assume a deep-structure analysis. The two positions are incommensurable. Certainly there was evolution in the era of the great learning theories but the cognitive revolution that came with the acceptance of

Piaget and Chomsky is a revolution, not evolution. The cognitive paradigm rejects the ideas of surface-structure analyses; it rejects the notion that you can understand complex behavior by studying simple behavior; it rejects the idea that you can understand human behavior by studying lower animals; and it accepts nativistic constraints on concepts. Behaviorism took a different position on all of these issues and that was a part of the more obvious hard core or paradigmatic world view of these scientists. None of the theorists identified by Gholson and Barker ever challenged these basic assumptions—at least, they have presented no evidence to support such a contention. They modified the theories as Gholson and Barker demonstrate quite clearly but, in so doing, they stuck to their paradigmatic guns. Push any one of them and you will find, not a deep-structure analysis of hypotheses, but a characterization of hypotheses as related to the stimulus events and defined in terms of stimuli and responses as definitely, although not as precisely, as Hull's ${}_{s}\dot{\bar{E}}_{r}$ (Hull, 1943).

We are talking about tacit acceptance of presuppositions about how the world is. They are seldom articulated or taught, they are acquired, as a part of the culture, by example. They are a part of the social matrix, which consists of the scientists in practice invoking the values, beliefs, and attitudes that influence their decisions about what is good science.

One of the problems in this entire endeavor is that it is not possible to discern the flow of a science at the time it is occurring because it is not possible to know what contributions being made today will, in the long run, be considered theoretically or empirically important to scientists in the field tomorrow. Consideration of the contributions to our theoretical journals makes the point. The papers are exciting enough at the time of submission to receive a recommendation for publication. Many of them, however, receive little attention thereafter. There are few papers that have long-lasting effects. On the other hand, if we wait until the scientists have made up their minds, we are reconstructing history in terms of what we assume must have happened in the minds of the scientists. In addition, we are reconstructing how those mental events in the minds of individuals interacted with the mental events occurring in the minds of other individual scientists to create a movement in the larger enterprise encompassing all of the scientists. We are, as they say, between a rock and a hard place in building a philosophy of science. More important, we come to see the point Weimer was trying to make when he argued that it is a psychology of inference and social interaction that is most likely to succeed in the endeavor. Although Kuhn may have been wrong in detail, he did see this point clearly and he tried to account for it.

Gholson and Barker show us that whereas Lakatos took us two steps away from Kuhn's insights, Laudan takes yet another step away, or is at a step back toward Kuhn. In any case, we are introduced to research traditions instead of research programs. The traditions allow for Kuhn's commitments and for Kuhn's competing theories within those commitments. The commitments, however, may also be modified by empirical testing although there is a relatively immune tacit subset, as Kuhn would agree. Traditions also allow for conceptual factors, mainly problematic ones, as Gholson and Barker suggest. It is not at all clear to me, however, why theoretical constructs such as equilibration, construction, assimilation, and organization are a liability if they cannot be directly tested unless we are regressing to surface structure analyses again.

Let me conclude by pointing out that everyone agrees that Kuhn was misinterpreted. Gholson and Barker make this point most clearly in their conclusion, in which they note both the contributions of Kuhn and the distortions of Kuhn's position. The distortions allowed the followers of Kuhn to offer their own perspectives on philosophy of science. At least some of the distortions destroy the most valuable contributions of Kuhn's analyses whereas others may be seen as clarifications, if we are to be kind, or as little more than relabeling of Kuhn's ideas if we are less generous. If we wish documentation of how commitment, irrationality if you wish, plays a part in intellectual endeavors, philosophical and scientific, I think we have a clear case provided in these papers as they describe how Kuhn's position has been torn asunder with the open admission that Kuhn never meant what was being criticized.

Every quotation I cited from Kuhn to counter example after example of misinterpretations of Kuhn came from his original book. The ideas were there from the very beginning. I am inclined to suggest that we go back and reread Kuhn and find out what he really did say and work from there. By this I do not mean that I am arguing for the status quo vis à vis Kuhn's original work. Instead, I think we need to recognize that Kuhn was correct that scientists are humans, humans who work and influence each other, by every means at their disposal, in social groups. We need to develop a psychology of the mental activities of scientists as pertains to their theoretical and research activities as individuals and as pertains to their social influences on each other in groups. How does a scientist, unable to know all there is to know about his discipline, make a decision that one view is correct and others are incorrect? How does the individual, having made up her mind that one view is incorrect, go about convincing others? Given alternative views, how does the group come to accept the view of one individual as opposed to another? How do groups coalesce with respect to a point of view? The solutions to these questions require a psychology of individuals and a social psychology based upon a reading of retrospective reports. Scientists do not work in vacuums. They are people working with people. They admire, hate, ridicule, respect, and ignore each other in both rational and irrational ways. They also have a vast and tacit knowledge system that guides their scientific efforts. Kuhn captured these ideas and scientists recognized them when reading his account. Philosophers, however, seem to find it difficult to accept them, which may be why, as Weimer pointed out, psychology and not philosophy may, in the long run, be better able to provide the answers to the fascinating issues raised in these papers.

REFERENCES

Beilin, H. The new functionalism and the Piagetian program. In E. K. Scholnick (Ed.), *New trends in conceptual representation.* Hillsdale, New Jersey: Erlbaum, 1983, in press.

Blumenthal, A. L. *Language and psychology.* New York: Wiley, 1970.

Hanson, N. R. *Patterns of discovery.* London and New York: Cambridge Univ. Press, 1958.

Hull, C. L. *Principles of learning.* New York: Appleton, 1943.

Kleindorfer, G.B., & Martin, J. E. The iron cage, single vision, and Newton's sleep. *Journal of Philosophy and Technology,* 1983, in press.

Kuhn, T. S. *The structure of scientific revolutions.* Chicago, Illinois: Univ. of Chicago Press, 1962.

Lakatos, I. Falsification and the methodology of scientific research programs. In I. Lakatos & A. Musgrave (Eds.), *Criticism and the growth of knowledge.* London and New York: Cambridge Univ. Press, 1970. Pp. 91–196.

Laudan, L. *Progress and its problems.* Berkeley, California: Univ. of California Press, 1977.

Overton, W., & Reese, H. W. Models of development: Methodological implications. In J. R. Nesselroade & H. W. Reese (Eds.), *Life-span developmental psychology: Methodological issues.* New York: Academic Press, 1973.

Palermo, D. S. Is a scientific revolution taking place in psychology? *Science Studies,* 1971, **1,** 135–155.

Popper, K. R. *Conjectures and refutations.* New York: Harper, 1963.

Spence, K. W. *Behavior theory and conditioning.* New Haven, Connecticut: Yale Univ. Press, 1956. Pp. 124–126.

Weimer, W. B. The history of psychology and its retrieval from historiography. I. The problematic nature of history. *Science Studies,* 1974, **4,** 235–258. (a)

Weimer, W. B. The history of psychology and its retrieval from historiography. II. The problematic nature of history. *Science Studies,* 1974, **4,** 367–396. (b)

Weimer, W. B. *Notes on the methodology of scientific research.* Hillsdale, New Jersey: Erlbaum, 1979.

COMMENTS ON BEILIN'S EPISTEMOLOGY AND PALERMO'S DEFENSE OF KUHN

Willis F. Overton
DEPARTMENT OF PSYCHOLOGY
TEMPLE UNIVERSITY
PHILADELPHIA, PENNSYLVANIA

In this paper I will briefly reply to some of the major points made by Beilin and Palermo as they relate to my original paper (see pp. 191–226). First, I wish to reassert and amplify my original comment that Beilin's analysis proceeds from a conventionalist framework. Taken as a whole, Beilin's paper is an excellent exemplification of the manner in which an empiricist epistemology, combined with a conventionalist–demarcationist strategy, interprets the role of underlying presuppositions (i.e., world views) in science. As stated in my original paper, the empiricist–conventionalist strategy must trivialize the impact of such presuppositions and this is exactly what Beilin does. Beilin's main attack on the influence of world views comes in the dogmatic assertion that the influence of the world view position "at least among philosophers of science, has considerably diminished, if not extinguished" (Beilin, p. 249, this volume). Which philosophers of science does Beilin refer to here? The one reference he made is to Suppe, who is, in fact, committed to an empiricist epistemology. In my opinion, Beilin's statement would be more accurate if it stated that among those philosophers of science who are committed to an empiricist epistemology the world view position has never had nor will ever have an influence. For an empiricist–conventionalist to accept the view that world views enter into the essential body of science would be to deny the central tenet of empiricism, that ultimately all knowledge depends on observation and only on observation.

Beilin also presents a more subtle attack on the influence of world views by

ADVANCES IN CHILD DEVELOPMENT
AND BEHAVIOR, VOL. 18

ISBN 0-12-009718-4

understating the role of the hard core in Lakatos' system and emphasizing the empirical predictive features of the system. Again, this is perfectly consistent with an empiricist–conventionalist interpretation. The hard core in Lakatos' system is the primary sphere through which metaphysical (world view) components enter into the essential body of science. But for Beilin, as for other empiricist–conventionalists, this is not acceptable and consequently the hard core is ignored or treated as a psychological or sociological curiosity that plays no essential role in science. Beilin carries this type of argument by omission even further by failing to consider that Laudan, in an even more detailed fashion than Lakatos, argues that metaphysical propositions enter into the essential body of science.

The fact that Beilin frequently interjects the term "rational" should not mislead the reader into the belief that he is sympathetic to a rationalist epistemology. As I pointed out in my original paper, there are both empiricist and rationalist models of rationality. Empiricist epistemological models claim that rationality is a product of observations of nature. Rationalist epistemological models claim that rationality is a product of mental activity and observation. As Lakatos states, "There is an important demarcation between '*passivist*' and '*activist*' theories of knowledge. 'Passivists' hold that true knowledge is Nature's imprint on a perfectly inert mind. . . . The most influential passivist school is classical empiricism. 'Activists' hold that we cannot read the book of Nature without mental activity, without interpreting it in the light of our expectations or theories" (Lakatos, 1978, p. 20). Investigators such as Kuhn, Lakatos, and Laudan all subscribe to a rationalist–activist model of rationality. Investigators such as Suppe, Shapere, and Beilin all subscribe to an empiricist–passivist model of rationality.

For Beilin, as for other empiricist–conventionalists, ultimately all legitimate scientific knowledge, reason, and rationality derive directly from fixed observational data free from the mental activity that constitutes interpretation. Beilin's "new functionalism" within this context is simply a heuristic device designed to order hard data. It is a new pigeonhole system that influences data in no important fashion. This understanding is radically different from Rychlak's (1977) more rationalist–activist analysis of functionalism and later mediational theorist analysis, in which he demonstrates that these positions continued to be influenced by mechanistic hard core commitments to a Lockean–Humean set of philosophical assumptions.

It is also not surprising that Beilin attacks the incommensurability issue. As stated in my original paper, this issue arose from the rationalist rejection of the idea of a neutral data base. For Beilin, as for other epistemological empiricists, the absence of a neutral fixed data base is intolerable and any such suggestion demands attack. Unfortunately, or fortunately—depending on one's perspective—the fact that pigeonhole systems can be modified has virtually no relevance to the problem of different general research programs or traditions (as distinguished from conventionalist theories) entailing different standards of evaluation.

Turning to Palermo's comments, I would first note that I do not count myself among Kuhn's detractors. As I think a careful reading of my paper will show, I believe that Lakatos and Laudan have extended Kuhn's work in ways that are quite compatible with it. Kuhn did focus on the individual difference factors that affect decision processes but such a focus does not preclude, as Kuhn himself stated, the search for rational rules of evaluation. Furthermore, although Lakatos makes no mention of a rational metric progress or anomaly weighting, Laudan does but to have specified these in my paper would have expanded it beyond any reasonable length.

Palmero asks about the validity of my analysis of the hard core and positive heuristics of the two research programs. This is a difficult question to answer. I think that the best answer I can give is that this analysis, in essence, is presented as a theory and it should be treated as any other theory, with respect to issues of validity. I make no pretense that the analysis is complete but I think that it presents a coherent and relatively adequate representation of ways in which different groups of scientists operate.

I would also argue that I do not waffle on the issue of incommensurability. I did not try "to invoke a neutral language" (Palermo, p. 226, this volume). Rather, I suggested that with respect to the communication issue it is possible to "withdraw, not to a pure observational language but to an observational language whose theoretical assumptions are not immediately at issue" (p. 222, this volume).

With respect to Palermo's concern that research programs address conceptual as well as empirical issues, I agree. In fact, Laudan extensively analyzes this point and if space had allowed I would have considered features of that discussion. However, I find it surprising that Palermo states that "we are less interested in the empirical problems than the underlying rules or principles which relate to the empirical but do not necessarily solve the empirical" (Palermo, p. 267, this volume). Palermo seems to come to this conclusion by confusing problem solution with prediction. In fact, the law of gravity solves a number of empirical problems, including the problem of ocean tides. It is difficult to imagine an abstract scientific principle or law that is not directed toward empirical problem solution.

As a final point, Palermo raises the question of whether my characterization of Wundt is accurate. It should be noted that in describing Wundt's commitment to an elementaristic analysis I was careful to qualify this by limiting it to the sphere of experimental psychology. In other domains, as I have pointed out in another paper (Overton, 1982), Wundt stands much closer to an organismic research program than to a mechanistic program.

REFERENCES

Lakatos, I. *The methodology of scientific research programmes: Philosophical papers* (Vol. 1). London and New York: Cambridge Univ. Press, 1978.

Overton, W. F. *Historical and contemporary perspectives of development*. Unpublished manuscript, 1982.

Rychlak, J. *The psychology of rigorous humanism*. New York: Wiley, 1977.

FROM KUHN TO LAKATOS TO LAUDAN

Peter Barker
DEPARTMENT OF PHILOSOPHY
MEMPHIS STATE UNIVERSITY
MEMPHIS, TENNESSEE

Barry Gholson
DEPARTMENT OF PSYCHOLOGY
MEMPHIS STATE UNIVERSITY
MEMPHIS, TENNESSEE

In our contribution to this volume (see pp. 227–244) we presented an analysis from the viewpoint of Imre Lakatos' methodology of scientific research programs (Lakatos, 1970, 1978). This was a conscious choice, intended to make the analysis more accessible to an audience already familiar with Kuhn and to show its applicability in both physics and psychology. Like Overton, however, we regard the work of Laudan (1977) as an advance over both Kuhn and Lakatos. Furthermore, we regard the work of Kuhn, Lakatos, and Laudan as a single coherent line of development. In what follows we will try to provide a brief overview of these developments. This will also clarify some of our earlier claims (see Barker & Gholson, this volume) and, perhaps, settle some of the perplexities for readers who, like Palermo, find it difficult to see why we accept some of Kuhn's ideas but not others.

ADVANCES IN CHILD DEVELOPMENT
AND BEHAVIOR, VOL. 18

ISBN 0-12-009718-4

I. Kuhn

Kuhn (1962) decisively redirected the philosophy of science away from the logical empiricist or *positivist* account that was then orthodox. The positivists limited their account of science to the categories of *theory* and *evidence* and the relationships between them. The two most important of these relationships were said to be "explanation" and "confirmation" (Brown, 1979). Kuhn's main contribution was to describe the important role supertheoretical entities, such as "world hypotheses," play in science. Kuhn (1962, 1970) called these types of entities *paradigms*. Lakatos (1970, 1978) renamed them *research programs* and Laudan (1977) dubbed them *research traditions*. Although each author attributed slightly different properties to them, in the interest of economy we will refer to all three as examples of a single sort of entity, here referred to generically as a "supertheory."[1]

A related attraction of Kuhn's early work concerned his stress upon the importance of metaphysics to science. According to positivist philosophy, metaphysics has no role in legitimate science and cannot even be discussed, because such discussion is said to be meaningless. Reese and Overton (1970), Palermo (1971), and Weimer (1974) quite rightly saw Kuhn's work as reintroducing to philosophers and scientists the pervasive influence of metaphysical assumptions, such as Pepper's (1942) "organismic" and "mechanistic" world hypotheses.

Kuhn's (1962) analysis was by no means a finished product. Although the key term *paradigm* passed into general usage, Kuhn admitted to an equivocation between two senses of the word (cf. Masterman, 1970), later distinguished as "disciplinary matrices" and "exemplars" (Kuhn, 1970). The general picture of science that emerged—long periods of paradigm-dominated normal science terminating in crisis and revolution—was problematic. Crises could not be identified, for example, in some of the most important revolutions, especially the Copernican revolution in astronomy (Gingerich, 1975). Perhaps the most important difficulty that emerged was the problem of incommensurability, with its implications for scientific progress. This was discussed at length in our earlier paper, in this volume. As we also made clear in the earlier paper, there was considerable confusion about whether more than one paradigm could exist in any given period of normal science (see Lakatos & Musgrave, 1970, for examples). Despite several admirable attempts, Kuhn (e.g., Kuhn, 1977) was unable to correct distortions of his work, many of which were adopted by both scientists

[1]In his later work, Kuhn (1970) replaced the idea of a supertheoretical entity with a more complex account. Although supertheories remain in the guise of "disciplinary matrices," they are subordinated to a detailed picture of science in terms of metaphysical models, symbolic generalizations, and exemplars.

and philosophers.[2] Reliable secondary sources have only recently become available (e.g., Brown, 1979; Gutting, 1980). Kuhn had, in any case, presented his early work as no more than a starting point (1970, p. ix), and we believe the accounts offered by Lakatos and Laudan are its direct descendants.

II. Lakatos

Kuhn never adequately specified the connection between paradigm and theory (Barker, 1982; Laudan, 1977).[3] Lakatos' first innovation was to specify this relationship with great clarity, and in so doing he also explicated further the role of metaphysics in science. Metaphysical assumptions appear as core principles that pass unchanged through all the theories of a research program, that is, through those theories that succeed one another as the program evolves. The sequence of theories itself constitutes the research program. The program, however, also has properties in addition to those contained in its specific theories: it has an associated ''heuristic,'' or plan of development, and it has a ''state of health,'' which may be progressive, stagnating, or degenerating—depending on the exact manner in which the last few theories in the program replaced one another. The concepts of progress and degeneration helped Lakatos solve the problem of incommensurability introduced by Kuhn by offering objective grounds for preferring one research program over a rival. Lakatos also recognized that research programs may change from progressive to degenerative and vice versa as they develop. A program's rate of progress can, and often does, change in relation to rivals. We consider one of Lakatos' most important contributions to be the identification, for the first time, of recurrent patterns of growth, decay, and revival in science.[4]

Laudan (1977) built on the work of Kuhn and Lakatos. His ''research tradition'' is most simply understood as a research program in which core commitments evolve with theory replacement. Like Overton, we regard Laudan's account superior to that of Lakatos. We intend to extend this analysis, using Laudan's categories, in a future paper, but we confine discussion here to his ideas that represent innovations in the tradition connecting him with Kuhn and Lakatos.

[2]Palermo's excellent discussion of incommensurability in the present volume (see pp. 259–272) shows that at least some scientists got the story straight.

[3]Palermo is, therefore, quite incorrect in saying that this distinction in Kuhn is ''more clearly articulated than Lakatos' distinction between hard core and protective belt'' (p. 261). For a clear explanation of the latter see our earlier paper in this volume.

[4]The diversity of patterns of scientific development specified in Lakatos' account should be contrasted with the linear progression of paradigms suggested by Kuhn, for whom scientific revolutions are irreversible (Barker, 1980).

III. Laudan

Laudan attempted to direct philosophy of science away from explaining facts and toward "solving problems." As already noted, the philosophy of science begun by Kuhn rejected the positivists' attempts to accommodate all of science in the categories of theory and observation (or experiment). On the positivist view, "explanation" was the primary relationship linking the two descriptive categories: theories explained observations. But Laudan also questioned the primacy of explanation. He argued that the dynamics of science are best understood as a search for new problem solutions. For this reason Overton spoke of research programs solving problems.

Having shifted our attention from explaining facts to solving problems, Laudan went on to note an unrecognized continuity between Kuhn and Lakatos. Both of the latter assumed that the appraisal of theories and supertheories (paradigms, research programs) depends almost exclusively on observational or experimental factors. For Kuhn, the source of crisis and revolution is an anomaly—an experimental failure or discrepancy between prediction and observation. For Lakatos, anomalies are the primary motivation for replacing theories in a research program. For Kuhn, the most important arguments in favor of a new paradigm involve solutions to anomalies that led its predecessor to crisis (1970, p. 153).[5] For Lakatos, the key to the victory of one research program over another is progress, in terms of the ability of the program's latest theories to yield successful new predictions.[6]

Laudan also pointed out that Kuhn and Lakatos neglected a second important element in the appraisal of scientific systems. Independent of experimental success or failure (in Laudan's vocabulary, their ability to solve empirical problems), theories and supertheories may be criticized on conceptual grounds. Notorious examples include Newton's circular definition of *mass* in *Principia Mathematica,* and the Cartesian attack on the concept of gravitational attraction as a relapse into Aristotelian "occult quality" explanations. Laudan identified two types of conceptual problems: concepts that are vague, circular, or ambiguous result in *internal* conceptual problems; new concepts that conflict with established notions in other scientific (or nonscientific) systems are *external* conceptual problems.

Thus, Laudan's appraisal is based on two sets of factors. A supertheory is preferred in comparison to rivals when its latest theory solves a maximum

[5]Other arguments are described by Palermo (this volume).

[6]In defense of Overton against Palermo, it should be noted that, for Lakatos, theoretical progress (new predictions) is *not* more important than empirical progress (verification of predictions). Theoretical progress may proceed for a long time with only occasional empirical confirmations, but these confirmations are essential. Lakatos provided no license for *unsupported* theorizing.

number of empirical problems and, at the same time, has a minimum number of conceptual liabilities.[7] This expands and adds some precision to Lakatos' judgments of progress, stagnation, and degeneration. Laudan, of course, retained Lakatos' concept of the heuristic and the notion that the judgment of a program's progress may change.

For Laudan, not all conceptual or empirical problems have equal weight. In addition, the cognitive importance of a given problem may change with historical circumstances. The judgment in favor of a given supertheory is therefore doubly relative: relative to the particular range of alternatives available and relative to the particular moment in history when the appraisal is made. Like Lakatos' appraisals, Laudan's are therefore revisable with changing historical circumstance. The explicit recognition given to extrascientific influences provides a natural way to accommodate social and psychological factors in supertheory appraisal. These are absent in Lakatos' account but, as pointed out by Palermo, are emphasized by Kuhn.

It is a curious fact that the specific categories Kuhn (1962) proposed have inspired little historical work. Even Kuhn's own later work makes no explicit use of them. Two clearly discernable lines of development, however, have followed from Kuhn's original ideas. One line, represented, for example, by Weimer and Palermo (1973), emphasizes the sociological aspect of Kuhn's account. The second line of development, which emphasizes the study of history in attempts to develop an adequate structural model of science, includes Lakatos and Laudan. Lakatos' (1968, 1970) work has stimulated a great deal of historical research that refined and extended his model. These studies range from the Copernican revolution (Lakatos & Zahar, 1978), early mechanical physics (Aant, 1972), nineteenth century physics (Howson, 1976), and the Einsteinian revolution (Zahar, 1976) to recent controversies in IQ theory (Urbach, 1974) and economics (Latsis, 1976). Despite our preference for Laudan, the work of Lakatos and his followers is warmly recommended. Laudan's own views of history (1981b; Frankel, 1980, 1981) are readily available, as are his criticisms of the sociological approach to science favored by Weimer and Palermo (Laudan, 1981a, 1982).

IV. History and Sociology

The historical and sociological orientations that developed from Kuhn's work are, of course, not completely incompatible. Consider, for example, how the weighting factors in Laudan's model accommodate facets emphasized by the

[7]This is a simplification. External conceptual factors may also count as assets. In addition, Laudan separated grounds for accepting a supertheory and grounds for deciding to pursue it (Laudan, 1977).

sociological approach. One of our criticisms of Lakatos' model is that it makes no allowance for multiple *competing* sequences of theories, all influenced by a single metaphysical orientation. Perhaps the best way to look at the dispute between those methodologists favored by Palermo and those we favor is to suggest they form competing theory sequences within a single metaphysical position, not in science but in the philosophy of science. All of these sequences begin with Kuhn. Palermo would branch from Kuhn to a (still to be formulated) psychology of inference and sociology of research communities. We also follow a branch from Kuhn, but it leads through the work of Lakatos and Laudan.

As Palermo puts it, a major part of our task is to make the implicit explicit. The role played by supertheories—and their attendant metaphysical assumptions—has long been implicit in psychology. Following Kuhn, it became possible and even respectable to try to make their role explicit (Palermo, 1971; Reese & Overton, 1970; Weimer & Palermo, 1973). Our understanding of the history and present state of given scientific disciplines rests, in part, upon the precision of this kind of analysis. Lakatos and Laudan have, in our opinion, presented important new developments that add to this precision.

We do not believe, however, that viewing science and its history through the broad world view (Pepper, 1942) lenses of mechanism and organicism (cf. Overton's and Palermo's papers, this volume) is likely to increase our understanding. World hypotheses simply lack the precision of research programs or paradigms. Pepper's categories, as is made clear by Palermo, only allow one to pigeonhole given theorists—and theories—and seem to imply that, at least in terms of broad metaphysical principles, neither the theorist nor the theory can change. Empirical work, however, suggests that theorists do not fit such neat categories (e.g., Coan, 1979). The fact that Tolman, for example, challenged Spence and others on their own turf does not necessarily mean he shared their behavioristic commitments. Similarly, as Laudan (1977) and Frankel (1981) show, both the hard core and the heuristic of a supertheory may change with successor theories.

As Lakatos pointed out, rationality works much slower than most people think. Thus, we cannot flatly claim the superiority of our approach over Palermo's or Overton's (our views are in agreement with Beilin's although his focus in this exchange is different). The choice between alternatives must be left to posterity. This is not, as Palermo suggests, because of human frailty, but rather because the most convincing arguments for one position over another involve *long-term* performance. History may be kinder in the end to sociologists than to the historians. We can all agree, however, that by resolutely turning our backs to positivism, we should set our feet on the path that begins with Kuhn, even if some cannot yet be persuaded to the second step with Lakatos, or to the third step with Laudan.

REFERENCES

Aant, E. *On a research program in early modern physics.* New York: Humanities, 1972.

Barker, P. Can scientific history repeat? *Philosophy of Science Association,* 1980, **1,** 20–28.

Barker, P. Uncle Ludwig's book about science. *Proceedings of the Southwestern Philosophical Society,* Suppl. to *Philosophical Topics,* October, 1982, 71–78.

Brown, H. I. *Perception, theory and commitment.* Chicago, Illinois: Univ. of Chicago Press, 1979.

Coan, R. W. *Psychologists: Personal and theoretical pathways.* New York: Irvington, 1979.

Frankel, H. Problem-solving, research traditions and the development of scientific fields. In P. D. Asquith & R. N. Giere (Eds.), *PSA 1980* (Vol 1). East Lansing, Michigan: Philosophy of Science Association, 1980. Pp. 29–40.

Frankel, H. The paleobiogeographical debate over the problem of disjunctively distributed life forms. *Studies in history and philosophy of science,* 1981, **12,** 211–259.

Gingerich, O. "Crisis" versus aesthetic in the Copernican revolution. In A. Beer (Ed.), *Vistas in astronomy* (Vol. 17). Oxford: Pergamon, 1975. Pp. 85–94.

Gutting, G. (Ed.). *Paradigms and revolutions.* Notre Dame, Indiana: Univ. of Notre Dame Press, 1980.

Howson, C. (Ed.). *Method and appraisal in the physical sciences.* London and New York: Cambridge Univ. Press, 1976.

Kuhn, T. S. *The structure of scientific revolutions.* Chicago, Illinois: Univ. of Chicago Press, 1962.

Kuhn, T. S. *The structure of scientific revolutions* (2nd ed., enlarged). Chicago, Illinois: Univ. of Chicago Press, 1970.

Kuhn, T. S. *The essential tension.* Chicago, Illinois: Univ. of Chicago Press, 1977.

Lakatos, I. Criticism and the methodology of scientific research programmes. *Proceedings of the Aristotelian Society,* 1968, **69,** 149–186.

Lakatos, I. Falsification and the methodology of scientific research programs. In I. Lakatos & A. Musgrave (Eds.), *Criticism and the growth of knowledge.* London and New York: Cambridge Univ. Press, 1970.

Lakatos, I. *The methodology of scientific research programmes.* London and New York: Cambridge Univ. Press, 1978.

Lakatos, I., & Musgrave, A. (Eds.). *Criticism and the growth of knowledge.* London and New York: Cambridge Univ. Press, 1970.

Lakatos, I., & Zahar, E. Why did Copernicus' research program supersede Ptolemy's? In I. Lakatos, *The methodology of scientific research programmes.* London and New York: Cambridge Univ. Press, 1978.

Latsis, S. J. (Ed.). *Method and appraisal in economics.* London and New York: Cambridge Univ. Press, 1976.

Laudan, L. *Progress and its problems.* Berkeley, California: Univ. of California Press, 1977.

Laudan, L. The pseudo-science of science. *Philosophy of the Social Sciences,* 1981, **11,** 173–198. (a)

Laudan, L. *Science and hypothesis.* Boston, Massachusetts: Reidel, 1981. (b)

Laudan, L. More on Bloor. *Philosophy of the Social Sciences,* 1982, **12,** 71–74.

Masterman, M. The nature of a paradigm. In I. Lakatos & A. Musgrave (Eds.), *Criticism and the growth of knowledge.* London and New York: Cambridge Univ. Press, 1970.

Palermo, D. S. Is a scientific revolution taking place in psychology? *Science Studies,* 1971, **1,** 135–155.

Pepper, S. *World hypotheses.* Berkeley, California: Univ. of California Press, 1942.

Reese, H. W., & Overton, W. F. Models of development and theories of development. In L. R.

Goulet & P. B. Baltes (Eds.), *Life-span developmental psychology*. New York: Academic Press, 1970.

Urbach, P. Progress and degeneration in the "IQ debate." *British Journal for the Philosophy of Science,* 1974, **25,** 99–135.

Weimer, W. B. The history of psychology and its retrieval from historiography. I. The problematic nature of history. *Science Studies,* 1974, **4,** 235–258.

Weimer, W. B., & Palermo, D. S. Paradigms and normal science in psychology. *Science Studies,* 1973, **3,** 211–244.

Zahar, E. Why did Einstein's research program supersede Lorentz's? In C. Howson (Ed.), *Method and appraisal in the physical sciences.* London and New York: Cambridge Univ. Press, 1976.

OVERTON'S AND PALERMO'S RELATIVISM: ONE STEP FORWARD, TWO STEPS BACK

Harry Beilin

DEVELOPMENTAL PSYCHOLOGY PROGRAM
CITY UNIVERSITY OF NEW YORK
GRADUATE SCHOOL AND UNIVERSITY CENTER
NEW YORK, NEW YORK

I. Overton

The revision of Overton's views of philosophy of science and its bearing on developmental theory, as well as the extended critique of our differing interpretations, are a significant addition to the debate Barker, Gholson, and I initiated that was the basis of the present exchange.[1]

My general reaction to Overton's paper is that in adopting the Lakatosian framework (and Laudan's extension of it), Overton uses the language of that formulation as a container for the same Kuhnian–Pepper proposals held earlier, with some slight compromises to the rationalist position. To use Overton's own argument, he has retained the hard core of his world view and has attempted to assimilate the rationalist position to it. However, in seeming to make Lakatos' position his own, the spirit and intent of Lakatos' theory is distorted. In addition, my own views are not accurately reported and what I have written on the relevant issues is ignored.

Overton's principal objectives are to show that world views (now transformed

[1]In the initial presentation of our critique of Kuhn and the *Weltanschauung* position (at the 1982 Southeastern Conference on Human Development), Overton was a discussant of those papers. We welcome the opportunity the present forum provides Overton for expanding upon his views, and for our own opportunity to reply to them.

ADVANCES IN CHILD DEVELOPMENT
AND BEHAVIOR, VOL. 18

ISBN 0-12-009718-4

into research programs or traditions) still provide the guidelines by which specific psychological theories are constructed, that such world views are essentially incompatible with one another (although not in as strong a fashion as Overton and Reese once believed), and that the organicist and mechanist distinction provides the most adequate integrative world views for developmental psychology. In addition, he accuses me of conventionalism and the view that the new functionalism is merely a simpler formulation among arbitrarily created distinctions.

First, to be identified as a conventionalist cannot be all bad in that Lakatos endorses at least a pinch of conventionalism himself: "I endorse to some extent both Le Roy's conventionalism with regard to theories and Popper's conventionalism with regard to basic propositions" (Lakatos, 1970, p. 176). The fact is, however, that I am not a conventionalist in the sense meant by Overton. I do not believe the "new functionalism" to be more elegant or simpler as a label or concept than the organicist–determinist distinction. Rather, I hold that the new functionalism idea accords better with the historical facts. I do not believe the organicist–mechanist distinction to be arbitrary either, or of no merit. This distinction was particularly useful at the time Pepper (1942) detailed his original analysis of "world hypotheses." It is just that they are less appropriate now to a description of the social sciences, particularly developmental psychology. If they do have utility, a case could be made that the Pepper "world hypotheses," which Overton has chosen to downgrade and ignore (formism and contextualism), provide a more apt description of aspects of present developmental psychology than does the organicist–mechanist contrast. What the organicist–mechanist distinction ignores is the history of the past 25 years that has thrust structuralist theories (of Levi-Strauss, Chomsky, Piaget, etc.) and functionalism (with information processing, linguistic pragmatics, hermeneutics, etc.) into the forefront of the social sciences.

In emphasizing that one's constructs have to bear the test of historical reality I imply a commitment to some form of empiricism and the cult of "hard data" observations. I plead guilty to the charge that I hold observation to be the ultimate arbiter of scientific theories (without at the same time believing that theoretical statements are reducible to observation statements). Despite Overton's implication to the contrary, so does Lakatos. "*Even then, experience still remains, in an important sense, the 'impartial arbiter' of scientific controversy.* We cannot get rid of the problem of 'empirical basis' if we want to learn from experience" (Lakatos, 1970, p. 131, italics in the original).

The emphasis on empiricism is not meant to detract from Lakatos' emphasis on rationality in science. But Overton's adoption of Lakatos is not in that spirit. Overton's effort is more in the spirit of retaining the subjectivist assumptions that go along with world views that are said to determine, by metaphysical and methodological *commitments,* how science is to be conducted and leads in turn to the impossibility (or great difficulty, in the newer, weak version) of communication among such world views. It is because of this conception that Overton most characteristically holds with Kuhn's incommensurability thesis, although most philosophers of science depart from the *Weltanschauung* thesis on the very same incommensurability issue. The difficulty for Overton is this: If he insists too strongly on the incompatibility or incommensurability of world views it would appear as if he is endorsing Kuhnian-type subjectivism. To deny it, however, is to deny the very quality that gives the *Weltanschauung* position its vigor and attractiveness. But then again, hardly anyone pays allegiance to that notion anymore. So instead, Overton substitutes the Lakatosian program, hard core and heuristic constructs for Kuhnian paradigms to protect his thesis and at the same time softens the incommensurability thesis to a weak form. The weak form holds that incommensurability can be eliminated by an appeal to "a currently more neutral language." In essence, Overton's solution is to suggest that when opponents confront one another at a point of incommensurability they withdraw and invoke an observation language whose theoretical assumptions are not at issue. In other words, they ignore the incommensurabilities. There are a number of problems with this proposal. First, the incommensurability issue did not arise from the rationalist rejection of the idea that there is no neutral observation language, as Overton claims. The issue had its origins with logical positivism itself and was later elaborated upon by the *Weltanschauung* group (Suppe, 1977). Next, incommensurability does not refer strictly to "lack of communication between rival world views." It means what the dictionary says it means; it is a lack of a common measure and the point at issue is whether there are such common measures for comparative evaluation among theories and whether some procedures are better than others (Barnes, 1982). Lakatos comments on incommensurability, as follows:

> I have not dealt with the Kuhn and Feyerabend claim that theories cannot be eliminated on any *objective* grounds because of the 'incommensurability' of rival theories. Incommensurable theories are neither inconsistent with each other, nor comparable for content. But we can *make* them, by a dictionary, inconsistent and their content comparable. If we want to eliminate a programme we need some methodological determination. This determination is at the heart of methodological falsificationism. (1970, p. 179)

In other words, for Lakatos the issue is no issue, the point is to look for methods that will lead to the rejection of theories, and in every science there are such methods. Overton's tactic protects his position from the most radical of subjectivism, but it does not tie it to the kind of methodological falsificationism to which a rationalist position like Lakatos' is at least in part committed.

As a last point on this issue, Overton claims, "as both Lakatos and Laudan argue, world views can and do form a necessary rational dimension to scientific research programmes and traditions." Lakatos, contrariwise, says, "One must never allow a research programme to become a *Weltanschauung*, or a sort of *scientific rigour*, setting itself up as an arbiter between explanation and non-explanation. . . . Unfortunately, this is the position which Kuhn tends to advocate'' (1970, p. 155). What Overton fails to realize is that the *Weltanschauung* conception, even in the weak form in which he wishes to weld it to research programs and traditions, is by its very nature, hard core if you will, subjectivist, and nonrational.

Now, briefly, to Overton's characterization of my views on the new functionalism; Overton says, in regard to my statement on functionalism (Beilin, p. 245, this volume), that the meaning of the term ''function'' is left undefined and, furthermore, that I include Piaget among the new functionalists. Overton should know fully well that the primary source for my discussion of the new functionalism was in an address given in 1981, which appears in even fuller form in print (Beilin, 1983). Overton knows this work because he has cited it. What I do in fact show is that ''function'' and ''functionalism'' have undergone significant changes in meaning and use in the history of psychology. That is the point, in fact. The new functionalists, despite their emphasis on function as process, have scrapped a number of the assumptions held by earlier functionalists. That is not a matter of blurring distinctions, unless one is committed to fixed and historically invariant category boundaries, which Overton appears to be. The flexibility of these boundaries is what makes it possible for Piaget, despite his self-styled characterization as a *structuralist* (1970), to encompass a fundamental commitment to functionalist analysis, which present day Genevans are increasingly emphasizing.

Overton's own description of historical developments in psychology is designed to reduce the structuralist–functionalist distinction to a mechanist–organicist world view difference. He is certainly entitled to do this. Yes, even on purely conventionalist grounds, but the critical issue is whether this is in keeping with actual historical trends and captures the nature of present day developmental psychology. In my view it does not, nor would it, I imagine, in the view of Eleanor Gibson, who also sees a new functionalism in contemporary psychology (Gibson, 1982). The two instances I cite bear this out. Overton's emphasis on Chomsky's supposed organicism ignores the momentous historical period that psychology and the other social sciences have been through. I know of few philosophers or social scientists who would claim the present era to be postorganicist rather than poststructuralist, and who see it as having been defined by other than Levi-Strauss, Chomsky, Piaget, the molecular biologists, and the like.

The other example I cite is information processing, certainly the most important development in psychology in the past 15 years. To see information-processing theories as merely mechanistic, which to some extent they are, is to ignore their view of humans as symbol processors, their willingness to entertain inferred mentalistic entities, and their view of organisms as active rather than reactive systems.

My point has been that in the era of the new functionalism much cross-adaptation has taken place. Functionalist theories increasingly assimilate structuralist elements to them, and structuralists are increasingly assimilating functionalist doctrines. A prime example is Overton himself, who in his analysis of the competence–performance distinction has argued that both competence (structuralism) and performance (functionalism) are required for an adequate developmental theory. So, despite Overton's plea for theories to be pure and true to their research traditions, Overton has been true "in his fashion," which turns out to be in the fashion of the new functionalism.

II. Palermo

Underlying Palermo's defense of the Kuhnian position is an unstated commitment to relativism, subjectivism, and the incommensurability and incompatibility of world views (with the latter confounded). Within this framework, Palermo takes as obvious that the history of science, like textual analysis, is open to the same kind of relativism. In the service of this view he accuses us of a too easy dismissal of Kuhn and a focus on rationality as the sole basis of scientific decision making. The latter point is least important to his argument and is most easily dealt with.

As will be clear from even a casual reading of what I have written, I do not hold that subjective and nonrational elements are excluded from scientific activity. They certainly have a role. But, to invoke a statistical metaphor, the question is how much of the variance is accounted for by such considerations. I believe the historical record, as open as it may be to interpretation (but not unlimited interpretation), does not show periods of normal science punctuated by revolutionary change. Instead, it shows periods of constant confrontation between research traditions, more in keeping with the description provided by Lakatos than by Kuhn. Palermo argues that Lakatos' position is Kuhn's reworked and made more precise. Lakatos' analysis has done much more than that. Its effect has been sufficient, together with the efforts of others, to create a major revision in attitudes toward the conduct of science. Kuhn's description of normal science, with its dominant paradigm, is not only *not* redefined by Lakatos, it is denied in its essence as it was also later denied by Kuhn. Kuhn's subjectivism, relativism, and sociologism are not reworked, they are rejected as critical factors in scientific change. Palermo is correct in perceiving that these elements are not totally denied, but Palermo fails to capture the dramatic differences in the Kuhn and Lakatos positions, dismissing as he does Lakatos as antihumanist and mechanist. In turn, Palermo appeals to common sense to justify Kuhnian subjectivism.

After all, he says, it had to be right or else it would not have struck a respondent chord in scientists. By the same argument we could say that subjectivism is wrong, in that Lakatos' rejection of Kuhn has had almost instant intuitive appeal to the rationality of both philosophers of science and scientists. Even worse, in the history of science intuitive appeal has led to the belief that the earth is flat, to phlogiston and ether theories, and these days, at least to some of the public, to astrology. These views lead Palermo to make a most astonishing statement: "In contrast, the efforts of Lakatos force scientists into a rational mold, a mold unfamiliar to the practitioners of science." I am willing to wager that not a single research report was rejected by the journal Palermo so successfully edited because it was too rational, but a good many were rejected because they weren't rational enough!

There is no question that the insights provided by Popper, Hanson, Kuhn, Feyerabend, Toulman, and others have done much to show that science is conducted in a social and psychological context that affects its conduct and history. It does not take much of a historical analysis, however, to show that radical subjectivism and relativism do not provide an adequate account of scientific activity. Nor do the sociological and psychological analyses of the kind suggested by Palermo offer adequate understanding of our own scientific history. The history of developmental psychology bears this out, as I have tried to show. Palermo, in commenting on this analysis, nevertheless concludes that functionalism, as I define it, is not a paradigm in Kuhn's sense or a research program in Lakatos' sense, principally because functionalists do not have a common set of commitments. What Palermo implies is that they do not have the kind of commitments that count as such, namely, those of mechanism or organicism. On the contrary, the commitments of functionalists are centrally concerned with accounting for behavior and cognition by universal and local processes, and with the argument that structure follows function rather than the reverse. Functionalists do differ among themselves in many ways, including how "deeply" they wish to go in positing inferred cognitive and other psychological entities. Their common goal, however, is more than a matter of functional "interests." For functionalists, the only satisfactory *explanatory* system is one that is function based. A single example should suffice. In addressing the question as to whether animals, like humans, have "thought" (theoretically, not a trivial question), the structuralist will decide the question on whether structural homologies can be established between the brains and (inferred) mental structures of animals and humans. The functionalist, on the other hand, will argue for or against the question on whether it can be established that animals and humans have similar or dissimilar mental functions or states. It is irrelevant to the functionalist as to whether brain or mental structures are alike. They argue, to use a computer analogy, that the same program (i.e., function) can run on machines of very different hardware (i.e., structure) (Stich, 1983). I submit that this commitment to a functionalist program is what principally identifies a most disparate group of contemporary theorists. Earlier functionalist periods showed the same disparate character.

Palermo indirectly raises a significant issue in questioning what constitutes a research paradigm, program, or tradition. I do not believe the diversity and complexity of different organizations of intellectual style within the sciences represented by these terms have been adequately delineated and described by Pepper, Kuhn, Lakatos, Laudan, or anyone else. Nonetheless, no matter how many categories or types of research traditions there may be, the new functionalism constitutes a consistent set of deep commitments shared by many developmentalists, including, if I might say so, Palermo himself.

REFERENCES

Barnes, B. A temperate rationalism. Review of W. H. Newton-Smith, ''The rationality of science.'' *Times Literary Supplement,* Feb. 19, 1982.

Beilin, H. *Piaget and the new functionalism.* Invited address to the annual symposium of the Jean Piaget Society, Philadelphia, April, 1982.

Beilin, H. The new functionalism and Piaget's program. In E. Scholnick (Ed.), *New trends in conceptual representation.* Hillsdale, New Jersey: Erlbaum, 1983.

Gibson, E. J. The concept of affordances in development: The renascence of functionalism. In W. A. Collins (Ed.), *Minnesota symposia on child psychology* (Vol. 15): *The concept of development.* Hillsdale, New Jersey: Erlbaum, 1982.

Lakatos, I. Falsification and the methodology of scientific research programmes. In I. Lakatos & A. Musgrave (Eds.), *Criticism and the growth of knowledge.* London and New York: Cambridge Univ. Press, 1970.

Pepper, S. C. *World hypotheses: A study in evidence.* Berkeley, California: Univ. of California Press, 1942.

Piaget, J. *Structuralism.* New York: Basic Books, 1970.

Stich, S. Beastly brainwork. Review of S. Walker, ''Animal thought.'' *Times Literary Supplement,* April 29, 1983.

Suppe, F. *The structure of scientific theories* (2nd ed). Urbana, Illinois: Univ. of Illinois Press, 1977.

AUTHOR INDEX

Numbers in italics refer to the pages on which the complete references are listed.

C

H

I

J

K

L

M

N

O

P

Q

R

S

T

U

V

W

XYZ

SUBJECT INDEX

S

T

V

W

X

Contents of Previous Volumes

Volume 11

Volume 12

Volume 13

Volume 14

Volume 15

Volume 16

Volume 17